IARIA

UBICOMM 2017

The Eleventh International Conference on Mobile Ubiquitous Computing, Systems, Services and Technologies

November 12 - 16, 2017

Barcelona, Spain

UBICOMM 2017 Editors

Timothy Arndt, Cleveland State University, USA

Evgeny Pyshkin, University of Aizu, Japan

Martin Ruskowski, German Research Center for Artificial Intelligence (DFKI), Germany Martin.Ruskowski@dfki.de

Aliane Loureiro Krassmann, Federal Institute Farroupilha – Federal University of Rio Grande do Sul, Brazil

Hiroaki Higaki, Tokyo Denki University, Japan

Printed from e-media with permission by:

Curran Associates, Inc.
57 Morehouse Lane
Red Hook, NY 12571

Some format issues inherent in the e-media version may also appear in this print version.

Printed by Curran Associates, Inc. (2017)

International Academy, Research, and Industry Association (IARIA)
412 Derby Way
Wilmington, DE 19810

Phone: (408) 893-6407
Fax: (408) 527-6351

petre@iaria.org

Additional copies of this publication are available from:

Curran Associates, Inc.
57 Morehouse Lane
Red Hook, NY 12571 USA
Phone: 845-758-0400
Fax: 845-758-2633
Email: curran@proceedings.com
Web: www.proceedings.com

Table of Contents

Performance Assessment of Time-Threshold Based Scheme over Soft Frequency Reuse (SFR) Scheme 1
Idil Candan

Analysis of the Usefulness of Mobile Eyetracker for the Recognition of Physical Activities 5
Peter Hevesi, Jamie Ward, Orkhan Amiraslanov, Gerald Pirkl, and Paul Lukowicz

Beware: Mobile and Web Application to Prevent Crimes against the Patrimony,Life, Body and Health 11
Alexa Tataje, Marco Florian, and David Mauricio

Using Hidden Markov Models and Rule-based Sensor Mediation on Wearable eHealth Devices 19
Gilles Irenee Fernand Neyens and Denis Zampunieris

Using Image Recognition for Testing Hand-drawn Graphic User Interfaces 25
Maxim Mozgovoy and Evgeny Pyshkin

On Providing Healthy Routes: A Case for Fine-Grained Pollution Measurements Using Mobile Sensing 29
Srinivas Devarakonda, Ruilin Liu, and Badri Nath

Hybrid Client/Server Rendering with Automatic Proxy Model Generation 37
Jens Olav Nygaard and Jon Mikkelsen Hjelmervik

'SER Analysis of Adaptive Threshold Based Relay Selection with 2-Bits Feedback for Type-2 Relays 41
Sung Sik Nam, Byungju Lim, Mohamed-Slim Alouini, and Young-Chai Ko

A Reward System for Collaborative Care of Elderly based on Distributed Ledger Technologies 46
Emilien Bai and Kare Synnes

Planning for Ubiquitous Learning in PLAN 56
Timothy Arndt

A Tool Rental Service Scenario - IoT technologies enabling a circular economy business model 60
Johanna Kallio, Maria Antikainen, and Outi Kettunen

Towards an Architecture to Multimodal Tools for e-Learning Environments 66
Andre da Silva, Fernanda Freire, and Flavia Arantes

Implementation Example with Ultra-Small PCs for Human Tracking System based on Mobile Agent Technologies 73
Masaru Shiozuka, Tappei Yotsumoto, Kenichi Takahashi, Takao Kawamura, and Kazunori Sugahara

Indoor Source Localization Using 2D Multi-Sensor Based Spatial Spectrum Fusion Algorithm 79

Taha Bouras, Di He, Wenxian Yu, and Yi Zhang

Probabilistic CCRN: Reliability Analysis of Ubiquitous Computing Scenarios Using Probabilistic Model Checking 85
Reona Minoda, Masakazu Ishihata, and Shin-ichi Minato

Using Brain-Computer Interface and Internet of Things to Improve Healthcare for Wheelchair Users 92
Ariel Teles, Mauricio Cagy, Francisco Silva, Markus Endler, Victor Bastos, and Silmar Teixeira

Enhancing the Affective Sensitivity of Location Based Services Using Situation-Person-Dependent Semantic Similarity 95
Antonios Karatzoglou and Michael Beigl

TPM Framework: a Comprehensive Kit for Exploring Applications with Textile Pressure Mapping Matrix 101
Bo Zhou, Jingyuan Cheng, Ankur Mawandia, Yujiang He, Zhixin Huang, Mathias Sundholm, Muhammet Yildrim, Heber Cruz, and Paul Lukowicz

Estimation of Relative Offset and Drift for Synchronization of Local Clocks in Wireless Sensor Networks 108
Ayako Arao and Hiroaki Higaki

A Quantitative Study on Live Virtual Machines Migration in Virtualized Computing Environment 115
Marcela Tassyany Galdino Santos, Edlane de Oliveira Gusmao Alves, and Anderson Fabiano Batista Ferreira da Costa

Management of Forest Fires Using IoT Devices 121
Josue Toledo-Castro, Ivan Santos-Gonzalez, Candelaria Hernandez-Goya, and Pino Caballero-Gil

ASUT : Advanced Software Update for Things 127
Juhyun Choi, Changue Jung, Ikjun Yeom, and Younghoon Kim

Towards Remote Control of Mobile Robots to Help Dependent People 129
Yvon Autret, Jean Vareille, David Espes, Valerie Marc, and Philippe Le Parc

MQTT-based Translation System for IoT Interoperability in oneM2M Architecture 137
Jiwoo Park, Geonwoo Kim, and Kwangsue Chung

High-performance Wireless Sensor Node Design for Water Pipeline Monitoring 141
Fatma Karray, Mohamed Wassim Jmal, and Mohamed Abid

An Extensible Edge Computing Architecture: Definition, Requirements and Enablers 148
Volkan Gezer, Jumyung Um, and Martin Ruskowski

GeSCo: Introducing an Edge Layer Between Cloud MES and Shop-Floor in Decentralized Manufacturing 153

Badarinath Katti, Michael Schweitzer, and Christiane Plociennik

Combining Edge Computing and Blockchains for Flexibility and Performance in Industrial Automation 159
Mauro Isaja, John Soldatos, and Volkan Gezer

Implementation of Interactive E-learning System Based on Virtual Reality 165
SeungJoon Kwon and HyungKeun Jee

Heads Up Displays (HUD) as a Tool to Contextualize the User in 3D Virtual Worlds 169
Aliane Loureiro Krassmann, Felipe Becker Nunes, Tito Armando Rossi Filho, Liane Margarida Rockenbach Tarouco, and Magda Bercht

UBICOMM 2017

Forward

The Eleventh International Conference on Mobile Ubiquitous Computing, Systems, Services and Technologies (UBICOMM 2017), held between November 12 - 16, 2017, in Barcelona, Spain, continued a series of events addressing fundamentals of ubiquitous systems and the new applications related to them.

The rapid advances in ubiquitous technologies make fruition of more than 35 years of research in distributed computing systems, and more than two decades of mobile computing. The ubiquity vision is becoming a reality. Hardware and software components evolved to deliver functionality under failure-prone environments with limited resources. The advent of web services and the progress on wearable devices, ambient components, user-generated content, mobile communications, and new business models generated new applications and services. The conference makes a bridge between issues with software and hardware challenges through mobile communications.

Advances in web services technologies along with their integration into mobility, online and new business models provide a technical infrastructure that enables the progress of mobile services and applications. These include dynamic and on-demand service, context-aware services, and mobile web services. While driving new business models and new online services, particular techniques must be developed for web service composition, web service-driven system design methodology, creation of web services, and on-demand web services.

As mobile and ubiquitous computing becomes a reality, more formal and informal learning will take pace out of the confines of the traditional classroom. Two trends converge to make this possible; increasingly powerful cell phones and PDAs, and improved access to wireless broadband. At the same time, due to the increasing complexity, modern learners will need tools that operate in an intuitive manner and are flexibly integrated in the surrounding learning environment.

Educational services will become more customized and personalized, and more frequently subjected to changes. Learning and teaching are now becoming less tied to physical locations, co-located members of a group, and co-presence in time. Learning and teaching increasingly take place in fluid combinations of virtual and "real" contexts, and fluid combinations of presence in time, space and participation in community. To the learner full access and abundance in communicative opportunities and information retrieval represents new challenges and affordances.

Consequently, the educational challenges are numerous in the intersection of technology development, curriculum development, content development and educational infrastructure.

The event was very competitive in its selection process and very well perceived by the international scientific and industrial communities. As such, it has attracted excellent contributions and active participation from all over the world. We were very pleased to receive a large number of top quality contributions.

The conference had the following tracks:

- Mobility
- Information Ubiquity
- Collaborative ubiquitous systems
- Users, applications, and business models
- Ubiquitous mobile services and protocols
- Ubiquity trends and challenges
- Ubiquitous networks
- Ubiquitous devices and operative systems
- Edge Computing in Factories of the Future
- Advances in Education with Ubiquitous 3D Applications

We take here the opportunity to warmly thank all the members of the UBICOMM 2017 technical program committee, as well as all the reviewers. The creation of such a high quality conference program would not have been possible without their involvement. We also kindly thank all the authors that dedicated much of their time and effort to contribute to UBICOMM 2017. We truly believe that, thanks to all these efforts, the final conference program consisted of top quality contributions.

We also gratefully thank the members of the UBICOMM 2017 organizing committee for their help in handling the logistics and for their work that made this professional meeting a success.

We hope that UBICOMM 2017 was a successful international forum for the exchange of ideas and results between academia and industry and to promote further progress in the field of ubiquitous systems and the new applications related to them. We also hope that Barcelona, Spain, provided a pleasant environment during the conference and everyone saved some time to enjoy the unique charm of the city.

UBICOMM 2017 Chairs

UBICOMM Steering Committee

Sathiamoorthy Manoharan, University of Auckland, New Zealand
Ann Gordon-Ross, University of Florida, USA
Jaime Lloret Mauri, Polytechnic University of Valencia, Spain
Radosveta Sokullu, Ege University, Izmir, Turkey
Michele Ruta, Technical University of Bari, Italy
Wladyslaw Homenda, Warsaw University of Technology, Poland
Hiroaki Higaki, Tokyo Denki University, Japan

UBICOMM Industry/Research Advisory Committee

Miroslav Velev, Aries Design Automation, USA
Cornel Klein, Siemens AG/Corporate Research and Technologies - Münich, Germany

Dmitry Korzun, Petrozavodsk State University, Russia
Carla-Fabiana Chiasserini, Politecnico di Torino, Italy
Volkan Gezer, German Research Center for Artificial Intelligence (DFKI), Germany
Shaohan Hu, IBM Research, USA
Elmano Ramalho Cavalcanti, Federal Institute of Education Science and Technology of Pernambuco, Brazil
Lars Braubach, Complex Software Systems | Bremen City University, Germany
Girish Revadigar, UNSW Australia and Data61|CSIRO, Sydney, Australia
Jon M. Hjelmervik, SINTEF Digital, Norway
Ming Jin, Lawrence Berkeley National Laboratory (LBNL) and UC Berkeley, USA

UBICOMM 2017
Committee

UBICOMM Steering Committee

Sathiamoorthy Manoharan, University of Auckland, New Zealand
Ann Gordon-Ross, University of Florida, USA
Jaime Lloret Mauri, Polytechnic University of Valencia, Spain
Radosveta Sokullu, Ege University, Izmir, Turkey
Michele Ruta, Technical University of Bari, Italy
Wladyslaw Homenda, Warsaw University of Technology, Poland
Hiroaki Higaki, Tokyo Denki University, Japan

UBICOMM Industry/Research Advisory Committee

Miroslav Velev, Aries Design Automation, USA
Cornel Klein, Siemens AG/Corporate Research and Technologies - Münich, Germany
Dmitry Korzun, Petrozavodsk State University, Russia
Carla-Fabiana Chiasserini, Politecnico di Torino, Italy
Volkan Gezer, German Research Center for Artificial Intelligence (DFKI), Germany
Shaohan Hu, IBM Research, USA
Elmano Ramalho Cavalcanti, Federal Institute of Education Science and Technology of Pernambuco, Brazil
Lars Braubach, Complex Software Systems | Bremen City University, Germany
Girish Revadigar, UNSW Australia and Data61|CSIRO, Sydney, Australia
Jon M. Hjelmervik, SINTEF Digital, Norway
Ming Jin, Lawrence Berkeley National Laboratory (LBNL) and UC Berkeley, USA

UBICOMM 2017 Technical Program Committee

Emad Abd-Elrahman, National Telecommunication Institute, Cairo, Egypt
Afrand Agah, West Chester University of Pennsylvania, USA
Taleb Alashkar, Northeastern University, Boston, USA
Mehran Asadi, Lincoln University, USA
Fredrick Awuor, Kisii University, Kenya / Academia Sinica, Taiwan
Liz Bacon, University of Greenwich, UK
Ali Balador, RISE SICS Västerås, Sweden
Matthias Baldauf, FHS St.Gallen, Switzerland
Felipe Becker Nunes, Federal University of Rio Grande do Sul (UFRGS), Brazil
Neil Bergmann, The University of Queensland, Brisbane, Australia
Simon Bergweiler, DFKI GmbH, German Research Center for Artificial Intelligence, Germany
Aurelio Bermúdez, Universidad de Castilla-La Mancha, Spain

Sun-Yuan Hsieh, National Cheng Kung University, Taiwan
Shaohan Hu, IBM Research, USA
Yu-Chen Hu, Providence University, Taiwan
Edward Y. Hua, Janus Research Group, Inc., USA
Malinka Ivanova, Technical University of Sofia, Bulgaria
Nafaa Jabeur, German University of Technology in Oman (GUtech), Oman
Chitra Javali, UNSW Australia and Data61|CSIRO, Sydney, Australia /
Fang-Zhou Jiang, Data61 | CSIRO & UNSW, Australia
Ming Jin, Lawrence Berkeley National Laboratory (LBNL), USA
Charalampos Kalalas, Centre Tecnològic de Telecomunicacions de Catalunya (CTTC) /
Universitat Politècnica de Catalunya (UPC - BarcelonaTECH), Spain
Fazal Wahab Karam, COMSATS Institute of Information Technology, Pakistan
Sye Loong Keoh, University of Glasgow, UK
Cornel Klein, Siemens AG/Corporate Research and Technologies - Münich, Germany
Reinhard Klemm, Avaya, USA
Vitaly Klyuev, University of Aizu, Japan
Sönke Knoch, German Research Center for Artificial Intelligence - DFKI GmbH, Germany
Thomas Kopinski, University of South Westphalia, Germany
Dmitry Korzun, Petrozavodsk State University, Russia
Konstantinos Kotis, University of Piraeus, Greece
Abderrafiaa Koukam, Université de Technologie de Belfort-Montbéliard, France
Jarosław Koźlak, AGH University of Science and Technology, Poland
Michal Kvet, University of Zilina, Slovakia
Soo Kyun Kim, Paichai University, South Korea
Philippe Lalanda, Université Grenoble Alpes, France
Frédéric Le Mouël, INSA Lyon, France
Dongman Lee, KAIST, Korea
Gyu Myoung Lee, Liverpool John Moores University, UK
Pierre Leone, University of Geneva, Switzerland
Xiuhua Li, University of British Columbia, Canada
Ruilin Liu, Rutgers - The State University of New Jersey, USA
Xiaodong Liu, Edinburgh Napier University, UK
Jaime Lloret Mauri, Polytechnic University of Valencia, Spain
Aliane Loureiro Krassmann, Federal Institute Farroupilha, Brazil
Derdour Makhlouf, University of Tebessa, Algeria
Elsa Maria Macias Lopez, University of Las Palmas De Gran Canaria, Spain
Elleuchi Manel, National Engineering School of Sfax (ENIS), Tunisia
Sathiamoorthy Manoharan, University of Auckland, New Zealand
Luis Marcelino, Polytechnic Institute of Leiria / Instituto de Telecomunicações, Portugal
Francesca Martelli, Institute for Informatics and Telematics (IIT) - Italian National Research Council (CNR), Italy
Sergio Martin, Universidad Nacional de Educación a Distancia, Spain
Nils Masuch, Competence Center Agent Core Technologies | DAI-Lab | TU Berlin, Germany
Natarajan Meghanathan, Jackson State University, USA

Daniela Micucci, University of Milano Bicocca, Milan, Italy
Reona Minoda, Hokkaido University, Sapporo, Japan
Moeiz Miraoui, University of Gafsa, Tunisia
Thuong Nguyen, CSIRO (Commonwealth Scientific and Industrial Research Organisation), Australia
Ryo Nishide, Kobe University, Japan
Andrea Giovanni Nuzzolese, STLab | ISTC-CNR, Rome, Italy
Kouzou Ohara, Aoyama Gakuin University, Japan
Satoru Ohta, Toyama Prefectural University, Japan
Carlos Enrique Palau Salvador, University Polytechnic of Valencia, Spain
Kwangjin Park, Wonkwang University, South Korea
K. K. Pattanaik, ABV-Indian Institute of Information Technology and Management Gwalior, India
Evangelos Pournaras, ETH Zurich, Switzerland
Elmano Ramalho Cavalcanti, Federal Institute of Education Science and Technology of Pernambuco, Brazil
Maurizio Rebaudengo, Politecnico di Torino, Italy
Valderi Reis Quietinho Leithardt, University of Vale do Itajai - Univali, Brazil
Girish Revadigar, UNSW Australia and Data61|CSIRO, Sydney, Australia
Abdallah Rhattoy, Moulay Ismail University | Higher School of Technology, Morocco
Marcos Rodrigues, Sheffield Hallam University, UK
Michele Ruta, Technical University of Bari, Italy
Prasan Kumar Sahoo, Chang Gung University / Chang Gung Memorial Hospital, Taiwan
Antonio José Sánchez Salmerón, Instituto de Automática e Informática Industrial | Universitat Politècnica de València, Spain
José Santa, University of Murcia, Spain
Floriano Scioscia, Technical University of Bari, Italy
Zary Segall, UMBC, USA
Hamed Shah-Mansouri, University of British Columbia, Vancouver, Canada
Alireza Shahrabi, Glasgow Caledonian University, UK
Vishakha Sharma, Georgetown University, Washington D.C., USA
Shih-Lung Shaw, University of Tennessee, Knoxville, USA
Haichen Shen, University of Washington, USA
Qi Shi, Liverpool John Moores University, UK
Kazuhiko Shibuya, Tokyo Metropolitan University, Japan
Catarina Silva, Polytechnic Institute of Leiria, Portugal
Radosveta Sokullu, Ege University, Izmir, Turkey
Angelo Spognardi, Sapienza University of Rome, Italy
Georgios Stylianou, European University Cyprus, Cyprus
Álvaro Suárez Sarmiento, University of Las Palmas de Gran Canaria, Spain
Apostolos Syropoulos, Greek Molecular Computing Group, Greece
Ryszard Tadeusiewicz, AGH University of Science and Technology, Poland
Yoshiaki Taniguchi, Kindai University, Japan
Adrian Tarniceriu, PulseOn SA, Switzerland

Performance Assessment of Time-Threshold Based Scheme over Soft Frequency Reuse (SFR) Scheme

Idil Candan
Computer Engineering Department, Middle East Technical University, Northern Cyprus Campus
Guzelyurt, Mersin 10 Turkey
email: cidil@metu.edu.tr

Abstract- **The Soft Frequency Reuse (SFR) scheme is used to make the cell-edge users get better performance and utilize the resource effectively. Applying Quality of Service (QoS) for cell-edge users in SFR scheme is a challenging issue. Time-Threshold based Scheme (TTS) is a call admission policy that is based on monitoring the elapsed time of the handoff calls and, according to a time threshold parameter, handoff calls are either prioritized or not. In this paper, the performance of SFR scheme in presence of TTS scheme (TTS-SFR) is investigated under different network conditions. The proposed scheme outperforms our previously proposed scheme in terms of handoff dropping (P_d), new call blocking (P_b) probabilities and utilization.**

Keywords - Call Admission Control; Soft Frequency Reuse; Handoff.

I. INTRODUCTION

The tremendous growth of wireless communication and mobile computing needs an ever increasing wireless spectrum. In order to support a number of simultaneous calls at the same time, radio resources have to be reused. Soft Frequency Reuse (SFR) scheme is one of the most promising Inter-Cell Interference Coordination (ICIC) schemes that has been introduced in Long Term Evolution (LTE) -Advanced networks [1]. The SFR scheme divides the available resource blocks (RBs) into two parts: cell-edge RBs and cell-core RBs. Cell-edge users are confined to cell-edge RBs, while cell-core users can access cell-center RBs and cell-edge RBs but with less priority than cell-edge users. This means that cell-center users can use cell-edge RBs only when there are remaining available cell-edge RBs available [1]. In literature, several approaches, such as [2] - [7], have been proposed for the performance analysis of different call admission control (CAC) schemes with SFR. In [2], the impact of new call bounding scheme with SFR using queuing analysis was discussed. In [3], the performance of SFR in presence of Uniform Fractional Guard Channel Scheme (UFGCS) was investigated. A fractional amount of bandwidth unit is allocated for handoff calls. In [4], an adaptive SFR algorithm was developed that dynamically optimizes subcarrier and power allocations for multicell wireless networks to improve system capacity. In [5], a new resource configuration strategy for SFR and an admission control algorithm that takes full account of the frequency planning of SFR was proposed. In [6], the effect of cutoff priority scheme in SFR was investigated using queuing analysis.

Several approaches for CAC schemes, such as [7] -[11], have been discussed to provide priorities to handoff requests and, since it is practically impossible to completely eliminate handoff drops, these schemes have advocated providing probabilistic QoS guarantees by keeping the handoff dropping probability below a certain level. The Guard Channel Scheme (GCS) in [12] gives priority to handoff calls by exclusively reserving channels for handoff calls. Although GCS decreases handoff dropping probability (Pd), it increases new call blocking probability (Pb) and may not utilize the system efficiently. On the other hand, according to the fully shared scheme (FSS), discussed in [12], all available channels in the cell are shared by handoff and new calls. Thus, the FSS scheme minimizes the new call blocking probability and maximizes system utilization. However, it is difficult to guarantee the required dropping probability of handoff calls. Usually, the GCS scheme is preferred by users since it decreases Pd, and the FSS scheme is preferred by service providers, since it maximizes system utilization. As mentioned before, handoff calls are prioritized in many schemes at the expense of blocking newly originating calls. Their claim is "forced termination of ongoing calls is more annoying than blocking of newly originating calls". We believe that this is true to some extent, as the annoyance is a fuzzy term which depends on the elapsed time of the ongoing call [13] - [15]. For example, dropping an ongoing voice call is very annoying if it does not last for a moderate duration, whereas it is not that much annoying if the call is coming to its end. Motivated by these arguments, the current work evaluates the performance of time-threshold based scheme over SFR scheme in terms of P_d , P_b and utilization. The performance of the system is evaluated via extensive simulation. The TTS scheme proposed in [15] is evaluated over SFR scheme. The rest of the paper is organized as follows: Section 2 summarizes the TTS scheme over SFR scheme. In Section 3, simulation parameters are presented. Section 4 presents the performance results. Finally, Section 5 summarizes some key achievements and conclusion.

II. TIME-THRESHOLD BASED SCHEME OVER SOFT FREQUENCY REUSE (SFR) SCHEME (TTS-SFR SCHEME)

In our scheme, we focus on a homogeneous multi-cellular system that has the same arrival times. This allows considering only one cell for performance study. Other cells interact through handoff call arrival process. The cell is divided into edge and core according to the soft frequency scheme.

Figure 1 below shows the flowchart of processing a voice call in TSS scheme over SFR scheme. According to the TTS-SFR scheme, after calculating the number of resource blocks required, the call type is determined. If there is any free RB available, then the new call is allocated. For handoff calls that have elapsed real time greater than or equal to time threshold t_e, if the sum of cell-edge RB and cell interior RB is less than total capacity, then the call is accepted. Otherwise, it is dropped. For handoff calls that have elapsed real time less than time threshold t_e, if the sum of cell-edge RB and cell interior RB is less than the total capacity, then the call is accepted. Otherwise, the required resource block is borrowed from a neighbouring new call and the call is accepted. If there are no cells left to borrow from, then the call is dropped.

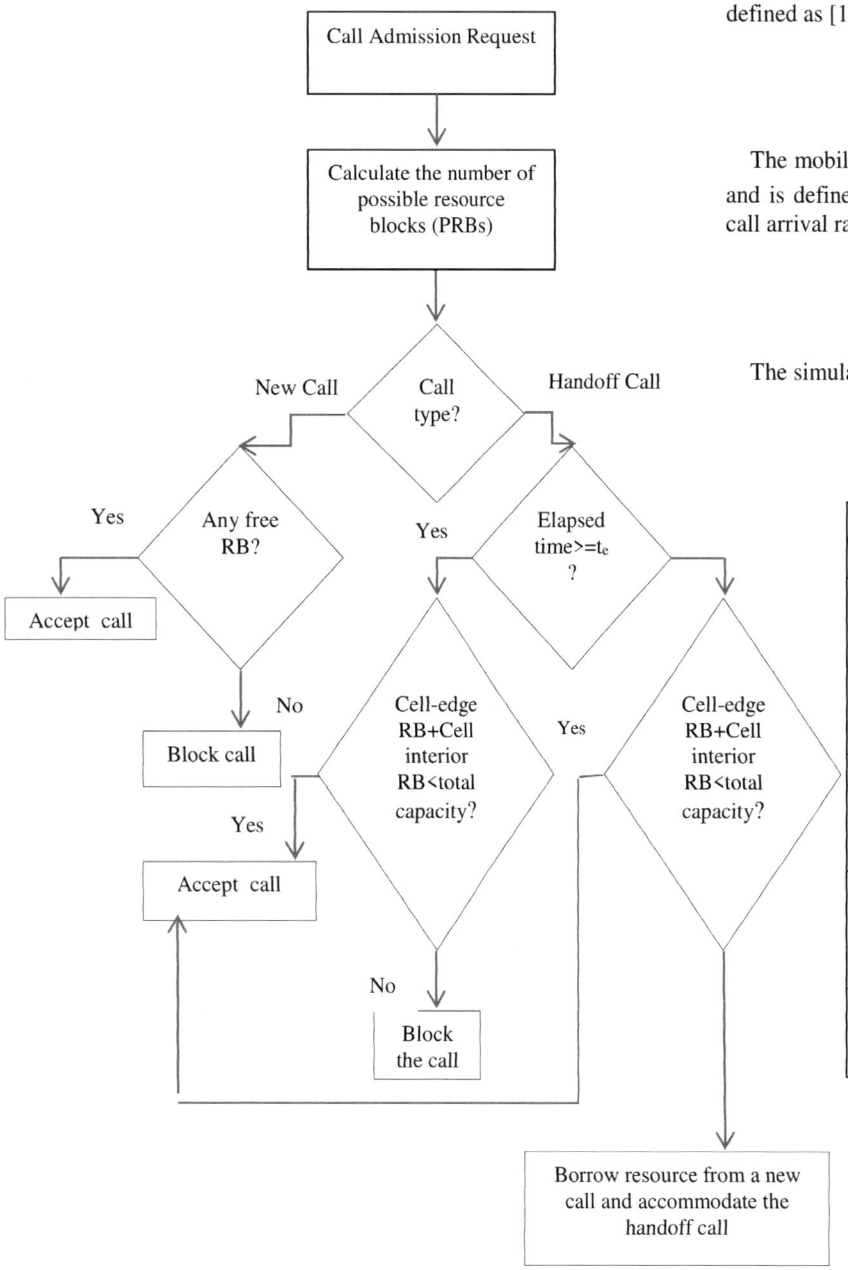

Figure 1. A Call Processing Flowchart

III. SIMULATION PARAMETERS AND PERFORMANCE METRICS

The simulation has been performed using the Java simulation tool [16]. During simulation, more than 30 runs are taken for each point in order to reach 95% confidence level. The inter-arrival times of new voice and handoff voice calls are assumed to follow Poisson processes with means $1/\lambda_n$,$1/\lambda_h$ respectively.

The call holding times follow exponential distribution with means $1/\mu_n$ for new calls, and $1/\mu_h$ for handoff calls.

The normalized offered load of the system (in Erlang) is defined as [12]

$$\rho = \frac{\lambda_n + \lambda_h}{B\mu} \qquad (1)$$

The mobility (γ) of calls is a measure of terminal mobility and is defined as the ratio of handoff call arrival rate to new call arrival rate, and can be written as [12]

$$\gamma = \frac{\lambda_h}{\lambda_n} \qquad (2)$$

The simulation input parameters used are given in Table 1.

TABLE I
SIMULATION PARAMETERS

Mobility(γ)	0.5, 1, 1.5
Load (ρ)	2 Erlangs
Time threshold values (t_{ev}, t_{ed})	15, 30, 60, 90, 120, 150, and 165 sec.
Total bandwidth (B)	10 MHz(50 RBs,180 kHz per RB)
New call average service time ($1/\mu_n$)	180 sec. (Exp. Dist.)
Handoff call average service time ($1/\mu_h$)	180 sec. (Exp. Dist.)
Average elapsed time of a handoff call	90 sec. (Unif. Dist.)

IV. PERFORMANCE RESULTS

The proposed scheme is evaluated for different time threshold (t_e) values. The performance measures obtained through the simulation are the blocking probability of new voice calls, the dropping probability of handoff voice calls (P_d) and utilization (U) of the system.

Figure 2 shows the voice handoff call dropping probability (P_d) versus elapsed time threshold (t_e) for mobility=3. It is seen that handoff dropping probability (P_d) decreases as elapsed time threshold (t_e) increases. The reason is that, as t_e increases, resource blocks are borrowed from new calls and handoff calls are accomodated.

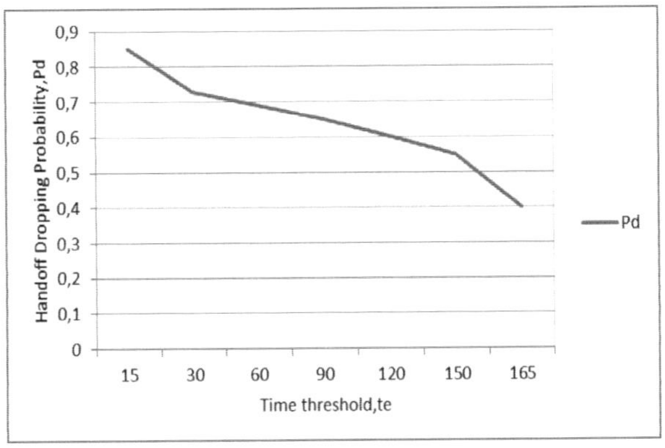

Figure 2. Dropping probability of voice handoff calls (P_d) versus time threshold (t_e) of the TTS-SFR scheme for load=2 and mobility=3

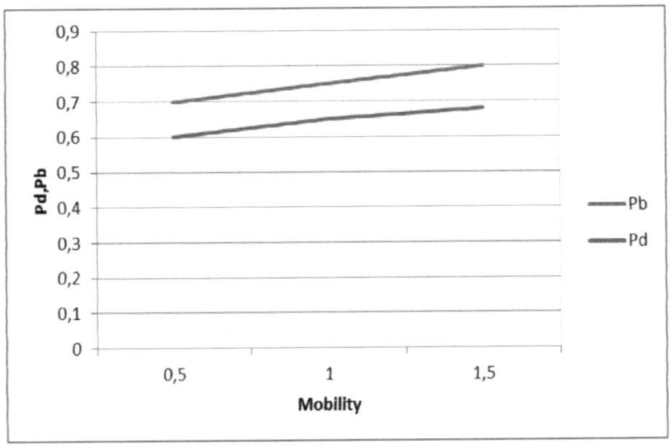

Figure 3. Dropping and blocking probabilities of calls (P_d,P_b) versus mobility of the TTS-SFR scheme for load=2 and te=90 sec

Figure 3 above shows the handoff call dropping probability (P_d) and new call blocking probability versus mobility for elapsed time threshold (t_e) = 90 sec. It is seen that both probabilities increase as mobility increases. This is because, as mobility increases, the number of handoff calls increases and more RBs are borrowed from the new calls.

Figure 4 below shows the blocking, dropping probabilities versus mobility for TTS and TTS-SFR schemes for t_e=90 sec. It is clear that the proposed scheme is superior to the previously proposed TTS scheme in terms of new call blocking and handoff dropping probabilities. In TTS-SFR scheme, if the sum of cell-edge RB and cell interior RB is less than the total capacity, a channel is borrowed from a new call to accommodate handoff call.

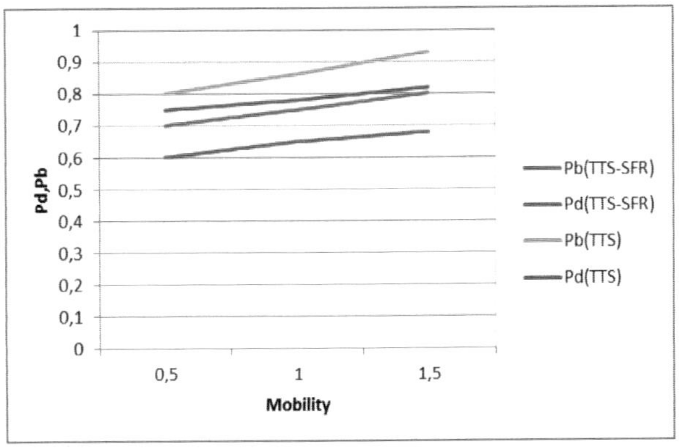

Figure 4. Dropping and blocking probabilities of TTS-SFR and TTS schemes versus mobility

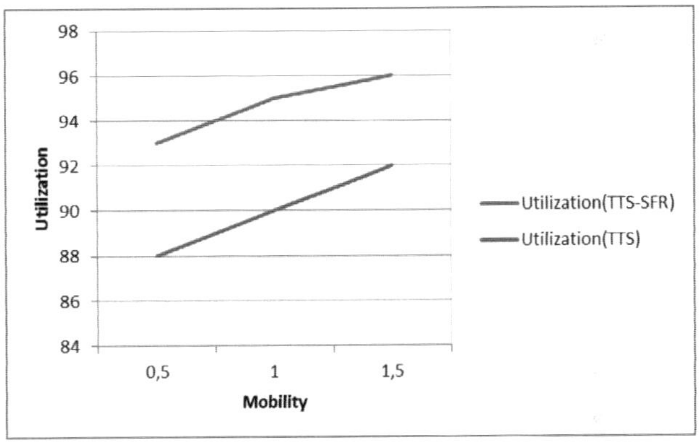

Figure 5. Utilization versus mobility for TTS and TTS-SFR schemes

Figure 5 above shows the utilization versus mobility for TTS and TTS-SFR schemes for t_e=90 sec. TTS-SFR performance is better than TTS in terms of utilization. This means channels are used more efficiently in the TTS-SFR scheme.

V. CONCLUSION

In this paper, a scheme called TTS-SFR is proposed and analyzed under different network conditions. According to the simulation results, the proposed scheme is superior to the previously proposed TTS scheme in terms of new call blocking probability, handoff dropping probability and utilization. There are a number of issues that will be addressed in our future research. We will be including multimedia data and queuing to the proposed model.

REFERENCES

[1] L. Shu, X. Wen, Z. Lin, W. Zheng, Y. Sun, "Queue Analysis of Soft Frequency Reuse Scheme in LTE-Advanced" 2nd International Conference on Computer Modeling and Simulation, pp.248-252, 2010.

[2] M. Safwat, A. Yehya, H. El-motaafy, "Performance Analysis for New Call Bounding Scheme with SFR in LTE-Advanced Networks", IEEE International Conference on High Performance Computing and Communications, pp.443-451, 2014.

[3] M. Safwat, H. M. El-Badawy, A. Yehya, H. El-Motaafy, "Performance Assessment for LTE-Advanced Networks with Uniform Fractional Guard Channel over Soft Frequency Reuse Scheme", Wireless Engineering and Technology, 2013, pp.161-170.

[4] M. Quin, W. Hardjawana, Y. Li, B. Vucetic, X. Yang, J. Shi, "Adaptive Soft Frequency Reuse Scheme for Wireless Cellular Networks", IEEE Transactions on Vehicular Technology, vol.64, no.1, pp.118-125, Jan 2015.

[5] Z. Lu, H. Tian, Q. Sun, B. Huang, S. Zheng, "An Admission Control Strategy for Soft Frequency Reuse Deployment of LTE Systems", 7th IEEE Consumer Communications and Networking Conference, pp.62-66, CCNC 2010.

[6] M. Safwat, H. M. El-Badawy, A. Yehya, H. El-mootaafy, "Analysis of Cutoff Priority SchemeImpact of Soft Frequency Reuse in LTE-Advanced Networks", Int.Journal of Scientific & Engineering Research, vol.4, Issue.10, October 2013.

[7] G. S. Kuo, P. C. Ko, M. L. Kuo, "A probabilistic resource estimation and semi-reservation scheme for flow-oriented multimedia wireless networks", *IEEE Communications Magazine*, vol. 39, pp. 135-141, February 2001.

[8] C. Oliveria, J. B. Kim, T. Suda, "An adaptive bandwidth reservation scheme for high-speed multimedia wireless networks", *IEEE J Select. Areas Commun.*, vol. 16, no. 6, pp. 858-874, August 1998.

[9] J. Y. Lee, J. G. Choi, K. Park, S. Bahk, "Realistic cell-oriented adaptive admission control for QoS support in wireless multimedia networks", *IEEE Trans. on Vehicular Tech.*, vol. 52, no. 3, pp. 512-524, May 2003.

[10] I.. Y. Kim, D. Lee, B. Lee, "Dynamic channel reservation based on mobility in wireless ATM networks", *IEEE Communications Magazine*, vol. 37, no. 11, pp. 47-51, November 1999.

[11] Z. Xu, Z. Ye, S. V. Krishnamurthy, S. K. Tripathi, M. Molle, "A new adaptive channel reservation scheme for handoff calls in wireless cellular networks", *Proc. of NETWORKING 2002 Technical Committee "Communications Systems" of International Federation for Information Processing (IFIP-TC6)*, pp. 672-684, May 2002.

[12] I. Katzela and M. Naghshineh, "Channel assignment schemes for cellular mobile telecommunication systems: A comprehensive survey", *IEEE Personal Communications*, pp. 10-31, June 1996.

[13] I. Candan, "Mobility and Queue Based Guard Channel Scheme for Cellular Networks", Proc. of 4th International Conference on Wireless Communications, Vehicular Technology,Information Theory and Aerospace/ElectronicSystems, Aalborg,Denmark, pp. 1-4, May 2014.

[14] I. Candan, "A Preemptive Time-Threshold Based Multi-Guard Bandwidth Allocation Scheme for Cellular Networks ", Proc. of the Sixth Advanced International Conference on Telecommunications,AICT 2010, Barcelona,Spain,May 2010.

[15] I. Candan and M. Salamah, "Analytical Modeling of a Time Threshold Based Bandwidth Allocation Scheme for Cellular Networks", Computer Communications, vol. 30, no. 5, pp. 1036 1043, 2007.

[16] http://www.um.es./fem/EjsWiki [accessed September 2016]

Analysis of the Usefulness of Mobile Eyetracker for the Recognition of Physical Activities

Peter Hevesi*, Jamie A. Ward*†, Orkhan Amiraslanov*, Gerald Pirkl* and Paul Lukowicz*‡
* German Research Center for Artificial Intelligence, Kaiserslautern, Germany
†University College London
‡University of Kaiserslautern
* peter.hevesi@dfki.de, † jamie@jamieward.net,
‡ orkhan.amiraslanov@dfki.de, § gerald.pirkl@dfki.de,
¶ paul.lukowicz@dfki.de

***Abstract*—We investigate the usefulness of information from a wearable eyetracker to detect physical activities during assembly and construction tasks. Large physical activities, like carrying heavy items and walking, are analysed alongside more precise, hand-tool activities like using a screwdriver. Statistical analysis of eye based features like fixation length and frequency of fixations show significant correlations for precise activities. Using this finding, we selected 10, calibration-free eye features to train a classifier for recognising up to 6 different activities. Frame-by-frame and event based results are presented using data from an 8-person dataset containing over 600 activity events. We also evaluate the recognition performance when gaze features are combined with data from wearable accelerometers and microphones. Our initial results show a duration-weighted event precision and recall of up to 0.69 & 0.84 for independently trained recognition on precise activities using gaze. This indicates that gaze is suitable for spotting subtle precise activities and can be a useful source for more sophisticated classifier fusion.**

Keywords–eyetracker; activity recognition; sensor fusion

I. INTRODUCTION

Understanding complex, self-organising, physical labour intensive work processes involving multiple persons is a key competence in applications like production line optimisation or construction management. Our research goal is to lay the foundation of a system, that is capable to analyse and understand such processes and provide hints for possible improvements. The first step towards that goal is to evaluate different unobstrusive sensing modalities that can be used in real word scenarios to detect physical activities of single group members. As part of this research, we investigated the usefulness of mobile eyetrackers for detecting physical activities.

Eyetracking is known to provide important insights about one's attention. Attention in turn is known to provide important indications of one's activity. As a consequence, as unobtrusive, affordable mobile eye trackers have started to emerge, there has been an increasing interest in using them for activity recognition [1]. To date the vast majority of such research had concentrated on activities directly related to visual attention and cognition (reading, watching TV, etc.) [2][3]. In this paper, we investigate the use of gaze information for the recognition of physical activities, specifically activities related to an assembly/construction task. In doing so, we focus on the following questions:

1) Can gaze information help spot subtle precise activities such as for example screw driving in a stream of heterogeneous physical activity data? Such spotting is a well known, hard problem in wearable activity recognition.
   One of the reasons, it is so hard, is the variability associated with the motions involved in many such activities (e.g., tightening a screw can be done with one hand, with two hands, with a screwdriver, or with a drill – all using a variety of grips). Another is the fact that many of the involved motions occur spuriously, for example during walking or random gesticulation. We hypothesize that the need to fix the gaze in a certain pattern during many such precise activities can help overcome those problems.
2) How fine grained is the discriminative power of gaze information for physical activities? Can it be used to distinguish activities on a fine grade or it is restricted to broad categories characterized by the need for an increased attention or focus level.
3) How strongly user and setting dependent is the gaze information?
4) How does gaze information compare to standard wearable activity recognition sensors such as accelerometers and sound? Can it complement such information?

We investigate these questions in an experiment where four participants have to build up a large TV wall (described previously in [4]). Note that the purpose of this work is not to present a highly optimized ready-to-use solution with the best possible recognition rate in the above specific application. Instead, it is to provide an initial analysis of the suitability of gaze tracking for physical activity recognition with respect to the questions above.

In Section II, we provide a brief overview of state-of-the-art methods in our research field. In Section III, we describe our experimental setup, used sensors and generated datasets. Our evaluation methodology including the proposed feature sets is described in Section IV and finally our results are presented and discussed in Section V.

II. RELATED WORK

Research into activity recognition using wearable sensing has continued to grow in recent years. Many studies deploy distributed body-worn or mobile inertial sensors to recognise a wide-range of physical activities (see [5] for an overview).

A common sensing modality is sound. In [6], Lu et al. introduce a mobile-phone based system for classifying ambient sound, voices and music. Previous works use multiple streams of audio to recognise social situations [7][8], or to infer collocation and social network information [9].

Combined sound and movement data obtained from the mobiles of groups was recently used to analyse pedestrian congestion at busy thoroughfares, making use of changes in people's step-intervals and ambient audio [10]. Wrist-worn microphones and accelerometers were first used together to detect hand-tool activities in a wood workshop scenario [11]. More recently, these sensors were used to recognise physical collocation and collaboration of co-workers performing a group task [4].

A. Eye-based activity recognition

Eye tracking is a widely used technique in human computer interaction (HCI), for example in assistive technologies for people with limited motor skills [12], and is used in a growing body of research in Ubicomp (e.g., on attention [2]). Typically, researchers are interested in the object of a user's gaze – what it is that the user is looking at – however, another approach is to analyse the patterns created by eye movement in different situations. Patterns of eye fixation and saccadic movement recorded from changes in the eye's electrical activity (electrooculography, or EOG), were first used in a wearable setting to detect reading activities while walking [1]. This work was then developed to detect activities such as writing, reading, watching a video, etc. [13]. An advantage of a pattern-based approach is that no calibration is needed with a worldview video. Platforms like Google Glass include the ability to record blink rate, which when combined with head movement can be an effective method for recognising activities [3].

Vidal et al. introduced a calibration-free, gaze interaction method based on tracking the smooth pursuit movements that occur when the eye follows a moving target [14]. And in [15] a commercial, wearable EOG system, the Jiins Meme, was used as a novel gestural input device based on a similar approach.

Closest to our research is the work in [16]. The authors proposed a system based on eyetracker and first person videos to recognise daily activities. However, this work focuses on activities directly related to gaze (e.g., reading, video watching) compared to our approach, where we want to detect rather physical activities (e.g., screw driving), where a direct gaze contact is not an essential part of the activity.

III. EXPERIMENT

We designed an experiment as a benchmark to evaluate different sensors and algorithms for group activity recognition.

A. Scenario

In the experiment, four participants collaborate to build a 2.5 meter high TV wall consisting of 8 large LCD screens, 3 base panels, 18 screen spacers, and more than 50 screws. The parts are stored in containers at a storage area which is separated by a ca. 25 meter long hallway from the assembly area.

The building phase included the following main steps: 1.) Unload screens (each screen weights 8 kg) and other TV parts from the containers, 2.) Carry items to the assembly area, 3.) Assemble and place base items, 4.) Lift screens onto the wall, 5.) Fix screens on the wall by tightening the screws. After the build phase and a short break the participants perform the reversed process: 6.) removing the screws, 7.) taking down the screens and other parts carefully, 8.) carrying back to the storage area, 9.) put them back into the containers.

Generally, the participants had the freedom to organise and execute the tasks as they thought it's best. The overall task takes usually from 40 minutes up to 1 hour.

B. Wearable sensors

As shown on Figure 1, the participants were equipped with a mobile eyetracker, a sound recording device with two separate microphones and three inertial measurement units.

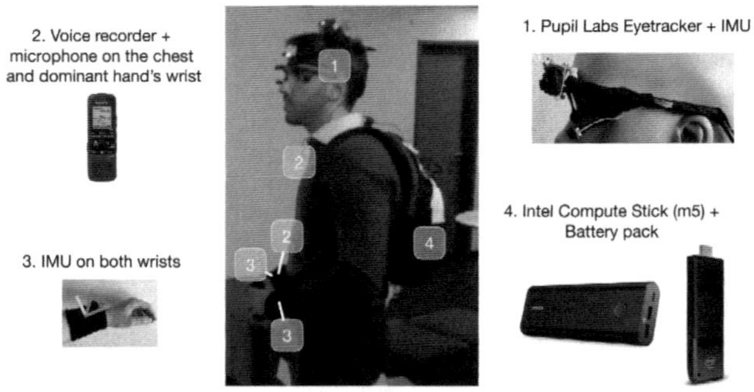

Figure 1. Recording setup for each participant includes an eyetracker connected to a small recording computer. Additional sensors: IMU on both arms and head, microphone on the wrist and at the chest.

a) Mobile eyetracker: The eyetracker setup consists of a head worn device from Pupil Labs [17] connected to an Intel Compute Stick with an m5 1.6 GHz processor as recording device (running Ubuntu 16.10). Both devices were powered by a portable 20100 mAh battery. The recording itself was done using Pupil Capture (v0.82) software. We implemented scripts to remotely control and monitor the recordings. The overall cost of this eyetracker setup is around 1600 Euros, which is significantly lower then many other commercially available mobile eyetracker solutions. This makes the setup better scalable for real world applications.

b) Inertial measurement unit (IMU): For tracking movements of the participants, they wore IMUs on both wrists and one on the head. The IMU devices record 3-axis acceleration, gyro, and magnetic field as well as 3D orientation with approximately 40 Hz.

c) Sound recorder: Each participant wore two microphones: one on the dominant hand's wrist and a second one attached on the chest. The microphones were connected to a voice recorder capable of recording stereo sound and were saved as the two channels of the sound file.

C. Datasets and labels

We created two datasets (referred to as dataset A and dataset B) by recording the above described experiment performed by two different group of participants. Each dataset includes IMU data, sound recording and eyetracker recordings (world camera video, eye camera video, eye and eye movement data, fixation events). To help the annotation process, four additional stationary cameras recorded the scene. Two cameras were recording the assembly area, one the storage area and one the hallway.

We created two label sets to analyse the discriminative power of the features, whether the system can distinguish single activities or rather just specific type of an activity.

a) Six class problem: The detailed label set includes six classes as follows:

1) Adjust: during these activities the subject is interacting (placing, taking or adjusting) with screws without any tool.
2) Screwdriver: subject tightens or loosens screws using screwdriver.
3) Drill: events when a participant tightens or loosens screws using a powerdrill with screwdriver attachment.
4) Carry: the times when one or two participants carry the heavy TV screens to or from the assembly area.
5) Screen placement: segments where screens are taken out of or placed back into the container or put on or taken off the TV wall.
6) Walk: person moves between assembly area and storage area (without carrying heavy objects).

b) One class problem: The second set looks only at the single class of Precise activities:

1) Precise Activity: mostly consists of small and precise movements. Typically it requires increased attention of the subjects. This includes the above labeled instances of screwdriver, adjust and drill events.

The ground truth labels for both sets were annotated using mainly the first person view (world camera) of the eyetracker recordings for each participant. The degree of freedom to organise and perform the experiment resulted often in unexpected event flows with lot of short interruptions and activity changes. This proved to be a real challenge for the labeling making low level event annotation nearly impossible, on the other hand this makes the data realistic. By keeping this in mind, we consider each ground truth label as a rough description what a participant is mainly doing in a given time interval of a few seconds up to a minute. Short interruptions (e.g., person taking additional screw from the desk or interacting with other participants) are not represented in this ground truth.

In total, we labeled 606 events with an overall length of ca. 260 minutes.

IV. Activity Recognition System

A. Features

For further analysis, we extracted features on the time series data of each participant using a centered sliding window of 30 seconds. The label for each sample is defined as the current ground truth event at the center of the window, or null if there are no active events for the current person.

a) Eyetracker features: One important eye movement feature is fixation (looking at something for a time period), because it could be an indicator of increased attention. The recording software already provides extracted fixation events described by start time and duration. A feature vector is easily calculated by sliding a window across this output and taking the sum of the fixation durations inside each window.

Figure 2 shows the correlation between the fixation length feature and a subject's activities. The temporal changes in the fixation length values are synchronous to the currently performed task (color on the top represent different activities). Statistical analysis confirms the relationship between an activity and fixation length values during it. The average fixation length for "drill" and "screwdriver" events is significantly higher than for any other activity which indicates that it might be a strong feature (see box-plot on the right side of Figure 2).

A similarly interesting feature can be extracted using the gap or duration between two fixations. A lower gap duration means that there are frequent fixations over a certain time, meanwhile a higher duration represent times when the participant is not looking at anything for a long time (scanning the environment).

Information about the pupil size, could help to distinguish dark and bright environments. Accommodation (change of viewing distance) can also cause changes of pupil size.

For this study, we calculated 10 eye-derived features for each sliding window: 1,2) average and median of the durations of fixation events starting or ending in the window, 3,4) average and median of the fixation gap values, 5,6) average of the pupil position in spheric coordinates (ϕ and θ) 7,8) standard deviation of the pupil position in spheric coordinates, 9) average pupil size, 10) standard deviation of the pupil size.

The above features are calibration-free meaning that the device displacement (or wrong calibration) does not influence the results.

b) Acceleration features: The 3-axis accelerometer signals (x,y,z) are combined to give a single orientation-invariant reading, $a = \sqrt{x^2 + y^2 + z^2}$, for each of the head, left, and right-wrist IMUs (a_h,a_l, and a_r). For each of these readings four standard features are calculated across a 1 second rolling window, these are: mean (μ), standard deviation (σ), short-term energy (E), and zero-crossing rate (ZC). ZC, a simple measure of dominant signal frequency, is calculated by counting the zero-crossings on each window after subtracting μ.

c) Sound features: Sound signals from each participant's dominant wrist, s_r (all were right-handed), and head, s_h, are downsampled from the recording rate of $44.1kHz$ to $8kHz$ (16 bit). Two features are extracted for each of these across a rolling window of 1 second: short-term energy, E, and zero-crossing rate, ZC. These features were chosen because of their widespread use in low-cost speech and audio analysis [18]. We also included an intensity analysis feature, calculated as $ia = \frac{E_r}{E_h} - \frac{E_h}{E_r}$, where E_r and E_h are the short term sound energies of the right-hand and head-recordings respectively. This measure can be used to distinguish sounds made closer to one microphone or another from sounds made further away from both [19]. For a sound made close to the hand, $ia > 0$, and for further away, $ia \approx 0$.

d) Feature sets: For each participant in each dataset, we created three feature matrices where each row represents the following features:

1) As baseline, we use the feature vector including the 12 acceleration and 5 sound features, since this is

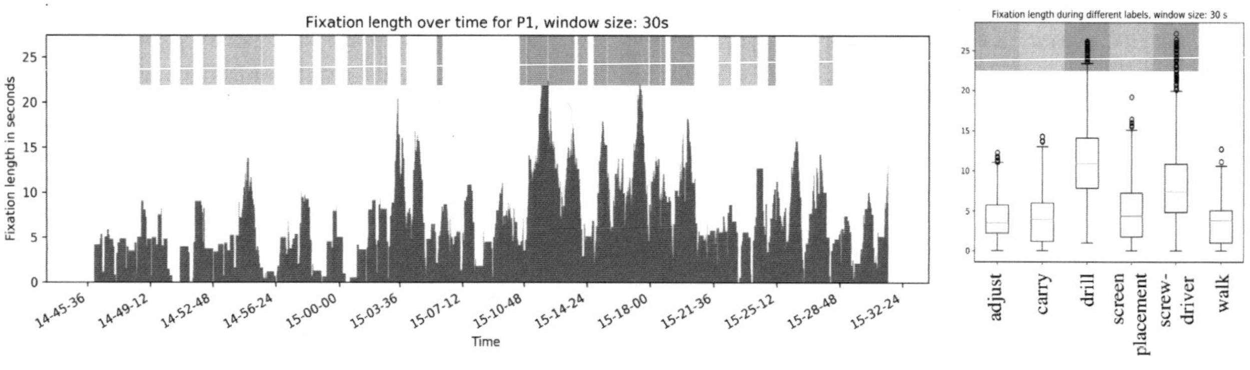

Figure 2. Left: sum of the lengths of each fixation event inside a 30 s window over time, the color on the top indicates the current activity of the subject. Right: statistical box plot about fixation length feature values during specific activities (see x axis) - same color scheme on top.

the most widespread approach. (Later referred as acc+snd)

2) The feature vector of the 10 eyetracker based features as described above is the topic of the main investigation in this paper (Later referred as eye)
3) For a preview, how well a combination of sensors performs, we combine simply the 12 acceleration and 5 sound features with the 10 eye-derived information to create a single feature vector for each time frame. (Later referred as all)

B. Evaluation methods

For evaluation, the features matrices are split up to training and test sets depending on the evaluation method. The training set is used then to train a Naive Bayes classifier. We applied several different standard classifiers, but found Naive Bayes to be sufficient for the purposes of the current work. Training and testing was implemented on Python using the scikit-learn toolkit [20].

In the testing phase, for each new samples (one row of the feature matrix) the classifier predicts an activity label. This is referred to as a frame based result. If sequential rows receive the same activity class predictions, these are merged together into an event. These predicted events are then used for event based evaluation.

a) Experiment dependent evaluation: The experiment dependent evaluations were performed on the primary dataset (dataset A). Ideally, the leave-one-person out would be the preferred method for training and evaluation. This approach however doesn't work well in this case because there are some activities performed almost exclusively by one participant. This leads to insufficient data for training.

Instead features are divided into six smaller sets, while trying to keep an equal distribution of samples for each label. A purely random selection of features for each split can result in a misleadingly high accuracy when samples from the same event are used for training and test. To avoid this the training and test samples are always strictly separated by the events they belong to. On the splits a six-fold cross validation was performed and the average scores were calculated over the iterations.

b) Experiment independent evaluation: In this evaluation, the performance of the recognition is tested on completely unseen data (not used for training in any way). The system is trained on all samples of a dataset B (including every person). The test is performed then on the extracted features of dataset A, which were not used for training at all in this case.

This indicates how well the system can generalize the results and handle later datasets without any additional training effort.

c) Frame based evaluation: Standard precision and recall values are calculated for the frame-based evaluation. Each predicted label is considered as true positive if it's equal to the sample's ground truth label or as false positive otherwise. A ground truth label is a false negative if the predicted label for the same sample is different.

d) Event based evaluation: In many cases it's more important to detect activity events rather than detecting each frame on an activity. For example, the information that a subject performed an activity is sufficient and the exact timings are less relevant. To get comparable results to the frame-based analysis, event based precision and recall values are calculated.

In the event based evaluation, we compare detection events with the ground truth. A detected event is considered as a true positive (TP_{det}) if it has an overlap with a ground truth event of the same activity (for the same participant) or as a false positive (FP_{det}) otherwise. Similarly ground truth events are labeled as true positives (TP_{gt}) if they are detected at least once otherwise as false negatives (FN_{gt}).

Analogous to the standard frame definitions the event-based metrics are calculated as:

$$precision = \frac{TP_{det}}{TP_{det} + FP_{det}} \quad (1)$$

and,

$$recall = \frac{TP_{gt}}{TP_{gt} + FN_{gt}} \quad (2)$$

V. Results and Discussion

The precision/recall results for different sensor combinations are given for the six class problem in Figure 3 and for the one class problem in Figure 4.

Before we go into discussion of individual issues, it is important to point out a general observation related to all

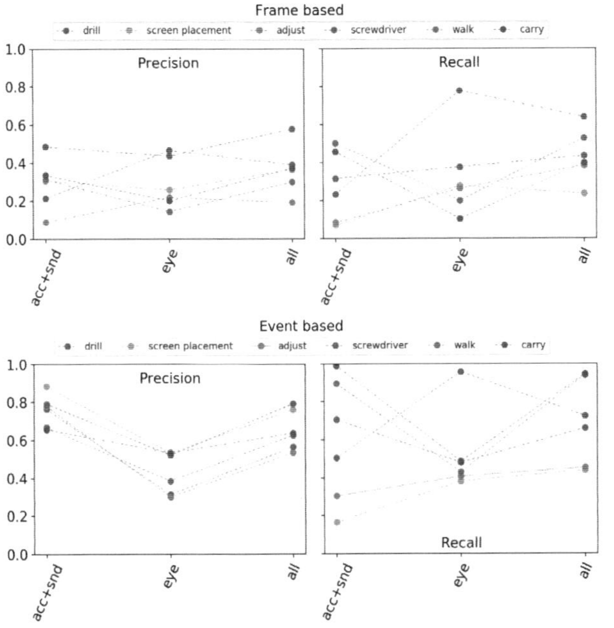

Figure 3. Six class, dataset dependent evaluation using different feature sets (acc+snd: acceleration and sound features, eye: eye features only, all: sound, acceleration, and eye). Top plots show frame, bottom plots show event-based precision and recall results.

results that involve gaze features: whereas acceleration and sound only results always show a big improvement when going from frame by frame to event based results (which is to be expected), this improvement is much smaller when gaze features are involved. Where in many cases eye features are better on frame level, acceleration/sound win on event level. The explanation of this fact is related to the way people's visual attention works. In very few cases, we keep our attention 100% on a single task. Instead, while focusing mainly on the main task, we tend to glance at other things (e.g., someone we speak to while tightening a screw). Since such distractions tend to be short, on frame level, they do not have much impact. However on event level, they fragment the result. Thus where there is in reality a single event, the system detects several separated by short breaks.

In our event evaluation, this means that what is a single insertion in the accelerometer data becomes several insertions in the eye related data. This is nicely illustrated by the duration-weighted normalized event results shown in Figure 4. The values are calculated as follows:

$$precision_{weighted} = \frac{\sum len(TP^i_{det})}{\sum len(TP^i_{det}) + \sum len(FP^i_{det})} \quad (3)$$

and,

$$recall_{weighted} = \frac{\sum len(TP^i_{gt})}{\sum len(TP^i_{gt}) + \sum len(FN^i_{gt})} \quad (4)$$

where $len(TP^i)$ means the length of the i-th true positive event (for false positive and false negative events analog). With this measure, small errors (short false positive or if a short event isn't recognized) are less significant. It can be seen that for the duration-weighted case, eye based features (1) significantly improve when moving to event based recognition and (2) are better than acceleration+sound case. On the other hand the non-weighted results get worse for event based evaluation and are lower than acceleration+sound. In future work, we will investigate more sophisticated temporal smoothing for eye based features to address this problem.

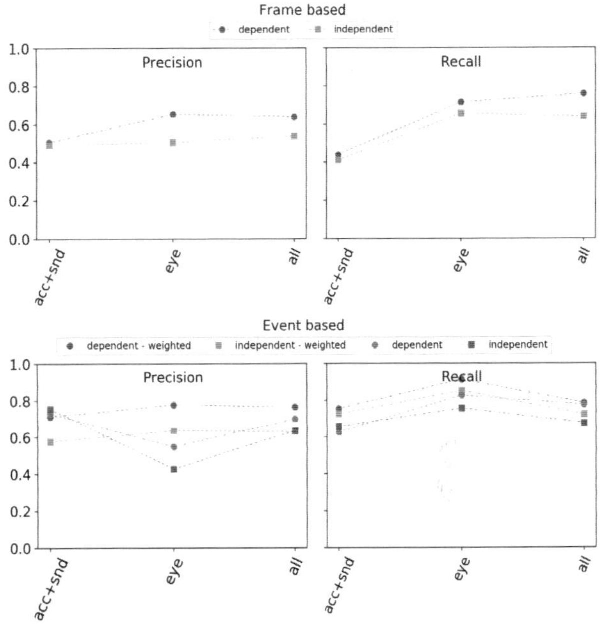

Figure 4. One class results for both dataset-dependent and independent evaluation. Frame (top) and event-based (bottom) precision and recall as well as event length weighted values are also represented. (acc+snd: acceleration and sound features, eye: eye features only, all: sound, acceleration, and eye)

With respect to the four questions raised in the introduction, the following can be said:

1) Gaze features seem clearly suitable for spotting subtle precises activities. Thus, for example, the weighted precision and recall for the one class problem in Figure 4 are 0.78 and 0.91 using the eye feature set (dataset dependent training).
2) As shown by the 6 class case (Figure 3), gaze based features allow a finer distinction then just a broad "Precise" activities class. Results for the screen placement, adjusting, and the individual types of screw driving are not perfect but well above random.
3) As a comparison of the experiment dependent and experiment independent results in all the graphs shows gaze based features are fairly robust with respect to different users (we have different subjects in the two experiments so that experiment (in)dependent means subject (in)dependent. Indeed the best performing combination (eye) in Figure 4 achieves a weighted event precision and recall of 0.69 & 0.84.
4) As can be seen in Figure 3, screen placement, adjusting and the individual types of screwdriving are resolved much better by gaze features then by acceleration+sound. Whenever acceleration and sound are not too bad, combining them provides further

improvement, which means that they do contain complementary information.

From the above, the focus of our future work will be on individualized recognition chains for each type of events (with subsequent plausibility like fusion), temporal smoothing for the gaze features on event level and combining eye gaze with image recognition methods for detecting visual context.

ACKNOWLEDGMENT

The work is funded by the German Federal Ministry of Education and Research (BMBF).

REFERENCES

[1] A. Bulling, J. A. Ward, H.-W. Gellersen, and G. Tröster, "Robust recognition of reading activity in transit using wearable electrooculography," in PERVASIVE, May 2008, pp. 19–37.

[2] M. Vidal, D. H. Nguyen, and K. Lyons, "Looking at or through?: Using eye tracking to infer attention location for wearable transparent displays," in Proceedings of the 2014 ACM International Symposium on Wearable Computers, ser. ISWC '14. New York, NY, USA: ACM, 2014, pp. 87–90. [Online]. Available: http://doi.acm.org/10.1145/2634317.2634344

[3] S. Ishimaru, K. Kunze, K. Kise, J. Weppner, A. Dengel, P. Lukowicz, and A. Bulling, "In the blink of an eye: Combining head motion and eye blink frequency for activity recognition with google glass," in Proceedings of the 5th Augmented Human International Conference, ser. AH '14. New York, NY, USA: ACM, 2014, pp. 15:1–15:4. [Online]. Available: http://doi.acm.org/10.1145/2582051.2582066

[4] J. A. Ward, P. Lukowicz, G. Pirkl, and P. Hevesi, "Detecting physical collaborations in a group task using Body-Worn microphones and accelerometers," in 13th Workshop on Context and Activity Modeling and Recognition (CoMoRea'17), Big Island, USA, Mar. 2017, pp. 268–273.

[5] A. Bulling, U. Blanke, and B. Schiele, "A tutorial on human activity recognition using body-worn inertial sensors," ACM Computing Surveys (CSUR), vol. 46, no. 3, 2014, p. 33.

[6] H. Lu, W. Pan, N. D. Lane, T. Choudhury, and A. T. Campbell, "Soundsense: Scalable sound sensing for people-centric applications on mobile phones," in Proceedings of the 7th International Conference on Mobile Systems, Applications, and Services, ser. MobiSys '09. New York, NY, USA: ACM, 2009, pp. 165–178. [Online]. Available: http://doi.acm.org/10.1145/1555816.1555834

[7] Y. Yang, B. Guo, Z. Yu, and H. He, "Social activity recognition and recommendation based on mobile sound sensing," in 2013 IEEE 10th International Conference on Ubiquitous Intelligence and Computing and 2013 IEEE 10th International Conference on Autonomic and Trusted Computing, Dec 2013, pp. 103–110.

[8] N. Eagle and A. S. Pentland, "Social network computing," in International Conference on Ubiquitous Computing. Springer, 2003, pp. 289–296.

[9] D. Wyatt, T. Choudhury, J. Bilmes, and J. A. Kitts, "Inferring colocation and conversation networks from privacy-sensitive audio with implications for computational social science," ACM Trans. Intell. Syst. Technol., vol. 2, no. 1, Jan. 2011, pp. 7:1–7:41.

[10] T. Nishimura, T. Higuchi, H. Yamaguchi, and T. Higashino, "Detecting smoothness of pedestrian flows by participatory sensing with mobile phones," in Proceedings of the 2014 ACM International Symposium on Wearable Computers, ser. ISWC '14. New York, NY, USA: ACM, 2014, pp. 15–18. [Online]. Available: http://doi.acm.org/10.1145/2634317.2642869

[11] J. A. Ward, P. Lukowicz, G. Tröster, and T. E. Starner, "Activity recognition of assembly tasks using body-worn microphones and accelerometers," IEEE Trans. Pattern Analysis and Machine Intelligence, vol. 28, no. 10, October 2006b, pp. 1553–1567.

[12] R. Barea, L. Boquete, M. Mazo, and E. Lopez, "System for assisted mobility using eye movements based on electrooculography," Trans. on Rehabilitation Engineering, vol. 10, no. 4, December 2002, pp. 209–218.

[13] A. Bulling, J. A. Ward, H. Gellersen, and G. Tröster, "Eye movement analysis for activity recognition," in (Ubicomp) Proceedings of the 11th international conference on Ubiquitous computing. New York, NY, USA: ACM, 2009, pp. 41–50.

[14] M. Vidal, A. Bulling, and H. Gellersen, "Pursuits: spontaneous interaction with displays based on smooth pursuit eye movement and moving targets," in Proc. UbiComp. ACM, 2013, pp. 439–448.

[15] M. Dhuliawala, J. Lee, J. Shimizu, A. Bulling, K. Kunze, T. Starner, and W. Woo, "Smooth eye movement interaction using eog glasses," in Proceedings of the 18th ACM International Conference on Multimodal Interaction. ACM, 2016, pp. 307–311.

[16] Y. Shiga, T. Toyama, Y. Utsumi, K. Kise, and A. Dengel, "Daily activity recognition combining gaze motion and visual features," in Proceedings of the 2014 ACM International Joint Conference on Pervasive and Ubiquitous Computing: Adjunct Publication. ACM, 2014, pp. 1103–1111.

[17] M. Kassner, W. Patera, and A. Bulling, "Pupil: An open source platform for pervasive eye tracking and mobile gaze-based interaction," in Adjunct Proceedings of the 2014 ACM International Joint Conference on Pervasive and Ubiquitous Computing, ser. UbiComp '14 Adjunct. New York, NY, USA: ACM, 2014, pp. 1151–1160. [Online]. Available: http://doi.acm.org/10.1145/2638728.2641695

[18] R. Bachu, S. Kopparthi, B. Adapa, and B. Barkana, "Separation of voiced and unvoiced using zero crossing rate and energy of the speech signal," in American Society for Engineering Education (ASEE) Zone Conference Proceedings, 2008, pp. 1–7.

[19] J. A. Ward, P. Lukowicz, and G. Tröster, "Roc analysis of partitioning method for activity recognition using two microphones," in Adjunct Proc. of the 3rd Int. Conf. on Pervasive Comp., vol. 191, May. 8-13 2005a.

[20] F. Pedregosa, G. Varoquaux, A. Gramfort, V. Michel, B. Thirion, O. Grisel, M. Blondel, P. Prettenhofer, R. Weiss, V. Dubourg, J. Vanderplas, A. Passos, D. Cournapeau, M. Brucher, M. Perrot, and E. Duchesnay, "Scikit-learn: Machine learning in Python," Journal of Machine Learning Research, vol. 12, 2011, pp. 2825–2830.

Beware: Mobile and Web Application to Prevent Crimes against the Patrimony, Life, Body and Health

Alexa Tataje[1], Marco Florián[1]
[1]Faculty of Engineering
Peruvian University of Applied Sciences UPC,
Lima, Peru
e-mail: {u201112163, u813651}@upc.edu.pe

David Mauricio[1, 2]
[2]Department of Computer Science, FISI
National University of San Marcos UNMSM,
Lima, Peru
e-mail: dmauricios@unmsm.edu.pe

Abstract—**Faced with the difficulty to know all the dangerous areas and find the latest information to avoid becoming the victim of a crime, this article proposes a mobile application for smartphones and smartwatches called *Beware*, which shows the dangerous zones within a specific geographical area according to the day and time of the week. This application also allows reporting emergencies to the corresponding emergency service entities and communicating events that put at risk the patrimony, life, body and health of other users and yourself. In addition, another Web application is proposed for the emergency service (police station, fire brigade or municipal patrols) responsible for receiving the emergency calls. User tests show that 14 out of 15 citizens consider that the proposed application is useful and very useful for public safety.**

Keywords-geolocation; mobile computing; crime prevention; smartwatch.

I. Introduction

Public safety is promoted worldwide to effectively safeguard the inherent human rights, particularly, the right to life, personal integrity, the inviolability of the home, and freedom of movement; however, over 1.5 billion people all over the world live in countries affected by violence, conflicts and high criminal rates; over 526,000 people are savagely murdered every year, which is slightly more than one person per minute [1].

The fight against citizen insecurity, in general, comes from the different government levels whether local, regional, central or federal, and is executed reactively, aimed to capture delinquents before or after the criminal activity takes place, or in a proactive manner by attacking the root causes of citizen insecurity. In both situations, the information and communication technologies are an essential tool. One way information technology is used for prevention are the so-called crime maps, which show information about the criminal activities within a geographical area. These are used in various countries, such as 'CrimeReports' [2] in the USA, 'InstaGIS' [3] in Chile, and 'Onde fui Roubado' [4] in Brazil. However, most are Web applications, which makes them less used than a mobile app. They do not present information in real time nor the crime intensity like a heat map.

This paper presents a smartphone and smartwatch mobile application that allows citizens to inform, in real time, about the security level of the area where they are located, and report any crime or possible crimes. It also proposes a Web application to be used by the police so they can see the criminal activities and act. The use of a smartwatch is justified due to its ease of use, low cost and lower theft risk compared to a smartphone. In addition, it is estimated that sales will be of 66.71 million units in 2017 [5] and by 2020 it will become one of the most sold wearables [6].

This article is organized in 5 sections. In Section 2, we present a review of mobile and Web applications related to crime maps. Section 3 describes the proposed mobile and Web applications. The use of these applications in an area of Lima, Peru, and its results are presented in Section 4. Finally, conclusions follow in Section 5.

II. Related Work

There are four important aspects to consider when developing a crime map mobile application: data collection, data analysis, architecture and related applications.

The data is the most important component for the whole crime map. It must be timely, significant and of quality; however, many times this information is not available or accessible, therefore the work in this context is aimed at building a criminal database from different sources. The collection of data from sources such as websites, news sites, blogs, social media, and Really Simple Syndication (RSS) feeds is presented in [10]. In [12], the data is collected based on the information obtained from interviews with the police, reports and the documentation in the occurrence books. A crowdsourcing based mobile application that allows people to send information about criminal activities is presented in [14]. In Beware, we decided to collect crime information from different governmental sources and to use crowdsourcing, allowing users to report crime events into the mobile application.

Once the crime information is obtained, it is analyzed to make decisions. The analysis could be about the criminal activity spatial (geographical) behavior, criminal records, crime trend, or urban infrastructure, among others. In [7], it is explained that a factor that could help reduce citizen insecurity is the analysis of the spatial behavior of the delinquents known within their activity space (Crime

Theory), since it can determine the likelihood of possible crime places. In [8], Sathyadeyan et al, include criminal records for the delinquents, the causes for crime occurrence, and every day crime factors. An emergency management system for public transport, based on a Geographic Information System (GIS), is proposed in [9], which includes the crime trend, and guides police officers might use to capture the delinquents. An analysis of the urban aspects related to criminal activities is studied in [15], where it is concluded that there is a correlation between the streets width, the number of construction floors, the type of facilities and neighborhood, and the criminal activities. In our approach, we not only count the occurrences of crime events in an area, but also take into consideration the aspects of the streets in that area that might represent a risk for people. This could be, for example, if the area has been abandoned or it has drug addicts rounding the streets (Table III).

Several architectures have been proposed for systems related to public safety. A client-server software architecture to determine more accurately the police location is presented in [11]; this considers that the mobile device should have an Assisted Global Positioning System (A-GPS) and be compatible with a HyperText Markup Language version 5 (HTML5) geolocation so it can connect with Google Maps API and the data center through JavaScript Object Notation (JSON). In [14], the architecture is designed around cloud development with the integration of GPS functions. In the same manner, in [13], the use of GPS is incorporated in the software architecture, and this consists of five layers: information knowledge layer, business support layer, data layer, business application layer, and user level. For our application, we considered to use GPS functionalities to capture, in real time, the user's current location, and use the Google Maps API to show him/her current map positions as well as the dangerous zones and crime events reported around.

There are several mobile applications related to public safety that take into consideration a crime map and allow reporting criminal activities. In [12], the authors added a search functionality for information about arrested people, the display of a map with the crime zones, and it also accepts alerts about new crime zones. [10] allows the police to receive information about the citizen's location – by GPS – and for him/her to receive information about the closest police station. In [13], six crowdsourcing mobile applications were evaluated, among which we mention: CrimeWatch Mobile, which displays the crimes reported within a 1-mile radius around the user current position; Community Against Crime, which sends email or Short Message Service (SMS) notifications about crimes reported by a registered or an anonymous user; CommunityAlert that includes reporting floods or fires, which are sent to the closest police station; and MyDistress, from where the closest police stations can be located. The application proposed in [14] also includes sending a report through short messages, and phone calls to all emergency contacts and institutions. A HTML5 based application that allows police officers to register a crime according to the GPS location at that very moment, attach pictures or videos related to the incident, and display on a map or chart the crimes reported, is proposed in [10]. In the Beware mobile application, it is not only possible to report a fixed type of event, as shown in Table II, but also any other incident or emergency as, for example, a land slide or flood. We added a type "other", which can be further explained by the user and viewable by others in the wall of events. Another useful feature added to the application is when a crime event (e.g. a house robbery or a fire incident) is reported close to a favorite location (e.g. your home, your university or your work) and a notification is sent to the user, so him/her can be timely informed.

Three mobile applications were selected to analyze their features. These applications were downloaded and installed on mobile phones that supported Android. Table I shows the summary of each criteria we used for this analysis.
Y = if the application complies with the feature.

TABLE I. SUMMARY OF ANALYSIS

Feature	Applications		
	Community Against Crime	***Community Alert***	***MyDistress***
View crime list	Y		
Share GPS coordinate to local authority	Y	Y	Y
View nearest police station		Y	Y
Send email/SMS about crimes	Y		
Share crime with others	Y	Y	Y
Share crime incident through social media	Y		
Send help alert to local authority		Y	Y
Send report to emergency contacts		Y	
Capture and share photo	Y		
Capture and share video	Y		
Integrate with a Web application	Y		
Coverage area	Malaysia Singapore	Australia	Malaysia Singapore

Based on the evaluation of the applications, it was observed that the three applications do not show the reports of crimes on a map. Only one of them allows to show them in a list (Community Against Crime). In the case of the Community Alert, it allows to notify the user's emergency contacts and shows the crime events, but in a general way and without evaluating if they are close to the user. Two of the applications have not been updated in 4 and 5 years, and none of the three applications perform an analysis of the information shared by their users. In comparison to Beware, the crime reports users share are used to create dangerous zones, as well as official police records. This way, it is possible to provide more reliable information, since there is a risk that they will register non-real crimes. In addition, hazards that exist on the streets (Table III) and the possibility of notifying emergency contacts are included to create dangerous areas. Additionally, the application notifies the user when entering a dangerous area, sends the location and report information to a local authority and the emergency contacts if requested, displays a map with the crimes closest to the user's location and a wall with the list of crimes that includes photographs.

III. BEWARE

A. *Background*

A mobile application called *Beware* has been developed. Its main objective is to warn citizens when they enter a dangerous area, report any crimes or risk events, and request assistance from an entity or emergency contact. To respond quickly to a criminal activity, the application has been designed to be used also by the security staff, police stations and fire stations. Also, with the information gathered, it is possible to generate a report of the crimes that are not reported to the police station and, in this way, create action plans.

Figure 1 shows the interaction between the citizen and the functionalities that Beware offers.

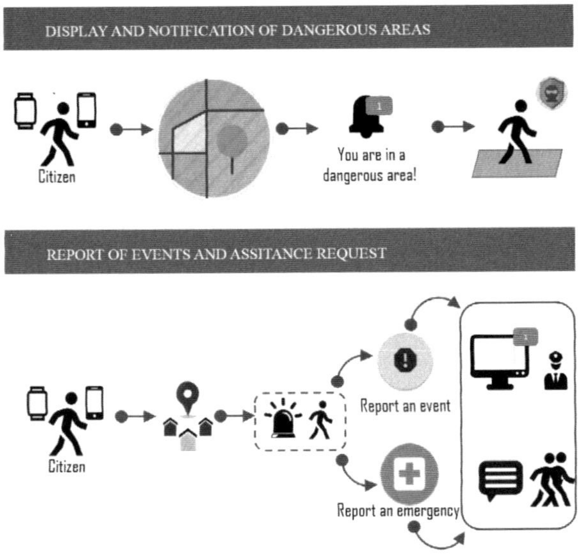

Figure 1. Beware flowchart.

B. *Development*

Data Analysis

The five steps for unstructured data analysis proposed in [8] and the criminal activities grouping given in [9] were considered. To collect data for the first time, public information sources were chosen, which are shown in Table II. After implementing the mobile applications for smartphones and smartwatches, these will be included as information sources for documenting new crimes.

TABLE II. PUBLIC INFORMATION SOURCES USED

Information source	Information used
Public Safety Local Plan	Crime map, Risk map, Critical points, Incidence detail about the crimes occurred
Surveillance staff opinion	Occurrences during their shift

The Public Safety Local Plans were reviewed to obtain a standard of the variables. We choose the most important variables that affect the citizen's patrimony, life, body and health. There were also interviews to obtain information, opinions and suggestions from the surveillance staff.

Regarding the data analysis, the most relevant crimes and risks were taken into consideration; these are listed in Table III. To identify delinquency patterns and trends within a specific place, the collected database was analyzed, which was spread according to the day of the week (7 days), hour range (every 6 hours), the amount of crime events (3 crimes or more) and how close these events are between each other (50 meters or less). The result of the analysis while identifying the pattern showed the places with the highest concentration of reported crimes, which, when manually grouped in polygons, form the areas with a delinquency index. The type of risks occurring in those polygons was also identified.

TABLE III. TYPE OF CRIME AND RISK

Type of crime	*Type of risk*
Burglary	Scarce lighting
Robbery of an establishment	Concentration of drug addicts
Personal theft	Abandoned area
Car parts theft	Concentration of alcoholics
Vehicle theft	Construction area
Scam	Street vendors
Micro drug trafficking	Informal bus stop
Clandestine prostitution	Frequent fights
Pernicious gang activities	

To obtain the areas prone to crime, we first identify the crime type level (Table IV), then the risk type level (Table V), and finally the crime percentage level that the created area contains. The crime type level refers to the occurrence degree and the crime priority at national level. The risk type level represents the degree it would harm a person while being near to a risk type, where the highest number is what would cause the most harm.

TABLE IV. CRIME TYPE LEVEL

Degree	Crime Type Level
5	Drugs and murder
4	Personal theft
3	Burglary, car parts or car theft
2	Robbery of an establishment, scams
1	Other (pernicious gang activities, clandestine prostitution, injuries)

TABLE V. RISK TYPE LEVEL

Degree	Risk Type Level
6	Concentration of drug addicts
5	Scarce lighting
4	Abandoned area
3	Concentration of alcoholics
2	Construction area
1	Other (street vendors, informal bus stop, frequent fights)
0	No risk

To qualify and visualize the crime level, the following concepts were taken into consideration. The crime percentage level within an area is the percentage that the criminal activities grouping represent compared to the total number of crimes that occurred within a day of the week and time range in that area. The danger value represents the amount of danger that exists in that area, and the danger level is the danger category to which each area belongs (Table VI). The danger value has been created from the International Standards Organization (ISO) 31000 risk management concepts, where the risk and type of impact are identified [16]. The risk represents the crimes and risks from Table III, and the type of impact are the levels in Tables IV and V.

TABLE VI. DANGER LEVELS

Classification	Lower Limit	Upper Limit
Very high	7.01	10
High	5.01	7
Medium	3.01	5
Low	1.01	3
Very low	0.00	1

The classification in Table VI is related to the ISO 31000, while the lower and upper limit ranges of the danger levels have been determined first by the maximum upper limit mean; from there, the areas with values higher than the midpoint were divided to be classified as "High" or "Very High". Meanwhile, values lower than the midpoint were established with a 2-difference-value interval for "Medium" and "Low", and finally, "Very Low" for values no greater than 1.

Equation (1) determines the danger value:

$$\text{Danger value} = \frac{(d + NPDP)}{2} + \frac{(NTD + NTR)}{2} \quad (1)$$

Where:

- **d:** Total crimes grouped in the area.
- **NPDP:** Percentage level of crimes within that area.
- **NTD:** Crime type level.
- **NTR:** Risk type level.

Each danger level is associated with a color, which can be seen when painting each dangerous area in the map of the mobile and Web applications (Table VII).

TABLE VII. DANGER LEVELS ACCORDING TO COLOR

Classification	Color	Value
Very high		c62828
High		d84315
Medium		ef6c00
Low		ff8f00
Very low		f9a825

Extract, Transform, Load (ETL) Structure

Aside from the information gathered, an ETL structure had to be done to elaborate the database. The data stored in the flat files and Web Services is extracted, then the transformation of the types of data from the corresponding fields takes place, and these are loaded into the database tables. For this, the quality of the data collected was verified wherever inconsistent terms were found, blank spaces and street names written backwards (e.g., Chavez Jorge instead of Jorge Chavez). The latter made it difficult to obtain the coordinates. To find the address where a crime occurred, it was necessary to make a connection with the Google Maps API to obtain the latitude and longitude through JSON, which were stored as spatial data in the database. The risks and crimes were associated to the geographical location (latitude and longitude), time, date, type and address where it occurred.

Software Architecture

The software architecture focuses on Model, View, and Controller (MVC), the geolocation services in the Google Maps API and the use of a cloud platform for the Web Services that the applications consume, as well as the PostgreSQL database with a PostGIS extension [17]. Next, the logical and physical architecture diagrams are shown.

Logical Architecture Diagram

In Figure 2, the logical architecture diagram describes the breakdown in the software architecture layer, which goes down to the level of the server containing them.

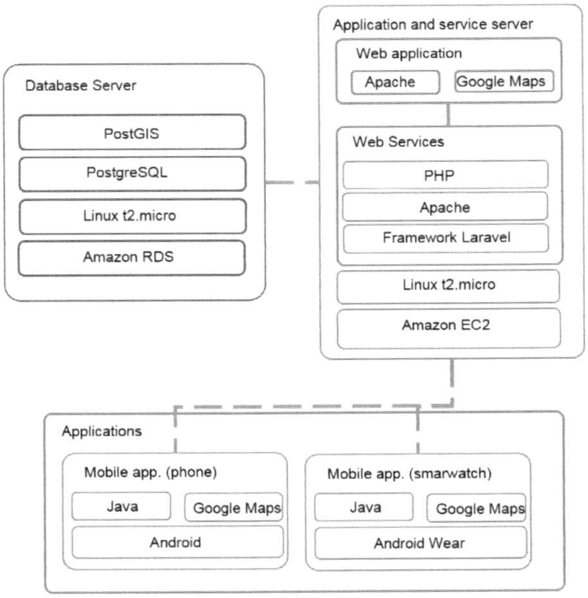

Figure 2. Logical architecture.

Physical Architecture Diagram

In Figure 3, the physical architecture diagram shows the Web Services and the Web application stored in the same Amazon Web Services Elastic Compute Cloud (Amazon EC2) instance. The Web application, Web Services and smartphone application require Internet to work, while the smartwatch application requires to be connected to the Internet via Bluetooth to the smartphone.

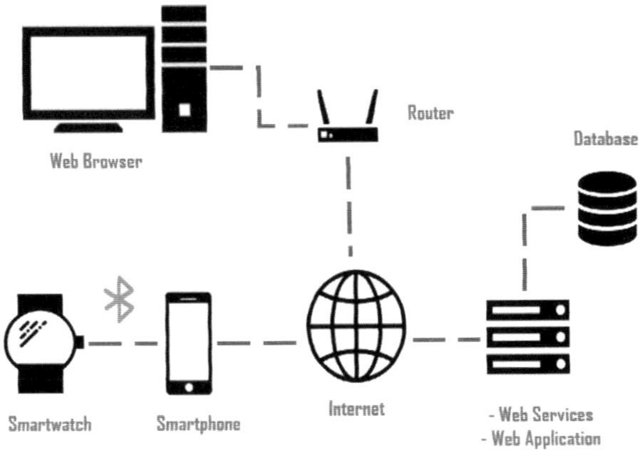

Figure 3. Physical architecture.

C. Final product "Beware"

Mobile Application

In the mobile application for smartphones (Figure 4), the users can see the areas with a security index and receive a notification when they are in one of them, register their emergency contacts, add their favorite places, enter relevant personal information that would be used in case they require medical assistance (blood type, allergies, medication), and report events according to their type. The users can also send their information and location automatically when requesting assistance through the alarm button. Aside from all this, they can view the reports from other users on a wall.

Figure 4. Mobile application interfaces for smartphones.

In the smartwatch application (Figure 5), users can see the map with a security index and receive a notification when they are in one of them, as well as request assistance quickly so the command center can obtain their location and personal information, and send a SMS to his/her emergency contacts.

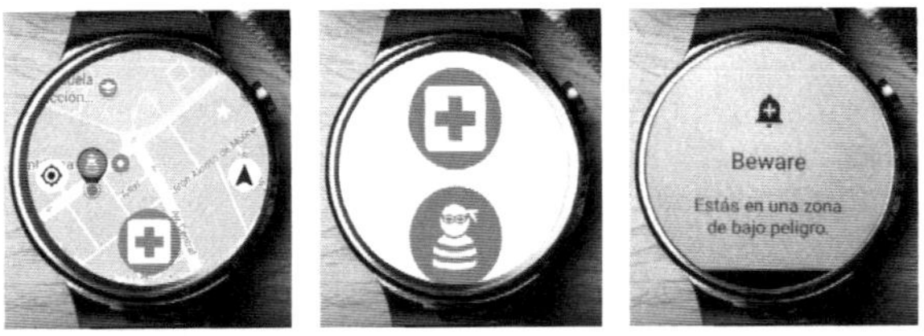

Figure 5. Smartwatch application interfaces.

Web Application

In the Web application (Figure 6), called Command Center, all the notifications that the users have made can be seen in real time. This platform is meant for the municipality patrols, where they register their security members. They are granted access through a Quick Response (QR) code generated by the mobile application. Inside the application, they can obtain all the information of an emergency event, such as the address, map location and information of the user who reported this emergency.

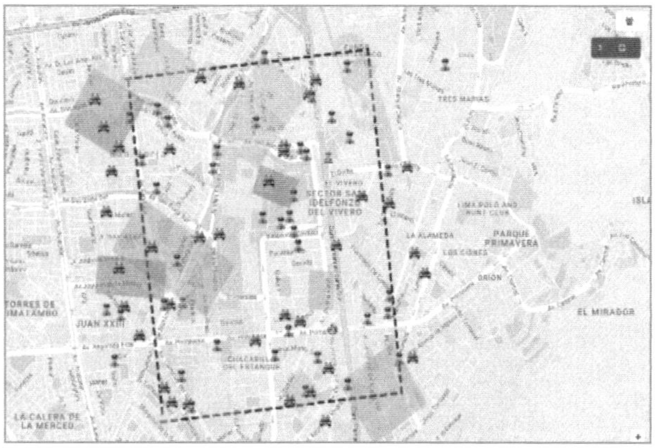

Figure 6. Web application interface (command center).

The access to this platform will be only for authorized security staff, since it shows the location of all the security staff that is on foot or inside a vehicle.

IV. VALIDATION

For the validation, we performed some tests and a survey about the usability, functionality and input from mobile and Web applications related to public safety.

A. Design

We performed a test to obtain the satisfaction level of the citizens from the Santiago de Surco district in Lima, Peru. In the first part, each participant would replicate the applications functionalities. For the second part, they had to answer questions about "Beware" after their experience with the application.

The sample area, in the Santiago de Surco district, was from the Primavera Bridge until the Peruvian University of Applied Sciences (UPC), from 13:00 to 18:00 hrs. on a Monday. Figure 7 shows the dangerous area and its danger level within the selected hour range and day of the week.

Prior to the test, the participants should have installed the mobile application "Beware" on their smartphones and two of them should have configured and installed it on their smartwatches. For the Web application, it was only necessary to have access to the URL, and the test user name and password.

Table VIII shows the characteristics of the participants who did the test.

Sex: F= Female, M= Male

TABLE VIII. CHARACTERISTICS OF THE PARTICIPANTS

Cod.	Age	Sex	Type of visit	Frequency (days of the week)	Type of device
P01	24	M	Health	Monday, Wednesday, Friday and Saturday	Smartphone
P02	28	F	Leisure	Friday, Saturday and Sunday.	Smartphone
P03	26	F	Studies	Friday, Saturday and Sunday.	Smartphone, smartwatch, Web
P04	30	F	Leisure	Monday, Tuesday, Friday, Saturday and Sunday	Smartphone
P05	18	F	Lives in the district	Everyday	Smartphone
P06	18	M	Studies	Monday to Thursday	Smartphone
P07	26	F	Lives in the district	Everyday	Smartphone
P08	18	F	Leisure	Friday	Smartphone
P09	24	F	Lives in the district	Everyday	Smartphone
P10	19	F	Leisure	Friday and Saturday	Smartphone
P11	28	M	Work	Monday, Tuesday and Thursday	Smartphone
P12	33	M	Studies	Tuesday and Thursday	Smartphone
P13	26	M	Work	Monday to Friday	Smartphone
P14	27	M	Work and lives in the district	Everyday	Smartphone
P15	28	F	Work	Monday to Friday	Smartphone

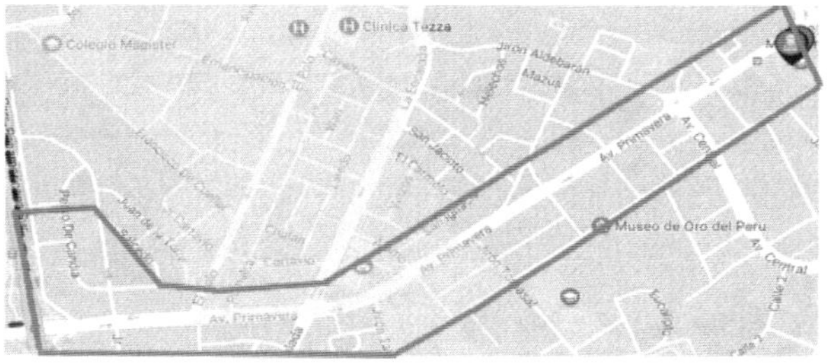

Figure 7. Area chosen for the test.

Table IX shows the questions the participants were asked once the mobile and web application test concluded.

TABLE IX. QUESTIONS ASKED

Cod.	Question
Q01	How much did the application help you to identify the dangerous areas?
Q02	How easy was it for you to use the application?
Q03	How useful do you consider the "Beware" application is?
Q04	How often would you use the application to report an emergency or event?
Q05	Would you recommend this application to identify which are the dangerous areas?

The scale used to measure the answers is in Table X.

TABLE X. MEASUREMENT SCALE

Scale	Score
Not at all	0
Very little	1
A little	2
Moderately	3
Very/Much	4
Extremely	5

B. Results

Table XI presents the results obtained per each respondent and the questions average. These results are interpreted in a qualitative way, matching the scores to the defined scales in Table X.

TABLE XI. SURVEY RESULTS

Cod.	Q01	Q02	Q03	Q04	Q05
P01	4	4	4	3	5
P02	4	3	4	4	4
P03	5	5	5	5	5
P04	5	5	5	4	5
P05	5	5	5	4	5
P06	5	5	5	5	5
P07	3	4	2	1	3
P08	4	0	5	3	5
P09	4	5	5	5	5
P10	5	5	5	5	5
P11	5	5	4	4	5
P12	4	5	4	2	4
P13	5	4	5	4	5
P14	4	5	5	5	5
P15	5	5	5	4	5
Average	4.47	4.33	4.53	3.87	4.73
Sample Standard Deviation	0.64	1.35	0.83	1.19	0.59

According to the survey results, in question 3, 90% of the participants consider the applications to be "Very useful" and "Extremely useful". Question 4 shows that 77% of the participants would frequently report events or emergencies. Questions 1 and 2 show how easy is to use the applications and that they help them "Much" to identify the dangerous areas.

It can also be observed that for participant P07, who lives in the district, the application helps him "Moderately" to identify the dangerous areas, while for most who visit the area a few days a week it helps them "Much".

In summary, it could be concluded that there is a favorable acceptance for applications that identify dangerous areas and their ease of use.

V. CONCLUSION AND FUTURE WORK

In this paper, a mobile application for smartphones and smartwatches was implemented. It displays and notifies which are the dangerous zones within a geographical area, and allows reporting emergencies and/or events. There is also a Web application to receive the emergency alerts from the users and manage the security staff who oversee these emergencies.

Public safety requires constant citizen participation since there is a lack of reporting in the police stations. Therefore, the use of GIS technologies helps to locate the exact place of a crime, analyze various factors that influence the reduction of citizen insecurity, and detect new places prone to crime. Another requirement is that all the criminal information should be stored in a single place to avoid losing data, and that at the same time it is presented in a friendly and updated manner.

The mobile application "Beware" for smartphones and smartwatches, allows citizens to be alert and take the necessary measures when entering into an unsafe area, so they can avoid becoming victims of a crime against their patrimony, life, body and health, as well as to participate in the reporting of criminal events that are not documented in the police stations, and safeguard their lives by sending an emergency report. The "Beware" Command Center allows the Municipality to know the crimes that occur during the day, detect new areas with a security index, know the location of their security staff so they can attend immediately to emergency alerts and, from the information gathered, create new action plans to reduce citizen insecurity.

The validation of the usability, functionality and security perspective of these applications is through a user experience test, which ended with a survey. It showed that the applications comply with the functionalities mentioned and that are easy to use. Also, the survey showed that the application helped to identify new dangerous areas that the participants were not aware of despite that they visit the place regularly. Thus, 14 out of 15 citizens consider that the proposed application is useful and very useful for public safety.

As for future work, we intend to develop an algorithm that generates automatically the dangerous areas from spatial data. This would decrease their creation and storage time. Likewise, we are also interested to use crowdsourcing.

REFERENCES

[1] UNDP: Issue Brief: Citizen Security Crisis Prevention and Recovery. United Natios Development Programme (2012). http://www.undp.org/content/dam/undp/library/crisis%20prevention/30012013_citizen_security_issue_brief(English).pdf?download, [retrieved: 2017, 08]

[2] http://www.crimereports.com/, [retrieved: 2017, 08].

[3] http://www.mapadeldelito.cl, [retrieved: 2017, 08].

[4] http://www.ondefuiroubado.com, [retrieved: 2017, 08].

[5] Garnet, "Gartner says Worldwide Wearable Devices sales to grow 18.4 percent in 2016", Febrero 2016. http://www.gartner.com/newsroom/id/3198018, [retrieved: 2017, 09]

[6] CCS Insight, "Wearables Momentum Continues", 2016. http://www.ccsinsight.com/press/company-news/2516-wearables-momentum-continues, [retrieved: 2017, 09]

[7] M. A. Tayebi, M. Ester, U. Glasser, and P. L. Brantingham, "CRIMETRACER: Activity Space Based Crime Location Prediction", ASONAM 2014 - Proceedings of the 2014 IEEE/ACM International Conference on Advances in Social Networks Analysis and Mining, pp. 472 – 480, 2014.

[8] S. Sathyadeyan, S. Gangadharan, and D. M. S., "Crime Analysis and Prediction Using Data Mining". 1st International Conference on Networks and Soft Computing, ICNSC 2014 – Proceedings, pp. 406 – 412, 2014.

[9] R. Liu, G. Su, W. Tang, and H. Su, "PTEMS: A Novel Public Transportation Emergency Management System Based on GIS", Proceedings of the 1st ACM SIGSPATIAL International Workshop on the Use of GIS in Emergency Management, 2015.

[10] W. Jakkhupan and P. Klaypaksee, "A Web-based Criminal Record System Using Mobile Device: A Case Study of Hat Yai Municipality", Proceedings - APWiMob 2014: IEEE Asia Pacific Conference on Wireless and Mobile 2014, pp. 243-246, 2014.

[11] T. Mantoro, Feriadi, N. Agani, M. A. Ayu, and D. Jatikusmo, "Location - Aware Mobile Crime Information Framework for Fast Tracking Response to Accidents and Crimes in Big Cities", Proceedings - 3rd International Conference on Advanced Computer Science Applications and Technologies, ACSAT, pp. 192-197, 2015.

[12] C. Oduor, F. Acosta, and E. Makhanu, "The Adoption of Mobile Technology as a Tool for Situational Crime Prevention in Kenya", IST-Africa Conference Proceedings, pp. 7 – 9, 2014.

[13] I. Ariffin, B. Solemon, and W. M. Luqman Wan Abu Bakar, "An Evaluative Study on Mobile Crowdsourcing Applications for Crime Watch", 2014 International Conference on Information Technology and Multimedia (ICIMU), pp. 335 – 340, 2014.

[14] S. T. Zeng and C. M Lee., "Personal Emergency Notification Application Design for Mobile Devices", 2014 International Symposium on Next-Generation Electronics, ISNE 2014.

[15] K. Leong and S. C. F. Chan, "A content analysis of web-based crime mapping in the world's top 100 highest GDP cities. Crime Prevention and Community Safety", pp. 1-22, 2013.

[16] http://www.poder-judicial.go.cr/controlinterno/index.php/informacion-general-gestion-de-riesgos?download=99:resumen-iso-31000-gestion-de-riesgos, [retrieved: 2017, 08].

[17] https://postgis.net, [retrieved: 2017, 08].

Using Hidden Markov Models and Rule-based Sensor Mediation on Wearable eHealth Devices

Gilles Irénée Fernand Neyens, Denis Zampunieris
University of Luxembourg
Luxembourg
Email:gilles.neyens@uni.lu, denis.zampunieris@uni.lu

Abstract—**Improvements in sensor miniaturization allow wearable devices to provide more functionality while also being more comfortable for users to wear. The Samsung Simband©, for example, has 6 different sensors Electrocardiogram (ECG), Photoplethysmogram (PPG), Galvanic Skin Response (GSR), Bio-Impedance (Bio-Z), Accelerometer and a thermometer as well as a modular sensor hub to easily add additional ones. This increased number of sensors for wearable devices opens new possibilities for a more precise monitoring of patients by integrating the data from the different sensors. This integration can be influenced by failing or malfunctioning sensors and noise. In this paper, we propose an approach that uses Hidden Markov Models (HMM) in combination with a rule-based engine to mediate among the different sensors' data in order to allow the eHealth system to compute a diagnosis on the basis of the selected reliable sensors. We also show some preliminary results about the accuracy of the first stage of the proposed model.**

Keywords–Wearable devices; Conflict handling; Hidden Markov Model; Autonomic Computing; Rule-based Systems; Sensor Mediation.

I. Introduction

In recent years, advances in sensor technology allow for comfortable wearable devices. This opens new possibilities in different areas as wearable social communities [1] and especially health care [2][3]. A patient can be monitored constantly at home in a non-invasive way, be it during his rehabilitation process [4] or to detect more elusive conditions that occur only in specific situations. There exist many different systems that have been developed to address these issues . One of these systems is the advanced care and alert portable telemedical monitor (AMON), which is capable of measuring an electrocardiogram (ECG), blood oxygen saturation, blood pressure and skin temperature and has integrated software for the real-time processing of the measured health parameters [2]. Another system that was developed is HeartToGo, which can continuously monitor and analyse an ECG in real time in order to detect cardiovascular diseases [3]. And, finally, LifeGuard[5] is a monitoring system, which is capable of measuring ECG, the respiration rate, the blood oxygen saturation, the skin temperature, the heart rate, the blood pressure and body movement.

Currently, Samsung is developing their own eHealth device with the Samsung Simband©. It provides several sensors including an ECG, a Photoplethysmogram (PPG), a Galvanic Skin Response (GSR) sensor, a Bio-Impedance (Bio-Z) sensor, an accelerometer and a thermometer, which are regrouped on a modular platform, which allows to easily integrate more sensors in the future.

A. Challenges

Most of the existing systems [3][5][4] either rely on only one sensor to estimate the state of the patient, or, when using multiple sensors, they still use them individually to detect anomalies in the patient's health. This might lead to erroneous results in the case one or maybe multiple sensors are malfunctioning, which can lead to false positive alarms, which could annoy the patient and make them reluctant to use the device or to false negative alarms, which are dangerous for the well-being of the patient monitored. Some systems tried to overcome this caveat by choosing reliability values for the different sensors [2]. This approach makes use of knowledge on which sensors are more likely to fail than others but fails to take advantage of the data gathered and analyzed by the different sensors. As more and more sensors are developed for wearable devices, the system should be able to use the power of these sensors combined in order to ensure a better monitoring of the patient. Thus, it is important for the system to be capable of mediating between the different sensors.

B. Contribution

Our contribution is twofold: First, we propose a method based on Hidden Markov Models (HMMS) to estimate the risk for different diseases that a patient could have. This is done by analysing the data from each sensor with specially trained HMMS. Secondly, we propose a model for an autonomic system for wearable devices that uses the state estimations from the HMMS in order to mediate between the different conflicting results.

The rest of this paper is structured as follows: The next section shows recent related work that has been done with regards to health care systems. In Section III, we describe the concepts of HMMS and how we use them in order to get different estimations for the state of the patient. In Section IV, we test the accuracy of the sensor analysis using HMMS and present the results. In Section V, we propose a structure for an autonomic system to mediate between the different sensors. Finally, in Section VI, we conclude and discuss future work.

II. Related Work

In this section, we will list and describe recent responsive healthcare systems. A very recent healthcare system is shown in [6]. The system has a total of 8 different sensors. However, the main focus of the study was to improve the energy consumption of the whole system and not the classification based on data from different sensors. In [7] and [8] an accelerometer sensor is used in order to help patients with their rehabilitation after a stroke.

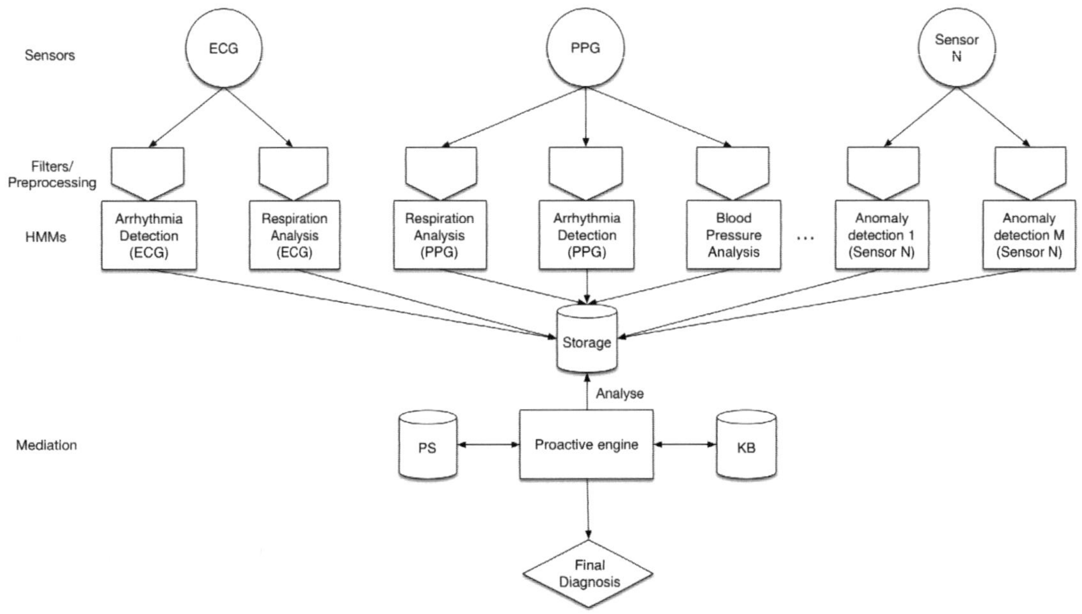

Figure 1: Detailed view of the system

These systems all have in common that they do not use the data from the different sensors together in order to improve the diagnosis. In fact, a recent survey and analysis of existing healthcare systems and applications, by Tsakalakis [9], showed that the current systems are missing the appropriate level of decision support and clinical evaluation. For example, in [10], the authors concentrate on ECG data in order to detect cardiovascular diseases. Another similar approach in order to detect pulse loss based on blood pressure data is presented in [11]. A little bit more sophisticated approach is described in [12] in which the authors not only use an ECG sensor but also an Electroencephalogram (EEG) in order to measure brain activity and an Electrogastrogram (EGG), which records the electrical signals of the muscles in the stomach. However, while they use multiple sensors, the diagnosis is done based on data from individual sensors.

In order to overcome some of these limitations, the authors in [13] proposed a multi-tier hierarchy that uses data from multiple sensors in combination with machine learning methods for disease recognition. In our system, we want to use a rule-based system in addition to machine learning methods to improve the accuracy of the diagnosis.

III. Hidden Markov Models for State Analysis

HMMS have been successfully used in many fields, be it for speech recognition [14][15][16], failure detection [17] or complex action recognitions [18].

Different studies also used them for ECG [19][20][21] and respiration analysis [22]. In this section, we will first give a theoretical overview about HMMS and then we describe how we integrated them into our system. Finally, preliminary test results are presented.

A. *Theoretical background*

An HMM models stochastic sequences as Markov chains where the states are hidden. HMMS consist of five parts [16] :

1) The number of states N in the model. Even though the states are hidden, they generally have a physical meaning. In the case of a patient, they can mean that the patient is in a low, medium, high or no risk state. We denote the individual states as S= $\{S_1, S_2, ..., S_N\}$ and the state at time t as q_t.
2) The number of distinct observation symbols. We denote the individual symbols as V= $\{v_1, v_2, ..., v_M\}$.
3) The state transition probability distribution A = $\{a_i j(k)\}$ where $\{a_i j(k)\} = P[q_{t+1} = S_j | q_t = S_j], \quad 1 \leq i, j, \leq N.$
4) The observation probability distribution B = $\{b_j(k)\}$ for every state j where $\{b_j(k)\} = P[v_k \text{ at } t | q_t = S_j], \quad 1 \leq j \leq N, 1 \leq k \leq M.$
5) The initial state distribution $\pi = \{\pi_i\}$ where $\pi_i = P[q_1 = S_i], \quad 1 \leq i \leq N.$

There are three fundamental problems for HMMS:

1) Given an observation sequence O= $O_1, O_2 ... O_T$ and a model $\lambda = (A, B, \pi)$, how do we compute $P(O|\lambda)$?
2) Given an observation sequence O= $O_1, O_2 ... O_T$ and a model $\lambda = (A, B, \pi)$, how do we find the most likely state sequence $Q = q_1, q_2, ..., q_T$)?
3) How do we optimise the model parameters A, B and π of the model λ in order to maximize $P(O|\lambda)$?

The solutions to the first and second problems can be both used for classification. With the solution to the first problem, we can calculate the probability that an observation belongs to a specific model. By doing this for different models, we can choose the model with the highest probability as classification.

The second problem can be solved easily by trying every possible state sequence and taking the one with the highest probability. As this method increases exponentially with the length of the observation sequence a more effective solution was developed: the Viterbi decoding algorithm [23] [24]. The Viterbi algorithm calculates the state sequence that has the highest probability to have generated a given observation sequence by only doing subsequent calculations for the partial path with the best probability, thus the complexity only increases linearly with the observation sequence length.

The third problem consists of training the model in such a way that, given a training observation sequence O, the parameters of the model $\lambda = (A, B, \pi)$ are adapted in order to maximise the probability of O given lambda. There does not exist an optimal solution for this problem, but there are several solutions to find local maxima for $P(O|\lambda)$ including the expectation maximisation algorithm [25], the segmental K-means algorithm [26] and the Baum-Welch algorithm [27].

In our system we use the Baum-Welch, also called forward-backward, algorithm in order to train the different HMMS. For the classification phase, we use the Viterbi decoding algorithm.

B. Structure

Some existing approaches already use HMMS in order to estimate the state of equipment [28] by analysing the data of several sensors of the same type simultaneously. In our approach, different HMMS are specialised to detect a specific disease or condition based on the data of different types of sensors, as shown in Figure 1. This means that there are different HMMS that are responsible for detecting the same disease, which in case of sensor malfunctioning can lead to conflicting results, as for example the ECG sensor could detect an arrhythmia while the PPG does not. Independent of possible conflicts, the results of the HMMS will be stored in a database where they wait for further analysis by the rule-based proactive engine, which will be discussed in Section V.

IV. Preliminary Experiments and Results

A. Experimental setup

For preliminary tests, we wanted to see how well HMMS can detect arrhythmias. To to this, we used the topology for a HMM described [19] (Figure 2) to distinguish between 3 classes of beats: supra ventricular, normal and ventricular. The individual states correspond to the different stages of a heartbeat. For the training and the testing phase, we used data from the MGH/MF Waveform Database [29][30], which contain three ECG leads and was sampled at a rate of 360 measurements per second as well as an annotation file by expert cardiologist that identified every heartbeat.

1) Initial parameters: Having good initial parameters for HMM is important to get satisfactory classification results [31]. In fact, the starting parameters have to be within one standard deviation [32] from the actual parameters in order to get accurate classification results. This is why, the starting parameters were calculated "manually" with a few samples of each class of heartbeat.

2) Training: Training is done for each class of heartbeat in a specific HMM for the class before they are regrouped in the final HMM described in Figure 2. Training is done using the Baum-Welch algorithm with records from the mgh001 file of the selected dataset.

3) State estimation: For the classification, we use the model from Figure 2. The sequence of states is calculated using the Viterbi algorithm.

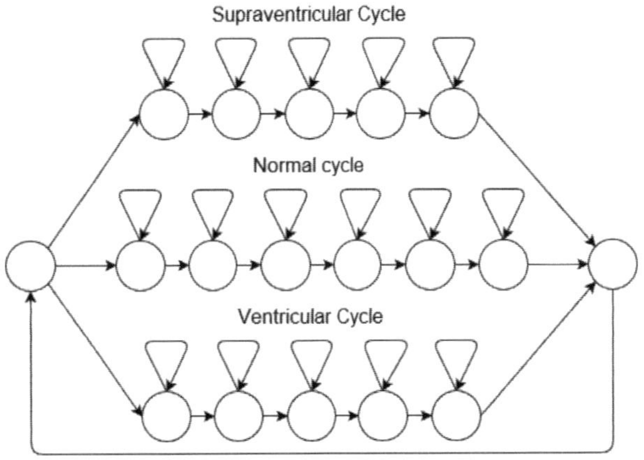

Figure 2: Markov model topology

TABLE I: CLASSIFICATION RESULTS

File	TP	FP	FN	TN	FP rate	Recall	Specificity
mgh001	11	824	1	1747	32.05%	91.67 %	67.95 %
mgh002	333	817	98	4320	15.90 %	77.26 %	84.10%
mgh003	7	1532	0	5449	21.95 %	100 %	78.05%

B. Results

The results are presented in Table I in terms of correctly determined arrhythmias (TP), correctly determined normal heartbeats (TN), false alarms (FP) and not detected arrhythmias (FN).

We see that the recall is actually quite high, as most of the arrhythmias were detected. However, the false positive rate is also high. By analysing the classification results, we found out that the HMM has difficulties to classify the period between heartbeats correctly, meaning that it often considers the period between heartbeats to be an arrhythmia.

The study done in [19] also has quite a lot of false positives depending on the data set used. While the number of false positives are not quite as high, they are still too high to use on an automated wearable system, as the patient would get annoyed really fast and switch the device of if he received notifications of detected problems all the time. In the next section, we propose a model of an autonomic system to try to overcome these difficulties.

V. A Model for an Autonomic eHealth System

A. Autonomic computing

Autonomic computing was introduced in 2001 by IBM [33], in an effort to reduce the need for human involvement in complex computing systems. Shortly afte,r a clearer definition of an autonomic system was developed [34][35]. Autonomic computing is the idea for a system to manage itself and to minimise human intervention. The goals and objectives of the system are ensured by a processing cycle, the MAPE loop, which stands for monitoring, analysing, planning and execution. Also, in order to be classified as an autonomic system, a system needs to exhibit at least the following self-properties, also called self-* properties: self-configuration, self-healing, self-optimisation and self-protection.

B. *System structure*

The self-managing aspect of these systems is ideal to use for the monitoring of patients on wearable systems. In Figure 4, we see a general overview of the system. As computing power on the wearable devices is quite limited, we consider the wearable device together with a smartphone as one autonomic system. The wearable device collects data with its sensors and forwards them to the smartphone on which the analysis part is done. A more detailed view of the analysis process is shown in Figure 1. It consist of two main steps: in the first step, filters pre-process the data coming from the sensors and pass it to the different HMMS for state analysis. The results from the HMMS are stored in a database, where they are analysed in a second step by a rule-based proactive engine in order to make a final diagnosis.

In the next section, we will discuss the structure of this rule-based engine that implements the properties of an autonomic system. Afterwards, we will then discuss what the job of the different self-properties is in a healthcare setting.

C. *Proactive engine*

A rule-based proactive engine was developed recently for different platforms (Windows, Android and iOS). Conceptually, the rules run in the engine [36] can be regrouped into scenarios [37] with each scenario regrouping rules that achieve a common goal.

Rules consist of 5 different parts: data acquisition, activation guards, conditions, actions and rule generation and are executed periodically. Both, activation guards and conditions, have to be satisfied in order for a rule to execute its actions. The activation guards are the triggers for a rule to consider taking actions while the conditions are the permissions of a rule. In order to decide, which rules can execute, all rules whose activation conditions are met are first put into a list. In Figure 3, the next steps of the rules' execution process is shown. The rules are split into two categories: diagnosis rules and conflict handling rules. In the first step, the diagnosis rules analyse the state probabilities provided by the HMMS and register appropriate actions that should be taken. As in this case, conflicting data is coming from the ECG and PPG sensor, conflicting actions are registered.

In the second step, the conflict handling rules detect conflicts based on the registered actions and resolve them by giving permissions to the different rules to execute their actions. This is done by calculations based on a chosen priority parameter and the probabilities coming from the HMM. As rules might execute more than one action, permissions are granted for individual actions.

Finally, in the last step the diagnosis rules check their permissions and execute the actions they are allowed to.

D. *Self-healing*

An autonomic system needs to be able to detect, diagnose and recover from problems occurring inside or also possibly outside the system in order to guarantee an acceptable uptime of the services provided.

In the case of a pervasive healthcare system, the data stream of the sensors might not be complete. For example, due to connection problems, data can be incomplete at times. If the data stream is disconnected for too long, the sensor will be marked as failed.

E. *Self-configuration*

An autonomic system needs to be able to configure and reconfigure itself in order to adapt itself to different situations, meaning that changes in the internal or external context should not prevent the system of achieving its objective(s).

Self-healing and self-configuration go hand in hand in this system as, as soon as the self-healing module detects problems in the system (in this case, most likely the sensors) and cannot repair them, the self-configuration module needs to adapt the internal parameters of the system in order to take the failures of some sensors into account for the decision making process. Some of the cases in which these two self-properties are used:

1) Failed sensors.
   Completely failed sensors can be detected easily as the stream of data to the system stops.
2) Malfunctioning sensors.
   Malfunctioning sensors can be difficult to detect as their malfunctioning could possibly be interpreted as health problems of the patient.
3) Removal of sensors.
   This should fall under the same category as failed sensors as removed sensors will simply stop sending data to the system.
4) Addition of sensors
   Adding new sensors is a challenge as not only does the system need to detect that there is a new sensor but it also needs to get an accurate description on how to use the data from the new sensor and how it should behave in relation to the data from the other sensors.
5) Recovery of failed or malfunctioning sensors
   The recovery of failed sensors should fall under the same category as adding new sensors.

F. *Self-optimisation*

An autonomic system always needs to try to improve itself based on different criteria as, for example, execution speed, accuracy, etc.

The self-optimisation module of this system tries to improve the accuracy of the decision making of the system regarding the diagnosis of the patients' illnesses.

This can be done by keeping track of the different decisions made in a Knowledge-Base and by analysing the behaviour of the patient that follows these decisions. Data kept in the Knowledge-Base include the decisions made, as well as the data from the sensors, and/or previous decisions that lead to this decision. For example, after a heart attack diagnosis, the system could check if the patient is still exercising and if his health parameters are stabilised again and conclude that next time it should not make the same diagnosis.

G. *Self-protection*

An autonomic system needs to be able to anticipate, detect, identify and protect itself from internal and external threats, in order to maintain its integrity and achieve security, privacy and data protection.

In an autonomic healthcare system the self-healing module needs to deal with the following issues:

1) Conflicts with self-healing
   While self-healing tries to keep sensors functioning as

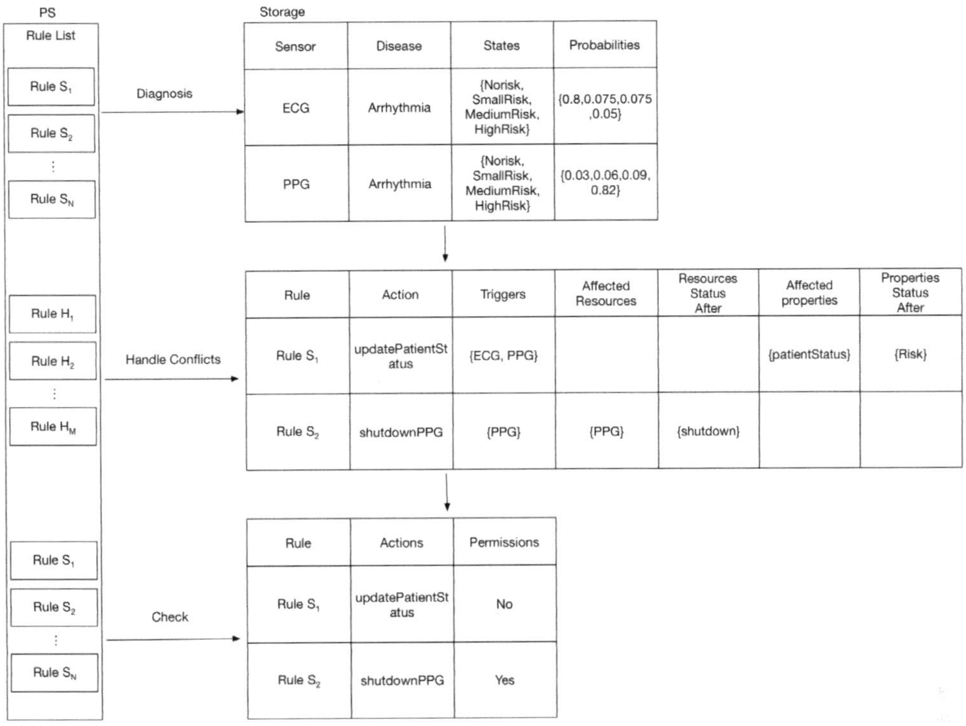

Figure 3: Proactive conflict handling

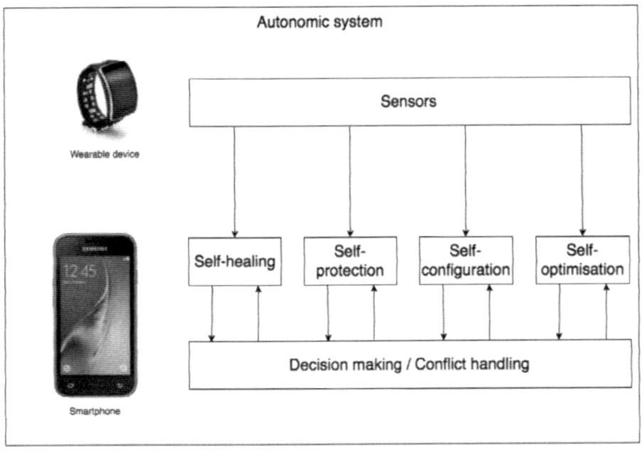

Figure 4: Autonomic healthcare system

long as possible, self-protection rather wants to shut the sensors down than to allow bad data to influence the integrity of the system.

2) Communication between smartphone and wearable device.
Data privacy and integrity is particularly important in E-Health systems. The communication between the wearable and the smartphone thus has to be secure in order to avoid privacy loss and even more importantly, manipulation of a patient's health parameters.

VI. Conclusion and Future work

We proposed an approach using HMMS combined with a rule-based system in order to diagnose the health state of a patient for wearable device. Our tests have shown that the false positive rate of individual HMM is quite high. This is one of the issues we plan to address with our system in the future by mediating between the data coming from different sensors. Additional tests are thus needed to see if the system proposed will be able to rescue the rate of false positives, while maintaining or even also improve the recall. In a second step, we will then also test the accuracy of the classification when one or more sensors are malfunctioning.

Another future work, in order to rule out possible errors related to the initial parameters of the HMM, is to improve the method in how these initial parameters are obtained. While we may, to some extent, rely on experts to provide this initial parameters estimation it would be more reliable to have the training algorithm adapt itself. In [38], Won et al. use genetic algorithms, in conjunction with the standard training algorithm for HMMS, in order to explore different starting conditions. Their study has shown that the addition of genetic algorithms, even with a naive implementation, lead to slightly superior classification results. We think that even slight improvements are important in a healthcare setting and plan to improve the training of the HMMS with a genetic algorithm.

References

[1] G. Kortuem and Z. Segall, "Wearable communities: augmenting social networks with wearable computers," IEEE Pervasive Computing, vol. 2, no. 1, 2003, pp. 71–78.

[2] U. Anliker et al., "Amon: a wearable multiparameter medical monitoring and alert system," IEEE transactions on information technology in biomedicine, vol. 8, no. 4, 2004, pp. 415–427.

[3] Z. Jin, J. Oresko, S. Huang, and A. C. Cheng, "Hearttogo: a personalized medicine technology for cardiovascular disease prevention and detection," in Life Science Systems and Applications Workshop, 2009. LiSSA 2009. IEEE/NIH. IEEE, 2009, pp. 80–83.

[4] R. A. Dobrican and D. Zampunieris, "A proactive solution, using wearable and mobile applications, for closing the gap between the rehabilitation team and cardiac patients," in Healthcare Informatics (ICHI), 2016 IEEE International Conference on. IEEE, 2016, pp. 146–155.

[5] C. W. Mundt et al., "A multiparameter wearable physiologic monitoring system for space and terrestrial applications," IEEE Transactions on Information Technology in Biomedicine, vol. 9, no. 3, 2005, pp. 382–391.

[6] A. M. Nia, M. Mozaffari-Kermani, S. Sur-Kolay, A. Raghunathan, and N. K. Jha, "Energy-efficient long-term continuous personal health monitoring," IEEE Transactions on Multi-Scale Computing Systems, vol. 1, no. 2, 2015, pp. 85–98.

[7] S. Patel et al., "A novel approach to monitor rehabilitation outcomes in stroke survivors using wearable technology," Proceedings of the IEEE, vol. 98, no. 3, 2010, pp. 450–461.

[8] T. Hester et al., "Using wearable sensors to measure motor abilities following stroke," in Wearable and Implantable Body Sensor Networks, 2006. BSN 2006. International Workshop on. IEEE, 2006, pp. 4–pp.

[9] M. Tsakalakis and N. G. Bourbakis, "Health care sensorâĂŤbased systems for point of care monitoring and diagnostic applications: A brief survey," in Engineering in Medicine and Biology Society (EMBC), 2014 36th Annual International Conference of the IEEE. IEEE, 2014, pp. 6266–6269.

[10] J. J. Oresko et al., "A wearable smartphone-based platform for real-time cardiovascular disease detection via electrocardiogram processing," IEEE Transactions on Information Technology in Biomedicine, vol. 14, no. 3, 2010, pp. 734–740.

[11] J. Rickard, S. Ahmed, M. Baruch, B. Klocman, D. O. Martin, and V. Menon, "Utility of a novel watch-based pulse detection system to detect pulselessness in human subjects," Heart Rhythm, vol. 8, no. 12, 2011, pp. 1895–1899.

[12] F.-S. Jaw, Y.-L. Tseng, and J.-K. Jang, "Modular design of a long-term portable recorder for physiological signals," Measurement, vol. 43, no. 10, 2010, pp. 1363–1368.

[13] Y. Hongxu and N. Jha, "A hierarchical health decision support system for disease diagnosis based on wearable medical sensors and machine learning ensembles," IEEE Transactions on Multi-Scale Computing Systems, 2017.

[14] X. D. Huang, Y. Ariki, and M. A. Jack, Hidden Markov models for speech recognition. Edinburgh university press Edinburgh, 1990, vol. 2004.

[15] M. Gales and S. Young, "The application of hidden markov models in speech recognition," Foundations and trends in signal processing, vol. 1, no. 3, 2008, pp. 195–304.

[16] L. R. Rabiner, "A tutorial on hidden markov models and selected applications in speech recognition," Proceedings of the IEEE, vol. 77, no. 2, 1989, pp. 257–286.

[17] F. Salfner and M. Malek, "Using hidden semi-markov models for effective online failure prediction," in Reliable Distributed Systems, 2007. SRDS 2007. 26th IEEE International Symposium on. IEEE, 2007, pp. 161–174.

[18] M. Brand, N. Oliver, and A. Pentland, "Coupled hidden markov models for complex action recognition," in Computer vision and pattern recognition, 1997. proceedings., 1997 ieee computer society conference on. IEEE, 1997, pp. 994–999.

[19] D. A. Coast, R. M. Stern, G. G. Cano, and S. A. Briller, "An approach to cardiac arrhythmia analysis using hidden markov models," IEEE Transactions on biomedical Engineering, vol. 37, no. 9, 1990, pp. 826–836.

[20] S. Hu, Z. Shao, and J. Tan, "A real-time cardiac arrhythmia classification system with wearable electrocardiogram," in Body Sensor Networks (BSN), 2011 International Conference on. IEEE, 2011, pp. 119–124.

[21] R. V. Andreão, B. Dorizzi, and J. Boudy, "Ecg signal analysis through hidden markov models," IEEE Transactions on Biomedical engineering, vol. 53, no. 8, 2006, pp. 1541–1549.

[22] T. Al-Ani, Y. Hamam, R. Fodil, F. Lofaso, and D. Isabey, "Using hidden markov models for sleep disordered breathing identification," Simulation Modelling Practice and Theory, vol. 12, no. 2, 2004, pp. 117–128.

[23] A. Viterbi, "Error bounds for convolutional codes and an asymptotically optimum decoding algorithm," IEEE transactions on Information Theory, vol. 13, no. 2, 1967, pp. 260–269.

[24] G. D. Forney, "The viterbi algorithm," Proceedings of the IEEE, vol. 61, no. 3, 1973, pp. 268–278.

[25] A. P. Dempster, N. M. Laird, and D. B. Rubin, "Maximum likelihood from incomplete data via the em algorithm," Journal of the royal statistical society. Series B (methodological), 1977, pp. 1–38.

[26] B.-H. Juang and L. R. Rabiner, "The segmental k-means algorithm for estimating parameters of hidden markov models," IEEE Transactions on Acoustics, Speech, and Signal Processing, vol. 38, no. 9, 1990, pp. 1639–1641.

[27] L. E. Baum and J. A. Eagon, "An inequality with applications to statistical estimation for probabilistic functions of markov processes and to a model for ecology," Bull. Amer. Math. Soc, vol. 73, no. 3, 1967, pp. 360–363.

[28] M. Dong and D. He, "Hidden semi-markov model-based methodology for multi-sensor equipment health diagnosis and prognosis," European Journal of Operational Research, vol. 178, no. 3, 2007, pp. 858–878.

[29] J. Welch, P. Ford, R. Teplick, and R. Rubsamen, "The massachusetts general hospital-marquette foundation hemodynamic and electrocardiographic database–comprehensive collection of critical care waveforms," Clinical Monitoring, vol. 7, no. 1, 1991, pp. 96–97.

[30] A. L. Goldberger et al., "Physiobank, physiotoolkit, and physionet," Circulation, vol. 101, no. 23, 2000, pp. e215–e220.

[31] L. R. Rabiner, B.-H. Juang, S. Levinson, and M. Sondhi, "Some properties of continuous hidden markov model representations," AT&T technical journal, vol. 64, no. 6, 1985, pp. 1251–1270.

[32] D. A. Coast, Cardiac arrhythmia analysis using hidden Markov models. UMI, 1988.

[33] A. C. Manifesto, "Ibms perspective on the state of information technology," http://www.research.ibm.com/autonomic/manifesto/, 2001.

[34] J. O. Kephart and D. M. Chess, "The vision of autonomic computing," Computer, vol. 36, no. 1, 2003, pp. 41–50.

[35] P. Lalanda, J. A. McCann, and A. Diaconescu, Autonomic computing. Springer, 2013.

[36] D. Zampunieris, "Implementation of efficient proactive computing using lazy evaluation in a learning management system (extended version)," International Journal of Web-Based Learning and Teaching Technologies, vol. 3, 2008, pp. 103–109.

[37] D. Shirnin, S. Reis, and D. Zampunieris, "Design of proactive scenarios and rules for enhanced e-learning," in Proceedings of the 4th International Conference on Computer Supported Education, Porto, Portugal 16-18 April, 2012. SciTePress–Science and Technology Publications, 2012, pp. 253–258.

[38] K.-J. Won, A. Prügel-Bennett, and A. Krogh, "Training hmm structure with genetic algorithm for biological sequence analysis," Bioinformatics, vol. 20, no. 18, 2004, pp. 3613–3619.

Using Image Recognition for Testing Hand-drawn Graphic User Interfaces

Improving Mobile Game GUI Tests with OpenCV Pattern Matching Methods

Maxim Mozgovoy, Evgeny Pyshkin
School of Computer Science and Engineering, Division of Information Systems
University of Aizu
Aizu-Wakamatsu, Japan
E-mail:{mozgovoy, pyshe}@u-aizu.ac.jp

Abstract—**This paper discusses the use of image recognition for constructing automated GUI tests for the applications with hand-drawn user interface components, such as mobile games. Specifically, this contribution addresses the use of OpenCV pattern matching algorithms and the choice of most appropriate combinations of methods for GUI testing of the upcoming Unity-based mobile game "World of Tennis: Roaring 20's". Our idea is to classify UI elements (including buttons, game control elements, static and movable objects) with respect to their appearance in different type of scenes present in the game, as well as to find pattern recognition methods providing the best similarity values to increase UI element recognition quality.**

Keywords-software testing; GUI; image recognition; similarity; mobile game.

I. INTRODUCTION

Human-centric systems and the systems based on human-computer interaction (HCI) technologies are substantially multidisciplinary [1]. Through the prospective of the HCI interdisciplinary analysis, we make the observation that models and methods originally developed in one research area (not necessarily "human-centric") are often transferred and applied to a completely new distinct application domain [2]. In this work, we make an effort to examine a good example of such a transdisciplinary connection, which is a nontrivial case of using image recognition algorithms for improving software non-native graphic user interface (GUI) testing automation process. Mobile game development is a particular area where such an approach can be useful.

Indeed, in mobile games (such as ongoing project "World of Tennis: Roaring 20's" where we are involved in [3] (see Figure 1)), GUI is often designed with using hand-drawn components. It makes difficult developing standard automated GUI tests and basic functional smoke tests since all screen elements are in fact plain graphical images, in contrast to "classic" native GUI control elements that we can easily access programmatically nearly in the same way as users do, in test scripts [4]. Furthermore, non-native GUI elements can change their position on the screen and might look differently on different devices with different resolution.

The paper has the following structure. In Section II we describe our approach in general. Section III describes how the experiments were organized. In Section IV we examine a number of problems to be resolved while implementing test scripts using pattern recognition methods. In Section V we briefly summarize the current state of this project and introduce the primary tasks for future work.

II. APPROACH

In our previous work, we demonstrated that identifying objects of interest on the screen (such as GUI elements or game characters) could not be completely reduced to the task of perfect matching of a bitmap image inside a screenshot [5]. There are several reasons:

- Onscreen objects may be rendered differently for different GPU/rendering quality cases;
- Screens vary in dimensions, so patterns might need scaling;
- Onscreen objects often intersect with each other, so it happens that one object hides another one or can be distorted because of such an interaction.

Figure 1. Actual screen of the "World of Tennis: Roaring 20's" mobile game.

Thus, the most straightforward way is to rely on approximate pattern matching. There are several tutorials where an idea of using image matching in creating test scripts is discussed [6][7]. OpenCV library [8] provides a number of methods for pattern recognition and can serve as a typical tool used for searching and finding the occurrences of the given pattern in a larger image. Basic OpenCV pattern matching methods can be accessed by using *matchTemplate()* function with a parameter defining a specific method among the variety of supported pattern matching methods [9][10]:

1. CV_TM_SQDIFF: square difference matching minimizing the squared difference between the pattern and the image area;
2. CV_TM_SQDIFF_NORMED: normalized version of the square difference matching (normalized methods are typically used when the effects of lightning difference between a pattern and an image should be reduced [10]);
3. CV_TM_CCORR: correlation matching method multiplicatively matching a template against the image and then maximizing the matched area;
4. CV_TM_CCORR_NORMED: normalized version of the correlation matching method;
5. CV_TM_CCOEFF: correlation coefficient matching method that matches a template against the image relative to their means and generates a matching score ranging from –1 (complete mismatch) to 1 (perfect match); and
6. CV_TM_CCOEFF_NORMED: normalized version of the correlation coefficient matching method.

As we know from different sources (such as [11]) the *matchTemplate()* function slides a template over the given area and computes similarity value in a range of [0..1] for each pixel location, thus maximizing pattern matching similarity. The function yields the best value as the final recognition similarity, so we are able to analyze the result from the viewpoint of GUI elements recognition quality.

An automated test consists of the following steps:

- Take a game screenshot (which is relatively time-consuming process that might take up to several seconds depending on a target mobile device);
- Detect the presence of a certain GUI element (using image recognition);
- React properly;
- Check the expected application behavior or program state; and
- Repeat the process.

III. First Experiments

For the first implementation of test scripts, we used *matchTemplate()* function and the pattern matching method TM_CCOEFF_NORMED. After experimenting with a number of test scripts, we realized that pattern matching reliability significantly depends on a recognition task. For example, simple button-like GUI elements (buttons, menus, tabs) can be recognized with high degree of similarity (0.90..0.98), according to OpenCV reports. Similarity score decreases to (0.63..0.65) for certain elements interfering with the background like menu item placed against the sky with moving clouds. This makes perfect template matching impossible in principle. Worse similarity values might occur even for the objects that are not graphically complex, but contain patterns distorted during rescaling: Figure 2 shows an example of low similarity score achieved for a simple edit box component.

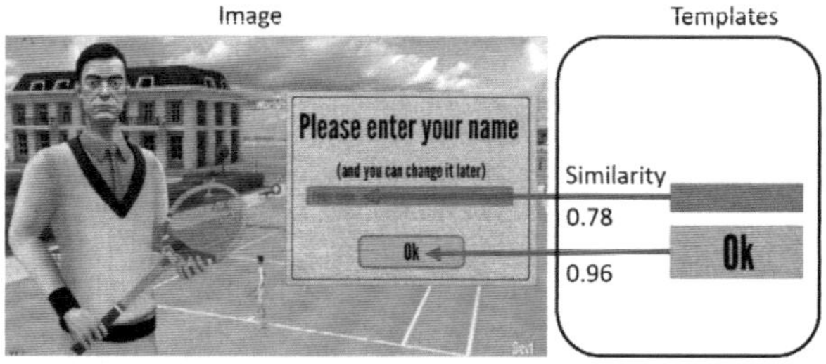

Figure 2. Template matching similarity varies for different UI elements.

Figure 3. Similary scores might differ depending on the device.

Even in the simplest cases, the similarity scores might differ depending on the device where the code is running. As Figure 3 illustrates, the scores for OK button range from 0.94 to 0.99 for different devices even if there is no any recognition complication such as "bad" background, surrounding or changing objects, etc. (apparently due to different screen resolutions and screen image scaling distortions). Table I summarizes this experiment.

TABLE I. EXPERIMENTING WITH OK BUTTON

Case	**Description of the test case**			
	Device	***Screen***	***Tap size***	***Similarity***
Figure 3 (a)	Xiaomi Redmi Note 3 Pro	1920x1080	1920x1080	0.99
Figure 3 (b)	iPad Air	2046x1536	1024x768	0.95
Figure 3 (c)	Doogee X5 Max Pro	1280x720	1280x720	0.94

There are also false positive cases, when the pattern matching algorithm detects the presence of a certain UI element, actually not shown on the screen.

Typically, such a false positive case might happen if some similar-looking graphical elements are confused with each other, especially when there are surrounding moving objects or complex background. One way to struggle with such cases is to try to match larger regions in order to include more context to a search request. For example, in the "World of Tennis: Roaring 20's", the Skip button is always placed next to a checkbox, so we can try to match the whole button/checkbox region. If there are several possible candidate elements, we can naturally report one having the highest similarity ratio with its identified match.

In principle, for test engineers, there is no much importance in achieving high similarity scores: we do not have to know whether a GUI element exists on the screen or not. We know that it *supposed* to be there. Otherwise, the test will fail (no expected element found). However, we believe that improving GUI element recognition will definitely facilitate the process of writing reliable application tests.

IV. PROBLEM STATEMENT

In matter terms, we face a purely interdisciplinary problem: the procedures for non-native GUI based software testing automation require the combined use of several technologies including traditional automated feature tests, functional testing frameworks, information retrieval, and image recognition.

As it follows from the observations mentioned in Section III, an important problem is to find optimal parameters of image recognition algorithms to maximize GUI elements recognition reliability, and therefore, to decrease the number of automated tests that might fail, not because of the software bugs, but due to the UI elements recognition defects.

There is a number of issues deserving particular attention. A typical problem in the process of initiating interaction between a testing framework and a fullscreen mobile application is to detect whether the device screen is upside down (it happens sometimes, and is not always detected correctly without pattern matching). For example, the first screen visible to the user of the "World of Tennis: Roaring 20's" is a "club view", so we can take some fragments of clubs and try to find them in the screenshots. Examples of club view elements are presented in Figure 4. We can also try to search the rotated fragments in order to diagnose that the screen is not in the position required for testing. Preliminary experiments show that, for such a problem, false positive cases might be a significant issue.

Figure 4. Club view template examples that can be used for checking screen orientation.

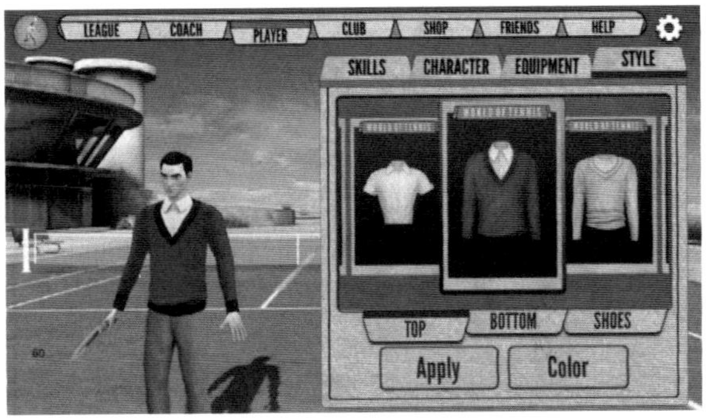

Figure 5. Standard UI controls: buttons, tabs, static images.

Even with relatively simple buttons (like those presented in Figure 5) there could be some problems:

a) Sometimes the game designers slightly change the buttons (in order to beautify them, make them slightly larger or smaller, change fonts, colors, etc.);
b) Sometimes buttons might be disabled, and the test scripts should be accurate enough to discern enabled and disabled buttons;
c) Sometimes there could be additional elements shown next to the button captions.

The challenge is to make sure that we still can match changing buttons in (a) and (c), but be able to distinguish them in (b).

There are also numerous moving objects on the screen. Suppose the test script needs to press on the character's head in the pictures shown in Figure 6. An animated head might make a perfect match difficult not only because of changes in object view itself, but also because of possible changes in the adjacent screen area (e.g., an airplane appeared in the sky, in our case). Hence, it might be required to work with a set of different images related to the same UI element and to perform a matching process for all of them. We have to consider a possibility to work with a larger region providing necessary context to avoid false positive recognition results.

Figure 6. Moving objects: the object view changes and the surrounding area might change as well.

Our hypothesis is that experimenting with different pattern matching algorithms will allows us to provide a number of recommendation for test script developers. These recommendations will provide hints, which algorithms are better to use in which test contexts.

V. CONCLUSIONS AND FUTURE WORK

Let us note that image recognition algorithms are rarely discussed within the scope of software testing, so we believe that advancing and improving the quality of the proposed approach will provide a feasible solution to be used as a part of integration pipeline in software development and testing. The special focus of this approach is on developing mobile applications (including mobile games) characterized by the presence of hand-drawn or non-native GUI components (for example, applications developed with Unity).

Our primary task is to arrange a number of experiments with real UI elements of different kind, real game screens of different size and resolutions and integrated with the tests running on real devices.

A big variety of UI components designed for the "World of Tennis: Roaring 20's" allows us to classify them in a number of classes including the following UI types:

- Button-like elements: buttons, edit boxes or similar;
- Static images: player portraits, field, etc.;
- Dynamic objects: moving player figures or similar.

We have to run pattern-matching algorithms for significantly different usage contexts: for example, in player settings window, club selection window, game selection window, ongoing game window, etc. We expect that for every combination (algorithm, UI element, usage context), the reported similarity values could give us better understanding how to improve the quality of test scripts and, therefore, how to make the next steps toward building a testing automation framework for mobile applications based on hand-drawn or non-native GUI components.

REFERENCES

[1] H. R. Hartson, "Human–computer interaction: Interdisciplinary roots and trends," Journal of Systems and Software, 1998 Nov 30, vol. 43(2), pp. 103-118.

[2] E. Pyshkin, "Designing human-centric applications: Transdisciplinary connections with examples," In Proc. of 2017 3rd IEEE International Conference on Cybernetics (CYBCONF), Exeter, UK, Jun 21-23, 2017, pp. 455-460.

[3] "World of tennis. project homepage," accessed: Jul 10, 2017. [Online]. Available: http://worldoftennis.com/.

[4] "Automating user interface tests," accessed: Jul 7, 2017. [Online]. Available:https://developer.android.com/training/testing/ui-testing /index.html.

[5] M. Mozgovoy and E. Pyshkin, "Unity application testing automation with appium and image recognition," in Tools and Methods of Program Analysis (TMPA-2017), 3rd International Conference on, 2017, Springer CCSI, vol. 779, in press.

[6] V. V. Helppi, "Using opencv and akaze for mobile app and game testing," (January 2016), accessed: Jul 7, 2017. [Online]. Available: http://bitbar.com/using-opencv-and-akaze-for-mobile-app-and-game-testing.

[7] S. Kazmierczak, "Appium with image recognition," (February 2016), accessed: Jul 7, 2017. [Online]. Available: https://medium.com/@SimonKaz/appium-with-image-recognition-17a92abaa23d\#.oez2f6hnh.

[8] "OpenCV Library," accessed: Jul 8, 2017. [Online]. Available: http://opencv.org/.

[9] "OpenCV: Template Matching, accessed: Jul 8, 2017. [Online]. Available: http://docs.opencv.org/master/de/da9/tutorial_template_matching.html.

[10] G. Bradski and A. Kaehler, "Learning OpenCV: Computer vision with the OpenCV library," O'Reilly Media, Inc., 2008.

[11] R. Laganière, "OpenCV Computer Vision Application Programming Cookbook," 2nd ed., Packt Publishing, 2014.

On Providing Healthy Routes: A Case for Fine-Grained Pollution Measurements Using Mobile Sensing

Srinivas Devarakonda, Ruilin Liu, Badri Nath
Department of Computer Science
Rutgers University, USA
e-mail: {skd70, rl475, badri}@cs.rutgers.edu

Abstract— **Extended periods of exposure to air pollution is a health hazard. For commuters, avoiding polluted areas to the extent possible can minimize long-term pollution exposure. Hence, it would be desirable to have an option in navigation systems to choose a route based on the pollution index of the route. However, sufficient data is not available to make an informed choice of routes based on pollution index. This choice is predicated upon availability of ubiquitous pollution measurements along the route segments. In this paper, we present a healthy route recommendation schema that uses spatially and temporally dense pollution measurements to recommend route options that avoid polluted road segments. These healthy routes were evaluated on a neighborhood scale using measurements from vehicular-based mobile sensors. Experiments using data generated by these mobile sensors demonstrate that significant reduction in pollution exposure can be achieved by taking a healthy route instead of the shortest route or the quickest route.**

***Keywords-** Air Quality; Mobile Sensing; Healthy Routes; Participatory Sensing; Navigation System.*

I. INTRODUCTION

According to the factsheet published by the World Health Organization [1], outdoor air pollution in cities and rural areas was estimated to have caused 3.7 million premature deaths worldwide in 2012. Major health effects associated with outdoor air pollution are respiratory and cardiovascular disease, lung cancer, asthma exacerbation and chronic bronchitis. Predominant outdoor airborne pollutants that contribute to these health effects are particulate matter (PM), ozone (O3), nitrogen dioxide, sulfur dioxide and carbon monoxide (CO). The effects of pollution depend on many factors – the concentration of the pollutant, the state of health of the person, the activity of the person and the duration of exposure.

During the 1996 Olympic games in Atlanta, efforts were made to reduce downtown traffic congestion. These efforts resulted in a prolonged reduction in O3 pollution and significantly lower rates of childhood asthma events [7]. The results show that reduction in traffic volume reduces air pollution measurably and improves the health. Another study reveals that utilizing a route away from motorized traffic could reduce bicycle commuter's exposure to particle number concentrations [5]. It was also seen that the inhaled dosage of pollution not only depends upon the pollution levels but also on the activity of the individual [8].

These studies show that, to reduce the effects of pollution one must either reduce the pollution or make an informed decision to avoid polluted areas. The latter serves as the motivation for our work in building a navigation system that uses spatially and temporally dense (fine-grained) pollution measurements in suggesting a healthy route choice instead of the shortest or the quickest route choices.

The healthy route choice is predicated upon the availability of accurate pollution measurements along the route segments. The difficulty in providing a healthy route choice is the lack of accurate ground-truth pollution measurements. The existing air pollution measurements are available for a non-representative sample of urban areas. Pollution is measured using expensive equipment located at a few select locations. Measurements from these stations are extrapolated over a large area using dispersion models. This data may not truly reflect the ground-truth measurements of pollutants. Localized variations in pollutant concentrations may not be truly represented by the published measurements based on modeled data. Consequently, individual exposure to pollutants on this basis is not fully known. Particularly in urban and metropolitan areas, an individual's daily pollution exposure levels are not truly quantified.

The availability of inexpensive sensors and the ubiquity of reliable cellular bandwidth have provided an impetus towards building and using mobile sensor systems to measure fine-grained pollution concentrations. The increase in the availability and usage of smartphones has seen an increase in the availability of personal pollution sensing devices. This gave rise to a new sensing paradigm – participatory sensing. The mobile sensing systems and personal sensors together are now providing a fine-grained pollution sensing opportunity.

In this paper, we present a navigation schema that generates a healthy route choice using fine-grained pollution measurements. We evaluated this schema on a neighborhood scale. Specifically, we evaluated the following:

- Is there a measurable reduction in pollution exposure on a healthy route as compared to the pollution exposure on the shortest route or the quickest route?
- What is the cost in terms of time and distance if a commuter chooses a healthy route recommendation?
- Is there a temporal variability to a healthy route or does it stay the same every day in a neighborhood?
- How does the choice of the pollutant affect the healthy route recommendation?
- Does the route recommendation differ depending on the mode of transport?

In Section II, we present related work. The details of the sensor systems deployed on public transportation, as well as the sensors used as participatory mobile sensing devices contributing to the fine-grained pollution measurements used in our study are presented in Section III. Details of route generation and the experiments are discussed in Sections IV and V, respectively. Results are presented in Section VI. During this study, there were several ideas that we identified were relevant to the generation of healthy routes but could not be investigated as part of the current work. These are discussed as future work items in Section VII. We provide our conclusions in Section VIII of the paper.

II. RELATED WORK

In an earlier work, Ribeiro et al. developed a healthy route planning system for pedestrians and cyclists to promote less polluting, economical and more equitable modes of transportation [11]. In this work, the healthy routes were calculated based on data collected and estimated through the simulation of noise levels and pollution indices derived from sparse measurement stations using dispersion models. In another study, Beheshtitabar et al. built a system that uses an alternate cost function to predict the bicycle route choice of a commuter based on cost function attributes chosen by the commuter [4]. The authors considered two types of cost function attributes – link-level factors, such as riding surface, riding incline, etc., and route level factors, such as travel time, presence of stop signs, etc. Both groups provided an alternate routing strategy specifically targeting pedestrians and cyclists. In our approach, we developed a system that generates fine-grained pollution measurements and used them to evaluate healthy navigational route choices for cyclists and drivers. We also evaluated the impact of choosing a healthy route in terms of increased time or distance. To the best of our knowledge, this is the first time a healthy route navigation system is developed based on multiple pollutants using fine-grained measurements and evaluated the trade-off between a healthy route choice and the quickest or shortest route choices.

III. HEALTHY ROUTING SYSTEM

In this paper, we evaluate healthy route choices for cyclists and drivers with the aim of minimizing a commuter's long-term pollution exposure. The factors that influence this decision are: the on-road pollution concentrations and the mode of transport. Pollutants that are found in higher concentrations near roads include PM, CO, oxides of nitrogen (NOx), and O3. Fine-grained measurements of these pollutants are required to provide a healthy route choice. The pollution considerations are different for cyclists and drivers. A cyclist is concerned with the ambient air pollution whereas a driver is concerned with the pollution inside the vehicle during their respective commutes. Irrespective of the modes of transport, a user may prefer to minimize exposure to a specific pollutant – for example one may choose to minimize PM exposure or to minimize O3 exposure. So, the considerations in providing a healthy route to a commuter are: on-road pollution measurements, inside the vehicle pollution measurements, pollution inventory as an input in route calculations and route generation.

A. *Pollution Measurements*

Two pollution-sensing models were used to collect the measurements in this study: public transportation sensors that are designed for use on public transportation vehicles to measure ambient pollution and personal mobile sensors that are used as participatory sensing devices to measure pollution inside vehicles. The sensor deployment schema is shown in Fig. 1.

1) *Public Transportation Sensors*

Public transportation sensor units are custom designed and built for use on public transportation infrastructure. We assembled sensor units for use on Rutgers University campus buses. One of the units was mounted on a car for experiments in areas not covered by the campus buses (Fig. 2).

These units are equipped with sensors to measure PM, CO, O3, nitrogen dioxide (NO2), temperature, humidity and pressure (see Table 1 for sensor specifications). The unit is powered by the vehicle battery and starts measuring pollution when the vehicle is powered up and put into service. Global Positioning System (GPS) location data, speed, date and time are attached to each pollution data point. Accumulated data points are uploaded every minute to a server deployed in the cloud. The data upload is done using the data channel of the cellular modem in the unit. These units provide the ambient pollutant measurements relevant for computing the healthy routes applicable to cyclists.

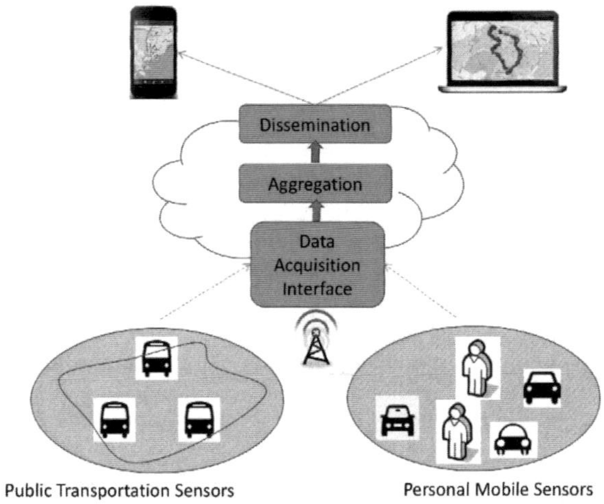

Figure 1. Sensor deployment schema.

Figure 2. Public transportation sensor mounted on a car for experimentation.

Figure 3. Personal mobile sensor mounted in a car near the vent.

TABLE I. PUBLIC TRANSPORTATION SENSOR SPECIFICATION

Sensor	Measures	Range
Figaro TGS5042	CO	0-10000 PPM
MICS 5525	CO	0-1000 PPM
MICS 2710	NO2	0.05 – 5 PPM
MICS 2610	O3	10-1000 PPB
Shinyei PMS1	PM	0.3 μm and larger
Shinyei PPD42NS	PM	1 μm and larger
Sharp GP2Y1010AU0F	PM	0.3 μm – 10 μm

2) *Personal Mobile Sensors*

As part of the participatory sensing model, we use NODE sensors from Variable Technologies for data collection [2]. These sensors connect to the user's IOS or Android smartphone over Bluetooth. We developed applications for IOS and Android platforms to communicate with and manage the NODE devices. GPS location data, speed, date and time are added to the pollution measurements collected by the smartphone application and are uploaded to the cloud server every minute over the phone's data channel. The user may choose to upload this data over Wi-Fi if data bandwidth is a constraint.

For our experiments, we use the NODE device to measure CO, temperature, pressure and humidity (see Table 2 for sensor specifications). The personal mobile sensor, when conveniently mounted inside a vehicle in front of the vent during the user's commute, can measure CO levels in the user's personal space (Fig. 3). In an earlier work, we have shown that the measurements inside the vehicle correlate well with outdoor values [6]. The personal mobile sensors provide the measurements relevant for computing the healthy routes applicable to drivers.

TABLE II. PERSONAL MOBILE SENSOR SPECIFICATION

Sensor	Measures	Range
NODE	CO	0-400PPM

The public transportation sensors and the personal mobile sensors send pollution data to a cloud server. We use Amazon Web Services (AWS) platform [12] to host our server in the cloud. The pollution measurements are stored in a PostgreSQL database [13]. The database has PostGIS [14] extension installed to add support for geographic objects and to allow location queries to be run. Data is post-processed to remove outliers and to apply calibration curves. The resulting dataset consists of pollution measurements, time, GPS location, and speed at the time of the measurement. Information whether the measurement is from inside a car or outside is also stored so that relevant measurement can be used in route calculations for cyclists and drivers. The cloud server provides these pollution measurements to users through a Web portal, as well as through the Android and IOS applications.

IV. ROUTE GENERATION BASED ON POLLUTION MEASUREMENTS

A neighborhood scale road segment graph was created for the Rutgers University College Avenue campus in New Brunswick, New Jersey. This is a directed graph with road intersections as graph nodes and roads as graph edges. Each road segment has a cost associated with it which includes the distance of the segment used for the shortest path calculation, the segment travel time used for the quickest path calculation and the average pollution index used for the healthiest path calculation. In our schema, we used PM and CO measurements for the pollution exposure values so that the healthy route can be calculated based on average PM or CO concentrations per road segment.

For each road segment, we stored the segment length, travel time, average PM and average CO concentrations per unit time. These values are obtained directly from the pollution inventory generated by the public transportation sensors and the personal mobile sensors. Segment lengths and segment travel times are used to calculate the shortest paths and the quickest paths, respectively. To calculate the healthiest path, the pollution load on each segment is required. A segment's pollution load at any given time is calculated based on the average pollution on the segment per unit time and the travel time on the segment.

We implemented Dijkstra lowest cost path algorithm with segment distance, segment travel time and segment pollution index as the costs to compute the shortest, quickest and healthiest paths, respectively.

V. EXPERIMENTS

Experiments were conducted in Rutgers University College Avenue campus in New Brunswick, New Jersey. Besides Rutgers University campus, the area has a transit train station, downtown businesses and a residential area. The neighborhood has a mix of pedestrians, cyclists and vehicular traffic. Because of this variability in the traffic mix, we chose this neighborhood for our experiments.

We measured CO concentrations inside the car using the personal mobile sensors placed near the car vent. The vent was set to a constant speed throughout the experiments. All the car windows were closed during data collection. PM, CO, NO2 and O3 outside the car were measured using a public transportation sensor mounted on the car. Inside-car measurements were used for route calculations for drivers and outside PM and CO measurements were used for route calculation for cyclists. Vehicular travel time on each segment was obtained from the measurements. Due to lack of transit data for cyclists in the test area, we assumed a constant speed of 10 mph in our route calculations for cyclists. Data was collected over a period of three days.

VI. RESULTS

During the tests, we observed significant temporal and spatial variations in the pollution measurements. Hence, a choice exists in selecting routes that avoid polluted road segments. The CO measurement data from two test runs on two different days shows the spatial and temporal variations in measurements (Fig. 4). On the map in Fig. 4, we display the CO data in three ranges instead of showing the discrete measurements so that spatial variations in pollution can be clearly differentiated. The graph in the inset shows CO measurements in parts per million (PPM) over time. Periodic data identifiers from the x-axis of the plot in the inset are marked on the map to show the corresponding location of the measurements.

The PM measurements were relatively steady due to a series of snowstorms in the area (Fig. 5). We believe that the few high readings observed were due to the re-entrained deicing treatment on the roads. Even though these readings had very little variation, we observed that average segment level PM concentrations showed variability so we went ahead and used these measurements in our healthy route evaluation. On the map in Fig. 5, we display the PM data in three ranges instead of showing the discrete measurements so that spatial variations in pollution can be clearly differentiated. The graph in the inset shows PM measurements in milligrams per cubic meter (mg/cum) over time. Periodic data identifiers from the x-axis of the plot in the inset are marked on the map to show the corresponding location of the measurements.

A. *Route choice and Pollution*

Using the inside-car CO measurements, we computed the shortest, quickest and healthiest paths between an arbitrary

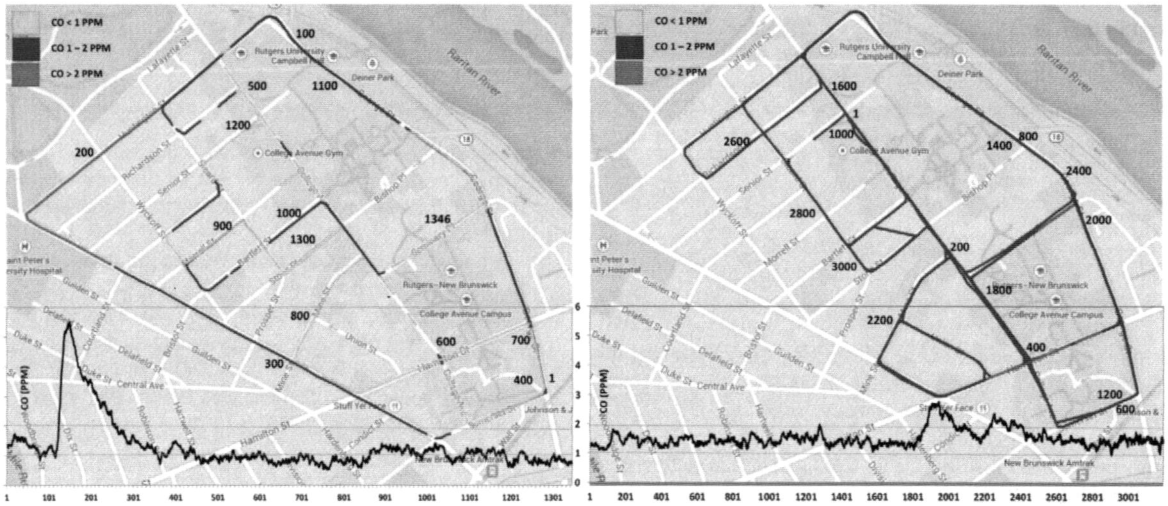

Figure 4. CO measurements in College Avenue campus during two test runs on two different days. Inset in each of the maps shows the time series plot of CO measurements. Periodic X-axis values are marked on map to correlate measurements shown in inset to corresponding location.

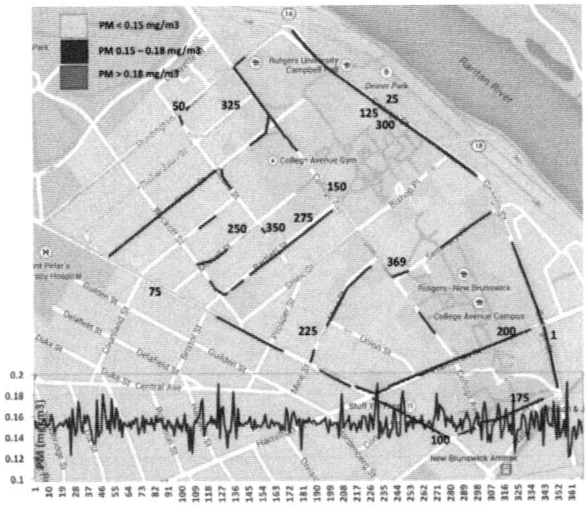

Figure 5. PM measurements in College Avenue Campus. Inset shows the time series plot of PM measurements. Periodic X-axis values are marked on map to correlate measurements shown in inset to corresponding location.

set of origin and destination (O/D) pairs. The exposure cost for the three route choices for 30 O/D pairs was calculated and plotted as scatter plot (Fig. 6). The CO exposure in the case of the shortest path and the quickest path has always been more than the exposure on a healthy route. The exposure is higher on the shortest path as compared to the exposure on the quickest path. It can be seen from Fig. 6 that, the healthy route's CO exposure of 10.19 PPM is much less than the corresponding exposure values of 30.2 PPM for the shortest path (data point marked as 1) and 17.0 PPM for the quickest path (data point marked as 2).

We quantified the percentage increase in the cumulative CO exposure on the shortest path and the quickest path as compared to the healthiest path for the 30 O/D pairs we evaluated (Fig. 7). It is seen that, on average there is an

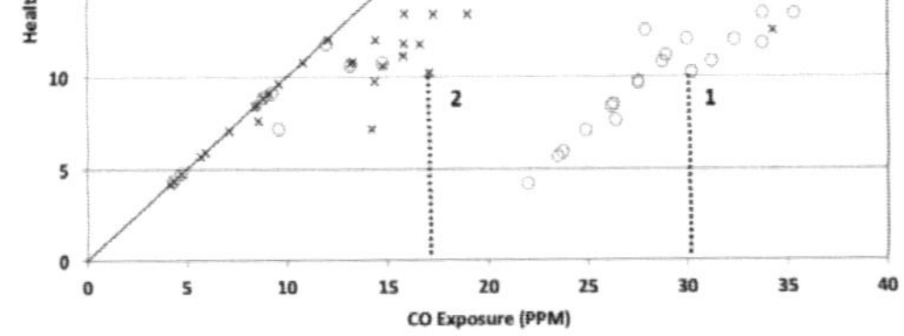

Figure 6. CO exposure on healthy route vs. CO exposure on shortest and quickest route. X-axis values for points 1 and 2 show the CO exposure values for shortest and quickest paths for a healthy route's CO exposure of 10.19 PPM.

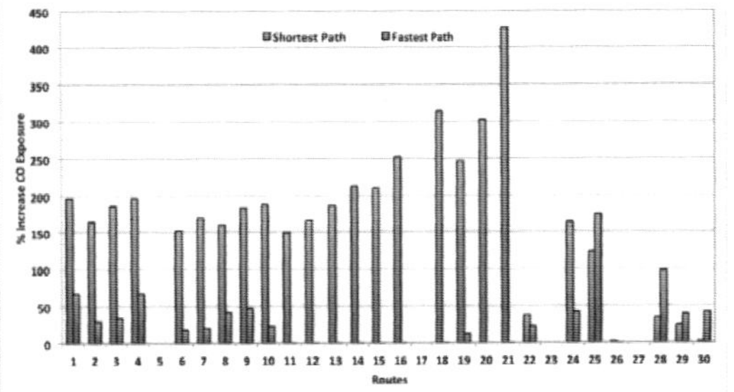

Figure 7. Increase in cumulative CO exposure in shortest and quickest paths over healthiest path in 30 origin-destination pairs.

increase of 160% in CO exposure if a shortest path is chosen. There was one instance where a 400% increase in CO exposure was recorded. In the case of the quickest route, the increase in CO exposure is not as predominant as in the case of the shortest path. On average, there is an increase of 45% in CO exposure when the quickest route is chosen. There were several instances of the quickest route where only a marginal increase in CO exposure was observed over the corresponding CO exposures on the healthiest route.

B. Cost of Healthy Route

In this section, we discuss the cost of the healthy route choice in terms of increase in time and distance of travel. We will use the same data set from the 30 O/D pairs we used before.

It is observed that in all the 30 O/D pairs we evaluated, there has been an increase in the distance and time of travel (Fig. 8). On average, there is an increase of about 8-9% in the distance travelled and about 30% in the time of travel. The maximum increase in the distance is about 50% and in time it is about 85%.

There is an additional cost to a healthy route choice due to the increased time and distance of travel. However, it is the choice of an individual – whether the benefits of a healthy route outweigh the additional costs of increased travel time and distance. There could be another choice provided to the user by the routing implementation to accept a threshold for the increased travel time and/or distance, beyond which the healthy route recommendation is not provided.

C. Healthy Route – Temporal Dependency

Pollution index for a route varies over time. To establish this temporal dependency, we calculated the healthy routes for the same O/D pairs (Fig. 9) using the CO measurements inside the car taken over two days.

It is seen that the healthy routes are different on the two days. Hence, static profiles of routes are not sufficient. Tests with different O/D pairs yielded similar results. The quickest routes were also different but we have not shown them in Fig. 9 for clarity.

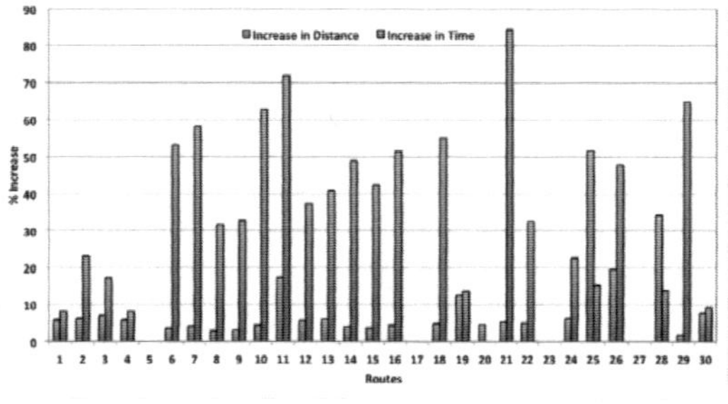

Figure 8. Percentage increase in distance and time on a healthy route corresponding to the shortest and quickest routes.

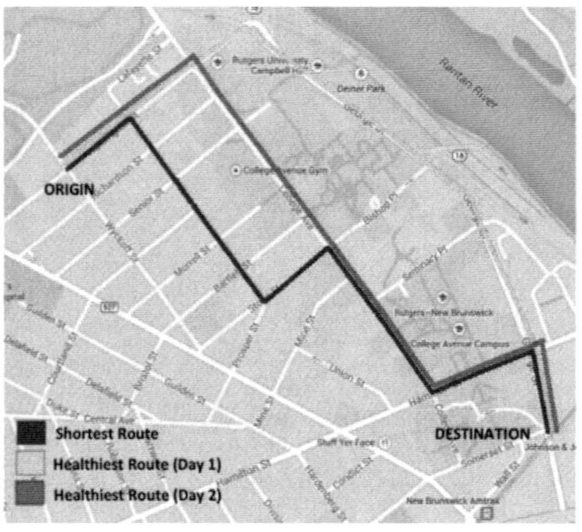

Figure 9. Healthiest route recommendations on two different days. Shortest route is also shown. Quickest route is omitted for clarity.

D. *Healthy Route – Dependency on Pollutant*

A user may prefer to base their healthy route choice on a specific pollutant. We evaluated this scenario using pollution measurements outside the car using PM and CO measurements for a cyclist. Currently, we only have CO measurements inside the car, so we used outside PM and CO measurements to evaluate this scenario.

Fig. 10 shows the route recommendation for a cyclist based on CO and PM measurements. We show the results for one O/D pair only, even though we observed similar results for other O/D pairs. A similar recommendation could not be evaluated for drivers due to lack of fine-grained measurements for pollutants other than CO.

E. *Healthy Route – Mode of Transport*

The healthy route recommendations for cyclists and drivers did not show any variation in the routes. The pollution exposure depends on the amount of time spent on a road segment. So, we think that the use of a constant speed of 10 mph in our calculations may be affecting the route calculations. Additional evaluation needs to be done when transit data becomes available for cyclists. Alternatively, we need to choose a test location where transit data for cyclists is available.

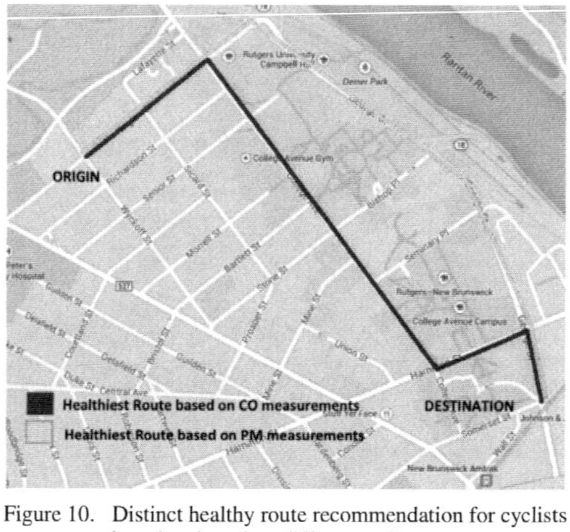

Figure 10. Distinct healthy route recommendation for cyclists based on based on different pollutants.

F. *Trade Off – Healthy Route and its Cost*

The left part of Fig. 11 shows the comparison between the increase in travel time on a healthy route and the increase in pollution on the quickest route. There is no clear distinction to choose one option over the other. A threshold function can help wherein an increase in travel time above a threshold on a healthy route - chooses the healthy route over the quickest route.

Fig. 11 shows the tradeoff between pollution exposure, distance and time. The right side of Fig. 11 shows the increase in pollution exposure along the shortest path plotted along with the increase in distance on the healthiest path. The proportional increase in pollution exposure far out-weighs the increase in travel distance on a healthy route.

VII. Discussion and Future Work

In this paper, we presented fine-grained pollution data as a choice in route selection. However, we have not discussed validation methods for our healthy route approach. Validation needed a large team divided into producers of fine grained pollution measurements and consumers of healthy route recommendations with a view to validate the correctness of the route recommendations. We did not have a large team at our disposal during these tests to conduct validation of our approach during our experimentation. However, during our tests we observed that the segment level pollution load and segment travel time remained relatively constant for a period of about 15-20 minutes. So, we use this to observe that our route recommendations are at least valid for this duration. A rigorous validation of our route recommendation will be taken up as part of a future work using data from sensors mounted on campus buses and participatory sensing using student groups.

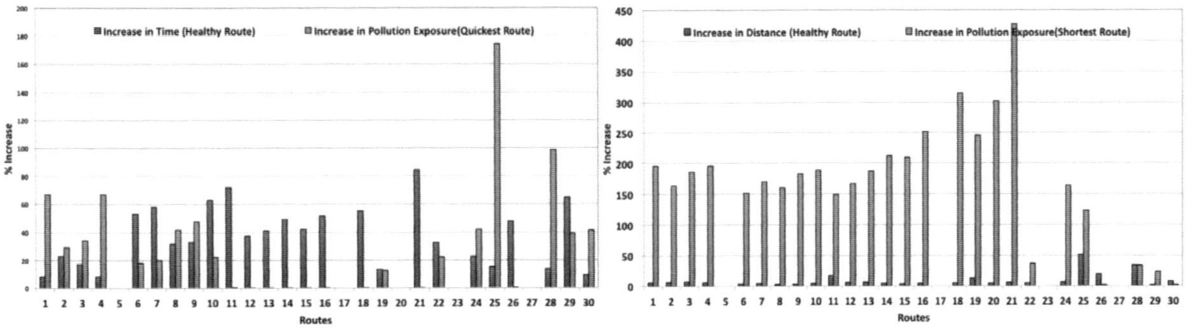

Figure 11. (Left) Percent increase in travel time for healthy route vs. percent increase in pollution for quickest route. (Right) Percent increase in distance for healthy route vs. percent increase in pollution for shortest route.

The healthy route recommendation depends on the availability of fine-grained pollution measurements. For areas with no pollution data, the available measurements in the near vicinity can be used to extrapolate on a micro scale based on the approach discussed by Ulyanik et al., [10].

Participatory sensing may not be contributing to fine-grained measurements in all areas. Using the model developed by Hudda et al., [9] outside the car pollution measurements can be used to derive the pollution exposure inside the vehicle. The inside-car measurements depend upon the comfort settings in the vehicle (ventilation settings, opening of windows, etc.) and the age of the vehicle. The model caters to all these variables. Similarly, it must be possible to derive outside car measurements based on measurements from inside the car. However, this needs further work in the future.

A healthy route recommendation need not be a static route generated at the start of the trip. Current navigation systems are capable of dynamic route updates based on road and traffic conditions. With the availability of fine-grained pollution measurements, it is trivial to reuse the existing dynamic route update capability to healthy routes as well.

Our study has been confined to a neighborhood scale due to lack of fine-grained pollution data. Even though our work is based on neighborhood scale data, we feel it can be easily extended as fine-grained measurements become available over a larger area. Consequently, the demand on existing navigation systems is additional storage to store per segment pollution attributes and the additional computation to generate healthy routes.

The sensitivity of healthy routes to seasonal variations needs additional study. The dependency on local weather conditions and its influence on the healthy route choice will require additional work in the future.

We did not include pedestrians in the current study. A pedestrian's pollution exposure depends on the mobility patterns and wait patterns in an urban setting. A separate study is required to provide similar insight into a pedestrian's pollution exposure during a day.

Once a healthy route recommendation is made, it will be interesting to study how users behave. For example, given a healthy route choice, how many cyclists and drivers adopt it at the cost of increased distance or time?

VIII. CONCLUSION

This paper presents a navigation system to provide healthy route recommendations using fine-grained pollution measurements contributed by participatory mobile sensors and public transportation sensors. We evaluated this model on a neighborhood scale and showed that the healthy route provides significant improvement in the pollution load on an individual when compared to the pollution loads on the shortest route or the quickest route. In addition, we also show that fine-grained measurements are essential for providing the healthy route recommendations daily. The healthy route recommendation need not be based on a single pollutant but can be a choice of pollutants. We evaluated this model for two modes of transportation, namely bicycles and automobiles.

ACKNOWLEDGMENT

This work has been supported in part by National Science Foundation (NSF) Grant CNS-1111811.

REFERENCES

[1] WHO factsheet http://www.who.int/mediacentre/factsheets/fs313/en/ [retrieved: September, 2017]

[2] NODE sensors http://www.variableinc.com/gas-sensing [retrieved: September, 2017]

[3] D. Allemann and M. Raubal, "Towards health-optimal routing in urban areas," In Proc. Second ACM SIGSPATIAL International Workshop on the Use of GIS in Public Health, pp. 56-59, 2013.

[4] E. Beheshtitabar, S. Aguilar Ríos, D. König-Hollerwöger, Z. Svatý and C. Rydergren, "Route choice modeling for bicycle trips," International Journal for Traffic and Transport Engineering 4, pp. 194-209, 2014.

[5] T. Cole-Hunter et al., "Utility of an alternative bicycle commute route of lower proximity to motorised traffic in decreasing exposure to ultra-fine particles, respiratory symptoms and airway inflammation–a structured exposure experiment," Environmental health 12, no. 1, 2013.

[6] S. Devarakonda et al., "Real-time air quality monitoring through mobile sensing in metropolitan areas," In Proc. Second ACM SIGKDD International Workshop on Urban Computing, 2013.

[7] M. Friedman, K. E. Powell, L. Hutwagner, L. M. Graham, and W. Gerald Teague, "Impact of changes in transportation and commuting behaviors during the 1996 Summer Olympic Games in Atlanta on air quality and childhood asthma," Jama 285, no. 7, pp. 897-905, 2001.

[8] K. Hu, T. Davison, A. Rahman, and V. Sivaraman, "Air Pollution Exposure Estimation and Finding Association with Human Activity using Wearable Sensor Network," In Proc. MLSDA 2014 2nd Workshop on Machine Learning for Sensory Data Analysis, 2014.

[9] N. Hudda and S. A. Fruin, "Models for predicting the ratio of particulate pollutant concentrations inside vehicles to roadways," Environmental science & technology 47.19, pp. 11048-11055, 2013.

[10] I. Uyanik, A. Khatri, P. Tsiamyrtzis and I. Pavlidis, "Design and Usage of an Ozone Mapping App," In Proc. Wireless Health 2014 on National Institutes of Health (WH '14). ACM, New York, NY, USA, DOI=10.1145/2668883.2668885 http://doi.acm.org/10.1145/2668883.2668885

[11] P. Ribeiro and J. F. G. Mendes, "Route planning for soft modes of transport–Healthy routes," In 17th International Conference on Urban Transport and the Environment, pp. 677-688, 2011.

[12] Amazon Web Services details https://aws.amazon.com/ec2/details/ [retrieved: October, 2017]

[13] PostgreSQL database details https://www.postgresql.org [retrieved: October, 2017]

[14] PostGIS spatial and geographic objects for PostgreSQL database http://postgis.net [retrieved: October, 2017]

Hybrid Client/Server Rendering with Automatic Proxy Model Generation

Jens Olav Nygaard
and Jon Mikkelsen Hjelmervik

SINTEF Digital
Applied Mathematics
Norway
Email: Jens.O.Nygaard@sintef.no,
and Jon.M.Hjelmervik@sintef.no

***Abstract*—A common problem in remote rendering setups is that of temporarily insufficient bandwidth and latency. For a proper experience of immersiveness, at least some rendering should be presented to the user, and it should appear to be responsive to user input, even in the presence of connection glitches. The all too familiar spinning hourglass symbol, or equivalent, will degrade such an experience. With the advent of Virtual Reality (VR) and Augmented Reality (AR), solutions to this become important even though connectedness in general is improving. We are dealing with a remote rendering of three-dimensional (3D) geometry being pushed to a lesser client, and what we in essence do is to replace a spinning hourglass symbol with an automatically client-generated approximation of the 3D geometry rendered on the client, responding to client-recorded user input. We call this a *proxy model*. Our main result is a system for automatically producing such proxy models on the client, from received images and depth buffers only, for showing on the client when remotely rendered frames do not arrive sufficiently fast.**

Keywords–Client-server; remote rendering; high latency; low bandwidth

I. Introduction

Hand in hand with increasingly powerful rendering engines comes ever increasing requirements on computational accuracy, power efficiency, data sizes, scaling properties, etc. This is also reinforced by popular cloud-based approaches and wireless usage patterns. An effect of this is that interactivity still is a difficult issue. We consider a client/server model for 3D rendering, addressing latency, bandwidth and scaling problems in a novel way.

We introduce a *proxy model*, defined as a temporary model to be shown and manipulated locally on a client while waiting for the appropriate image from a connected server. Producing such proxy models can be difficult for many kinds of 3D data, like in our main case in which we have an oil reservoir viewer [1] that renders large *corner point grids*, together with faults, oil wells, and more; see Figure 1 for an example of both a full server-side rendering, and automatically generated proxy models rendered in Google Chrome. Our solution is to pass depth information from the server along with ordinary rendered images. From this, a rudimentary 3D model is built, and with the Red, Green and Blue (RGB) image as a texture, this model can be manipulated and rendered on the client while waiting for the next update from the server. If the client does not change the position or orientation of the model too much, this proxy model rendering integrates seamlessly with the slower stream of server-rendered frames. Even if bandwidth and latency is not a problem, it may be desirable to let a server of limited capacity serve many simultaneous users, hence limiting the effective server time available for each one. Suitable scaling may still be achieved using our solution. This is currently being commercialized as a part of the result of a recently finished European Union (EU) project called CloudFlow [2].

In Section II, we review some previous and related work, before we consider our contribution in Section III. This is further split into three subsections, in Subsection III-A we consider the server side part of the system, in Subsection III-B, the client side and in Subsection III-C we consider automatic parameter tuning during use of the system. We discuss results in Section IV, before we finally sum up in Subsection V.

II. Previous work

Our approach has some similarities to *Image Based Rendering* (IBR) techniques [3], with the difference that an important IBR problem would be the reconstruction of a depth map from images, while we have access to the full depth map from a rendering pass. Another way to use depth maps similar to what we do, is for "immersive streaming", see, e.g., [4], where focus is on depth map compression, an issue that we also consider. Another work focused on similar streaming and geometry compression, is Teler [5]. Also, [6] contains some of the same ideas as our work, with respect to image-based rendering acceleration. A very early work aiming at the same kind of "inter-frame rendering", is Mark et al. [7]. Here, several frames are warped, and subsequently combined, in order to avoid large unpainted areas caused by occlusion. This corresponds to our use of several proxy models, each from a pair of (rgb, depth)-images, the main difference being that they work on separate pixels, while we use larger, textured "splats". Our method avoids their slightly complicated meshing, discontinuity detection and final image composition stage. Common to many IBR-algorithms is also that of stitching together 3D or 2.5D point clouds. We could do this for our 2.5D maps fetched from the server, but it is unclear if the benefit would outweigh the cost. Our approach differs from many similar ones, in that we use existing depth maps to distill and render temporary geometry, rather than retrieveing the depth maps from images. We observe that these 2.5D height maps are exactly what "3D cameras" (time-of-flight and other range image sensors) produce, but most authors considering these are typically building more complex geometries before

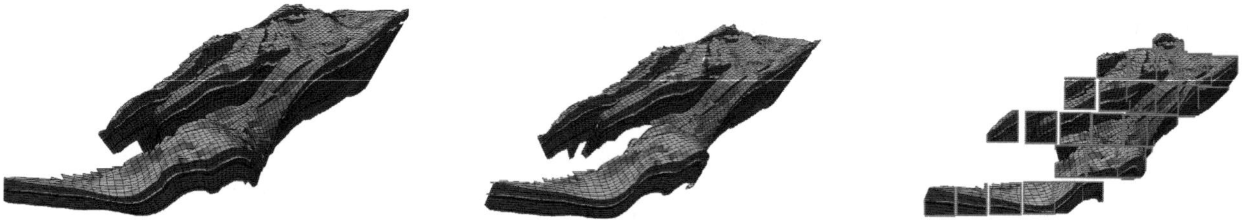

Figure 1. Oil reservoir viewer showing one server-rendered and two client-rendered images of automatically generated and slightly rotated proxy models. For (b), parameters are chosen to produce the best possible image, and in (c) we want to highlight artifacts and implementational details. See the text for further discussion.

visualization, see [8]. Another approach is that of [9]. They use websockets where we use the http protocol, a more significant difference is that we get away with transferring a lot less data due to our adaptive compression ratio depending on continuous bandwidth and latency measurements. In [10], Pajak et al. considers remote rendering and streaming of frames rendered from a dynamical 3D model, we are quite agnostic to the source of imagery. Their setup requires more powerful clients than ours, due to the use of the Open Graphics Library (OpenGL) vs. Web Graphics Library (WebGL), but they will also have higher fidelity. A special case is provided for in the rendering of stereo images. In this case, the 3D disparity is limited, while the rendering cost is doubled, since two views per frame is needed. In [11], this is exploited to make a solution tailored to such stereo synthesis; performance approaches that of rendering non-stereo, with a minimization of depth disparity artifacts. Occlusion and disocclusion holes are avoided by warping quads rather than pixel and filling in with previous images.

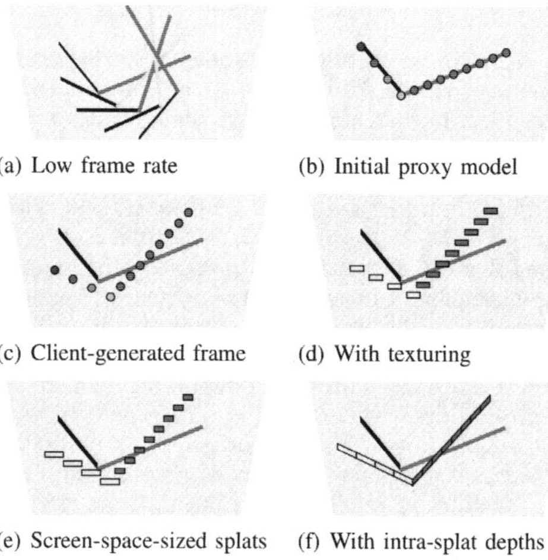

Figure 2. Bird's view of 3D model (solid lines) and proxy model renderings.

III. THE AUTO PROXY ALGORITHM

Since the depth buffer is a height map seen from the observer, it does not contain information about occluded scene elements. Our approach assumes that small transformations of this height map still will give good approximations of the scene. In Figure 2 below, a sequence of three server-rendered images (thick lines) is shown, together with intermediate client-rendered proxy models with different features that will be discussed in Section III-B.

A. The server side

The server renders the 3D model into a framebuffer, and in the process generates a depth image that we also send to the client. Since this adds to the data being sent, it must be kept to a minimum. We have found that reducing the spatial resolution of the depth image (for instance by a factor of $1/16$) only degrades the proxy model imperceptibly. We also encode each depth value in the range $[0, 1]$ as a 16 bit fixed point number, and the bundling of the depth image with the RGB image then imposes just a small data overhead. Further compression may bring this down even more, but the cost of compression/decompression must also be considered. One proposed solution is to be found in [12], which promises to be fast both for the compression and decompression stages.

B. The client side

When the client receives an RGB and depth image, together with view transformations, it builds a proxy model from this. This model can then be transformed and rendered directly, or it can be combined with other proxy models the client already has in store, see Section III-B2.

As indicated by Figure 2 (b), the received height map does not allow us more than concluding where a set of points belong on the 3D model, i.e., we have little topologic information. Since the information from the depth map can only contain the foremost point along any ray from the observer, it is said to be in 2.5D, as opposed to 3D. The simplest thing the client can do, is just to transform and render the set of 3D points with color sampled from the server-rendered image, as is illustrated in Figure 2 (b).

Rendering a 3D point for each depth fragment available may tax a thin client, and it may be necessary to use a smaller number of primitives and instead render each with a larger number of pixels on the client side, a *splat*. A set of such splats for a given depth image we call a *proxy model*. By rendering splats, we get fewer "false connections" than if we connect 3D points and reconstruct topology, but we risk getting more "holes" in our models. We can render each splat as a fixed geometry, e.g., a disk or rectangle, with the correspondig color from the image, see Figure 2 (c), where we have introduced a transformation local to the client. We will briefly describe some improvements to this. Note that other possibilities include building and maintaining a 3D occupancy mesh, computing a distance field from which iso-surfaces can be extracted, etc.

1) Texturing: Each splat produces many client pixels, necessitating an "intra-splat" fragment texturing for which we need a local texture coordinate transform. A first approximation is for the client to assume that the corresponding part of the server's model is planar in a region around the given point. If this is the case, a local 2D texture transformation will provide a good approximation to the intra-splat texturing to be performed on the client. Let P_c and P_s be projection matrices on the client and server, respectively, and M_c and M_s corresponding view matrices. For the splat centered in $\mathbf{v}_{i,j} = (x_j, y_i, z_{i,j})$, to be centered on the client's canvas at screen coordinate $\mathbf{p}_{i,j} = P_c M_c M_s^{-1} P_s^{-1} \mathbf{v}_{i,j} = U\mathbf{v}_{i,j}$, the texture coordinate transformation to be used is,

$$T = \begin{pmatrix} \frac{1}{n_x} & 0 \\ 0 & \frac{1}{n_y} \end{pmatrix} \begin{pmatrix} \mathbf{s}_x & \mathbf{s}_y \end{pmatrix}^{-1} \begin{pmatrix} \frac{w}{n_x} & 0 \\ 0 & \frac{h}{n_y} \end{pmatrix} = A \begin{pmatrix} \mathbf{s}_x & \mathbf{s}_y \end{pmatrix}^{-1} B,$$

where A maps the "client's splat region" (in $[0,1]^2$) to the corresponding texture area, $(\mathbf{s}_x \ \mathbf{s}_y)^{-1}$ maps the "client's screen space splat area" to $[0,1]^2$, and B provides a scaling factor to fill the *viewport* of size $w \times h$ with $n_x \times n_y$ splats laid out in a grid, when $M_c = M_s$. We obtain $\mathbf{s}_x$ and $\mathbf{s}_y$ by evaluating proxy model positions followed by perspective division and transformation into window coordinates,

$$\mathbf{p} = U \begin{pmatrix} x \\ y \\ d \\ 1 \end{pmatrix}, \mathbf{p}_{x+\Delta x} = U \begin{pmatrix} x+\Delta x \\ y \\ d_{\Delta x} \\ 1 \end{pmatrix} \text{ and } \mathbf{p}_{y+\Delta y} = U \begin{pmatrix} x \\ y+\Delta y \\ d_{\Delta y} \\ 1 \end{pmatrix},$$

where $d = 2D(x,y)-1$, $d_{\Delta x} = 2D(x+\Delta x, y)-1$, and $d_{\Delta y} = 2D(x, y+\Delta y)-1$ are depths sampled from the received depth buffer D and transformed to $[-1,1]$. With a w-component set to one, we have in effect done a perspective division, so that we are in clip space and multiplication with U is appropriate. Note that Δx and Δy are not unique, we use

$$\Delta x = n_x/\text{width}(D) \quad \text{and} \quad \Delta y = n_y/\text{height}(D),$$

but something larger may also be used. These are used for looking up depth image samples, and the calculation of $\mathbf{s}_x$ and $\mathbf{s}_y$ is really a gradient approximation, so we should not make them too large either.

This leaves us $\mathbf{p}$, $\mathbf{p}_{x+\Delta x}$ and $\mathbf{p}_{y+\Delta y}$ in clip coordinates, and from this we get corresponding window coordinates $\mathbf{s}$, $\mathbf{s}_{x+\Delta x}$ and $\mathbf{s}_{y+\Delta y}$, from which we finally get splat spanning vectors

$$\mathbf{s}_\delta = \mathbf{s}_{x+\delta} - \mathbf{s} = \frac{L}{2\delta} \left(\frac{\mathbf{p}_{x+\delta}.xy}{\mathbf{p}_{x+\delta}.w} - \frac{\mathbf{p}.xy}{\mathbf{p}.w} \right),$$

with $\delta = \Delta x$ or $\delta = \Delta y$, L is viewport size, either w or h, and we have used the "shader notation" for vector components. The client renders a large `glPoint` for each splat, with texture coordinates $(s,t)'$, and each fragment then looks up the server-rendered image at position

$$\begin{pmatrix} s \\ t \end{pmatrix} + T \begin{pmatrix} u \\ v \end{pmatrix} = \begin{pmatrix} s \\ t \end{pmatrix} + T \left(\texttt{glPointCoord} - \tfrac{1}{2} \right)$$

where (u,v) are "intra-splat texture coordinates". When the assumption that the geometry is locally planar does not hold, e.g., if the splats are very large, or they originate from a curved or non-smooth part, this may look slightly odd, see Figure 3. The figure shows splats for which depths are sampled on different planar regions at an angle to one another, causing contortions when large splats cover more than one such planar region.

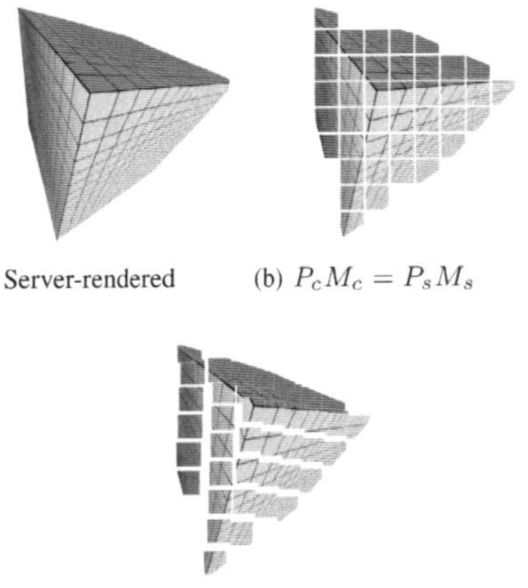

(a) Server-rendered (b) $P_c M_c = P_s M_s$

(c) $P_c M_c \neq P_s M_s$

Figure 3. Notice the corner and edges, parameters are chosen to display effects of different planes meeting at edges.

When the geometry is not planar, T produces the wrong result for parts of a splat. Two ways to remedy this could be to choose either more and smaller splats, or introduce more complex texture transformations. Note that using a more sophisticated texture coordinate transform may amount to performing the same work as for more and simpler transforms. The latter may be regarded as exactly a better "global" texture transform implementation.

2) Other splat considerations: **Splat sizing** Each splat should be rendered into a number of client pixels according to the new splats' 3D position. To achieve this, we use the vectors $\mathbf{s}_{\Delta x}$ and $\mathbf{s}_{\Delta y}$ from the previous section, and in addition, we scale the splats up a bit so that they overlap. Hence, we can render rectangular window-aligned splats with less risk of getting uncovered areas when interactively rotating and scaling the model on the client. In most cases this removes the problem visualized in Figure 3.

Splat depth fragments For larger splats, it makes sense to also compute and use depth fragments on the client. The "intra-splat" depth values can easily be fetched from the depth image, just as the texture is looked up for color. Not all clients support this WebGL extension.

Splat set replacement algorithms We mainly concern ourselves with proxy models defined as sets of splats, and it makes sense to keep a set of such models on the client, then we may combine them to cover larger ranges of client-side transformations. One can imagine a plethora of *splat set replacement algorithms*. We have tested three approaches that all retain a constant number of proxy models. The first is to replace the one with a viewing direction differing the most from the newly received model. The second simply replaces the oldest one in store. The third replaces a proxy model k if the replacement results in the following objective function being reduced,

$$\text{coverage} = \sum_{i=1}^{n} \sum_{j \neq i}^{n} (\angle(\mathbf{camdir}_i, \mathbf{camdir}_j)^2, \qquad (1)$$

where n is the number of proxy models available, **camdir** is the direction in which the camera was looking when a particular model was generated, and the model to be replaced is the one that minimizes (1) after replacement.

C. Auto-tuning

It is important that the process of generating and sending proxy model data from the server itself does not slow down transmission. There are mainly three sources of delay for server-rendered images to the client; high latency, low bandwidth, and slow server-rendering. In the first case, it seems prudent to have a good proxy model on the client, which can be used for longer time and for a wider range of client-side transformations. In the two other cases, it is important for the proxy model generation/transmission to be cheap/fast, both in order to get the proxy model to the client and keep from delaying the server-image more than necessary. These demands are not always compatible.

We have adopted an adaptive specification of proxy model data from the server involving a more light-weight image (lossy Joint Photographic Experts Group (JPEG) compression with adaptive quality control) while interaction is ongoing. Also, reduced resolution of the depth buffer sent from the server is used. Another possibility is to let the client dynamically set the number of splats, number of proxy models, etc.

IV. Results and Discussion

We have tested the proposed algorithms through the Tinia framework [13], which is a programming framework for setting up and managing client/server based interactive visualization applications. As client, we use Google Chrome, code is written in standard Javascript/WebGL. The auto-proxy implementation is invisible to the application, so all existing Tinia-applications will have the feature available. The algorithm is minimally intrusive in that only the depth buffer will have to be added to the rendering output of the application. We have tested several smaller test cases, but also on a larger oil reservoir viewer.

The reservoir viewer utilizes several OpenGL Shading Language (GLSL) shaders to render reservoir cells, boundaries, tubular wells, etc., and visualizes a 3D model that is not trivial to reduce in complexity. It is typically also very large, so rendering it on a thin client is prohibitive. With the automatic proxy model, we obtain interactive frame rates with limited connection from a lightweight client. For a comparison of a server-rendered image and a client-rendered proxy model that is slightly rotated on the client, see again Figure 1. In Figure 1 (a), the full server-rendered image is shown, and in (b) and (c), a slightly (about 10 degrees) rotated proxy model is rendered on the client. In (b), parameters are chosen for best possible results, while in (c), we want to highlight effects, so it uses a small number of non-overlapping large splats. One can easily spot areas not well covered, and areas where the texture coordinate transform T does not produce optimal results.

V. Conclusion and Future Work

The most attractive feature of the method described is the automated generation of the proxy model. Problems with compression and simplification of existing geometries is bypassed altogether. The automatic proxy model implementation is invisible to the application. There are several directions in which we would like to follow up and improve this concept, a couple of these are,

- **Proxy model replacement algorithms** Obtaining good results with a minimal set of proxy models.
- **Depth compression** We would like to ivestigate other approaches than just truncation, see, e.g., [12].
- **Deferred shading** With a normal map more advanced shading could be done on the client. Such a map could also be constructed from the depth map.

References

[1] SINTEF, "Cloudviz — direct visualization in the cloud," Project website: https://www.sintef.no/projectweb/heterogeneous-computing-expired/projects/cloudviz/, January 2010, website, retrieved: 2017-10-18.

[2] CloudFlow: Computational cloud services and workflows for agile engineering. Seventh Framework Programme (FP7) under grant agreement number 609100. Website, retrieved: 2017-10-18. [Online]. Available: http://eu-cloudflow.eu/ (2017)

[3] M. M. Oliveira, "Image-based modeling and rendering techniques: A survey." RITA, vol. 9, no. 2, 2002, pp. 37–66.

[4] P. Verlani and P. J. Narayanan, "Proxy-based compression of $2\frac{1}{2}$-d structure of dynamic events for tele-immersive systems," in Proceedings of 3D Data Processing, Visualization and Transmission (3DPVT), Atlanta, GA, USA, June 18-20 2008.

[5] E. Teler, "Streaming of complex 3d scenes for remote walkthroughs," Master's thesis, School of Computer Science and Engineering, The Hebrew University of Jerusalem, December 2001.

[6] I. Yoon and U. Neumann, "Web-Based Remote Renderingwith IBRAC (Image-Based Rendering Acceleration and Compression)," Computer Graphics Forum, 2000, pp. 321–330.

[7] W. R. Mark, L. McMillan, and G. Bishop, "Post-rendering 3d warping," in Proceedings of the 1997 Symposium on Interactive 3D Graphics, ser. I3D '97. New York, NY, USA: ACM, 1997, pp. 7–ff. [Online]. Available: http://doi.acm.org/10.1145/253284.253292

[8] A. Kolb, E. Barth, R. Koch, and R. Larsen, "Time-of-flight sensors in computer graphics (state-of-the-art report)," in Proceedings of Eurographics 2009 - State of the Art Reports. The Eurographics Association, 2009, pp. 119–134, retrieved 2017-10-18. [Online]. Available: http://www2.imm.dtu.dk/pubdb/p.php?5801

[9] C. Altenhofen, A. Dietrich, A. Stork, and D. Fellner, "Rixels: Towards secure interactive 3d graphics in engineering clouds," Transactions on Internet Research (TIR), vol. 12, no. 1, Jan. 2016, pp. 31–38.

[10] D. Pajak, R. Herzog, E. Eisemann, K. Myszkowski, and H.-P. Seidel, "Scalable remote rendering with depth and motion-flow augmented streaming," Computer Graphics Forum, vol. 30, no. 2, 2011, pp. 415–424. [Online]. Available: http://dx.doi.org/10.1111/j.1467-8659.2011.01871.x

[11] P. Didyk, T. Ritschel, E. Eisemann, K. Myszkowski, and H.-P. Seidel, "Adaptive image-space stereo view synthesis," in Vision, Modeling and Visualization Workshop, Siegen, Germany, 2010, pp. 299–306.

[12] P. Lindstrom, "Fixed-rate compressed floating-point arrays," IEEE Trans. Vis. Comput. Graph., vol. 20, no. 12, 2014, pp. 2674–2683. [Online]. Available: http://dx.doi.org/10.1109/TVCG.2014.2346458

[13] C. Dyken et al., "A framework for opengl client-server rendering," 2013 IEEE 5th International Conference on Cloud Computing Technology and Science, 2012, pp. 729–734.

Symbol Error Rate Analysis of Adaptive Threshold Based Relay Selection with 2-Bits Feedback for Type-2 Relays

Sung Sik Nam, Byungju Lim, Young-Chai Ko
Korea University, Korea
Email:{ssnam, limbj93, koyc}@korea.ac.kr

Mohamed-Slim Alouini
KAUST, Saui Arabia
Email: slim.alouini@kaust.edu.sa

***Abstract*—In this paper, we address the performance analysis of the extended adaptive threshold based relay selection (ATRS) scheme for multiple type-2 relays. More specifically, the symbol error rate (SER) analysis of 2-bits feedback based ATRS scheme is presented. For validation of our analytical results, derived analytical results are cross-verified with results obtained via Monte-Carlo simulations. Some selected results show that with more refined feedback information, the potential performance degradation caused by the minimum (i.e., 1-bit) feedback can be compensated, especially with a 1-bit increase in terms of feedback data rate and additional single comparison process in terms of complexity.**

Keywords–Symbol-Error Rate (SER); closed-form solutions; limited feedback; relay selection; type-2 relays.

I. Introduction

Recently, in [1], the adaptive threshold based relay selection (ATRS) scheme with minimum (i.e., '1-bit') feedback information was proposed by complying with the specifications for type-2 (or user equipment (UE)) relay to meet backward compatibility with the LTE-Advanced standard [2] [4]. Type-2 relay must be transparent to the end user (D) and the retransmitted signal from a selected relay is seen at D, like from the source (S) [1] [2]. If S only has the information of average channel gain of R-D link, like type-2 relay relaying, then the end-to-end error performance is degraded severely due to the insufficient information about R-D link. Here, to meet such backward compatibility required for type-2 relay, one of the possible solutions for selecting relay is that the relay selection process is performed at the transmitter (i.e., the source). In [3], it is done at end user and it turns out that [3] increases the complexity due to selection processing at end user, which is undesired for the mobile UE with limited complexity. In this transmitter-oriented scheme unlike the conventional receiver-oriented method, the relays (Rs) can use in the limited feedback information to the source about channel status information and then the source can use them for selecting the best relay. Based on these observations, in [1], the author proposed the threshold-based relay selection method that requires the minimum feedback load (i.e., '1-bit feedback information').

With [1], there is no need to feedback the full channel information to S that may cause a system overhead. This overhead caused by the channel status information (CSI) exchange is the bottleneck of practical implementations so that the reduction of overhead due to the required CSI exchanges is crucial. Instead of transmitting the full channel information, each relay simply reports to S about its R-D link status (e.g., "unacceptable" or "acceptable"). Then, S selects the relay with the highest S-R link gain among acceptable relays which have "acceptable" R-D link status. Therefore, with ATRS proposed in [1], there is no need to exchange the control (scheduling) message between Rs and D and as a result, it lead to satisfy the backward compatibility with type-2 relay. Further, [1] provides bandwidth efficiency and reduced complexity while it still provides an acceptable performance.

However, with the ATRS scheme [1], there may exist a potential performance degradation caused by applying the minimum (i.e., '1-bit') feedback information instead of the full CSI. More specifically, it is likely to mistakenly discard some links with better R-D channel links. For example, there may exist a relay that does not provide better S-R link compared to the scheduled relay among selected candidates only with two levels R-D link status information. Here, this potential performance degradation can be compensated with more refined feedback information. More specifically, instead of selecting acceptable or unacceptable relays with one threshold, by adopting one more threshold as shown in Figure 1, the status of each relay according to its R-D link gain is classified as three levels (i.e., "unacceptable", "good", or "better"). Then, after selecting each best relay from the good candidate group and the better candidate group, respectively, S selects the best one among these two relays. Here, since each relay needs to notify one of R-D link status among three status levels, 2-bit-based feedback is required. Therefore, with this 2-bits feedback based ATRS scheme, the potential performance degradation can be compensated with a 1-bit increase in terms of feedback data rate and additional single comparison process in terms of complexity.

Based on these observations, in [5], one more threshold was adopted. According to [5], by adopting one additional threshold to '1-bit feedback' based ATRS scheme [1], system can provide the symbol error rate (SER) performance very close to that of the perfect feedback case. Although the possibility of missing better channel links can be eliminated, the authors of [5] provided the SER performance results only from the computer simulations without any analytical derivations. Since the SER results from simulation show the performance only for the tested parameter range, we need the versatile analytical performance results which provide important insight on general range of parameter values [6]–[8]. However, we still need an accurate and efficient performance analysis, since, as far as we are aware, the general performance analysis results are not currently available.

Main Contributions: In this work, we statistically analyze the SER performance of '2-bits feedback' based ATRS scheme for multiple type-2 relays. More specifically, the closed-form result of SER is derived and validated with results obtained via Monte-Carlo simulations. Note that the derived closed-form results of SER can be easily evaluated numerically in the standard mathematical packages, such as MATHEMATICA, MATLAB and MAPLE.

The rest of the paper is organized as follows. In Section II, we present the system and channel models including the mode of operation. Then, we provide in Section III the SER performance analysis for M-ary phase-shift keying (PSK) signaling based on the statistical analysis. Finally, some selected results are provided followed by concluding remarks, in Sections IV and V, respectively.

II. System and Channel Models

Similar to [1], we assume that all channel links are quasi-static (or block flat fading) and mutually independent, which means that the channels are constant within one transmission duration, but vary independently over different transmission durations. In addition, the fading conditions follow Rayleigh fading model. In the performance analysis, we assume that all relays are statistically identical.

We also consider a network with multiple type-2 relays and decode-and-forward (DF) protocols [9] [10], where a source node, S, communicates with a destination node, D, with the help of multiple type-2 relays, R_i, (there exist N possible relays). The channel gains of S-D, S-R$_i$, and R$_i$-D links are denoted by $h_{s,d}$, h_{s,r_i}, and $h_{r_i,d}$ which are assumed zero-mean complex Gaussian random variables with variances $\delta^2_{s,d}$, δ^2_{s,r_i}, and $\delta^2_{r_i,d}$, respectively.

Each node has only one omni-directional antenna. Therefore, all the nodes operate on half-duplex mode. Furthermore, it is assumed that each relay knows the CSI of its S-R$_i$ link and CSI of its R$_i$-D link based on ACK/NACK from end user (D) [1] [2]. More specifically, based on the system model of the type II relay shown in [1] [2], each relay can overhear the reference signal including ACK/NACK signal periodically sent from D to S. Such overheard signals can be used for estimating each R-D link quality by comparing with pre-determined thresholds. Therefore, it is possible to partially feedback the R-D link channel conditions to S [1]. Given some form of network block synchronization, carrier and symbol synchronization for the network can build equally between the individual transmitters and receivers. Exactly how this synchronization is achieved, and the effects of small synchronization errors on performance, is beyond the scope of this paper.

In the relay selection scheme, similar to [1], we assume TDD mode where $h_{s,d}$ and h_{s,r_i} are known at S, and $h_{r_i,d}$ are known at R, but $h_{r_i,d}$ must be fedback to S by R that causes system overhead. Here, we extend the proposed ATRS scheme with '1-bit feedback information' in [1] as '2-bits feedback information' based scheme by adopting two thresholds to improve the SER performance while slightly increasing system complexity. Note that [5] shows that more specific information assures better R-D channel condition for the best relay, resulting in an improved SER performance [5].

The relay selection strategy is similar to the ATRS scheme with 1-bit feedback [1]. In [1] [5], the relay selection protocol proposed in [11] is adopted to compensate the drawbacks of the

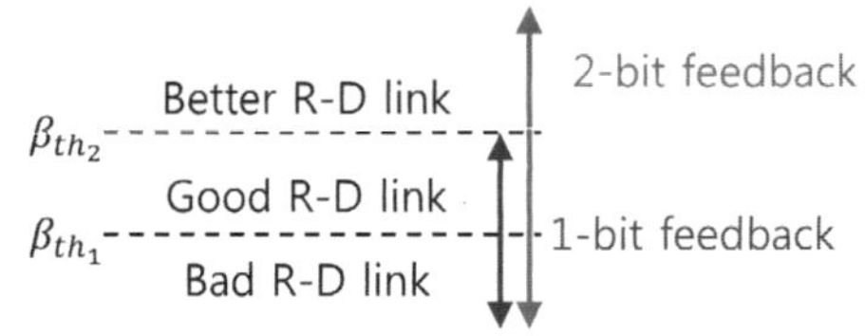

Figure 1. ATRS with 2-bit feedback.

performance degradation due to the limited feedback. In [11], they proposed the relay selection protocol using a modified harmonic mean, which is an appropriate metric to represent the relay's ability on how much help a relay can offer. According to [11], the optimal relay is the one which has the maximum value of the relay's metric, which is a modified version of the harmonic mean function of its source-relay and relay-destination instantaneous channel gains. Therefore, if multiple relays are available and we need to choose one relay only, then the relay with maximum value in terms of the modified harmonic mean is selected. Similarly, in [5], the optimal relay is the one which has the maximum value of the modified version of the harmonic mean among candidate relays. Specifically, the scheme with limited feedback information selects the relay, which maximizes the modified harmonic mean of S-R and R-D links: i) S transmits both to all relays and to D; ii) D transmits an ACK/NACK message, which is overheard at multiple relays to acquire information about the R-D links; iii) eligible relays must communicate their eligibility to S; iv) S selects the best relay in terms of the modified harmonic mean. Here, the main difference of the 2-bits feedback based scheme compared to [1] is to quantize the R-D link with three levels, i.e., "unacceptable", "good" or "better" as shown in Figure 1. The quantized R-D channel gains value can be written as $\beta_{r_i,d} \in \{0, \beta_{th_1}, \beta_{th_2}\}$ (for $i = 1, 2, \ldots, k$ and $k \leq N$). More specifically, in the first stage, each relay notifies S of being "better" or "good" if

$$\begin{aligned} &\beta_{r_i,d} \geq \beta_{th_2} \longrightarrow \text{available with a better link condition,} \\ &\text{or} \\ &\beta_{th_2} > \beta_{r_i,d} \geq \beta_{th_1} \longrightarrow \text{available with a good link condition,} \\ &\text{for } i = 1, 2, \ldots, k_2, \end{aligned} \tag{1}$$

where $k_1 + k_2 = k$, $\beta_{x,y} = |h_{x,y}|^2$, and β_{th_j} (for $j = 1, 2$) is the threshold ($\beta_{th_1} < \beta_{th_2}$). Similar to [1], since such relays are considered as candidates for the best relay and their SNR values are one of the two threshold values (i.e., β_{th_1} or β_{th_2}), choosing the relay who can maximize the modified harmonic mean function of S-R and R-D channel gains based on the S-R link condition will select the best relay. Specifically, the source selects one candidate from the 'better' candidate group whose R-D channel gain exceeds the threshold β_{th_2} is $\beta_b = \max\{\beta_{s,r_1}, \beta_{s,r_2}, \ldots, \beta_{s,r_{k_2}}\}$ and the other candidate from the 'good' candidate group whose R-D channel gain below the threshold β_{th_2} but exceeds the threshold β_{th_1} as $\beta_a = \max\{\beta_{s,r_1}, \beta_{s,r_2}, \ldots, \beta_{s,r_{k_1}}\}$. Then, the source chooses the best S-R link from these two candidates to maximize the modified harmonic mean of S-R and R-D channel gains. Consequently, the optimum relay will have a metric, which is equal to $\max\{\beta_{k_1^*}, \beta_{k_2^*}\}$, where $\beta_{k_1^*} = \frac{2q_1q_2\beta_{th_1}\beta_a}{q_1\beta_{th_1}+q_2\beta_a}$, $\beta_{k_2^*} = \frac{2q_1q_2\beta_{th_2}\beta_b}{q_1\beta_{th_2}+q_2\beta_b}$, $q_1 = \left(\frac{M-1}{M} + \frac{\sin(2\frac{\pi}{M})}{2\pi}\right)^2$ and

$q_2 = \left(\frac{3(M-1)}{2M} + \frac{\sin\left(2\frac{\pi}{M}\right)}{\pi} - \frac{\sin\left(4\frac{\pi}{M}\right)}{8\pi}\right)$, especially for $P_1 = P_2$. If there exists no candidate ($k = 0$), the source randomly chooses one relay among N relays similar to [1].

For cooperative transmission (upon reception of NACK) in the second stage, the best relay forwards data to the end user if decoding is performed correctly and otherwise, the relay remains idle. In addition, we also assume that the system has the total power constraint of $P = P_1 + P_2$, where P is the total maximum transmit power available, P_1 and P_2 are the transmit powers at the source and at the selected relay, respectively. Further, we also assume maximal-ratio combining (MRC) for the signals from source and selected relay to destination, for which the destination estimates the CSI for coherent detection. Then, the instantaneous SNR of MRC output can be evaluated as $\gamma_{s,r_i,d} = \frac{P_1\beta_{s,d} + P_2\beta_{r_i,d}}{\sigma_n^2}$ given in [1].

III. Performance Analysis

In this section, by adopting the performance analysis framework applied in [1], the SER performance of the ATRS scheme with 2-bits feedback is analyzed for M-PSK signaling. With the help of [1], the average SER conditioned on the number of candidates k_1 and k_2 can be formulated as

$$\overline{\text{SER}}_{\text{total}} = \sum_{k_1}\sum_{k_2} \overline{\text{SER}}\,(k_1, k_2)\, P\,(K_1 = k_1, K_2 = k_2)\,, \tag{2}$$

where $\overline{\text{SER}}\,(k_1, k_2)$ is the SER at the destination when there are k_1 candidate relays with 'good' R-D links and k_2 candidate relays with 'better' R-D links and $P\,(K_1 = k_1, K_2 = k_2)$ is the probability of having candidate relay subsets of size k_1 and k_2. In deriving $P\,(K_1 = k_1, K_2 = k_2)$, the problem can be simplified as "How many candidate relays in each group ('good' and 'better') exist?" because we assume that all the relays are statistically identical. As a result, the probability of having k_1 and k_2 candidates follows the multinomial distribution [12]. Therefore, we can obtain the probability of having k_1 and k_2 candidates in each group as

$$\begin{aligned} P(K_1 = k_1, K_2 = k_2) &= \frac{N!}{k_1!k_2!(N-k_1-k_2)!} \\ &\times \left(e^{-\frac{\beta_{th_1}}{\delta^2_{r,d}}} - e^{-\frac{\beta_{th_2}}{\delta^2_{r,d}}}\right)^{k_1} \left(e^{-\frac{\beta_{th_2}}{\delta^2_{r,d}}}\right)^{k_2} \left(1 - e^{-\frac{\beta_{th_1}}{\delta^2_{r,d}}}\right)^{N-k_1-k_2}. \end{aligned} \tag{3}$$

In deriving $\overline{\text{SER}}\,(k_1, k_2)$, if there is no relay for co-operation mode, the direct transmission is performed. Otherwise, the relay cooperation mode is performed. As a result, we can formulate $\overline{\text{SER}}\,(k_1, k_2)$ with two SER terms of the direct transmission mode and the relay cooperation mode as

$$\begin{aligned} \overline{\text{SER}}\,(k_1, k_2) =& P_e(s, r_i|\, k_1, k_2)\, P_e(s, d) \\ &+ [1 - P_e(s, r_i|\, k_1, k_2)]\, P_e(s, r_i, d|k_1, k_2)\,, \end{aligned} \tag{4}$$

where $P_e\,(s, r_i|k_1, k_2)$, $P_e\,(s, d)$, and $P_e\,(s, r_i, d|k_1, k_2)$ represent the conditional decoding error at the best relay, the SER for direct transmission, and the conditional SER for cooperative transmission, respectively. Then, we need to evaluate three conditional decoding error terms at the best relay in (4).

A. For the conditional decoding error at the best relay, $P_e\,(s, r_i|\, k_1, k_2)$

In this case, we overall need to consider two cases, separately. More specifically, if the $\beta_{k_2^*} > \beta_{k_1^*}$, the relay for cooperation is selected from k_2 candidates and otherwise, the relay for cooperation is selected from k_1 candidates as

$$\begin{aligned} P_e(s, r_i|\, k_1, k_2) =& \int_0^\infty P_e(\beta) p_{s,r_{1,i}}(\beta\,|K_1 = k_1, K_2 = k_2) d\beta \\ &+ \int_0^\infty P_e(\beta) p_{s,r_{2,i}}(\beta\,|K_1 = k_1, K_2 = k_2) d\beta, \end{aligned} \tag{5}$$

where $P_e(\gamma)$ is the SER formula for M-PSK, $P_e(\gamma) = \frac{1}{\pi}\int_0^{\frac{(M-1)\pi}{M}} e^{-\frac{b\gamma}{\sin^2\theta}} d\theta$, given by [1] [8] and $b = \sin^2(\pi/M)$ and M is the modulation order of PSK. For case 1) (i.e., $\beta_{k_2^*} > \beta_{k_1^*}$), we can rewrite as the function of β_a and β_b

$$\begin{aligned} \beta_{k_1^*} > \beta_{k_2^*} &\Leftrightarrow \frac{1}{q_2 * \beta_b} + \frac{1}{q_1 * \beta_{th2}} > \frac{1}{q_2 * \beta_a} + \frac{1}{q_1 * \beta_{th1}} \\ &\Leftrightarrow \frac{1}{\beta_a} - \frac{1}{\beta_b} < \frac{q_2}{q_1}\left(\frac{1}{\beta_{th2}} - \frac{1}{\beta_{th1}}\right). \end{aligned} \tag{6}$$

Then, if we let $X = \frac{1}{\beta_a}$ and $Y = \frac{1}{\beta_b}$, then the valid integral regions of β_a and β_b become $0 < \beta_a < \infty$ and $0 < \beta_b < \frac{\beta_a}{1 - A\beta_a}$, respectively, where $A = \frac{q_2}{q_1}\left(\frac{1}{\beta_{th_2}} - \frac{1}{\beta_{th_1}}\right)$ $(A < 0)$.

Similarly, for case 2) (i.e., $\beta_{k_2^*} < \beta_{k_1^*}$), we can rewrite as the function of β_a and β_b

$$\begin{aligned} \beta_{k_1^*} < \beta_{k_2^*} &\Leftrightarrow \frac{1}{q_2 * \beta_b} + \frac{1}{q_1 * \beta_{th2}} < \frac{1}{q_2 * \beta_a} + \frac{1}{q_1 * \beta_{th1}} \\ &\Leftrightarrow \frac{1}{\beta_a} - \frac{1}{\beta_b} > \frac{q_2}{q_1}\left(\frac{1}{\beta_{th2}} - \frac{1}{\beta_{th1}}\right). \end{aligned} \tag{7}$$

In this case, we consider two cases separately for mathematical convenience. More specifically, for case 2)-i) (i.e., $Y > -A$), the valid integral regions of β_a and β_b become $0 < \beta_a < \frac{\beta_b}{1 + A\beta_b}$ and $0 < \beta_b < \frac{1}{-A}$, respectively. Otherwise (i.e., for case 2)-ii)), the valid integral regions of β_a and β_b become $0 < \beta_a < \infty$ and $\frac{1}{-A} < \beta_b < \infty$, respectively. As results, (5) can be rewritten as the following three integral terms

$$\begin{aligned} &\int_0^\infty P_e(\beta) p_{s,r_{1,i}}(\beta\,|K_1 = k_1, K_2 = k_2)\, d\beta \\ &= \int_0^\infty \frac{1}{\pi} \int_0^{\frac{(M-1)\pi}{M}} e^{\left(\frac{-b\beta_a}{\sin^2\theta}\right)} \int_0^{\frac{\beta_a}{1 - A\beta_a}} \frac{k_2}{\delta^2_{s,r_i}} e^{-\frac{\beta_b}{\delta^2_{s,r_i}}} \left(1 - e^{-\frac{\beta_b}{\delta^2_{s,r_i}}}\right)^{k_2 - 1} \\ &\quad \frac{k_1}{\delta^2_{s,r_i}} e^{-\frac{\beta_a}{\delta^2_{s,r_i}}} \left(1 - e^{-\frac{\beta_a}{\delta^2_{s,r_i}}}\right)^{k_1 - 1} d\beta_b d\theta d\beta_a, \end{aligned} \tag{8}$$

and

$$\begin{aligned} &\int_0^\infty P_e(\beta) p_{s,r_{2,i}}(\beta\,|K_1 = k_1, K_2 = k_2)\, d\beta \\ &= \int_0^{-\frac{1}{A}} \frac{1}{\pi} \int_0^{\frac{(M-1)\pi}{M}} e^{\left(\frac{-b\beta_b}{\sin^2\theta}\right)} \int_0^{\frac{\beta_b}{1 + A\beta_b}} \frac{k_1}{\delta^2_{s,r_i}} e^{-\frac{\beta_a}{\delta^2_{s,r_i}}} \left(1 - e^{-\frac{\beta_a}{\delta^2_{s,r_i}}}\right)^{k_1 - 1} \\ &\quad \frac{k_2}{\delta^2_{s,r_i}} e^{-\frac{\beta_b}{\delta^2_{s,r_i}}} \left(1 - e^{-\frac{\beta_b}{\delta^2_{s,r_i}}}\right)^{k_2 - 1} d\beta_a d\theta d\beta_b \\ &\quad + \int_{-\frac{1}{A}}^\infty \frac{1}{\pi} \int_0^{\frac{(M-1)\pi}{M}} e^{\left(\frac{-b\beta_b}{\sin^2\theta}\right)} \frac{k_2}{\delta^2_{s,r_i}} e^{-\frac{\beta_b}{\delta^2_{s,r_i}}} \left(1 - e^{-\frac{\beta_b}{\delta^2_{s,r_i}}}\right)^{k_2 - 1} d\theta d\beta_b. \end{aligned} \tag{9}$$

In (8), after applying the binomial theorem [13], (8) and then with the help of the integral identity [14, Eq. (07.33.07.0001.01)] and Taylor series expansions of exponential functions [13], the closed-form expression of (8) can be obtained as

$$\sum_{j=0}^{k_2-1}\sum_{l=0}^{k_1-1}\binom{k_2-1}{j}\binom{k_1-1}{l}k_2k_1\frac{(-1)^{j+l+1}}{1+j}$$
$$\times\left[\sum_{n=0}^{\infty}F_1\left(\frac{\left(1+l+\frac{b\delta^2_{s,r_i}}{\sin^2\theta}\right)\left(\frac{A\delta^2_{s,r_i}}{1+j}\right)^n}{U\left(n,0,-\frac{1}{A}\left(\frac{b}{\sin^2\theta}+\frac{1+l}{\delta^2_{s,r_i}}\right)\right)}\right)-F_1\left(1+l+\frac{b\delta^2_{s,r_i}}{\sin^2\theta}\right)\right], \tag{10}$$

where $U(a,b,z)$ is Tricomi's confluent hypergeometric function [14, Eq. (07.33.02.0001.01)] and $F_1(x(\theta))$ is given in [1, Eq. (22)] as $F_1(x(\theta))=\frac{1}{\pi}\int_0^{\frac{(M-1)\pi}{M}}\frac{1}{x(\theta)}d\theta$. Here, $U(a,b,z)$ and $F_1(x(\theta))$ can be evaluated in the standard mathematical packages. Note that the expression in (10) involves an infinite summation for the term of n. However, it is found that the summand in (10) decay exponentially (or slightly faster) with the increase of n, because Stirling's approximation specifies that $n!$ grows as $\exp(n\ln n)$ [13]. As results, due to the factorial term in Tricomi's confluent hypergeometric function, $U(\cdot,\cdot,\cdot)$, as the function of n, a truncated summation with a finite number of terms can reliably achieve a required accuracy.

For the first integral term in (9), after applying binomial theorem and then expanding the exponential function as a Taylor series similar to previous case, with the help of [15, (3.381.3)], the closed-form expression of the first integral term in (9) as the function of $F_1(\cdot)$

$$\sum_{j=0}^{k_2-1}\sum_{l=0}^{k_1-1}\binom{k_1-1}{l}\binom{k_2-1}{j}k_1k_2\frac{(-1)^{j+l}}{1+l}\left[\sum_{n=0}^{\infty}\frac{1}{n!}\Gamma\left(1-n,-\frac{1+l}{A\delta^2_{s,r_i}}\right)\right.$$
$$\left(\frac{A^2(\delta^2_{s,r_i})^2}{1+l}\right)^{-n}e^{\frac{j-l}{A\delta^2_{s,r_i}}}F_1\left(e^{-\frac{b}{A\sin^2\theta}}\left(1+j+\frac{b\delta^2_{s,r_i}}{\sin^2\theta}\right)^{1-n}\right)$$
$$\left.-e^{\frac{1+j}{A\delta^2_{s,r_i}}}F_1\left(e^{-\frac{b}{A\sin^2\theta}}\left(1+j+\frac{b\delta^2_{s,r_i}}{\sin^2\theta}\right)\right)\right]. \tag{11}$$

For the second integral term in (9), similarly, after applying the binomial theorem and then simply integrating over β_b, the closed-form expression can be obtained as

$$\sum_{j=0}^{k_2-1}\binom{k_2-1}{j}k_2(-1)^j e^{\frac{1+j}{A\delta^2_{s,r_i}}}F_1\left(e^{-\frac{b}{A\sin^2\theta}}\left(1+j+\frac{b\delta^2_{s,r_i}}{\sin^2\theta}\right)\right). \tag{12}$$

B. For the SER for direct transmission, $P_e(s,d)$

In this case, the PDF of S-D link is independent of the number of candidates and its channel gain follows the exponential distribution. Therefore, the SER of directly transmission from source to destination can be evaluated as

$$P_e(s,d)=\int_0^{\infty}P_e(\beta)p_{s,d}(\beta)d\beta=\frac{1}{\pi}\int_0^{\frac{(M-1)\pi}{M}}\frac{\sin^2\theta}{\sin^2\theta+b\delta^2_{s,d}}d\theta. \tag{13}$$

Then, the closed-form expression of (13) can be simply obtained as

$$P_e(s,d)=F_1\left(1+\frac{b\delta^2_{s,d}}{\sin^2\theta}\right). \tag{14}$$

C. For the conditional SER for cooperative transmission, $P_e(s,r_i,d|k_1,k_2)$

In this case, the conditional SER for cooperative transmission at D when each candidates are k_1 and k_2 can be formulated by considering two cases (s.t. 'good' or 'better')

$$P_e(s,r_i,d|k_1,k_2)$$
$$=P\left[\beta_{k_1^*}>\beta_{k_2^*}|K_1=k_1,K_2=k_2\right]\int_0^{\infty}P_e(\beta)p_{s,r_{1,i},d}(\beta)d\beta$$
$$+P\left[\beta_{k_1^*}<\beta_{k_2^*}|K_1=k_1,K_2=k_2\right]\int_0^{\infty}P_e(\beta)p_{s,r_{2,i},d}(\beta)d\beta. \tag{15}$$

In (15), we need to evaluate two integral terms. For the first integral term, it can be evaluated by performing the integration of the exponential function over β. Therefore, we can obtain the closed-form expression of (15) as

$$\int_0^{\infty}P_e(\beta)p_{s,r_{1,i},d}(\beta)d\beta$$
$$=F_1\left(\left(\frac{e^{\frac{\beta_{th_1}}{\delta^2_{r,d}}}-e^{\frac{\beta_{th_2}}{\delta^2_{r,d}}}}{e^{-\frac{b\beta_{th_2}}{\sin^2\theta}+\frac{\beta_{th_1}}{\delta^2_{r,d}}}-e^{-\frac{b\beta_{th_1}}{\sin^2\theta}+\frac{\beta_{th_2}}{\delta^2_{r,d}}}}\right)\left(1+\frac{b\delta^2_{r,d}}{\sin^2\theta}\right)\left(1+\frac{b\delta^2_{s,d}}{\sin^2\theta}\right)\right). \tag{16}$$

For the second integral term, similar to (16), we can obtain the closed-form expression as

$$\int_0^{\infty}P_e(\beta)p_{s,r_{2,i},d}(\beta)d\beta=F_1\left(e^{\frac{b\beta_{th_2}}{\sin^2\theta}}\left(1+\frac{b\delta^2_{r,d}}{\sin^2\theta}\right)\left(1+\frac{b\delta^2_{s,d}}{\sin^2\theta}\right)\right). \tag{17}$$

In (15), the probability where the R-D link of the selected relay is 'good' can be evaluated as

$$P\left[\beta_{k_1^*}>\beta_{k_2^*}|K_1=k_1,K_2=k_2\right]=\int_0^{\infty}\frac{k_1}{\delta^2_{s,r_i}x^2}e^{-\frac{1}{\delta^2_{s,r_i}x}}\left(1-e^{-\frac{1}{\delta^2_{s,r_i}x}}\right)^{k_1-1}$$
$$\left(\int_{x-A}^{\infty}\frac{k_2}{\delta^2_{s,r_i}y^2}e^{-\frac{1}{\delta^2_{s,r_i}y}}\left(1-e^{-\frac{1}{\delta^2_{s,r_i}y}}\right)^{k_2-1}dy\right)dx, \tag{18}$$

where $A=\frac{q_2}{q_1}\left(\frac{1}{\beta_{th_2}}-\frac{1}{\beta_{th_1}}\right)$. Here, by applying the binomial theorem to the inner integral term and then with the help of Taylor series expansions of exponential functions [13], with the help of the integral identity [14, Eq. (07.33.07.0001.01)], we can finally obtain the closed-form expression of (18) as

$$P\left[\beta_{k_1^*}>\beta_{k_2^*}|K_1=k_1,K_2=k_2\right]=\sum_{l=0}^{k_2-1}\binom{k_2-1}{l}\frac{(-1)^l k_2}{1+l}$$
$$\times\left[1+\sum_{j=0}^{k_1-1}\sum_{n=0}^{\infty}\binom{k_1-1}{j}\frac{k_1(-1)^{j+1}}{1+j}A^{-n}U\left(n,0,\frac{-1-j}{A\delta^2_{s,r_i}}\right)\left(\frac{1+l}{\delta^2_{s,r_i}}\right)^n\right]. \tag{19}$$

Similarly, with (19), the probability where the R-D link of the selected relay is 'better' in (15) can be evaluated as

$$P\left[\beta_{k_1^*}<\beta_{k_2^*}|K_1=k_1,K_2=k_2\right]=1-P\left[\beta_{k_1^*}>\beta_{k_2^*}|K_1=k_1,K_2=k_2\right]. \tag{20}$$

IV. NUMERICAL RESULTS

In this section, as a validation of our analytical results for the SER performance, we compare in Figure 2 the analytical results with the simulation results obtained via Monte-Carlo simulation over i.i.d. Rayleigh fading channels. Here, for the fair comparison of the SER performance between 1-bit and 2-bits feedback based schemes, we consider the equal power allocation and the fixed threshold, especially to show the effect of more refined feedback information on the SER performance. Note that the derived analytical results match the simulation results and we believe that it is available to accurately predict the performance with them.

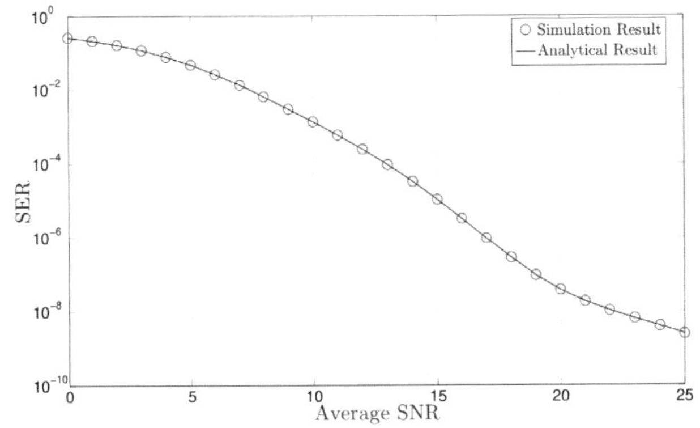

Figure 2. Performance comparison between the simulation and analytical results with $N = 6$, $\beta_{th_1} = 10$dB, $\beta_{th_2} = 12$dB, and $\overline{\gamma}_{SR} = \overline{\gamma}_{RD} = \overline{\gamma}_{SD} = \overline{\gamma}$.

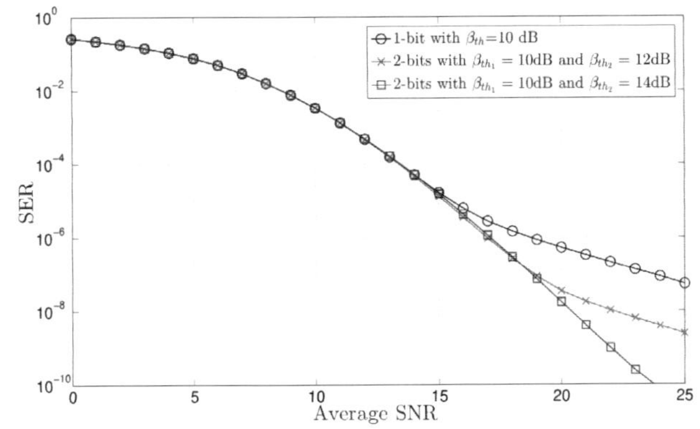

Figure 3. SER performance with varying threshold values and $\overline{\gamma}_{SR} = \overline{\gamma}_{RD} = \overline{\gamma}_{SD} = \overline{\gamma}$ for $N = 6$.

Figure 3 shows that as our original expectation, the proposed ATRS scheme with 2-bits feedback information achieves better performance than 1-bit feedback based scheme. More specifically, the possibility that the 2-bits feedback based scheme can provide the better performance compared to the 1-bit feedback based scheme is high because through one additional bit in terms of a feedback information and one additional comparison operation in terms of the complexity, the 2-bits feedback based scheme has the higher ability to compensate the potential performance degradation. Further, if we consider that the S-R link condition of each candidates selected from both 'better' and 'good' candidate groups is similar, the performance improvements of the 2-bits feedback based scheme is getting increasing compared to the 1-bit feedback based scheme as the threshold, β_{th_2}, increases.

V. CONCLUSIONS

In this paper, we analyzed the SER performance of the extended ATRS scheme based on '2-bits feedback' information as closed-form expressions. For validation of analytical results, derived analytical results were cross-verified with results obtained via Monte-Carlo simulations. Based on some selected results, we confirmed that with more refined feedback information, the potential performance degradation caused by the 1-bit feedback can be compensated, especially with a 1-bit increase in terms of feedback data rate and additional single comparison process in terms of complexity.

ACKNOWLEDGMENT

This work was supported by Institute for Information & communications Technology Promotion(IITP) grant funded by the Korea Government(MSIT)(2014-0-00552,Next Generation WLAN System with High Efficient Performance) and the MSIP(Ministry of Science, ICT and Future Planning), Korea, under the ITRC(Information Technology Research Center) support program (IITP-2017-H8501-16-1019) supervised by the IITP(Institute for Information & communications Technology Promotion).

REFERENCES

[1] S. C. Park, D. I. Kim, and S. S. Nam, "Adaptive threshold based relay selection for minimum feedback and channel usage," *IEEE Trans. Wireless Commun.*, vol. 10, pp. 3620-3625 , Nov. 2011.

[2] E. Hossain, D. I. Kim, and V. K. Bhargava, *Cooperative Cellular Wireless Networks*, Cambridge University Press, 2011.

[3] F. A. Onat, T. Fan, H. Yanikomeroglu, and H. V. Poor, "Threshold based relay selection in cooperative wireless networks," *in Proc. GLOBECOM'08*, pp. 1-5, New Orleans, USA, Dec. 2008.

[4] S. S. Nam, D. I. Kim, and H.-C. Yang, "Modified dynamic DF for type II UE relays," *in Proc. IEEE WCNC'12*, Paris, France, pp. 1402-1407, Apr. 2012.

[5] K. Oh and D. I. Kim, "Relay selection with limited feedback for multiple UE relays," *in Proc. Computational Science and Its Applications (ICCSA 2011)*, pp. 157-166, Santander, Spain, June 2011.

[6] G. L. Stüber, *Principles of Mobile Communications*, 2nd ed., Norwell, MA: Kluwer Academic Publishers, 2001.

[7] T. S. Rapapport, *Wireless Communications: Principles and Practice*, 2nd ed., Upper Saddle River, NJ: Prentice Hall, 2002.

[8] M. K. Simon and M.-S. Alouini, *Digital Communications over Generalized Fading Channels*, 2nd ed., New York, NY: John Wiley & Sons, 2004.

[9] A. Sendonaris, E. Erkip, and B. Aazhang, "User cooperation diversity. Part I and Part II," *IEEE Trans. Commun.* , vol. 51, pp. 1927-1948, Nov. 2003.

[10] J. N. Laneman, G. W. Wornell, and D. N. C. Tse, "An efficient protocol for realizing cooperative diversity in wireless networks," *in Proc. IEEE ISIT'01*, pp. 294, Washington D.C., June 2001.

[11] A. S. Ibrahim, A. K. Sadek, W. Su, and K. J. R. Liu, "Cooperative communication with relay-selection: when to cooperate and whom to cooperate with?" *IEEE Trans. Wireless Commun.*, vol. 7, pp. 2814-2827, July 2008.

[12] A. Papoulis, *Probability, Random Variables, and Stochastic Processes*, 3rd ed., New York, NY: McGraw-Hill, 1991.

[13] M. Abramowitz and I. A. Stegun, *Handbook of Mathematical Functions*, New York, NY: Dover Publications, 1972.

[14] I. Wolfram, Research, Mathematica Edition: Version 8.0. Champaign, IL, USA: Wolfram Research, Inc., 2010.

[15] I. S. Gradshteyn and I.M. Ryzhik, *Table of Integrals, Series, and Products*, 7th ed., San Diego, CA: Academic Press, 2007.

A Reward System for Collaborative Care of Elderly based on Distributed Ledger Technologies

Emilien Bai and Kåre Synnes
Luleå University of Technology
Luleå, Sweden
e-mail: emibai-6@student.ltu.se, unicorn@ltu.se

Abstract— **This paper presents the design and implementation of a reward system for collaborative care of elderly based on distributed ledger technologies. The work is motivated by the demographic change, where an aging population consequently increases the need for care. This causes a great tension in our society, as care resources become increasingly constrained, both regarding costs and availability of care staff. Much of the daily care of the elderly is today done by family members (spouses, children) and friends, often on a voluntarily basis, which adds to the tension. The core idea of this work is to help broaden the involvement of people in caring for our elderly, enabled by a system for collaborative care. The proposed system benefits from recent advances in distributed ledger technologies, which similarly to digital currencies, are build on the ability for mutual agreements between people who do not know each other. The system also benefits from recent gamification techniques to motivate people to collaborate on a larger scale through performing simple daily tasks. The system builds on rewards automatically given when these smart contracts are fulfilled, a gamification technique that is believed to maintain motivation of the volunteers. In this paper, we thus describe a reward system designed to connect elderly and volunteers by mutual agreements implemented as smart contracts.**

Keywords- Blockchain; Collaborative Care; Gamification.

I. INTRODUCTION

The aging population has been identified as a challenge for the future in a Swedish study from 2013 [1]. In May 2012, 18.8% of the total population of Sweden was 65 years old or older. This part of the population is expected to reach 20.5% in 2020 and 25.9% in 2060. The main difficulties identified are to finance welfare of the aging population, as well as meeting the increasing demand of service provision. The demand on staff is expected to increase by 210 000 caregivers by 2030 in Sweden, while the supply is expected to stay quite the same. Also, this situation will probably result in a widened financial gap between the cost of welfare and state revenues. The trend of an aging population is confirmed to be worldwide by a United Nations report from 2015, which focuses on the oldest persons (aged 80 years or more) [2].

Much of the daily care (such as performing daily tasks like shopping for groceries, cleaning, cooking, etc) are often performed by informal carers such as family members, or friends. The burden this places on spouses and children of the elderly can often be very high, reducing the quality of life not only for the elderly being cared for but also for these informal carers.

It is thus clear that a broader engagement of our society in caring for our elderly is needed, where voluntary contributions also can be rewarded (besides the altruistic satisfaction of being helpful, pro-bono). Not everyone would of course require such rewards, but motivating a larger cohort of our fellow people may require both short and long term perceived benefits. Examples of short term benefits may be making people's contributions visible in the society or being able to trade work, and long term benefits may include being able to get help back in kind (If I help now, then I will get help later). This leads to the following research question:

How can a system for collaborative care of elderly be designed and implemented to engage and motivate people to contribute with daily tasks on a voluntary basis?

The aim of this work is thus to develop an application intended to connect the population who may need help in common daily tasks with people who may provide voluntarily help. The aim is not to replace workers specialized in health care, but to reduce their work charge where it is possible and therefore instead leave them more time to do important and skilled tasks for the elderly.

Ultimately, by reducing the proportion of paid care, the application may also contribute to decreasing the cost of care for the aging population, without degrading the quality of care.

The rest of the paper is organized as follows. In section II, we present a state of the art concerning distributed ledger technologies, blockchains as well as smart contracts. In section III, we introduce the methodology used in order to develop the system. Section IV focuses on the implementation and design of the system. In section V, we present the design of the gamification aspect. In section VI, we discuss how the designed system fills the needs of our research question and point out some limitations. Finally, we conclude this paper in section VII.

II. STATE-OF-THE-ART

The rapid digitization of our society is key to alleviating the tension on our care systems, where recent technological and methodological advances bring great potentials to enable an increasingly collaborative care. One example is communication technologies, where access to mobile computing now is nearly ubiquitous and where we now at any time can engage in our social networks. A recent example is Distributed Ledger Technologies (DLT), including the notions of Blockchains and Smart Contracts, which are introduced in this section together with novel methodologies for user engagement, namely Gamification.

A. *Distributed Ledger Technologies (DLT)*

A distributed ledger (also called a shared ledger) is a consensus of replicated, shared and synchronized digital data geographically spread across multiple nodes (sites, countries or institutions) [3]. There is no central administrator or centralized data storage. Instead, a peer-to-peer network is required together with consensus algorithms to ensure that replication and consistency is maintained across the nodes of the distributed ledger.

The most popular distributed ledgers are based on public or private blockchains, which employ a chain of blocks to provide secure and valid achievement of distributed consensus. The first Blockchain was conceptualized in 2008 by Satochi Nakamoto [4] and implemented in 2009 for the digital currency Bitcoin. The example of bitcoin demonstrates the huge potential of blockchains for mutual agreements between two parties without the need of a trusted third party. For example, the volume of daily bitcoin transactions has been over 175 000 since April 2016 [5].

Distributed ledger technologies are expected to have a disruptive effect in our society, especially concerning mutual agreements, as they show many advantages: 1) agreements made on top of the blockchain do not need a trusted third party, and 2) each transaction needs to be signed by its sender using asymmetric encryption, which removes the need of an authentication layer in applications as this is directly handled at the blockchain level.

B. *Blockchains*

Blockchains are distributed databases for transaction processing, and they are well suited for financial transactions but not limited to such applications. The use of blockchain technology also extends to non-financial applications and is for example considered for supply chains, asset management or electronic health records.

All transactions are stored in a single ledger and ordered by time. The ledger represents the current state of the system and is replicated across every node. The transactions are broadcasted to the network and accepted if valid, by distributed consensus mechanisms, and are then grouped into a block, which is to be added to the blockchain. The last, and key, operation is to compute an ID for this block before storing it on the blockchain.

This operation can be done by solving a complex mathematical problem, based on the previous block index (this takes around 10 minutes for the Bitcoin blockchain). Once an ID has been computed, the network adopts it and begins to work on the next block. The process of computing an ID in this way is called **proof-of-work** and it makes the blockchain immutable since changing an existing block requires to compute the ID for all the following blocks while the blockchain continues to grow.

This operation can also be done using a **proof-of-stake**, where the miner is chosen in a deterministic way. This method is more energy efficient and safer to attacks if using a monetary blockchain.

Every transaction on a blockchain is signed, using asymmetric key cryptography, ensuring its provenance. The nodes in the network check the transaction conformity (a user can only spend the money he owns from previous transactions and can only perform a transaction in his own name: this is verified thanks to the cryptographic signature), authorization (a user can only perform a transaction in his own name) and resistance to censorship.

If a transaction conforms to the protocol, it will be added to the ledger without any party being able to discard it. All transactions can be processed peer-to-peer without the need of a trusted third party, since a blockchain network does not rely on any central authority but on a distributed consensus.

C. *Public and Private Blockchains*

This study began with a review of existing blockchain technologies, which revealed two main categories of ledgers: public or private.

A public blockchain is a ledger for which anyone executes transactions or mines blocks. Since anyone can modify a public blockchain, they offer a high replication rate, but this is also what makes public blockchains slow and less energy-efficient. Since anybody can contribute to public blockchains, it also offers pseudonymity where a user is only identified by an address and all the transactions referring to this address can be read.

A private blockchain does not allow everyone to join. It usually belongs to a single company, running the chain and validating transactions. The level of decentralization is not as good as in public blockchains, but performance is generally significantly higher. Indeed, when located on a public blockchain, a decentralized application represents only a small proportion of the entire system instead of representing the majority of it and, therefore, gains efficiency. It allows for greater privacy since users are chosen and known. However, private blockchains are therefore not resistant to censorship.

D. *Permissioned and Non-permissioned Blockchains*

Our study also identified two subcategories of blockchains: permissioned or non-permissioned. In a permissioned blockchain, each node has a limited role. It may only be allowed to validate transactions, mine new blocks, execute smart contracts (see below) on the blockchain or perform transactions with the chain assets. On the contrary, a non-permissioned blockchain allows any node to take any role. Table I illustrates the resulting categorization of studied blockchains.

TABLE I. CHAIN CLASSIFICATION

	Non-permissioned	Permissioned
Public	Ethereum[6], Bitcoin[4], Iroha[7]	Ripple[8]
Private		Fabric[9], Burrow[10], Openchain[11], Multichain[12]

E. Smart Contracts

In 1994, Nick Szabo defined smart contract as [13]:

"A smart contract is a computerized transaction protocol that executes the terms of a contract. The general objectives are to satisfy common contractual conditions (such as payment terms, liens, confidentiality, and even enforcement), minimize exceptions both malicious and accidental, and minimize the need for trusted intermediaries. Related economic goals include lowering fraud loss, arbitrations and enforcement costs, and other transaction costs."

Smart contracts are a way to enforce a legal agreement without the need of a trusted third party. It consists of computer code, stored on the blockchain and its execution can change the state of the blockchain. It profits from blockchain immutability to ensure that the terms cannot be modified. Thus, smart contracts cannot be modified and the result of an action is predictable and not corruptible. A high level in data integrity (as well as a good log level in case of breach in contracts design) is therefore ensured.

F. Bitcoin and Etherum Smart Contracts

The Bitcoin blockchain can only run a single smart contract, where the Bitcoin blockchain only ensures that the sender actually owns the tokens he wants to send in a transaction. As a consequence, a receiver cannot refuse a transaction.

Ethereum is the biggest public platform for smart contracts [6] which provide a Turing complete language for smart contracts executing in a virtual machine environment and whose completeness is guaranteed by gas: it is the system used by the Ethereum blockchain that limits the number of computation cycles during execution [6].

Smart contracts are triggered when they receive a transaction and they process transaction data in order to change the state of the contract. This modification is replicated across the network and there are therefore some limitations in the smart contracts design [14]: it is difficult to link smart contracts with outside world events, or make use of external services automatically (without a transaction). If a contract is waiting for data from the outside world and it does not receive the same data on every node, this creates a conflict on the chain. On the contrary, if a contract must call an external Application Programming Interface (API), which will trigger an action, it cannot determine which node is responsible to actually make the call.

Smart contracts are thus not well suited to ensure payments outside the chain, but they remain a very efficient way to condition fund transfer inside a chain. They are also not well suited to hide confidential data, especially on a public chain since every node replicates the database.

G. Involver

Our technical review only identified one mobile application for volunteering, an application called "Involver". It is defined as a social volunteering platform [15].

The goal of this application is to bring together potential volunteers with partner organizations that need help. Every cause a volunteer can help with is ordered based on location, subjects and skills needed. The rewards are brought by sponsors and take the form of non-monetary advantages.

The application also offers to certify the number of volunteering hours on professional social networks. It also includes a social aspect emphasizing the fact that volunteering is more interesting with friends. This example illustrates the need of a trusted third party (in this case the application) when agreements are made between volunteers and organizations.

Involver is however more of a start-up than a scientific platform. It is also not aimed at manipulating sensitive data, as this kind of information is to be held out of the application, by the organizations themselves if need be.

III. METHODOLOGY

A. Gamification Definitions

The word gamification appeared for the first time around 2002, when Nick Pelling used it for its consultancy business [16]. Gamification is according to Hutoari and Hamari [17] *"a process of enhancing a service with affordances for gameful experiences in order to support user's overall value creation."*

Deterding et al [18] propose a more general definition of gamification as *"the use of game design elements in non-game contexts"*. This definition is supported by the distinction made between games and play, with gaming being more structured by rules and more competitive. Game elements are defined as elements that are characteristics to games, found in most (but not necessarily all) games and found to play a significant role in gameplay.

Since gamification has been a trending topic, it prompted a lot of academic studies, which showed gamification to be present in many different contexts such as learning (e.g., Duolingo[19]), exercise (e.g., Fitocracy[20]), work and more.

B. Gamification, Rewards and Volunteers

The gamification aspect is part in the final application as an incentive for volunteers to use it. A review of studies concerning gamification by Hamari, Koivisto, and Sarsa [21] showed that, globally, gamification has positive effects and benefits on users where it is used. Gamification have a positive impact on the behavior of users, but also a psychological impact, acting on motivation, attitude or enjoyment of users while filling tasks. The gamification aspect is expected to motivate users and maintain their involvement.

Gamification can also be coupled with rewards in order to extend the scope of the gamification to the real world. A reward system can thus be seen as a natural part of a gamification system. For example, it can be used as a mechanism to engage, motivate and compensate users who volunteer their time and services for collective purposes.

Volunteers' motivations to help have been shown to be more based on intrinsic rewards (to fulfill psychological needs). However, small and non-expensive rewards are also appreciated and encouraging, where, generally, the goal is not to spend as much in a reward as the cost to pay someone [22]. The vision of combining gamification with real-world rewards allows reaching both fully altruistic people, who probably would not use the rewards or would not see it as an essential part of the application, as well as an audience needing more recognition to maintain its motivation.

C. *Achievements and Badges*

Achievements are a really common part in gamified applications. They are usually associated with badges and find their origin in merit-badges given to boy scouts of America since 1911. In 2003, Wikipedia started Wikipedia's Barnstars [23], aimed at rewarding contributors for their involvement on the platform. Another example of successful use of achievements is the Foursquare badges [24], which encouraged people to complete tasks in real life in order to unlock them. Furthermore, all games published on the Microsoft Xbox Live [25] platform are required to have achievements. A study by Anderson et al [26] showed that badge placement in an application can have an effective influence on user behavior and also affect his/her use of the application. However, a study by Montola et al [27] concludes that achievements globally have a positive effect on motivation but can sometimes be confusing for some users if they are not introduced properly. In summary, badges can be efficient incentives and are relatively cheap to implement in an application.

D. *The Hamari and Eranti Achievement Framework*

According to the framework designed by Hamari and Eranti [28], an achievement can be divided in three main parts.

Firstly, an achievement has a signifier, which is the visible part of an achievement and conveys information about it. It consists of a name that set the theme of the achievement and hints at the completion logic for it. The signifier also includes a visual, which completes the name and often has two states, unlocked where the visual is faded and completed where the visual gets fully colored. Finally, the signifier has a description, which describes what is required from the user to complete the achievement and what can be gained by completing it.

Secondly, an achievement also consists of a completion logic. It consists of a trigger, a pre-requirement (specific date, already completed achievement), a conditional requirement to determine if the action is triggered and also a multiplier, which determines how many times the three first parts have to be completed to unlock the achievement.

Thirdly, achievements carry rewards to show the user the achievement that has been completed. When added to a game, achievements completion can be a way to unlock in-game rewards. The external part of the reward is often the fact that these achievements are displayed publicly.

E. *Leveling*

Leveling based on experience points is an easy way for the user to keep track of his progress. It was originally used in role playing games, and then extended to any type of games. The logic behind leveling is quite simple: when performing a task, the user receives points, and then when a certain amount is reached, the user advances a level. In games, earning levels is often linked to gain or progress skills for the avatar. In a gamified application, advancing a level is a recognition of the skills acquired by the user in real life: it can also allow a user to access more advanced features. In games, points are earned when completing a mission/quest: in gamified applications, points are delivered when the user completes the task the app is trying to help with. For example, points can be delivered when a volunteer completes an offer, based on the number of tokens earned. However, when the user spends his tokens, he keeps the same number of points.

An important part of a levelling system is the threshold: it represents the number of points needed to reach the next level. Usually, the first levels have a low threshold, in order to keep the user motivated and show quick progress. Then, once the user has been significantly engaged, thresholds get bigger to be more challenging and therefore more rewarding.

IV. IMPLEMENTATION

Based on the pros and cons listed above, the Burrow blockchain has been chosen because it is fast, provides a smart contract virtual machine (VM) and the permission layer allows controlling the access rights. As the system works with sensitive data, it benefits from the privacy a private blockchain provides. The permission layer allows limiting the number of addresses allowed to mine blocks or create contracts on the chain. Our chain is therefore only dedicated to our system and does not spoil resources for other contracts. It also uses a proof-of-stake consensus mechanism which is better adapted to the use of a private blockchain, since every mining node is known and trustworthy. A proof-of-stake consensus is also more energy efficient and faster than using proof-of-work.

A. *System Goals*

The designed system is intended to connect elderly with volunteers who can help them with everyday life tasks, which do not require any specialized skills (for example in health care). The goal is not to replace health care workers but to reduce their workload where it is possible in order to give them more time for specialized tasks. As an incentive, volunteers receive a non-monetary reward, a token based on time spent to help and eventually resources involved in tasks, as the use of a vehicle for example. These tokens can be used to buy rewards as coupons or advantages / discounts in local shops or non-monetary advantages. On top of this, gamification aspects using points and badges is added to keep volunteers motivated.

Users of the platform need to register by giving their identity. Their personal data is stored encrypted and only revealed to other users if they share a task (tasks can also be referred to as offers or task offers from elderly users). Once users are registered, an authority is charged of verifying the information and grants the permissions according to the user status. An elderly user is allowed to create task offers: they describe the mission, specify a time slot and duration, and a type for the task (gardening, shopping, accompanying, etc.). The reward amount is computed according to the offer specifications. Once the offer is created, volunteer users can see it and read its specifications: if a volunteer is available and able to fulfill the task, he can commit to it. From there, the elderly user can access his/her contact information to schedule the task more precisely. Once the task is accomplished, the volunteer needs to claim the reward. The elderly user can then confirm that the offer has been fulfilled: this action triggers the issuing of tokens for the volunteer who helped. With these tokens, the volunteer will be able to buy rewards. Rewards are added by rewarders. These rewards contain a description, a price and a code, delivered only when the reward is bought. This is illustrated in the activity diagram below, see Figure 1.

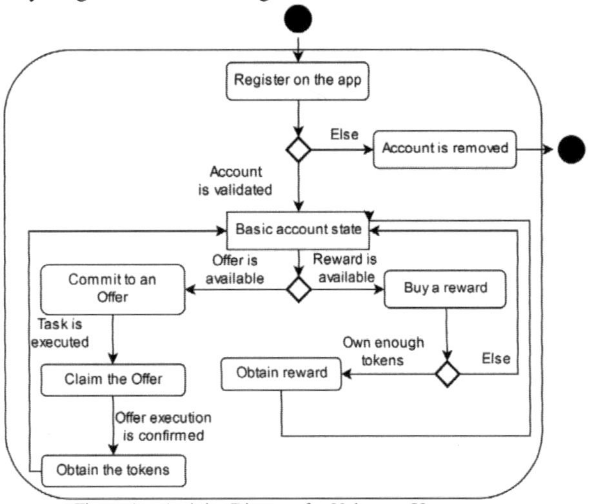

Figure 1. Activity Diagram for Volunteer Users

B. Global Design

The system back-end is built on top of a blockchain with smart contracts to handle agreements between the users. It has four main contracts handling the different parts of the system: these contracts form a database while they also ensure system consistency. They store contracts which are created depending on users' needs.

The bank contract handles the tokens for each user: the only way to issue tokens is to confirm that a task offer has been fulfilled. The only way to use these tokens is to spend them to buy rewards. The bank contract stores the balance for each user and ensures that the user actually owns enough of them before spending them.

The user contract is used to store user data, one part being visible for everyone (using pseudonimity) and sensitive data stays encrypted and is only revealed when a task links two users. This contract is also used to handle permissions for each user: permissions are set by an authority according to the status of the user: depending of his permission level, a user can or cannot perform some actions in the application (that is, only a volunteer user can commit and claim an offer).

A contract is used to store offers plus commit, claim and confirm their execution. An offer is a task, proposed by an elderly user for which help from a volunteer is needed. Offers thus are smart contracts with properties and states: the states of the offer evolve during the course of the agreements but properties are immutable. This evolution is described in Figure 2. Finally, a contract is used to store and buy available rewards. Rewards are added by partner rewarders in a limited availability and bought by volunteers.

The blockchain handles authentication of users for these actions, allowing a mutual agreement between different users without the need of a trusted third party, once the registration is complete. The blockchain also guarantees the content of agreements since contracts cannot be discreetly modified. The division of the application is described in Figure 3.

C. Detailed Architecture

The system is built on the Monax blockchain, Burrow [9], a fork of the Ethereum blockchain allowing working with a permissioned ledger: this permission layer also allows using a proof-of-stake mining mechanism. Another difference compared to unpermissioned ledger is that nodes can have restrictions on how they can contribute: some can be dedicated to validate nodes, while others handle permissions or receive transactions.

Contracts are developed using Solidity [29], an object-oriented programming language for smart contract development. The application is developed following an action-driven architecture coupled with a five types model.

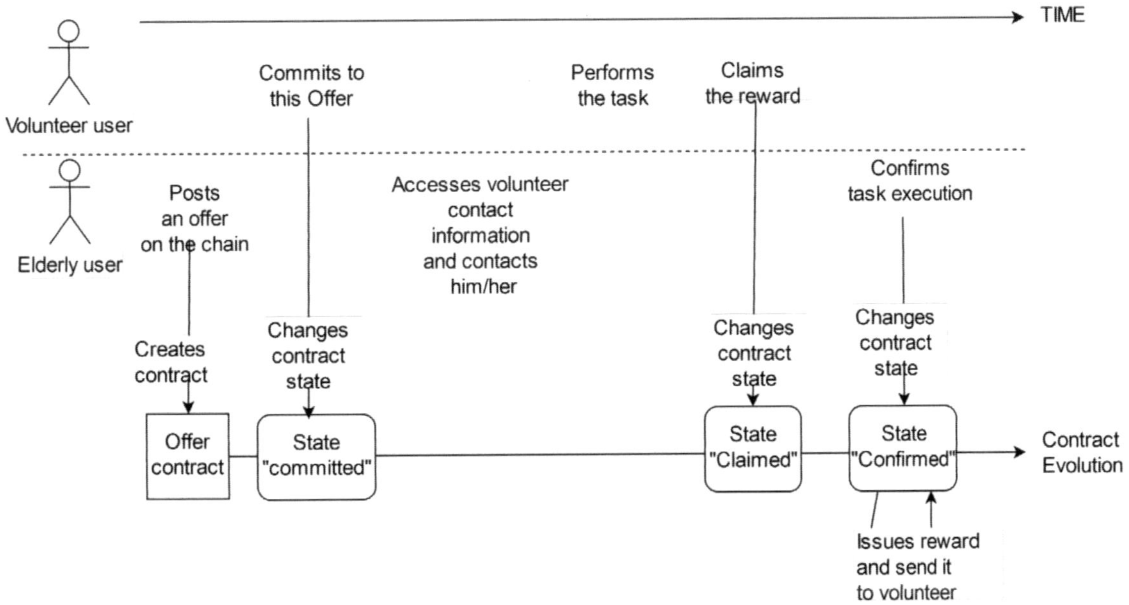

Figure 2. Offer Evolution

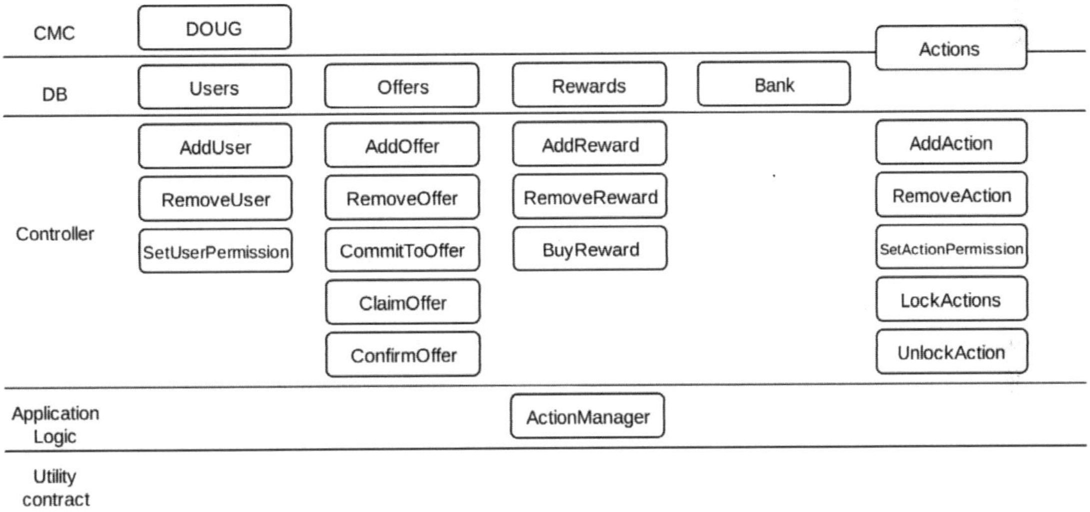

Figure 3. The Five Types Model

The five types model suggests splitting the application using different kind of contracts. Database contracts, where data is stored, can be read or updated. Controllers contracts operate on database contracts, and can operate on multiple databases instead of one (for example read user's permissions from one database and then operate on another). A third type of contract is contracts managing contracts (CMCs) where other contracts are kept in view and can be replaced if needed. They provide single point of entries to the system, which is useful when a system uses many contracts and therefore also many addresses when these contracts needs to be updated. Application logic contracts (ALC) are contracts specific to an application and they perform multiple operations using controllers and other contracts. Finally, utility contracts can be seen as libraries: they perform a specific task, without modifying the state of other contracts and can be used without any restrictions.

The five types model effectively separate actions used to interact with databases contracts. Actions are thus focused on small parts and modifications of the system. Actions are stored in a CMC. This architecture allows the system to be updated more easily than if using full controller contracts. A full controller would handle every interaction with database contracts. Any simple modification to a simple function implies the full contract replacement, which infer heavy interaction with the chain. As a result, actions can be dynamically replaced without the need of modifying a complete controller contract.

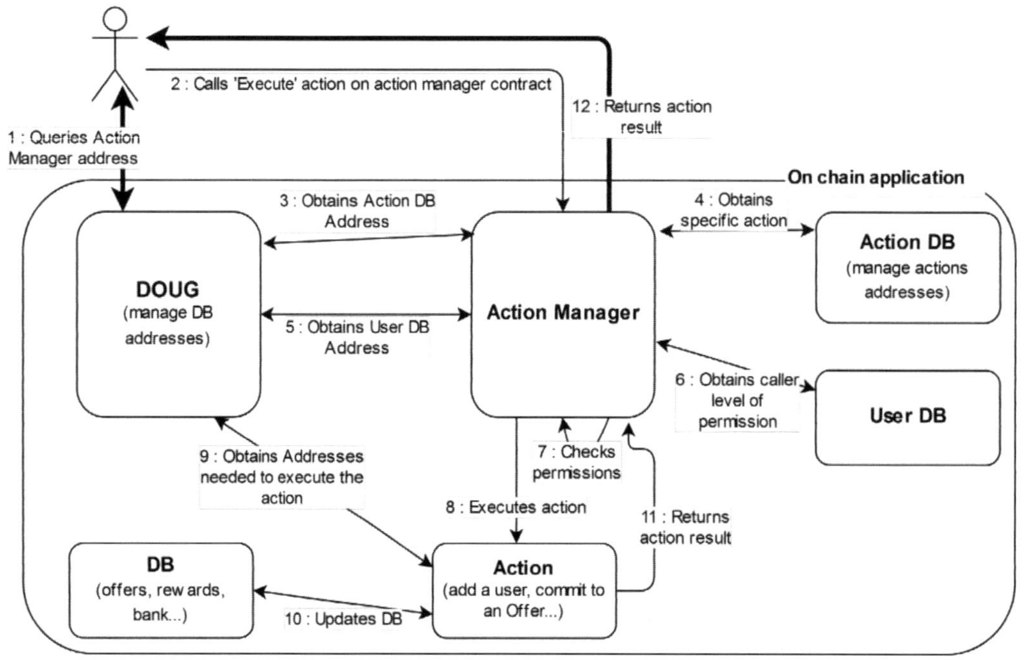

Figure 4. Execute Action Process

The main CMC is a Decentralized Organization Upgrade Guy (DOUG) storing all databases' contracts of the system and especially, the action database. The action database is also a CMC and works with an action manager calling this database in order to find the actions to execute. By following this architecture, a user can interact with the system knowing only the address of the DOUG and the databases public APIs. On the developer side, maintenance operations are simple because actions can be easily updated (replacing an action in the database is an action itself) without the need of updating every interface as long as the DOUG contract stays the same (and therefore keeps the same address).

Since action replacement is an integrated part of the application, this also allows using multiple developer accounts with the right permission level instead of locking the system by limiting updates to only its creator. The process of executing an action is described in Figure 4.

D. *Interface*

In order to keep the system as decentralized as possible, the user credentials are not kept in a database. The most suitable solution is to let users manage their own credentials and this can be done using a mobile or desktop application acting as a Bitcoin wallet. Another solution to store credentials can be paper wallets: these are cardboard-cards with flash-codes or text-written credentials. This can be a solution to effectively handle permissions and verify user information by sending them credentials using for example standard post. The credentials on paper-wallets can afterwards be stored in a mobile application or required to be scanned for every action performed through the application. This solution has not been chosen in the prototyping step, but should be considered in a following step.

The user then interacts with the blockchain through a Representational State Transfer (REST) API. Every node used as a validator for the blockchain is also used to host an API server, allowing a good level of decentralization.

The use of an installed application instead of a web based application also limits the number of request needed for developing the gamification aspects, since, as a Bitcoin wallet, this kind of application does not need to store every transaction but only those concerning users. The developed application used for testing is illustrated in Figure 5.

E. *Technical limitations*

The system was first designed to be as modular as possible: every action had its own execute method, taking various numbers of arguments. Since this modularity implies no real inheritance, the action manager had to use low-level calls, a Solidity feature where a function is called at a specified address without knowing the contract API at the caller level. These low-level calls return a boolean only indicating if the call succeeded or not (but not the actual return value). This solution has been abandoned since it created a lot of problems in data formatting for arguments at the action manager level and afterwards at the action level. The absence of a relevant return value was also a performance issue since it implied to check every action execution afterward. Finally, the choice has been made to use a formatted schema for the execute method of every action, covering all the current cases, and ignoring some useless parameters for some of the actions contracts. This choice reduces genericity but improve the reliability and performances of the system.

Some gamification aspects have been limited by the use of smart contracts as databases. This layout is not really efficient when querying many contracts and therefore limits some features such as ranking between all users.

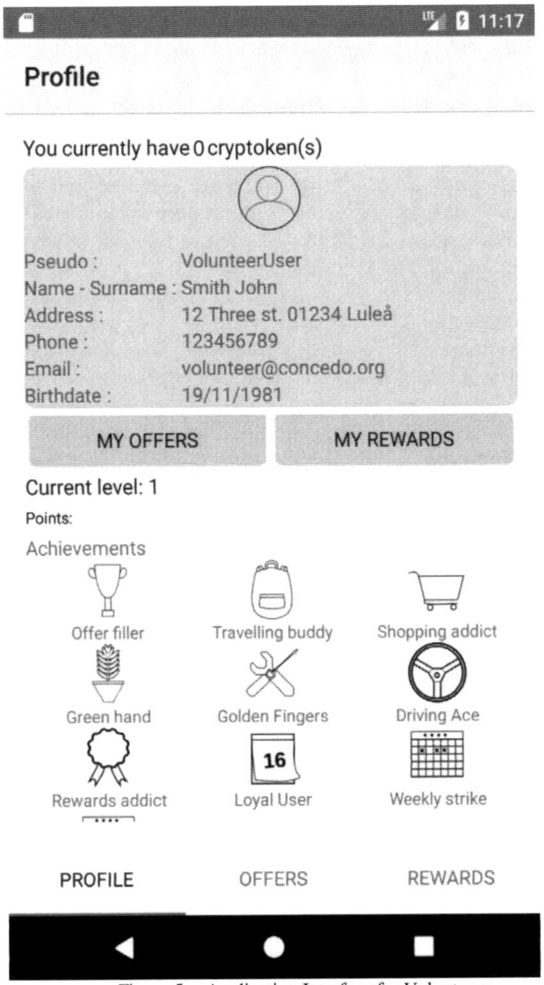

Figure 5. Application Interface for Volunteers

V. GAMIFICATION DESIGN

The choice for our application is to limit the gamification aspect to the frontend in order to reduce the volume of interaction with the back-end and therefore improve performance. Badges fit really well with this vision. Achievements are well oriented towards volunteers, as they are the target we try to motivate. The achievements implemented have two main objectives. The first objective is to serve as a tutorial, where these achievements appears when doing really basic actions (such as to commit to an offer or getting a validated account) and are supposed to show the possibilities of the application while also introduce the achievement system. The second objective is to maintain motivation and encourage involvement. The achievements for this objective are focused on quantity and regularity: it consists in fulfilling a defined number of offers (typed or not), buying rewards, keep checking the app and keep fulfilling offers every week/month to create strikes.

The achievements implemented in the application are detailed in Table II.

TABLE II. LIST OF ACHIEVEMENTS

Achievement / Multiplier	Step 1	Step 2	Step 3
Complete X offers	10	50	100
Buy X rewards	10	50	100
Complete X offers- Gardening	5	20	50
Complete X offers- Shopping	5	20	50
Complete X offers- Driving	5	20	50
Complete X offers- DIY	5	20	50
Complete X offers- Accompanying	5	20	50
Use the app for X days	30	180	360
Complete X offers in a week	2	4	6
Complete X offers in a month	4	8	15

The Hamari and Eranti Achievement Framework, as detailed above, have been utilized to design the achievements for the application. Since no formal study have been found regarding leveling curve formulas, and since in game examples are often based on experience points gains varying depending on level, the following formula has been chosen in order to progressively increase the levelling thresholds:

$$t_1 = 30$$
$$t_{n+1} = t_n + \frac{l_n}{5} \quad (1)$$

The chosen initial threshold (to pass from level 1 to level 2) is 30. Since points are approximately equivalent to minutes, this allow users to gain levels quite quickly at first, then require more engagement to level-up further. The progression of points needed is illustrated in Figure 6.

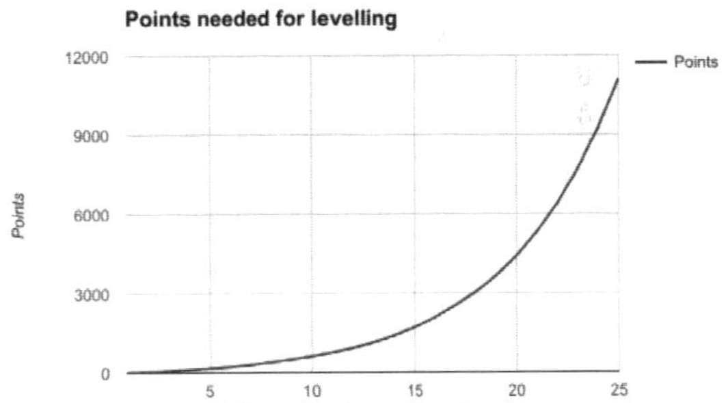

Figure 6. Levelling Curve

Levels can be seen as a simplified achievement since it can be associated with a name and a visual status. The chosen completion logic, focusing more on specific task completion, is however simplified in comparison to an achievement focused on global progress. Gaining points also happens more often than unlocking an achievement.

VI. DISCUSSION

How can a system for collaborative care of elderly be designed and implemented to engage and motivate people to contribute with daily tasks on a voluntary basis?

A system for collaborative care of elderly should come as a complement to the "classical" care system. It means that it should be efficient to help professional workers while keeping the costs low and the elderly population safe. The costs problem can be treated by implying volunteers in the process of elderly care and creating a system where moderation needs are low. Distributed Ledger Technologies (DLT) appear to be interesting by their performance in handling mutual agreements between parties not knowing each other. Such a system only requires moderation at registration and then can handle itself efficiently. Such an application should be mobile in order to integrate itself efficiently in daily life for both volunteers and rewarders.

Even if the system benefits from the advantages of the blockchain on mutual agreements, it also shows some limitations due to the fact that it requires many interactions with the outside world. Firstly, the designed system can be abused by two parties knowing each other and agreeing on hypothetical tasks in order to issue tokens. This bias can partly be solved by limiting the number of offers an elderly user can post every week/month. The risk is to disadvantage honest users who need a lot of help, while only curbing abuses. However, since every commitment can be publicly visible, these abuses could be detected and user banned although this implies more authority regulation than just certifying user identity at registration. It therefore reduces the interest in using such a trust-based system.

Another issue comes from the fact that the system does not allow nuances: a task offer will either be confirmed or not. Even if task confirmation could be coupled with a notation system, weighting the reward would be really dependent on personal appreciation. In the worst situation, an offer is not completed at all and this case is not automatically disadvantageous for the abuser while it can have negative consequences for the elderly user. Nevertheless, this situation is the same in every system implying trade between nonprofessional users (such as in carpooling services for example), and require an impartial arbiter to be resolved.

Finally, another bias that could possibly appear is the preference for the most rewarding offers at the expense of the smaller ones. Even if rewards are calculated based on the efforts needed for their fulfillment, the least demanding offers could be discouraging because of the external efforts it can imply.

VII. CONCLUSION

Care of elderly is an important and sensitive topic which raises many and various concerns. The need for care will grow and volunteering will have to take part in this care in order to maintain reasonable costs for the society, as well as a sufficient level of services. A service to establish contact between people needing help and people willing to volunteer therefore is well motivated. This kind of system creates mutual agreements between users not necessarily knowing each other and can therefore take advantage of distributed ledger technologies.

Smart contracts are most efficient with on-chain agreements but show limitations when interfacing with outside-chain events. Interfacing with such events require additional control points during the course of the agreements, to keep consensus between users. This reduces the interest in comparison with traditional, often centralized, systems between non-professional users.

In conclusion, the system described here still benefits from inherent DLT advantages, such as a high level of decentralization, thus a high availability, and strong data consistency. These advantages make it interesting to develop the possible links between blockchains and the outside world to allow for a higher level of automation of services such as collaborative care.

VIII. FUTURE WORK

This proof-of-concept system and prototype would be required to be evaluated with real users, first in small scale through participatory design and then in larger scale to ensure statistical certainty of results. The current project can be seen as a feasibility study to pave the way for this future work that would require more extensive resources.

The next development step in this project would consist in working on a new agreement protocol that could for example involve a third-party user of the system to settle and confirm or not the task execution. This could be associated with an appreciation system working both ways: the elderly user evaluates the service he received in terms of motivation or punctuality (the goal is not to judge the skills) while volunteers could rate the offer description accuracy and the reception received. By adding a rating system for both tasks and users, it should motivate users to provide a quality service and filter abusive users or at least point them out. Using smart contracts, we can imagine to automatically suspend accounts who received a very bad appreciation in order to clarify the situation with the authority running the service.

We could also think of adding more filters to offers based on the elderly user preferences and needs: for example, some tasks may require a valid driving license that can be authenticated at registration: then, only users with a valid driving license would be able to see and commit to these offers. One last feature that can be investigated is a bidding system allowing volunteers to compete on committing to an offer and therefore not base the system on a first-come, first serve model. This would probably allow a selection focused more on the volunteer motivation.

A future step would also be to include more in-life elements, starting with paper wallets in order to authenticate users for the first meeting or while claiming a reward. Offer passwords, needed to claim the offer, shortly evoked in the precedent paragraph taking the form of matrix bar-code only readable by the mobile application could be used as a proof of the meeting while complicating frauds.

ACKNOWLEDGMENT

This work was conducted as an internship at Luleå University of Technology, Sweden, in collaboration with INSA Lyon, France. The work was sponsored by Concedo, an industry-academia exchange project, between Luleå University of Technology and Ericsson Research, funded by Vinnova. The authors would like to thank Johan Kristiansson at Ericsson Research for invaluable insights into Distributed Ledger Technologies, Blockchains and Smart Contracts.

REFERENCES

[1] P. M. Office, "Future challenges for Sweden", 2013, [Online], Available: http://www.regeringen.se/49b6cf/contentassets/389793d478de411fbc83d8f512cb5013/future-challenges-for-sweden--final-report-of-the-commission-on-the-future-of-sweden, [retrieved: 10, 2017].

[2] U. N. D. of Economic and S. A. P. Division, "World population ageing 2015", 2015, [Online], Available: http://www.un.org/en/development/desa/population/publications/pdf/ageing/WPA2015_Report.pdf, [retrieved: 10, 2017].

[3] UK Government, Office for Science, "Distributed Ledger Technology: beyond blockchain", 2016, [Online], Available: http://www.ameda.org.eg/files/gs-16-1-distributed-ledger-technology.pdf, [retrieved: 09, 2017].

[4] S. Nakamoto, "Bitcoin: A peer-to-peer electronic cash system", 2008, [Online], Available: http://bitcoin.org/bitcoin.pdf, [retrieved: 09, 2017].

[5] www.blockchain.info, "Confirmed transactions per day", [Online], Available: https://blockchain.info/charts/n-transactions [retrieved: 09, 2017].

[6] V. Buterin, "A next-generation smart contract and decentralized application platform", 2013, [Online], Available: https://github.com/ethereum/wiki/wiki/White-Paper, [retrieved: 09, 2017].

[7] Iroha, "White Paper", 2016, [Online], Available: https://github.com/hyperledger/iroha/blob/master/docs/iroha_whitepaper.md , [retrieved: 09, 2017].

[8] Ripple, "Solution Overview", 2013,[Online], Available: https://ripple.com/files/ripple_solutions_guide.pdf, [retrieved: 09, 2017].

[9] "Welcome to Hyperledger Fabric", edited 2017, [Online], Available: https://hyperledger-fabric.readthedocs.io/en/latest/, [retrieved: 09,2017].

[10] "The Monax Platform", edited: 2017, [Online], Available: https://monax.io/platform/, [retrieved: 09, 2017].

[11] "Openchain - Blockchain Technology for the Enterprise", edited: 2017, [Online], Available: https://www.openchain.org/, [retrieved: 09,2017].

[12] G. Greenspan, "MultiChain Private Blockchain — White Paper", 2015, [Online], Available: https://www.multichain.com/white-paper/, [retrieved: 09, 2017].

[13] N. Szabo, "Smart Contracts: Building Blocks for Digital Markets," 1996.

[14] G. Greenspan, "Why many smart contract use cases are simply impossible", 2016, [Online], Available: https://www.coindesk.com/three-smart-contract-misconceptions/, [retrieved: 09, 2017].

[15] "Involver – Social Volunteering", 2015, [Online], Available: www.getinvolver.com, [retrieved: 09, 2017].

[16] A. Marczewski, "Gamification: a simple introduction", 2013, [Online], Available: https://books.google.se/books?id=IOu9kPjlndYC, [retrieved: 09, 2017].

[17] K. Huotari and J. Hamari, "Defining gamification: a service marketing perspective", in Proceeding of the 16th International Academic MindTrek Conference, ser. MindTrek '12. New York, NY, USA: ACM, 2012, pp. 17–22, doi:10.1145/2393132.2393137.

[18] S. Deterding, D. Dixon, R. Khaled, and L. Nacke, "From game design elements to gamefulness: Defining gamification", in Proceedings of the 15th International Academic MindTrek Conference: Envisioning Future Media Environments, ser. MindTrek '11. New York, NY, USA: ACM, 2011, pp. 9–15, doi:10.1145/2181037.2181040.

[19] "Duolinguo", edited 2017, [Online], Available: https://www.duolingo.com/, [retrieved: 09, 2017].

[20] "Fitocracy", edited 2017, [Online], Available: https://www.fitocracy.com/, [retrieved: 09, 2017].

[21] J. Hamari, J. Koivisto, and H. Sarsa, "Does gamification work? – a literature review of empirical studies on gamification", in the 47th Hawaii International Conference on System Sciences, Jan 2014, pp. 3025–3034.

[22] M. H. Phillips and L. C. Phillips, "Volunteer motivation and reward preference: an empirical study of volunteerism in a large, not-for-profit organization", SAM Advanced Management Journal, 2010, pp. 12–19.

[23] Wikipedia, the free encyclopedia, "Wikipedia:Barnstars", 2004, [Online], Available: https://en.wikipedia.org/wiki/Wikipedia:Barnstars, [retrieved: 09, 2017].

[24] "Foursquare", edited 2017, [Online], Available: https://www.foursquare.com, [retrieved: 09, 2017].

[25] "X Box Live", edited: 2017, [Online], Available: https://www.xbox.com/en-US/live, [retrieved: 09, 2017].

[26] A. Anderson, D. Huttenlocher, J. Kleinberg, and J. Leskovec, "Steering user behavior with badges", in Proceedings of the 22Nd International Conference on World Wide Web, ser. WWW '13. New York, NY, USA: ACM, 2013, pp. 95–106, doi:10.1145/2488388.2488398.

[27] M. Montola, T. Nummenmaa, A. Lucero, M. Boberg, and H. Korhonen, "Applying game achievement systems to enhance user experience in a photo sharing service," in Proceedings of the 13th International MindTrek Conference: Everyday Life in the Ubiquitous Era, ser. MindTrek '09. New York, NY, USA: ACM, 2009, pp. 94–97 doi :10.1145/1621841.1621859.

[28] J. Hamari and V. Eranti, "Framework for Designing and Evaluating Game Achievements," in Proceedings of DiGRA 2011 Conference: Think Design Play, 2011, [Online], Available: http://www.digra.org/wp-content/uploads/digital-library/11307.59151.pdf, [retrieved: 09, 2017].

[29] "The solidity programming language", 2015, [Online], Available: https://github.com/ethereum/wiki/wiki/The-Solidity-Programming-Language, [retrieved: 09, 2017].

Planning for Ubiquitous Learning in PLAN

Timothy Arndt
Department of Information Systems and Department of Electrical Engineering and Computer Science
Cleveland State University
Cleveland, OH, USA
t.arndt@csuohio.edu

Abstract— **The rise of e-Learning as a primary platform for higher education promises to open up higher education to a wider range of learners than ever before. In order to best cater to this ever more diverse group of students, a personal learning system, which reflects the individual student's learning style and needs, would be valuable. Such a system would successfully integrate a user's learner profile, as well as his or her social networks, and big data sources, as well as time and location information in order to support ubiquitous learning. In this paper, we review PLAN (Personal Learning AssistaNt), our model for personal recommendation systems for students of higher learning and explore how ubiquitous learning fits in with our system.**

Keywords- ubiquitous learning; e-learning; personalized learning; recommendation systems.

I. INTRODUCTION

In [1] we presented a formalism for our personal learning assistant called PLAN (Personal Learning AssitaNt). The formalism integrates Big Data (learning and social network) analytics, a finite state transducer which acts as a recommender system for the learner, the learner's calendars, location, a learner profile, etc. into a complete system for assisting the student to achieve his or her personalized goals. The aggressiveness of the recommendations can be controlled by the user. We laid out several scenarios of the system in action which help to explain how it will be used in practice. The cloud-based architecture of the system with a mobile app user interface was also described. The formalism is currently being implemented as a prototype system for experimentation purposes.

Previously, we reported the results of a survey of university students on their attitude towards ubiquitous e-learning [2]. The attitudes reported were quite positive. This confirms the impressions one has that today's generation of students is not only open to, but desirous of ubiquitous learning platforms to help them reach their learning goals.

Therefore, we have begun to consider adding support for ubiquitous learning to the prototype system currently being developed based on our PLAN formalism. This paper reports our initial reflections on this subject. The next section is a brief survey of some previous research in the area of ubiquitous learning. Section 3 gives our reflections on how ubiquitous learning can be integrated into the prototype learning recommendation system currently being developed based on our prototype. Section 4 gives some further discussion and sketches future research.

II. RELATED RESEARCH

Much research has been done in recent years on ubiquitous learning. In this section, we will briefly review a small portion of that work.

A review of research trends in mobile and ubiquitous learning as reported in selected journals between 2001 and 2010 is given in [3]. The authors use the definition of ubiquitous learning as 'learning anywhere and at anytime'. Ubiquitous learning experiments have been carried out in classrooms, museums, labs, as well as outdoors, for example observing nature in a natural science class.

The authors chose six major technology-based learning journals and looked for studies in the given area published between 2001 and 2010. They found 154 total articles which met their criteria and noted that the number of publications increased greatly starting in 2008. One expects that this trend has continued. They also found that while the US authors contributed the most publications in the first four years of the study, Taiwanese authors had a very large number of contributions in the later years, and other countries were well represented as well.

A very influential system for ubiquitous language learning is reported in [4]. Two different systems are actually described. The first, JAPELAS (JApanese Polite languagE Learning Assisting System) is a context-aware language-learning support system for learning Japanese polite expressions. JAPELAS provides the learner with the correct polite Japanese language expressions based on the learner's situational context and personal information. This is especially appropriate, since Japanese polite expressions are very context-sensitive.

The second system, TANGO (Tag Added learNinG Objects), uses RFID (Radio-frequency identification) tags to detect objects near the learner and to provide him with educational information concerning those objects. This was an early example of the importance of RFID technology in ubiquitous learning.

The basic criteria, strategies, and research issues of context-aware ubiquitous learning are given in [5], which also identifies the check items for the development of such learning environments.

Technology which enables context-aware learning via ubiquitous computing includes sensors and actuators, RFID tags and cards, wireless communication, smartphones, PDAs (Personal Digital Assistants), and wearable computers. A ubiquitous system interoperates spontaneously with changing environments incorporating these and other technologies. A ubiquitous system must seek out new devices as they come into range, and interact with those devices. These devices form part of the user's context, and must be incorporated by a ubiquitous learning system in order to support a form of the pedagogical theory of constructivism.

The authors define their context-aware ubiquitous learning as learning with mobile devices, wireless communications and sensor technology. Such learning systems are more specialized than the broader mobile-learning systems since they focus much more closely on the users' contexts (e.g. location and body temperature). Contexts include: personal contexts sensed by the system; environmental contexts sensed by the system; feedback from learner via the mobile learning device; personal data retrieved from databases; environmental data retrieved from databases. These are called situation parameters by the authors, and based on them, twelve models for conducting context-aware ubiquitous-learning activities are defined.

The notion of context-aware ubiquitous learning environments for peer-to-peer collaborative learning is the topic of [6]. The author sees the ubiquitous learning environment as providing an interoperable, pervasive, and seamless learning architecture to integrate three major dimensions of learning resources – learning collaborators; learning contexts; and learning resources.

Ubiquitous learning must provide innovative and effective ways to identify and utilize learning collaborators, learning contexts and learning resources. In other words, the context of the learner is key to this type of learning. Virtual learning communities, which provide geographically dispersed users a means to collaboratively learn, have been described, without being precisely defined. It is recognized, though, that the collaboration is an important element of such communities.

Collaborative efforts of users to manage knowledge, enhance the reservoir of knowledge, and to help each other accumulate and build knowledge in a given domain is a key component of virtual learning communities. The author uses a peer-to-peer approach to building a system for ubiquitous learning environments for collaborative learning.

An ontology based context model is used to describe the context of learners and services. The Protégé system [8] is used to build the learner ontology and service ontology. Three context acquisition methods are then used: form filled, context detection and context extraction in order to obtain context information. In order to define the functionality of the peer-to-peer collaborative learning system, a study which identifies the most wanted learning services in such a system is used. The services are: who is currently online; instant message; learning content search; personal annotation; and recording of personal learning portfolio. The system developed supports these services, as well as multimedia real time group discussion. A scenario for the usage of the peer-to-peer system is given.

The question of how effective and meaningful learning is in a ubiquitous learning context is considered in [7]. While ubiquitous learning seems to be a great idea, and is certainly exciting for researchers and teachers, we need to be sure that the techniques that we are using are providing meaningful learning experiences to learners and are not inefficient or do not lead to reduced learning experiences, especially for low-achieving learners.

The authors investigate the impact of a meaningful learning-based evaluation on ubiquitous learning, in order to enhance the system being evaluated. A quasi-experiment is described in which both post-evaluation and refined ubiquitous learning activities are adopted for the experimental group, while a control group works without the proposed evaluation method. The results show that the evaluation technique can be used to greatly enhance the outcomes and learning effectiveness, especially in the case of low-achieving learners. High-achieving learners did not have such dramatic results. In sum, a meaningful learning-based evaluation method is an effective way to find out how the ubiquitous learning environment needs to be improved.

III. PLAN

In this section we will describe our personal learning assistant PLAN (Personal Learning AssistaNt) [1].

A personal learning assistant supports a user in achieving desired learning goals. The formal definition of a personal learning assistant is described in this section.

A personal learning assistant uses multiple sources of information to provide appropriate recommendations and alerts when active. Some data are collected through the direct interaction with the user, while other data are mined by searching across available data sources. The first source of information used by the personal learning assistant comes from the user's learning profile. An additional source of information is provided by the user's social network from which desired data are extracted. Finally, additional data are mined from the multiple data sources available across the networks.

Mining significant data from data sources means to be able to identify data that can be of interest to the user. So, while an event can be considered interesting for achieving a learning goal, that event could be irrelevant if the user is unable to participate in it. This means that there are constraints that should be taken into account in order to select significant data and provide useful recommendations.

The two primary constraints come from the spatial and temporal information associated with the user. The temporal information is derived from a calendar. The spatial information is derived from the user's geolocation which, from the implementation point of view, is associated with the GPS (Global Positioning System) coordinates extracted from the sensor of the device where the personal assistant has been launched from. The amount of information produced by the personal learning assistant could be very large and overwhelm the user. A level of aggressiveness must be used to customize the personal learning assistant to a user-desired level. An aggressiveness level of 0.0 will result in no recommendations being generated by the personal learning assistant, while 1.0 will result in a maximum number of recommendations being generated.

The activity of the personal learning assistant PLAN is formally described by a learning finite state transducer

(LFST). The LFST moves from state to state in order to reach the desired learning goals and in each transition produces zero or more outputs.

When the system is initialized for a user, the PLAN generates the user's learner profile based on an interactive process with the user, as well as on the basis of a default profile. The learner profile may be refined as the learning process advances. The system also interrogates the user to determine the user's set of learning goals. The learner profile and learning goals are then used by the system to generate the LFST.

Data is mined from key-value data stores, as well as from the user's social networks, using traditional data mining processes. This results in knowledge items being discovered as data mining proceeds. Each time a knowledge item is discovered, the state transition function may result in a transition to a new state in the LFST. Calendar events from the user's calendar set may also be generated as time passes. These calendar events are treated as knowledge items by the LFST.

A state transition generally results in zero or more recommendations (i.e. the output function of the LFST) being made to the learner (e.g. to take a section of a particular source). On the other hand, some action of the learner may result in a state transition (e.g. the user successfully completing a course).

The architecture of the system is structured as a mobile app which communicates with a cloud service which performs the main share of the computation. The PLAN Cloud Service interacts with standard data mining processes which run in the cloud and which work on two categories of data: the key-value data stores and the user's social networks. The key-value data stores represent the raw matter used for learning analytics. Sources of the data which can be analyzed include institutional data about students, courses, applicants, as well as a particularly rich field to mine for data - that are associated with online courses and Course Management Systems (CMS) [9].

In addition, the data mining processes interact with the student's social networks – both online social networks such as Facebook and Twitter, as well as more informal social networks such as those identified by email and text message communication as well as those which are deduced by examining the course rosters of the courses the students are enrolled in. These social networks form another important asset in the student's learning process, being sources of expertise in course topics, various university processes, job markets and so on. The data mining processes can interact with online social networks through the APIs (Application Programming Interface) that they provide and through the more informal social networks through custom processes which may be developed.

IV. Discussion and Future Research

In this section, we discuss how ubiquitous learning can be added to the PLAN model discussed in section 3.

A number of issues related to ubiquitous learning can be identified from the related research as surveyed in section 2, including the following.

- Context-aware
- Sensor networks and RFID
- Peer-to-peer communication
- Resource discovery
- Learner discovery
- Collaborative learning
- Others

How are these issues handled in PLAN, and if they are not currently handled in PLAN, can the PLAN model be extended so that they are handled? We will look briefly at these issues in the following.

The current PLAN system model handles context-awareness in a limited way. The current location is one of the parameters of the model and can be used to generate a suggestion which the learner can choose to follow or not, as he should desire. The graph associated with LFST forms a type of context, but not, certainly, as specific as the ontology-based context of [6]. Further work on incorporating context-awareness into the system, possibly via system-driven user interrogation, would be useful.

Sensor networks (sensors and actuators) and RFID are not currently supported by the PLAN system. The PLAN system is oriented towards higher education learning, while most of the ubiquitous learning scenarios involving RFID, etc. are oriented towards primary and (somewhat) secondary schools, for instance learning in a museum. This is a bit of a different emphasis on ubiquitous learning from ours, where we are more concerned with enabling students to learn at anytime than interacting with (a limited set of) real-world objects. If desired, we could extend our model by incorporating sensor networks as a component, as we do social networks.

Peer-to-peer communication is enabled in our system through our incorporation of a learner's social networks. By accessing the location or other data of a learner, along with those of his friends/classmates in his social networks, PLAN can suggest collaboration with other learners. The actual communication is outside of the model, and how it is implemented will depend on the software/tools used in the implementation.

Resource discovery is not specifically foreseen in our model. It could be incorporated by reference to the data mining process which continuously discovers knowledge used to make suggestions. Resource discovery techniques can be modeled as one particular type of data mining process. It might also be useful to make resource discovery more apparent/specific in the PLAN model.

Learner discovery in the PLAN model is already foreseen and is accomplished through the use of social networking platforms and the geolocation information associated with users of those platforms. This could be extended to a more general learner location process if multiple learners are using the PLAN system, since the location information of users is one of the system parameters.

Collaborative learning is supported by inclusion of users social networks as in the above paragraphs on peer-to-peer communication and learner discovery. A more precise mechanism for knowledge sharing could be incorporated for multiple users of the PLAN system.

As the above considerations show, while PLAN has many aspects which support ubiquitous learning currently, there are many ways in which it could be enhanced to further support ubiquitous learning. We are currently implementing a prototype system, and will consider modifying and/or extending the system in such ways. These decisions and the prototype system itself will be reported in a future publication.

REFERENCES

[1] T. Arndt and A. Guercio, "A Formalism for PLAN – a Big Data Personal Learning Assistant for University Students", Journal of e-Learning and Knowledge Society, vol. 12, no. 2, 2016.

[2] T. Arndt and A. Guercio, "Ubiquitous E-Learning: Student Attitudes and Future Prospects", GSTF Journal on Computing, vol. 4, no. 1, October 2014.

[3] G.-J. Hwang, and C.-C. Tsai, "Research Trends in Mobile and Ubiquitous Learning: A Review of Publications in Selected Journals from 2001 to 2010," British Journal of Educational Technology, vol. 42, pp. 65-70, 2011.

[4] H. Ogata and Y. Yano, "Context-Aware Support for Computer-Supported Ubiquitous Learning," Proceedings the 2nd IEEE International Workshop on Wireless and Mobile Technologies in Education, 2004, pp. 27-34.

[5] G.-J. Hwang, C.-C. Tsai, and S. Yang, "Criteria, Strategies and Research Issues of Context-Aware Ubiquitous Learning," Educational Technology & Society, vol. 11, 81-91, 2008.

[6] S. Yang, "Context Aware Ubiquitous Learning Environments for Peer-to-Peer Collaborative Learning," Educational Technology & Society, vol. 9, 188-201, 2006.

[7] Y.-M. Huang and P.-S. Chiu, "The Effectiveness of the Meaningful Learning-Based Evaluation for Different Achieving Students in a Ubiquitous Learning Context," Computer & Education, vol. 87, 243-253, 2015.

[8] https://protege.stanford.edu. [Accessed: October 2017]

[9] S.K. Patel, V.R. Rathod, and J.B. Prajapati. "Performance Analysis of Content Management Systems-Joomla, Drupal and Wordpress." International Journal of Computer Applications 21.4 (2011): 39-43.

A Tool Rental Service Scenario

IoT technologies enabling a circular economy business model

Johanna Kallio, Maria Antikainen, Outi Kettunen
VTT Technical Research Centre of Finland Ltd.
Finland
Email: johanna.kallio@vtt.fi, maria.antikainen@vtt.fi, outi.kettunen@vtt.fi

Abstract—**Internet of Things (IoT), sensors, wireless networks, cloud computing and big data analytics are technological innovations that have the power to transform traditional businesses. These technologies can enable and accelerate a circular economy on a broader scale. We aim at providing information on how to disrupt current prevailing linear business models by employing digital data and IoT technologies. We give the reader a short overview of IoT technologies affecting the incumbents of industry. We present the current deployment of a tool rental service experiment and develop a scenario anticipating the possible future of the tool rental service. The envisioned tool rental scenario provides understanding on the effects of digital technologies and helps companies in identifying more sustainable and circular business models.**

Keywords-circular economy; IoT; scenario; tool rental service; sensors; networking; cloud computing; data analytics.

I. Introduction

The concept of a circular economy describes an economy with closed material loops. The circular economy focuses on reusing materials, and creating added value in products through services and technology-enabled smart solutions. This implies that the concept of the circular economy is a continuous development cycle that aims to keep products, components and materials at their highest utility and value at all times, distinguishing between technical and biological cycles [1]. If EU manufacturing sector would adopt a circular economy business model, net material costs savings could worth up to 570 billion euros per year and growth opportunities 320 billion euros by 2025 [1][2]. The circular concept fosters also wealth and employment generation against the backdrop of resource constraints [3][4]. This transformation from linear "take-make-dispose" economy to circular one requires disruptive innovation in business models and technologies.

The Internet of Things (IoT) is considered as being one of the key enablers for enhancing the circular economy at large [2]. We define IoT as a computing concept where internet enabled physical objects (e.g., sensors, actuators, tags, smart machines) can network and communicate with each other to achieve greater value and services by exchanging data and producing new information [5][6]. IoT relies on the three pillars related to the ability of smart objects: i) *to be identifiable*, ii) *to communicate* and iii) *to interact*. When object can sense the environment and communicate, they become tools for understanding complexity and responding to it [5].

Advancement in IoT technologies is making the current linear take-make-dispose economy more and more efficient, but still fails to address resource and natural capital issues. However, this new connectivity between emerging technologies and economy also offers the opportunity to re-think the underlying system and support the development of a circular economy. By combining the principles of circular economy with IoT technologies, there may be greater opportunity to scale new business models more effectively [7].

In this paper, we will present a circular economy based tool rental service scenario. First, we take a look at the main principles of circular economy in Section II. Then, in Section III, we present an overview of potential IoT technologies enabling the circular economy business. In Section IV, we describe the current deployment of the tool rental service, as well as develop the scenario for the future developments. Finally, Section V concludes the paper and provides some indicators for future work.

II. Circular Economy

A circular economy is commonly defined as an industrial system that is restorative or regenerative by intention and design [8][9]. In the circular economy, new business models are developed to reduce the need for virgin raw materials and to generate sustainable growth. The basic approach of the circular economy is to eliminate waste by designing out of waste. Products are designed and optimized for a cycle of disassembly, reuse and refurbishment, or recycling, with the understanding that economic growth is based on reuse of material reclaimed from end-of-life products rather than extraction of resources. Circular design makes products easier to disassemble in preparation for their next round trip. Reuse means the use of a product again for the same purpose in its original form or with little enhancement or change. Refurbishment means a process of returning a product to good working condition by replacing or repairing major components that are faulty or close to failure, and making 'cosmetic' changes to update the appearance of a product, such as cleaning, changing fabric, painting or refinishing. Any subsequent warranty is generally less than issued for a new or a remanufactured product, but the warranty is likely to cover the whole product (unlike repair). Accordingly, the performance may be less than as-new. [1].

In a circular economy, the concept of *user* replaces that of *consumer*. Unlike today, when a consumer buys, owns and disposes of a product, in the circular economy, durable products are leased, rented or shared whenever possible [1]. If goods are sold, new models and incentives motivate consumers (users) to return or reuse the products or their components and materials at the end of their primary use. New performance-based business models are instrumental in translating products designed for reuse into attractive value proposals. IoT technologies and digitalization in general have potential to disrupt current prevailing linear business models [10]. For example, the incumbents of the media and music industries have bitterly experienced the enormous forces of start-ups' new business models based on digital data and IoT technologies.

III. ENABLING IOT TECHNOLOGIES

The concept of combining computers, sensors and networks to monitor and control devices has existed for decades [11]. The recent advances in digital technologies are not only limited to embedded technologies, wireless communication protocols and small devices, but also huge amounts of data are being generated and can be utilized to improve businesses. In this section, we give a short overview of the potential IoT technologies affecting the circular economy.

A. Sensors

Recent advances in wireless technologies and electronics have enabled the development of low-cost, low power and multifunctional sensors that are small in size and can communicate in short distances. Typically, these sensors consist of sensing, data processing and communication components. The deployment of sensors is mainly driven by three factors; decreasing price, improving computational power and smaller size, which enables their integration into smartphones and other small devices [12].

Sensors are often categorized based on their power sources, i.e., *active* or *passive*. Active sensors emit energy in environment, while passive sensors passively receive energy that is produced externally to the device. Passive sensors require less energy, but active sensors can be used in harsh environmental conditions. Sensors can measure for example a position, motion, pressure, temperature or humidity of a device or surroundings [13].

B. Networking

Data collected with sensors need to be communicated to other locations for integration and analytics. Internet Protocol (IP) is an open protocol that provides unique addresses to various Internet-connected devices. IP networking represents a scalable and platform-independent technology having interoperability as the most essential objective. There are two IP versions, IP version 4 (IPv4) and IP version 6 (IPv6), which is the next generation protocol designed to provide several advantages over IPv4 [14].

Network technologies can be classified as wired or wireless. The main advantage of a wireless network is that users and devices can move around freely within the area of the network and get an internet connection, while wired connections are still useful for relatively more reliable, secured and high-volume network routes. The choice of technology depends mostly on the geographic range to be covered [15].

The most common short-range wireless network technologies are Bluetooth [16], Near Field Communication (NFC) [17], Radio Frequency Identification (RFID) [18], Wi-Fi [19] and ZigBee [20]. Respectively, the most commonly employed wide range wireless network technologies are cellular technology, such as 3G or 4G, and Low Power Wide Area Network (LoRaWAN) [21].

C. Cloud-based platforms

An IoT platform enables interaction between devices and users. With cloud technology, platform's computation and storage resources can be made available on a need basis, without requiring major investment in new hardware or programming.

Many vendors, such as Microsoft, HP, IBM and Oracle, provide commercial cloud-based IoT platforms for connecting sensors and actuators to the Internet. In addition, several open-source IoT platforms are available and often propose their own communication or middleware solutions. Reference [22] gives an evaluation of a number of available proprietary, as well as open-source, IoT platforms.

D. Data integration

Data communication includes a set of protocols that have been built for high volumes and large networks of assets. The most of IoT platforms are implemented with the Representational State Transfer (REST) API, which also enables an easy integration with other web services [23].

Constrained processing capabilities and limited battery resources restrict communication in sensor systems. Typical sensor application and data communication protocols considering processing capability and energy consumption are REST-based Constrained Application Protocol (CoAP) [24], Message Queue Telemetry Transport (MQTT) [25], and Extensible Messaging and Presence Protocol (XMPP) [26].

Data processing methods can be divided in two categories. *Batch processing* starts with data acquisition and storing and continues with processing of already stored information. Apache Flume [27] focuses on a flexible architecture, enabling the use of a variety of data sources and sinks. Another example of getting the data and sending it somewhere else at very large scale is Kafka [28].

Especially new IoT applications require real-time processing of information, where data items are processed as soon as they become available. This is called *stream processing* and it facilitates real-time action on the data, as well as filtering and aggregating it for efficient storage. Some new frameworks, such as the Apache tools Samza [29], Storm [30] or Flink [31], have been created for tackling the real-time processing of streams of information.

Performance and scalability requirements shift the choice of data storage towards column-oriented NoSQL databases. Apache HBase [32] is one of the most popular columnar databases offering rea-time access to very large tables with time-series support available via KairosDB [33]. In addition, Apache Cassandra [34] can be augmented with time-series operation. In fact, time-series databases, like InfluxDB [35], are yet another interesting storage technology.

E. Data analytics

Data analytics is driven by cognitive technologies, which are able to perform tasks that formerly only humans used to be able to do. Typically, the field of data analytics is divided into three different categories: a) descriptive analytics describing what the data looks like, b) predictive analytics predicting what is going to happen, and c) prescriptive analytics describing what should happen to reach the goal [36].

Some of the cognitive technologies that are increasingly adopted and can be deployed in predictive and prescriptive analytics are shortly described below:

- **Machine learning** refers to compute systems' ability to learn without being explicitly programmed. Machine learning explores the development of algorithms that can learn from and make predictions on data. Machine learning algorithms are often categorized as being *supervised* or *unsupervised.* Supervised algorithms can apply what has been learned in the past to new data, e.g., parametric/non-parametric algorithms, support vector machines, kernels, neural networks. Unsupervised algorithms can draw inferences from datasets, e.g., clustering, dimensionality reduction, recommender systems and deep learning [37].
- **Computer vision** refers to the ability of computers to identify objects, scenes and activities in images. Computer vision includes methods for acquiring, processing, analyzing and understanding digital images. Certain techniques, for example, allow for detecting the edges and textures of objects in an image [38]. The application of computer vision includes for example robotics, remote sensing and process control.
- **Robotics** refers to the interdisciplinary engineering and science that involves the design, manufacture and operations of robots, as well as software for their control and data processing. Recent advances in artificial intelligence, communications and sensors have produced more intelligent, capable and sensing robots. In practice, these developments enable robots to replace human labor in manufacturing task, as well as in a growing number of service jobs, such as maintenance [39]. For example, recent research [40] shows that robotics and automation of manufacturing processes translates into optimizing processes in the material and energy consumptions, which are important targets of the circular economy.

IV. TOOL RENTAL SERVICE

In this section, we describe how the previously presented digital technologies, namely sensors, networking, cloud-based platforms, data integration and data analytics, can be applied to a tool rental service to promote the circular economy. We present a rapid experiment of the tool rental service and develop a scenario anticipating the possible future of the tool rental service. Our aim is to afford understanding on the possibilities of digital technologies enabling more sustainable and circular business models.

A. Approach

Our AARRE project (Capitalising on Invisible Value - User-driven Business Models in the Emerging Circular Economy) explored user-driven circular business models and collaborated with multiple Finnish companies, Finnish organizations and Finnish decision makers in the circular economy field. The idea of a tool rental service is to offer an alternative for purchasing of tools, such as electric tools and cleaning equipment, which are used infrequently in urban economy. This kind of sharing economy can be an ecological option in certain conditions and on the other hand facilitates the storage problem of goods in urban housing [41].

The planning and rapid experimenting of the tool rental scenario is based on several discussions with eight AARRE project researchers, one start-up entrepreneur and various companies. The goal of our empirical study is to provide input for the discussion on how to disrupt current prevailing linear business models by employing digital data and IoT technologies.

B. Current deployment of the tool rental service

Our AARRE project conducted a rapid experimental tool rental service called Liiteri [42] in collaboration with Finnish IT-startup CoReorient [43] and hardware store K-Rauta. The other co-operation partners were Helsinki Region Environmental Services Authority HSY, Technology Industries of Finland, SER-kierrätys, City of Espoo, Purjebägit Oy, Kierrätysverkko Oy, Metrosuutarit.fi, Pyörähuoltoovelle.fi and Kauppahalli24.fi.

Liiteri is an online platform, where consumers can rent electric tools and house cleaning equipment. By registering as a Liiteri user, the consumer can choose the desired product and renting date via online platform. In addition, the payment is made via the online service at the same time. When the payment has been processed, the consumer gets an access code to the 24/7 Liiteri self-service point, which is an intelligent container in the city centre of Helsinki. The consumers can pick up the rented gear any time from the Liiteri self-service point, where there are good public transport connections. Alternatively, the consumer can choose a crowdsourced PiggyBaggy home delivery service [44]. An initial experiment to examine the utility of the Liiteri tool rental service was conducted and reported in another study [41].

C. IoT-enabled scenario for the tool rental service

In this section, we present an IoT platform based future scenario for the Liiteri tool rental service by employing digital data and IoT technologies. Figure 1 presents the developed scenario, which aims to provide understanding of the anticipated possibilities of sensors, networking, cloud-based platforms, data integration and data analytics.

A beacon is a node aware of its location (e.g., equipped with Bluetooth) [45] and it can send signals to smartphones or other mobile devices. For example, the consumer's smartphone can interact with beacons placed in the Liiteri self-service point via a Liiteri mobile application (later referred to as the Liiteri app). Bluetooth-based *beacons can be used for mobile door opening* when entering the 24/7 Liiteri self-service point [46]. Furthermore, the beacons can enable consumers to be recognized when entering the 24/7 Liiteri self-service point and *help them easily to find the selected tool or other rented gear with nearby notifications feature*. A payment for the selected product can be discharged using a *beacon-based mobile payment* or a more conventional online payment service provided by the Liiteri app.

The rental profile including demographic data and browsing history from the Liiteri app can be stored in the cloud-based Liiteri database and analysed for *personalized recommendations*. The Liiteri app can also allow the consumers to *access product information and reviews* to help them make their decision. At home, the consumers can be provided with a *guided usage service* by scanning the tool (equipped with beacon) with their phone. The Liiteri app makes it easier for the consumers to get useful information and even a guided replacement service in case of a broken part can be possible.

Sensors can measure for example acceleration, temperature, vibration and humidity of tools or parts of the tools. *The sensor data can be exploited in business intelligence* in many ways, such as in *condition-based maintenance* (CBM). CBM is a maintenance procedure based on the information collected through conditions monitoring and can be used for *diagnostics* and *prognostics* [47]. Prognostics based maintenance is often called as predictive maintenance. CBM of the tools can employ multiple sensor data fusion and analytics platform (either on-premise or cloud-based) to assess current failures (diagnostics) and possible future failures (prognostics). In our Liiteri scenario, the tools can be equipped with budget sensors connected to the cloud-based analytics platform. The sensor data can be stored in the Liiteri database and further analysed in batches with different data analytics techniques, such as machine learning, for diagnostics and prognostics purposes. The sensor data, especially concerning usage and failures, can be utilized in refurbishment activities and turn refurbishment into a potential and accessible option. The *predictive maintenance service* can 'maintain the tools before they break' in order to increase the lifetime of tools, and improve safety and usage experience of the tool rental service. A trivial consequence from refurbishment and increasing the lifetime of tools is decreasing the use of natural resources and waste.

A prognostics model employing machine learning can be developed for calculating a Remaining Useful Lifetime (RUL) and considering sustainability aspects in decision-making, i.e., deciding when maintenance is economically viable, environmentally bearable and equitable compared to reuse, remanufacture or recycle [48]. The tool usage data collected with sensors and the consumer feedback can be analysed to *improve future product design and performance.*

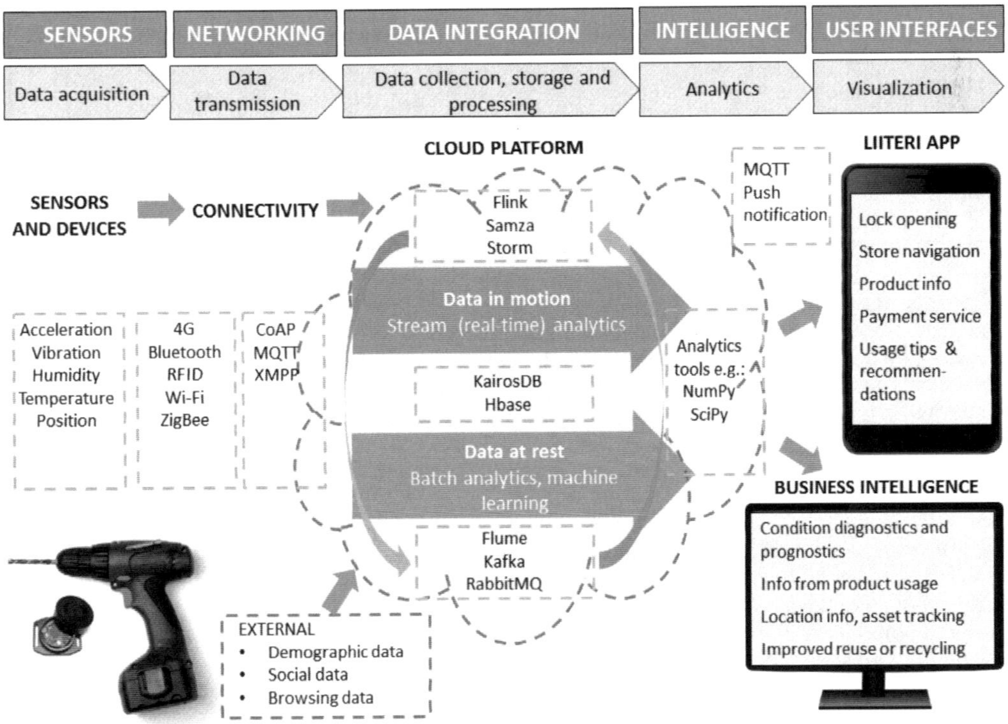

Figure 1. The IoT-enabled tool rental service business scenario.

In addition, the collected data can be analysed *to specify the recycling or disassembly* activities in order to maintain both economic and environmental value of the parts as high as possible.

The cloud-based Liiteri platform can also collect data about *the location of the tool and provide a connection with next user.* This promotes collaboration among consumers and facilitates crowdsourced delivery from user to user. During the delivery process, communication can be handled via the Liiteri app. *The deliverer can earn points*, which she or he can spend for the tool rental or redeem for cash. Home delivery service of the tools, in turn, can utilize the *real-time navigation information and the customer's location information for route planning and optimization of delivery routes* to reduce driving time, fuel consumption and exhaust gases.

V. CONCLUSIONS

IoT technologies and digitalization in general enable novel business models based on the circular economy. As a result, they offer a great potential to disrupt current prevailing linear business models [49]. This study contributes to the discussion on circular economy by providing a future IoT-enabled scenario for future development paths. The tool rental service scenario uses sensors, networking, cloud computing and data analysis technologies for selling services instead of goods, for designing products for regeneration and for creating added value through services. Generally, offering services instead of selling goods reduces the environmental footprint of product manufacturing and the private ownership of goods. At its best, this study awakes discussion among companies on how to create circular economy business by employing digital data and IoT technologies.

The scenario planning of this study has been qualitative and it includes researchers' own subjective interpretation. The previous study [41] examined the utility of the Liiteri tool rental service and the results indicated that renting could be an attractive choice to consumers if crucial consumer expectations are identified and met. This attitudinal change is partly attributable to technological improvements, such as widespread digital cloud platforms, which make sharing of goods easier. On the other hand, especially young people prefer services to ownership of goods.

In order to proceed towards commercial utilization of the presented concept, further work on the IoT-enabled tool rental service scenario includes addressing multiple technical, usability, and profitability aspects, in addition to the environmental viewpoint. The main technological challenges include the overall cost-efficient logistics on large scale, data security, interoperability of IoT sub-systems, and interface with the consumers. The usability of the service must meet or exceed the level of current modern competing e-commerce platforms. Overall, the business challenges are the same as for e-commerce services in general. To be commercially viable, the service must maximize the user satisfaction and minimize the costs through intelligent use of IoT technologies. Future work needs to evaluate which parts of the system are efficient as automated, and which parts should be managed by human operators, resulting in an optimal profitability. Full examination is needed on the types of products that provide most benefit from the circular economy service concept in terms of environmental benefit. Moreover, next steps of future research endeavours could focus on implementation of a next generation IoT-enabled circular economy service for a larger group of people, with the systematic collection of consumer experiences for further service improvement.

Despite the various remaining challenges, there is a growing amount of consumers that see the environmental friendliness as an added value factor. This could facilitate the accumulation of consumers in the early phases of development, towards ultimately better collaboration between the human use of technology and the environment.

ACKNOWLEDGMENT

This research has been conducted as a part of the AARRE (Capitalising on Invisible Value – User-Driven Business Models in the Emerging Circular Economy) project. The authors would like to express their gratitude to the Green Growth Programme of the Finnish Funding Agency for Innovation (Tekes), the Technical Research Centre of Finland (VTT), the case companies and other parties involved in the AARRE project.

REFERENCES

[1] Ellen Mac Arthur foundation. "Towards the Circular Economy vol 1: Economic and business rationale for an accelerated transition", 2012.

[2] J. Manyika, M. Chui, J. Bughin, R. Dobbs, P. Bisson, P. and A. Marrs. "Disruptive technologies: Advances will transform life, business, and the global economy", McKinsey Global Institute, 2016.

[3] P. Ghisellini, C. Cialani and S. Ulgiati (2015). "A review on circular economy: the expected transition to a balanced interplay of environmental and economic systems." Journal of Cleaner Production 114, 2016, pp. 11-32. doi:10.1016/j.jclepro.2015.09.007

[4] A. Wijkman and S. Kristian. "The circular economy and benefits for society." Jobs and Climate Clear Winners in an Economy Based on Renewable Energy and resource Efficiency, 2015.

[5] D. Miorandi, S. Sicari, F. De Pellegrini and I. Chlamtac. "Internet of things: Vision, applications and research challenges." Ad Hoc Networks 10(7), 2012, pp. 1497-1516.

[6] J. Buckley. "From RFID to the Internet of things: pervasive networked systems", Final Report on the Conference organised by DG Information Society and Media, Networks and Communication Technologies Directorate, March 2006.

[7] A. Morlet et al. "Intelligent assets: Unlocking the circular economy", Ellen Mac Arthur foundation, 2016.

[8] J. Butterworth et al. "Towards the Circular Economy vol 3: accelerating the scale-up across global supply chains", Ellen MacArthur Foundation, 2014.

[9] D. A. R. George, B. C. Lin, and Y. Chen, "A circular economy model of economic growth". Environmental Modelling & Software 73, 2015, pp. 60-63. doi:10.1016/j.envsoft.2015.06.014

[10] M. E. Porter and J. E. Heppelmann. "How smart, connected products are transforming competition". Harvard Business Review, 92(11), 2014, pp. 64-88.

[11] M. Weiser, M. (1991). "The computer for the 21st century". IEEE pervasive computing, 1(1), 2002, pp. 19-25.

[12] J. Greenough. "The Internet of everything 2016", BI Intelligence, 2016.

[13] J. Fraden. Handbook of modern sensors: physics, designs, and applications. Springer Science & Business Media, 2015.

[14] The IPv6 Forum n.d. http://www.ipv6forum.com/ (Accessed Jul 14, 2017)

[15] N. Kaur and S. Monga. "Comparisons of wired and wireless networks: A review". International Journal of Advanced Engineering Technology, V(II), 2014, pp. 34-35.

[16] Bluetooth. "A look at the basics of Bluetooth technology" n.d. http://www.bluetooth.com/Pages/Basics.aspx (Accessed Jun 20, 2017).

[17] NearFieldCommunication.org n.d. http://nearfieldcommunication.org/ (Accessed Jun 20, 2017).

[18] R. Want. "An introduction to RFID technology". IEEE Pervasive Computing, 5(1), 2006, pp. 25-33.

[19] Wi-Fi Alliance n.d. http://www.wi-fi.org/ (Accessed Jun 20, 2017).

[20] ZigBee website n.d. www.zigbee.org/ (Accessed Jun 20, 2017).

[21] LoRa Alliance www-pages n.d. https://www.lora-alliance.org/what-is-lora/technology (Accessed Jun 20, 2017).

[22] J. Mineraud, O. Mazhelis, X, Su and S. Tarkoma. "A gap analysis of Internet-of-Things platforms". Computer Communications, 89, 2016, pp. 5-16.

[23] M. Kovatsch, S. Mayer and B. Ostermaier. "Moving application logic from the firmware to the cloud: Towards the thin server architecture for the internet of things". In: Innovative Mobile and Internet Services in Ubiquitous Computing (IMIS), 2012 Sixth International Conference on. IEEE, 2012. pp. 751-756.

[24] Z. Shelby, K. Hartke and C. Bormann. The Constrained Application Protocol (CoAP) n.d. https://tools.ietf.org/html/rfc725 (Accessed Jun 20, 2017).

[25] MQ Telemetry Transport (MQTT) V3.1 Protocol Specification (2010) n.d.http://www.ibm.com/developerworks/library/ws-mqtt/ (Accessed Jun 20, 2017).

[26] A. Iivari, T. Väisänen, M. Ben Alaya, T. Riipinen and T. Monteil. "Harnessing XMPP for Machine-to-Machine Communications & Pervasive Applications". Journal of Communications Software & Systems, 10(3), 2014, pp. 163-178.

[27] Apache Flume 1.5.2 User Guide — Apache Flume n.d. http://flume.apache.org/FlumeUserGuide.html (Accessed Jun 20, 2017).

[28] Apache Kafka n.d. https://kafka.apache.org/ (Accessed Jun 20, 2016).

[29] Apache Samza n.d. http://samza.apache.org/ (Accessed Jun 20, 2017).

[30] Apache Storm n.d. https://storm.apache.org/ (Accessed Jun 20, 2017).

[31] Apache Flink: Scalable batch and stream processing n.d. https://flink.apache.org/ (Accessed Jun 20, 2017).

[32] HBase – Apache HBaseTM Home n.d. http://hbase.apache.org/ (Accessed Jun 20, 2017).

[33] KairosDB n.d. https://kairosdb.github.io/ (Accessed Jun 20, 2017).

[34] The Apache Cassandra Project n.d. http://cassandra.apache.org/ (Accessed Jun 20, 2017).

[35] InfluxDB - Open Source Time Series, Metrics, and Analytics Database n.d. http://influxdb.com/ (Accessed Jun 20, 2017).

[36] T. H. Davenport. "Competing on Analytics". Harward Business review, 84(1), 2016, p. 98.

[37] S. Boyd, N. Parikh, E. Chu, B. Peleato and J. Eckstein, J. "Distributed optimization and statistical learning via the alternating direction method of multipliers". Foundations and Trends® in Machine Learning, 3(1), 2011, pp. 1-122.

[38] S. Russell and P. Norvig, P. "Artificial intelligence: a modern approach". Prentice-Hall, Egnlewood Cliffs, 1995.

[39] M. Chui, J. Manyika and M. Miremadi. "Where machines could replace humans – and where they can't (yet)". McKinsey Quarterly, July 2017.

[40] V. F. Soporan, M. Crişan, T. Lehene and A. L. Pop. (2016, June). "Methodology for appreciation the manufacturing castings from perspective of circular economy". In IOP Conference Series: Materials Science and Engineering, 133(1), June 2016, p. 012063.

[41] M. Antikainen, M. Lammi and H. Paloheimo. "Creating value for consumers in CE - Tools as a service". In: ISPIM Innovation Symposium. The International Society for Professional Innovation Management (ISPIM), June 2017, p. 1.

[42] Liiteri n.d. www.liiteri.net (Accessed Sep 26, 2017)

[43] CoReorient n.d. www.coreorient.com (Accessed Sep 26, 2017)

[44] Piggy Paggy Beta n.d. www.piggybaggy.com (Accessed Sep 26, 2017)

[45] M. L. Sichitiu and V. Ramadurai. "Localization of wireless sensor networks with a mobile beacon". In: Mobile Ad-hoc and Sensor Systems, 2004 IEEE International Conference on. IEEE, 2004. p. 174-183.

[46] J. Potts and S. Sukittanon. "Exploiting Bluetooth on Android mobile devices for home security application". In: Southeastcon, 2012 Proceedings of IEEE. IEEE, 2012. p. 1-4.

[47] A. K. Jardine, D. Lin and D. Banjevic. "A review on machinery diagnostics and prognostics implementing condition-based maintenance". Mechanical systems and signal processing, 20(7), 2006, pp. 1483-1510.

[48] B. Iung and E. Levrat, E. "Advanced maintenance services for promoting sustainability". Procedia CIRP, 22, 2014, pp. 15-22.

[49] M. Antikainen, M. Lammi and T. Hakanen. "Consumer service innovation in a circular economy – the customer value perspective". In: Proceedings of ICServ2016 Conference. The 4th International Conference on Serviceology (ICServ2016), September 2016.

Towards an Architecture to Multimodal Tools for e-Learning Environments

André Constantino da Silva
IFSP, NIED/UNICAMP
Hortolândia, Brazil
e-mail: andre.constantino@ifsp.edu.br

Fernanda M. P. Freire, Flávia L. Arantes
NIED/UNICAMP
Campinas, Brazil
e-mail: ffreire@unicamp.br, farantes@unicamp.br

Abstract— **e-Learning environments are applications that use the Web infrastructure to support teaching and learning activities; they are designed to have good usability using a desktop computer with keyboard, mouse and high-resolution medium-size display. Devices equipped with pen and touch sensitive screen have enough computational power to render Web pages and allow users to navigate through the e-learning environments. But, pen-based or touch sensitive devices have a different input style, decreasing the usability of e-learning environments due the interaction modality change. To work on mobile contexts, e-learning environments must be improved to consider the interaction through pen and touch. In our previous work, we presented InkBlog, Multimodal Editor, and InkAnnotation: three multimodal tools for e-learning environments. Based on these previous works, we propose a generic architecture for multimodal tools for e-learning environments, describing common components to treat data generated by pen and touch that can be generalized to treat other modalities.**

Keywords- architecture for multimodal tools; multiple platform and multidevices; e-Learning environments.

I. INTRODUCTION

e-Learning environments, such as Moodle [1], SAKAI [2], TelEduc [3], Ae [4], are applications that use the Web infrastructure to support teaching and learning activities. The e-Learning environments are designed to support a variety of users and learning contexts, but they are designed for conventional computers, usually equipped with keyboard and mouse as input and a medium screen and speakers as output, a limited set of interaction styles for nowadays devices. These modalities, and the technology that support them, shape the teaching and learning activities done in the e-Learning environments; they focus on reading and writing skills.

Mobile devices, such as smartphones and tablets, are becoming increasingly popular; most of them have touch screen displays, Internet access and enough computing power to process Web pages. So, it is possible to access Web applications to read and to post content through mobile devices. But, it is important to consider that most of e-Learning tools are developed to be accessed by desktop computers equipped with keyboard, mouse and a medium size display; in our previous work we described that when a user interface designed for a set of interaction styles is accessed by a different set of interaction styles the users face interaction problems [5]. Another problem is that it is not possible to take advantage of the interaction style features; for example, in a desktop computer, users use the keyboard for typing the content that will be posted. In a pen-based computer without handwrite recognition, users need to type each letter pressing the pen on the respective key of a virtual keyboard. This way of writing text takes a lot of time, makes the writing task boring and does not take advantage of the main purpose of the pen, namely, handwriting and doing sketches easily. In the case of touch sensitive screen, the user can touch the virtual keyboard to write the post, but it is not possible to do sketches.

So, we believe that the e-learning environments and tools that compose them need to be improved to be easier to use in a variety of devices and contexts, e.g., areas which need sketches or drawing, such mathematics; or the environment must be sensitive about the device the user is using or the user's location. So, our research group is developing some tools that take advantage of the interaction styles available on the user device. An obstacle are the few papers already published on multimodal architectures for Web applications, in particular e-learning tools, and lack of models. So, we propose a generic architecture for multimodal tools of e-learning environments.

Section II presents a literature review about e-learning environments, multimodality and multimodal systems. Section III presents our previous work about development of multimodal tools for e-learning environments. In Section IV, we propose a generic architecture for tools that compose e-Learning environments and need to manipulate multimodal inputs, allowing this kind of system to be more adaptable to the context and to reach ubiquity. The last section presents the conclusion and future work.

II. LITERATURE REVIEW

The World Wide Web has changed since its invention from a static to a highly dynamic media in the recent years; so, the term "Web 2.0" was coined in 1999 to describe the Web sites that use technology beyond the static pages and its uses for collaborative, user-centric content production and interactive content access [6]. Safran, Helic, and Gütl [7] describe that in literature the marks of Web 2.0 include: (i) social phenomena, such as the Web for participation, (ii) technology for significant change in Web usage, and (iii) design guidelines for loosely coupled services. The Web 2.0 allows users to interact and collaborate with each other in social networking sites, weblogs, podcasts, wikis, video sharing sites and other sort of tools.

One kind of Web applications that have some Web 2.0 features is e-Learning environments, as Moodle [1], SAKAI

[2] and Ae [4]. They are applications with tools to support teaching and learning activities though the Web. Tools in these environments allow users to create content, communicate with other users and manage the virtual space. Tools like chat, forums, portfolios, repositories are widely used, and tools that explore the audio and video resources for user communication, such as instant messenger and video-conferences, are becoming common among these environments.

HyperText Markup Language (HTML) is used for any Web application to describe the page interface and its content. Usually, in Web applications where users post text, there is a rich text editor to allow users without HTML skills to write formatted text. In desktop computers, the users use the keyboard to typewrite the letters, and use the mouse to point and trigger text format functionalities (some of them have shortcuts to be triggered by the keyboard). Since the rich text editors have a direct manipulation interface similar as text editor applications, it is easy to be used in desktop computers equipped with mouse and keyboard.

The HTML has some improvement defined in the last version, the HTML5, related to support of multimedia, making it easily readable by humans and consistently understood by computers and devices [8]. HTML5 adds the new <video>, <audio> and <canvas> tag elements, as well as the integration of Scalable Vector Graphics (SVG, a vector image format for two-dimensional graphics based on eXtended Markup Language - XML) content and Mathematical Markup Language (MathML, an XML based-format to describing mathematical notations) to integrate mathematical formulae into Web pages. These features are designed to easily include and handle multimedia and graphical content on the Web without having proprietary plugins and Application Programming Interfaces (APIs) installed.

The <canvas> tag allows for dynamic, scriptable rendering of 2D shapes and bitmap images; it is a drawable region defined in HTML code with height and width attributes. JavaScript code may access the area through a full set of drawing functions similar to those of other common 2D APIs, thus allowing for dynamically generated graphics.

Another evolution in HTML is standardizing how the browser must handle events from touch and pointer inputs [9]. The World Wide Web Consortium (W3C) specified that "The Touch Events specification defines a set of low-level events that represent one or more points of contact with a touch-sensitive surface, and changes of those points with respect to the surface and any Document Object Model (DOM) elements displayed upon it (e.g., for touch screens) or associated with it (e.g., for drawing tablets without displays)". This specification was done thinking of devices equipped with a stylus, such as a tablet, and defines event types for: (i) when a user touches the surface (touchstart), (ii) when a user removes a touch point from the surface (touchend), (iii) when a user moves a touch point along the surface (touchmove), (iv) to indicate a touch point has been disrupted (touchcancel). Having different event types for input data generated by each hardware gives flexibility for the developers to define the actions to be triggered for each input data.

W3C defines XML formats for non-primitive data to allow exchange of a wide variety of data on the Web and elsewhere; one example is Ink Markup Language (InkML) [10]. The InkML provides a common format for exchanging ink data between components, such as handwriting and gesture recognizers, signature verifiers, sketches, music and other notational languages in applications. The InkML serves as data format for representing ink gathered by an electronic pen or stylus. It is possible to find some uses of InkML, such as Microsoft Word 2010 which supports electronic ink in text review and the InkML JavaScript Library [11], that offers some functions to allow InkML digital ink to be referenced within Web pages and rendered directly into the HTML5 <canvas> tag.

Considering the technology breakthrough that HTML5 proposes, most Web sites use HTML5 to impress users through content exhibition. Few developers consider the user input interaction styles, so they develop Web pages for users with keyboard and mouse on desktop computers which are not appropriate for touch devices. But, this scenario is changing with the smartphone and tablet popularization: the Web designers need to think about the other interaction styles, such as touchscreen and pen-sensitive devices.

In pen-based devices, when the user moves the pen on the screen, the pen trace should result in electronic ink that must be treated by the application to be rendered and stored. But, desktop applications that running on Tablet PCs do not treat electronic ink, so it is necessary to incorporate special applications to treat the electronic ink to have the benefits of the pen interaction style.

Multi-touch in Web applications is more common in games. Johnson [12] presents a tutorial to include features of multi-touch in Web applications, such as handling the touchstart, touchmove and touchend event types. Since we wanted the users to draw with their fingers in touchscreen devices, these event types call functions to start a line, to compose the line, and to stop to draw a line, respectively. To allow multi-touch, it was necessary to store the data from each finger in an array. The browser sends to the function that will handle the user interaction an event object with the *changedTouches* attribute, a collection with data from one or more modified touch points. To identify finger´s move it is possible to use the event´s *identifier* attribute; this value was used as index in the array to put the data in the correct line. To avoid the browser from scrolling the page when the user moves the fingers on the screen, the event´s functions *preventManipulation()* and *preventDefault()* were called.

These technologies allow Web applications be adapted considering the device (and considering their input hardware). In particular, mobile devices and wireless networks allow users to interact with a Web application anytime and anywhere.

Modality is a used term to define a mode in which the user data input or a system output is expressed. The communication mode refers to the communication model used by two different entities to interact [13]. Nigay and Coutaz [14] define modality as an interaction method that an agent can use to reach a goal, and it can be described in general terms such as "speech" or in specific terms such as "using microphones". Bernsen [15] claims that two modalities are not equivalent because they differ in relation to strengths and weaknesses of expressiveness and also in relation to the perceptual, cognitive and emotional systems of the human being. It is also important to understand that device switching can result in changing platform and/or interaction modality. In terms of the system´s usability, therefore, we can find two types of interaction problems when we change devices: those coming from the modality changing and those from the platform changing [5].

For monomodal systems, designers are not limited to choose only one modality. But, in multimodal systems, they can choose many modalities, that, used together, increase the system flexibility and provide other benefits. Interfaces with this characteristic are called multimodal interfaces and the systems are called multimodal interaction systems.

Multimodal systems are present in the Human-Computer Interaction (HCI) literature, and to make them easier to understand and build multimodal systems, some works present a general architecture model for these systems. Multimodality can increase the usability, accessibility, convenience, and flexibility of an application [13], four desirable requirements for e-learning environments. But to build a multimodal e-learning environment it is not a trivial task, it is necessary to deeply understand the e-learning environments, their use and technology, and define an architecture that considers components of multimodal interaction and of e-learning environments, and the Web platform restrictions. To define these components and their communications, we propose an architecture for multimodal e-learning systems.

Some models of Tablet PCs are equipped with touchscreen too, so the user can interact with the keyboard, mouse, track pad, pen or using his/her fingers. Since the touch has become a common way to interact with digital applications, mainly on mobile devices, e-learning environments need to be improved to manipulate data from this input device.

Multimodal interaction is a research proposal to turn the interaction between humans and machines more natural, i.e., closer to the interactions between two humans, and have the benefits to increase the usability, flexibility and convenience [16][17]. Mayes [18] defines multimodal interaction systems as systems with the capacity to communicate with the user by different communication modes, using more than one modality, and automatically gives or extracts meaning. According to Oviatt [13] "Multimodal interfaces process two or more combined user input modes (such as speech, pen, touch, manual gesture, gaze, and head and body movements) in a coordinated manner with multimedia system output". Lalanne et al. [17] describe multimodal interaction systems, or multimodal systems, that allow users to interact with computers though many data input modalities (e.g., speech, gesture, eye gaze) and output channels (e.g., text, graphics, sound, avatars, voice synthesis). Multimodal systems need to process all input done by the user to identify and process the desired action and generate the output using the appropriate modes. Dumas et al. [16] present a generic architecture for multimodal systems composed by the following components: i) input recognizers & processors, ii) output synthesizers, iii) fusion engine, iv) fission module, v) dialog management and vi) context, user model and history manager. The last four components (components iii, iv, v, vi) make up the Integration Committee.

To implement a multimodal system for Web it is necessary to consider both the multimodal architecture and the Web architecture. Gruenstein et al. [19] present a framework to develop multimodal interfaces for Web, namely, the Web-Accessible Multimodal Interface (WAMI) Toolkit. The framework defines tree client-side components (Core GUI, GUI Controller and Audio Controller) and four more server-side components (Web Server, Speech Recognizer, Speech Synthesizer, and Logger). The user interacts with the Core GUI, described using HTML and JavaScript, and the Audio Controller, a Java Applet to receive the audio input. The collected data is sent to server to be treated by the Speech Recognizer and the Web Server components. The components Core GUI, GUI Controller, Audio Controller and Speech Recognizer can be classified as the input recognizers & processors of the Dumas et al.´s architecture. The Speech Synthesizer can be classified as output synthesizers of the Dumas et al.´s architecture. The WAMI toolkit is focused on speech plus keyboard and mouse modes, but the framework can be expanded to include other modes through definition of new components.

III. PREVIOUS WORK

In our previous work, we developed several tools for TelEduc [3] and Ae [4] e-learning environments. Due the penetration of smartphones in the society, we started to develop tools for these environment that take advantage of the smartphones input hardware and their mobility. The first one was InkBlog, the second was InkAnnotation and the MultiModal Editor was the last one. All tools are described in this section.

A. *InkBlog*

In e-Learning environments, Weblog [20] is a communication and collaborative tool that aims to promote the sharing of messages among participants through an area named blog. Users can publish texts, images, audio, videos and links, sharing their opinions, in posts typically displayed in reverse chronological order (the most recent post appears first) and allowing visitors to leave comments. In this way, blogging can be seen as a form of social networking.

The InkBlog [21] (Fig. 1) was created to make it easier to handwrite posts and comments in a blog using a stylus in pen-based devices. The approach to develop the InkBlog was to extend the Weblog tool with components to generate and manipulate the electronic ink in the user interface, representing the electronic ink in InkML format. Before that, a usability test was done to identify problems when user interacts with pen. Changes in the Weblog´s architecture (Fig. 2) and user interface (Fig. 1) were done to support input data from stylus. In the architecture, we added a component to receive data from the pen, the InkController component, and a component to renderer this data as electronic ink, the InkRenderer component. Both components, the InkController and the InkRenderer, make up the InkEditor, which is a handwritten text editor for Web pages that renders the electronic ink and receives the input data generated by the stylus.

The pen input data is received by the InkController, which transforms each point of the trace into coordinate points following InkML format. The user can choose the trace´s color and the width by selecting the button options on the right-hand side (Fig. 3). When the user points out and presses the pen into a color or width button, the next traces will have the brush attributes set to look like the selected options.

The InkRenderer, the other InkEditor component, draws the traces of a handwritten post on the user screen (Fig.1). The InkRenderer´s code, the electronic ink data in InkML format and the HTML page are sent to the client over the HTTP protocol (Fig. 2) to display the page with posts. After all the data and code arrived in the client, the InkRenderer reads the InkML data found inside the tag canvas, and draws the electronic ink for each trace, taking into account the ink formatting. The InkRenderer was developed using the InkML JavaScript Library.

To post a new message, the user can choose the input hardware (keyboard or pen) by selecting the icon on "input from:" field, to type the text using a keyboard or to handwrite a post with a stylus (Fig. 3). When the user chooses the pen, she will write a handwriting post, the browser will hide the text editor and show the InkEditor, where the user will use the stylus to handwrite. When the user touches the InkEditor within the pen and draws a trace, the InkController will listen to the user actions, getting the dots that compose the trace. Each dot is recorded and a line connecting the preceding point to the new point is drawn

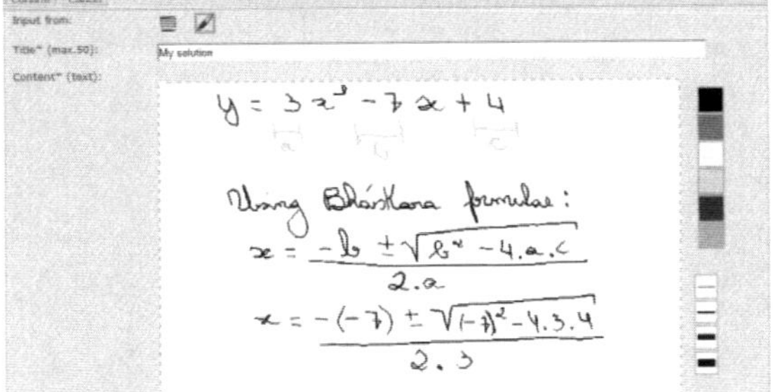

Figure 1. Using InkBlog to handwrite a post using a stylus.

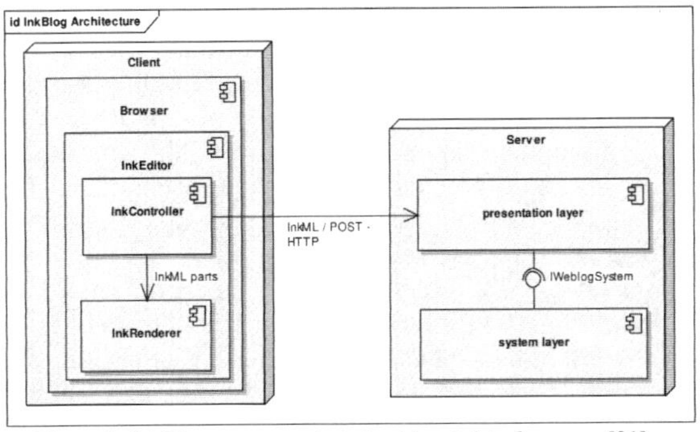

Figure 2. InkBlog components to treat input data from pen [21].

until the user releases the pen. After the pen is released, the InkController will generate the InkML´s trace node for the new trace. The user can draw as many traces as she wants and all of them will be stored and will compose the InkML data. When the user finishes to handwrite the post, she will click the "Confirm" button and the generated InkML data will be sent to the server to be stored.

Some changes were needed in the Web application to distinguish textual content from typewriting content and to show the correct editor in the post view. The changes are done in the presentation layer. The other layers have not been changed.

The client device needs to have a compatible HTML5 browser to run the InkEditor. The InkEditor uses InkML to represent the handwriting data and the Canvas HTML attribute to draw the traces on the screen.

It is also possible to handwrite comments and post them. The process is similar to the process described above.

B. *InkAnnotation*

InkAnnotation [22] is a tool for review of documents, pictures and sketches by handwriting comments using a pen-based tablet or computer (Fig. 3). There are two ways to use this tool. In this first case, the InkAnnotation will be similar to a whiteboard where the user can handwrite or sketch on a blank space or over an uploaded document.

Another use is embedding the InkAnnotation inside

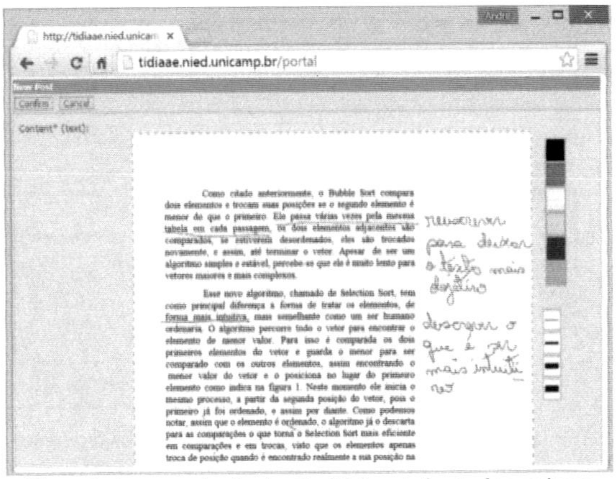

Figure 3. An example of using the InkAnnotation tool to review a document.

another e- tool, e.g., the Portfolio tool. Portfolio is a space each user can use to typewrite an item or do files upload, e.g., PDF files, Word files, and pictures. When the user wants to handwrite a Portfolio item to review it, the user triggers the option "Do Annotation with Ink", and a new window will be open with the document as background. This document will be drawn using the canvas tag, allowing the user to handwrite or sketch over it (Fig. 3).

To treat the data generated by a pen, we reused the InkRenderer and InkController. When the user touches the interface within the pen and draws a trace, the InkController will listen to the user actions, getting the dots that compose the trace. Each dot is recorded and a line connecting the preceding point to the new point is drawn until the user releases the pen. After the pen is released, the InkController will generate the InkML´s trace node for the new trace. The user can draw as many traces as she wants and all them will be stored and will compose the InkML data. When finished handwriting the review, the user will click in the "Confirm" button and the generated InkML data will be sent to the server to be stored. Since we used HTML5, any browser that supports it can render the electronic ink drawn by the InkRenderer.

Figure 4. An example of using the Multimodal Editor tool to write a multimodal text.

C. *Multimodal Editor*

The Multimodal Editor (Fig. 4) is a tool for producing multisemiotic texts: texts composed of different forms of representation - images, audios and videos, besides written and spoken language [23][24]. The most common (and old) multisemiotic texts are those that add written text and images and are still widely used today in newspapers, magazines, advertisements. The point, therefore, is that we read more multisemiotic texts than we actually produce such texts. In the development of Multimodal Editor, we assumed that mobile learning is related more to the learner than to technology, since it is the learner who moves. He is the center of learning and the technology allows him to learn in any context [25].

To allow the Multimodal Editor to treat the data generated by a pen, we developed two new components to capture and treat the ink, which are similar to the previous InkRenderer and InkController. However, in this case, the controller generates a SVG draw instead of a InkML file. So, when the user touches the interface within the pen and draws a trace, the controller will listen to the user actions, getting the dots that compose the trace. Each dot is recorded and a line connecting the preceding point to the new point is drawn until the user releases the pen. After the pen is released, the controller will generate the SVG´s trace node for the new trace. Since we used HTML5, any browser that supports it can render SVG files, so the InkRenderer is the browser´s SVG renderer.

IV. Architecture for Multimodal tools

By analyzing the architecture of each developed tool, we can generalize an architecture for multimodal tools for e-learning environments (Fig. 5). For each modality, a component to receive the data and represent in a way that can be processed and also trigger a system function. In Fig 5.

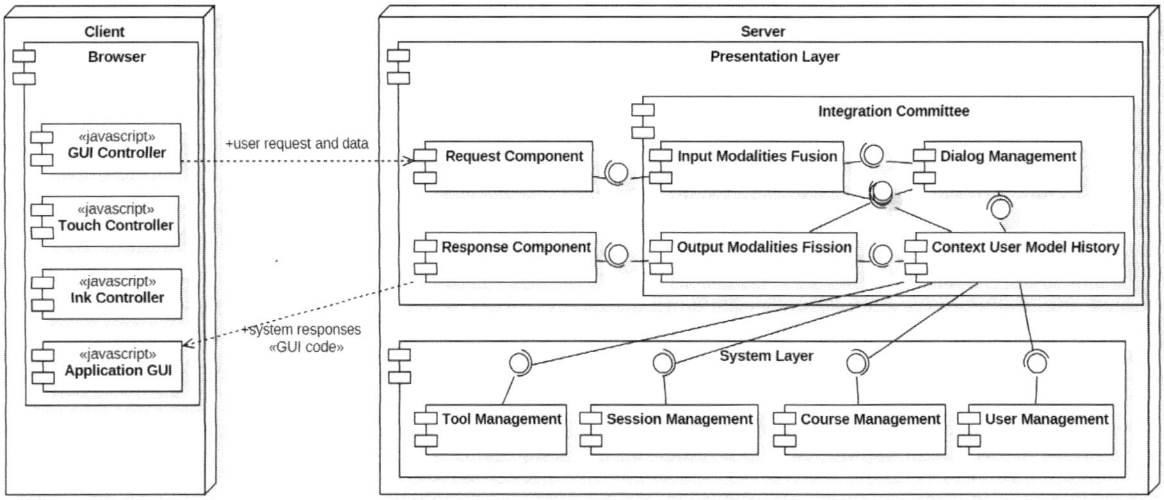

Figure 5. A generic architecture for multimodal tools to e-learning environments.

we specified some components to treat data from touch (Touch Controller), mouse+keyboard (GUI Controller) and pen (InkController), and to render the user interface (Application Renderer) and to render the digital ink (Ink Renderer). The components need to send their data to the server, who receives it by the Request Component (following a Web architecture).

When the devices allow the user to interact with more than one modality, the system can decide how the user can trigger a specific function. This responsibility is that of the Context-aware component and it needs to be configured by the developer since each tool has different functions. The idea is to combine the power of input modalities, e.g., in Tablet PCs. For the devices that have capacity to distinguish the origin of the input data, it is possible to use the data from the pen to generate the electronic ink and the data from touch to scroll the screen or to trigger another gesture, such as selection and zoom.

V. CONCLUSION

e-Learning environments are applications that use the Web infrastructure to support teaching and learning activities. To post text, there is a rich text editor to allow users who do not have HTML programming skills to write formatted text. This solution has good usability on desktop computers, but when the user interacts with a pen or by touch, he/she needs to type each letter using a virtual keyboard, so the usability, most specifically, the efficiency, decreases and makes the writing task boring. Another problem is the difficulty to draw sketches using the mouse.

In our previous work, we developed three multimodal tools (InkBlog, InkAnnotation and Multimodal Editor). Based on the knowledge acquired developing these tools, we propose a generic architecture for multimodal tools for e-learning environments, made up of components that treat the data of each modality and perform a system functionality depending on the used modality and available modalities.

As future work, we are developing a context-sensitive component. Since users consider the device´s characteristics, in particular the input hardware, e.g., in devices with pen and touch sensitive screens, users can use a pen to trigger some functions and they can use touch to trigger other functions. In case of devices with only touch sensitive screens, users interact with the fingers to trigger all functions. Another future work aims to provide the developed components so developers of e-learning environment´s tools can improve their tools with multimodality.

ACKNOWLEDGMENT

Authors thank CNPq for grants in the project No. 462478/2014-9.

REFERENCES

[1] Moodle Trust, "Moodle.org: open-source community-based tools for learning," Available at <http://moodle.org>. [retrieved: Jul. 2013]

[2] SAKAI Environment, "Sakai Project | collaboration and learning - for educators by educators," available at <http://sakaiproject.org>. [retrieved: Jul. 2013]

[3] TelEduc Environment, "TelEduc - Distance Learning," available at <http://www.teleduc.org.br>. [retrieved: Jul. 2013]

[4] Ae Project. "Ae - Electronic Learning Environment," available at <http://tidia-ae.iv.org.br/>. [retrieved: Nov. 2013]

[5] A. C. da Silva, F. M. P. Freire, and H. V. da Rocha, "Identifying Cross-Platform and Cross-Modality Interaction Problems in e-Learning Environments," Proc. of 6th International Conference on Advances in Computer-Human Interactions (ACHI 2013), IARIA, February 2013, pp. 243-249.

[6] T. O'Reilly, "What Is Web 2.0 - Design Patterns and Business Models for the Next Generation of Software," available at <http://www.oreillynet.com/pub/a/oreilly/tim/news/2005/09/30/what-is-web-20.html>. [retrieved: Nov. 2013]

[7] C. Safran, D. Helic, and C. Gütl, "E-Learning practices and Web 2.0," Proc. of International Conference on Interactive Collaborative Learning (ICL 2007), Kassel University Press, Sep. 2007, pp. 1-8.

[8] R. Berjon, T. Leithead, E. D. Navara, E. O´Connor, and S. Pfeiffer, "HTML5 - A vocabulary and associated APIs for HTML and XHTML W3C Candidate Recommendation, " available at <http://www.w3.org/TR/html5/>. [retrieved: Nov. 2013]

[9] D. Schepers, S. Moon, M. Brubeck, and A. Barstow, "Touch Events" available at < http://www.w3.org/TR/touch-events/>. [retrieved: Nov. 2013]

[10] Y. Chee et al., "Ink Markup Language (InkML) W3C Recommendation," available at <http://www.w3.org/TR/InkML/> [retrieved: Nov. 2013].

[11] T. Underhill, "InkML JavaScript Library," available at <http://inkml.codeplex.com/>. [retrieved: Nov. 2013]

[12] T. Johson, "Handling Multi-touch and Mouse Input in All Browsers – IEBlog – Site Home – MSDN Blogs," available at < http://blogs.msdn.com/b/ie/archive/2011/10/19/handling-mu lti-touch-and-mouse-input-in-all-browsers.aspx> [retrieved: Nov. 2013].

[13] S. L. Oviatt, "Advances in Robust Multimodal Interface Design", in IEEE Computer Graphics and Applications, vol. 23, no. 5, Sep. 2003, pp. 62-68, doi: 10.1109/MCG.2003.1231179.

[14] L. Nigay and J. Coutaz, "A Generic Platform for Addressing the Multimodal Challenge". Proc. of 13th Conference on Human Factors in Computing Systems (SIGCHI 1995), ACM Press / Addison-Wesley Publishing Co., May 1995, pp. 98-105, doi: 10.1145/223904.223917.

[15] N. O. Bernsen, "Multimodality Theory", in D. Tzovaras (Ed.) Multimodal User Interfaces: From signal to interaction, Berlim, Alemanha: Springer-Verlag Berlin Heidelberg, 2008, pp. 5-28.

[16] B. Dumas, D. Lalanne, and S. Oviatt, "Multimodal Interfaces: A Survey of Principles, Models and Frameworks", in Human-Machine Interaction, D. Lalanne and J. Kohlas, Eds. Berlin: Springer Berlin / Heidelberg, 2009, pp. 3-26, doi: 10.1007/978-3-642-00437-7_1.

[17] D. Lalanne, B. Dumas, and S. Oviatt, "Fusion Engine for Multimodal Input: A Survey", in Proceedings of the 11th International Conference on Multimodal Interfaces (ICMI-MLMI´09), ACM Press, 2009, pp. 153-160, doi: 10.1145/1647314.1647343.

[18] T. Mayes, "The 'M' Word: Multimedia interfaces and their role in interactive learning systems", in Multimedia Interface Design in Education, A. D. N. Edwards and S. Holland, Eds. Berlin: Springer-Verlag, 1992, pp. 1-22, doi: 10.1007/978-3642-58126-7_1.

[19] A. Gruenstein, I. McGraw, and I. Badr, "The WAMI Toolkit for Developing, Deploying, and Evaluating Web-Accessible Multimodal Interfaces". Proc. of 10th International Conference on Multimodal Interfaces (ICMI 2008), ACM Press, Oct. 2008, pp. 141-148, doi: 10.1145/1452392.1452420.

[20] J. Ray. "Welcome to the blogosphere: The educational use of blogs". Kappa delta pi Record, 2006, pp. 175-177.

[21] A. C. da Silva, H. V. da Rocha, "InkBlog: A Pen-Based Blog Tool for e-Learning Environments," in Bridging Disciplinary Boundaries: Issues in Informing Science and Information Technology, vol. 10, May 2013, pp. 121-135.

[22] A. C. da Silva, "InkAnnotation: An Annotation Tool for E-Learning Environments," Proc. of The 2015 International Conference on e-Learning, e-Business, Enterprise Information Systems, and e-Government (EEE 2015), Universal Conference Management Systems & Support, July 2015, pp. 73-74.

[23] F. M. P. Freire, F. L. Arantes, A. C. da Silva, and L. E. L. Vascon, "Estudo de viabilidade de um Editor Multimodal: o que pensam os alunos?," Proc. of the XX Congreso Internacional de Informática Educativa (TISE 2015), v. 11, Universidad de Chile, Dec. 2015, pp. 109-119.

[24] F. L. Arantes, F. M. P. Freire, Jan Breuer, A. C. da Silva, R. C. A. de Oliveira, and L. E. L. Vascon, "Towards a Multisemiotic and Multimodal Editor", Journal of Computer Science & Technology, v. 17, n. 2, oct 2017, pp. 100-109.

[25] M. Ally and J. Prieto-Blázquez, "What is the future of mobile learning in education? Mobile Learning Applications in Higher Education", Revista de Universidad y Sociedad del Conocimiento (RUSC), v. 11, n. 1, 2014, pp. 142-151. DOI: http://dx.doi.org/10.7238/rusc.v11i1.2033.

Implementation Example with Ultra-Small PCs for Human Tracking System Based on Mobile Agent Technologies

Masaru Shiozuka[†‡], Tappei Yotsumoto[†‡],
Kenichi Takahashi[‡], Takao Kawamura[‡], Kazunori Sugahara[‡]

[†]System Engineering Department,
Melco Power Systems Co. Ltd.
Kobe, Japan
email: {Shiozuka.Masaru@zd, Yotsumoto.Tappei@zb}.MitsubishiElectric.co.jp

[‡]Graduate School of Engineering,
Tottori University
Tottori, Japan
email: {takahashi, kawamura, sugahara}@eecs.tottori-u.ac.jp

Abstract—**In order to take security measures and crime prevention measures, companies have introduced human monitoring systems. However, operators are required to monitor many devices, such as cameras and sensors to track suspicious persons. We have proposed an automatic human tracking system based on mobile agent technologies. In this paper, we propose an implementation example with Ultra-Small PCs for the human tracking system. By using this Ultra-Small PCs, it is possible to construct a low cost human tracking system that is highly extensible.**

Keywords-Human tracking; Mobile agent; Raspberry Pi; Beacon.

I. INTRODUCTION

In order to take security measures and crime prevention measures, companies have introduced human monitoring systems. Operators monitor suspicious persons using cameras and sensors. However, if the number of cameras and tracking targets increase, tracking all targets must be difficult. As a result, operators could lose targets.

We have proposed an automatic human tracking system based on mobile agent technologies [1][2]. This system tracks targets by mobile agents instead of operators. The automation of tracking persons can reduce the burden of tracking and the number of incorrect tracking instances. There is another usage example of this system, that is, this system can track customers' behavior in department stores or collect their movement information for marketing decisions.

This paper proposes an implementation example with Ultra-Small PCs for human tracking system based on mobile agent technologies. Due to the recent advances in Internet of Things (IoT) devices, the costs of these Ultra-Small PCs have been lower. These Ultra-Small PCs, such as Raspberry Pi [3], can connect to the Internet, equip many sensors and easily collaborate with each other. We consider that we can construct human tracking system with low cost and highly extensible by using these Ultra-Small PCs.

We evaluate our implementation by the correctness of human tracking. We introduce the system into a real-life office, where a target person walks around. Then we observe and see if mobile agents can track the person correctly.

The remainder of this paper is structured as follows. In Section II, we provide a survey of related works. Section III illustrates the overview of our human tracking system. Section IV explains an implementation example. In Section V, the implementation is evaluated. Concluding remarks are provided in Section VI.

II. RELATED WORK

[4] and [5] proposed the method that tracks persons by analyzing a shooting range of camera. We propose the method that tracks persons by using many sensors, and we illustrate the simple implementation of the algorithms. When the system tracks persons, the system uses a Beacon Tag to identify each person. The burden of carrying a Beacon Tag is smaller because the Beacon Tag is compact.

Correa [6] proposed the method that tracks a person by analyzing a received signal strength indication (RSSI) value. We propose the method that can easily extend the area of tracking persons by placing sensors depending on the size of the floor. In our system, each sensor only needs to know its neighbor relation sensors, that is, each sensor does not need to know where all sensors are placed. By constructing the system like this, it is easy to connect or disconnect to or from the network. Suwa [7] also proposed the method that tracks a person by using a RSSI value of Bluetooth Low Energy (BLE). The system sends a RSSI value to a database server and estimates the persons' positions. Our system does not need such servers.

Stefano [8] proposed the system that supports visitors to browse artworks in museums. The system presents the cultural information when visitors come close to the artworks. In order to track the persons, visitors need to wear wearable

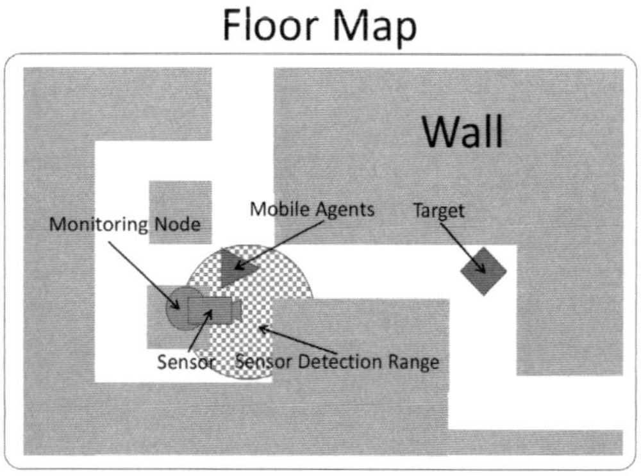

Figure 1. System Overview

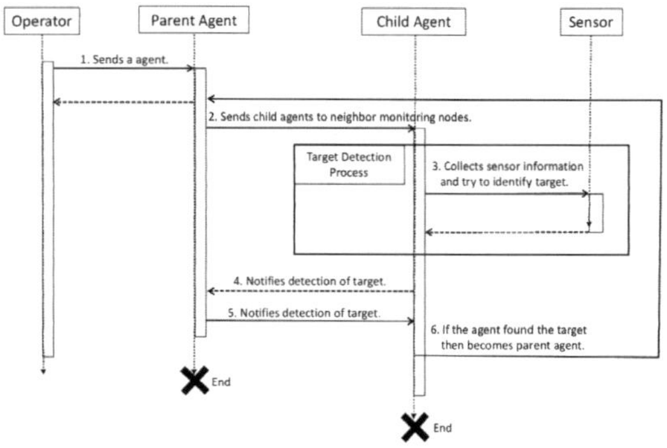

Figure 2. Human Tracking Algorithm

devices which collect the radio of Bluetooth and images of artworks.

In our system, the target person only needs to have the small Beacon Tag. Our system can keep the cost low even if the number of target persons increases because the Beacon Tag is compact and low price.

III. Human Tracking System Based on Mobile Agent Technologies

In this section, we explain the human tracking system in detail.

A. *System Overview*

Figure 1 shows our human tracking system overview. This system consists of the following elements.

- A Target is a person who is being tracked.
- A Sensor is a device which collects surrounding information and sends it to the connected monitoring node, that is, a Beacon receiver or a camera is a sensor. A sensor needs to be placed together with a monitoring node.
- A Sensor Detection Range is a range of detection which can track targets, such as a radio reception range or a camera's shooting range.

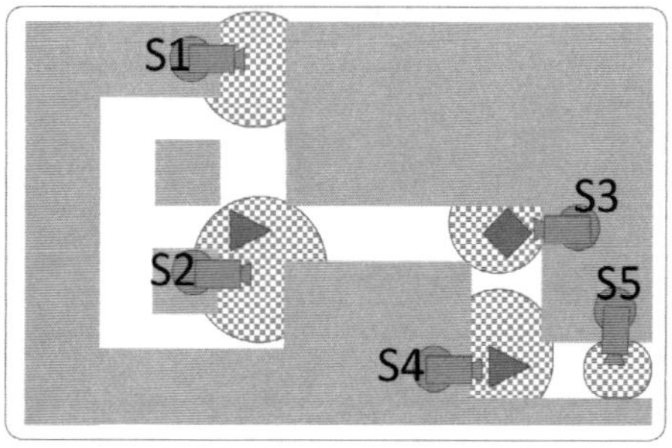

Figure 3. Example Of Neighbor Relations

- A Monitoring Node (referred to as a node) is a device which collects sensor information of Beacon Tags or cameras. The node constructs networks between each node.
  We define neighbor relations of each node. The node provides an execution environment for mobile agents.
- A Mobile Agent (referred to as an agent) is a program which identifies and tracks a person using sensor's information. An agent has features data (e.g., facial features, Beacon IDs) of a target person. A human tracking is implemented by moving an agent between nodes.

B. *Human Tracking Algorithm*

Figure 2 shows human tracking algorithm by using agents. A target is tracked using the following 6 steps.

1. In order to track a target, an operator sends an agent with feature data to the node where the target is.
2. When the agent arrives at the node, the agent creates its copies and sends them to other nodes. We define an original agent as a parent agent, and a copied agent as a child agent.
3. Child agents collect information from the node where they are sent. Each agent identifies persons using the sensor information and feature data. If it identifies a target person, it goes to step 4. If not, retries step 3 from head.
4. The child agent notifies the target detection to the parent agent.
5. The parent agent notifies the target detection to all child agents, and exits.
6. The child agent who detects the target becomes a new parent agent and goes to step 2, the other child agents exit. By repeating steps 1 to 6 agents can move nodes and automatically track the target.

C. *Neighbor Relations Of Nodes*

1) *Algorithm To Calculate Neighbor Nodes*

In order to move child agents between nodes, we define neighbor relations of nodes which a node has the possibility of passing next time. Child agents move to nodes based on these neighbor relations. For example, Figure 3 shows the floor map where S1 to S5 are placed. There are five nodes on this floor. Suppose a target person is in the S3 node, then the S2 and the S4 are only possible nodes that the target person passes next because the aisle from the S2 node to the S4 is a single road. Therefore, the neighbor relations of the S3 node are the S2 node and the S4 node. If the person passes the S1 node or S5 node, the person needs to pass the S2 node or the S4 node previously.

We define the algorithm to calculate relations between nodes. Defining vectors *S*, *B*, *D* and *P* as a set of node points, a set of branch points, a set of a sensor detection points and a set of all these points, respectively, we can obtain matrix *X* and *Y*, as $S{\times}P$, as $P \times P$, respectively. Here, matrix elements of *X* and *Y* are defined as follows:

$$X_{ij} = \begin{cases} 0, & \text{where the monitoring range of the camera } S_i \text{ does not include the point } P_j. \\ 1, & \text{where the monitoring range of the camera } S_i \text{ includes the point } P_j. \end{cases} \quad (1)$$

$$Y_{ij} = \begin{cases} 0, & \text{where the point } P_i \text{ and the point } P_j \text{ are not neighboring each other.} \\ 1, & \text{where the point } P_i \text{ and the point } P_j \text{ are neighboring each other.} \end{cases} \quad (2)$$

When $E_{ij} \geq 1$ in (3), the neighboring camera is overlapped with (n-1) points away from the monitoring range of the camera S_i.

$$E = X \bullet Y^n \bullet X^T \quad (3)$$

2) Neighbor Relations Localized Algorithm

In order to enhance the extension of neighbor relations, we define neighbor relations localized algorithm. By localizing the neighbor relation, each node does not need to know all the nodes on the floor but to know some nodes which have localized relationship. Matrix Xs_{ij} and Ys_{ij} are defined as follows.

$$Xs_{ij} = \begin{cases} 0, & \text{where the monitoring range of the camera } S_i \text{ does not include the point } Ps_j. \\ 1, & \text{where the monitoring range of the camera } S_i \text{ includes the point } Ps_j. \end{cases} \quad (4)$$

$$Ys_{ij} = \begin{cases} 0, & \text{where the point } Ps_i \text{ and the point } Ps_j \text{ are not neighboring each other.} \\ 1, & \text{where the point } Ps_i \text{ and the point } Ps_j \text{ are neighboring each other.} \end{cases} \quad (5)$$

Then, the neighbor nodes are calculated as follows.

$$Es = Xs \bullet Ys \bullet Xs^T \quad (6)$$

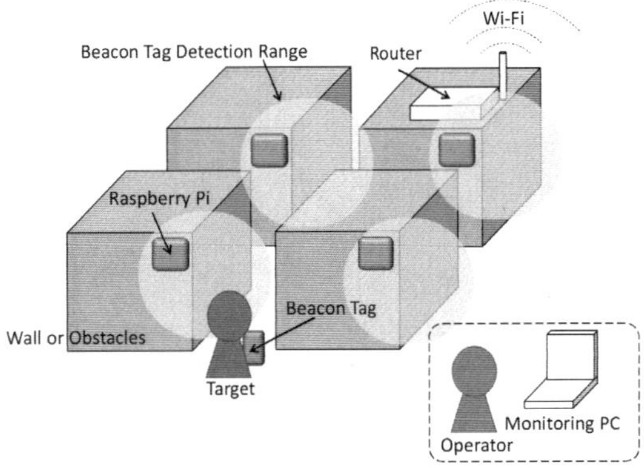

Figure 4. System Architecture

TABLE I. SYSTEM CONSTRUCT DEVICES

Raspberry Pi	
Machine model	Raspberry Pi 2 Model B
CPU	ARM Cortex-A7 900MHz
Memory	1GB RAM
OS	Raspbian GNU/Linux 8
Java	version 1.8.0
Bluetooth Dongle	PLANEX BT-Micro4
Wireless Wi-Fi Device	BUFFALO WLI-UC-GNM2
Beacon Tag	Aplix MB004
Monitoring PC	
OS	Windows7
Web Browser	IE11

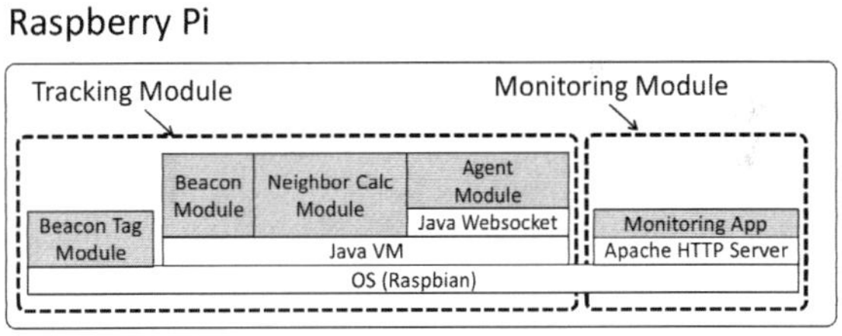

Figure 5. Software Architecture

IV. IMPLEMENTATION

In this section, we explain the implementation with Ultra-Small PCs of the human tracking system.

A. System Architecture

Figure 4 shows the system architecture. We use a Raspberry Pi as a node. One Raspberry Pi works one node. Table 1 shows the details of devices. Each Raspberry Pi is equipped with a Wireless Wi-Fi Device to connect to Wi-Fi and with a Bluetooth Dongle to receive the radio signal of the Bluetooth [9] from Beacon Tag which a target person has. Each node is connected to the router. We use the Bluetooth Dongle as a sensor. Our system can use a camera as a sensor. But we did not adopt camera systems because of their cost and their hard setting and managing points of view.

Moreover, by using cameras, privacy issues have to be considered. Finally, we use a monitoring PC to track the target persons.

B. Tracking Flow

The flow of tracking a person using this system architecture is as follows. Operators send an agent with feature data to the node where the target is. The feature data consist of a set of data, namely a person id and a Beacon Tag id. The person id identifies a person. A Beacon Tag id identifies a Beacon which the person has. When the person approaches a Raspberry Pi, the Bluetooth Dongle detects the person. The agent on the Raspberry Pi analyzes the radio of Bluetooth, and if the Beacon Tag id corresponds to the feature data, the agent judges that the person is the target.

C. Implementation Detail

Figure 5 shows the software architecture. There are two modules, as follows: the left-hand tracking module which is placed in all Raspberry Pi, and the right-hand monitoring module which is placed in an arbitrary Raspberry Pi.

1) Tracking Module

The tracking module implements the human tracking function. This module consists of four sub modules.

- The Beacon Tag Module implements a function that receives a radio signal from the Beacon Tag. We implemented it in C language and used BlueZ [10] whose open source projects provide Bluetooth stack protocol library. When this module receives a radio signal from the Bluetooth, it passes the radio signal to a Beacon Module.
- The Beacon Module is implemented in Java language and connects to a Beacon Tag module by TCP sockets and reads the radio signal of the Bluetooth.
- The Neighbor Calculation Module implemented in Java language obtains the neighbor relations and decides the destination where agents are sent to.
- The agent module is implemented in Java language and provides four functions as follows.
  - Sends a parent agent with the feature data to an arbitrary Raspberry Pi.
  - Identifies the target person by the radio signal of the Bluetooth from the Beacon Module.
  - Sends child agents based on the neighbor relations to the nodes. The child agents are serialized when they are sent, and de-serialized when they arrive at the next node.
  - Notifies the tracking information to the monitoring module by Websocket [11]. The tracking information consists of the agent status (parent or child), tracking human id, and its IP address.

2) Monitoring Module

The monitoring module is implemented in JavaScript and uses Websocket. This module shows the target person and child agents to the Web Browser on a floor map. To display the map, we use the Open Layers [12], which is an open source project map display library.

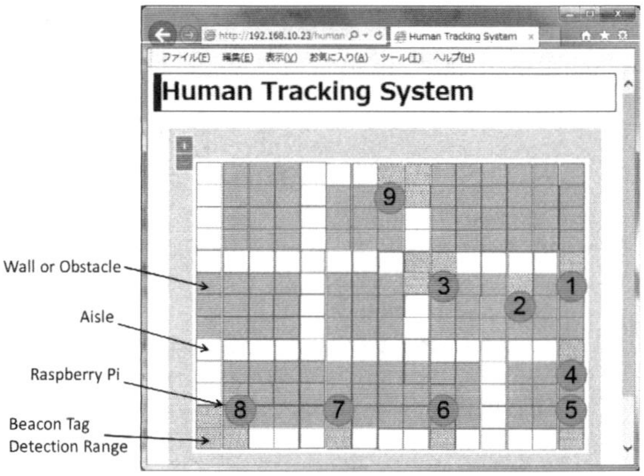

Figure 6. The Monitoring PC Web Browser

Figure 7. Example of installing a Raspberry Pi

TABLE II. NEIGHBOR RELATIONS OF NODES

Node Number	Neighbor Relation Nodes
1	2, 3
2	1, 3
3	1, 2, 4, 5, 6, 8, 9
4	3, 5, 6, 8, 9
5	3, 4, 6, 8, 9
6	3, 4, 5, 7, 8, 9
7	6, 8
8	3, 4, 5, 7, 9
9	3, 4, 5, 6, 8

V. EXPERIMENT

In this section, we evaluate our implementation of the human tracking system. We introduce the system into a real-life office.

A. Environment

Figure 6 shows the view of the monitoring PC using a Web browser. The map shows that it is one floor, the gray

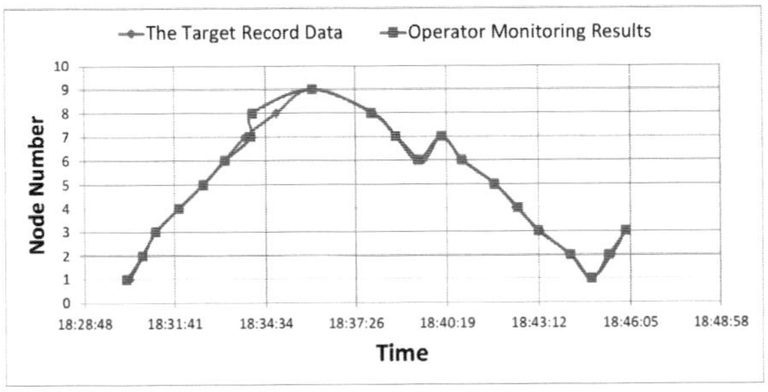

Figure 8. The First Experiment Result

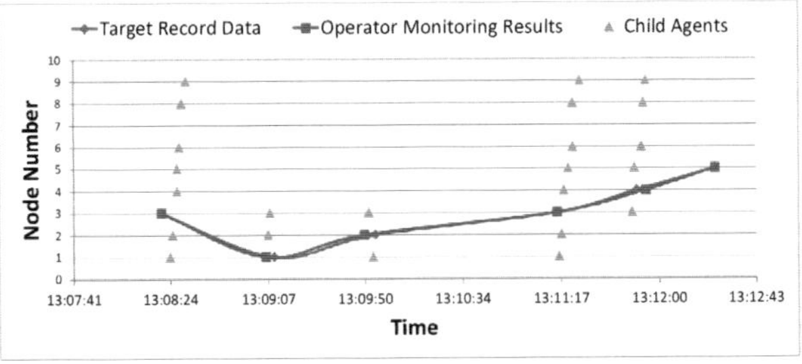

Figure 9. The Results Of Child Agents Moving

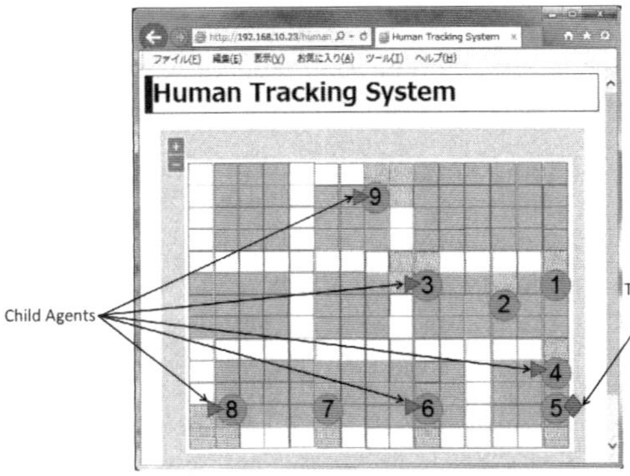

Figure 10. The Monitoring PC Web Browser at Node 5th

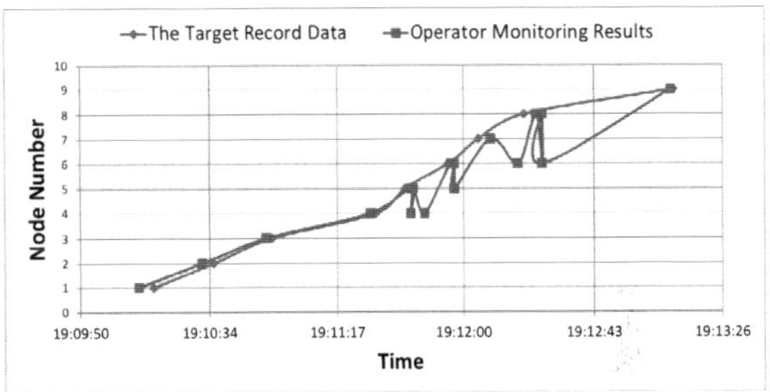

Figure 11. The Second Experiment Result

blocks are walls or obstacles, such as bookshelves or desks. The white blocks are aisles. The width and height of these blocks are about 2m. The horizontal length is about 30m, and the vertical length is about 25m. The green blocks are sensor detection areas. The numbers in the green circles are nodes (Raspberry Pi). Figure 7 shows an example of installation of a Raspberry Pi. The Raspberry Pi units are set on walls, bookshelves or desks. We set nine Raspberry Pi units on the floor and we set one router in the center of the floor. Table 2 shows the neighbor relation of nodes. For example, node number 1 has node neighbor relations with nodes number 2 and 3. Each Raspberry Pi unit is set more than 4 meters apart from other Raspberry Pi units.

B. Methods

The target person walks on the floor with a Beacon Tag. When the person passes the nodes, the person records the time and the node number. At the same time, the operator records the time and the node, watching the monitoring PC by using a Web browser. To compare both results, if the time and the position are close, the tracking by agents is correct.

In order to evaluate the correctness of tracking by agents, we conducted two kinds of experiments as follows.

1) First Experiment

The person walks slowly and stops for about 10 seconds to wait for the node to detect him.

2) Second Experiment

The person walks at normal pace.

C. Results

1) First Experiment Result

Figure 8 shows the result of the first experiment. The target person moved to the nodes as follows.

$$1\rightarrow2\rightarrow3\rightarrow4\rightarrow5\rightarrow6\rightarrow7\rightarrow8\rightarrow9\rightarrow8\rightarrow7\rightarrow6\rightarrow7\rightarrow6\rightarrow5\rightarrow4\rightarrow3\rightarrow2\rightarrow1\rightarrow2\rightarrow3$$

The first experiment shows that the agents were able to track the person correctly.

Moreover, we confirmed that the algorithm showed in Section II works correctly. Figure 9 shows the results of the sent child agents. The target person moved to the nodes as follows.

$$3\rightarrow1\rightarrow2\rightarrow3\rightarrow4\rightarrow5$$

The triangles in Figure 9 are the child agents. The child agents that line up vertically and correspond to the same time are the agents that are sent from the same parent agent previously. It can be seen that the human tracking worked correctly because the target moved to the nodes where the child agents were.

Figure 10 shows an example of the monitoring PC Web browser. The target was node 5. The rectangle at node 5 is the target person and the triangles at nodes 3, 4, 6, 8, 9 are the child agents.

2) Second Experiment Result

Figure 11 shows the result of the second experiment. The target person passed to nodes as follows.

$$1\rightarrow2\rightarrow3\rightarrow4\rightarrow5\rightarrow6\rightarrow7\rightarrow8\rightarrow9$$

The second experiment shows that the agents were able to track the person almost correctly. The monitoring result shows that it shifted a little on the way from the actual target positions. As the cause of these results, we consider that it is the timing when the child agent detected the target and made itself the new parent agent. Each agent communicates asynchronously. Therefore, when the new parent agent is invoked, the old parent still existed. As a result, the plural parents existed at the different nodes. For example, when the target was at node 5, the operator's monitoring results show that the target was at node 5 and at node 4. This means that the old parent agent was at node 4. In the next moment, the old parent agent exited asynchronously.

We consider that this is not a serious problem because the agent could track the person correctly in the end.

VI. CONCLUSION AND FUTURE WORK

This paper proposes an example of implementation using Ultra-Small PC Raspberry Pi for a human tracking system based on mobile agent technologies. We introduced the system to a real-life floor and evaluated the correctness of the implementation and tracking algorithms.

We have proposed the tracking method in the circumstance where some nodes are down or the sensor misses the tracking person [2]. In this paper, we evaluated the case that the person walks at a normal pace. However, when the person runs around, the sensor may not be able to detect the person. We are going to evaluate these methods and situations in the future.

In case when the nodes are placed very close, where the nodes are placed within 2 meters, the Beacon Tag is detected by these nodes at the same time. We need to manage this situation by changing the strength of the radio of Beacon Tag in the future.

REFERENCES

[1] T. Yotsumoto, K. Tanigawa, M. Tsuji, K. Takahashi, T. Kawamura, and K. Sugahara, "Automatic Human Tracking System using Localized Neighbor Node Cluculation," Sensors & Transducers, Vol. 194, No. 11, pp. 54-61, 2015.

[2] T. Yotsumoto, M. Shiozuka, K. Takahashi, T. Kawamura, and K. Sugahara, "Hidden neighbor relations to tackle the uncertainness of sensors for anautomatic human tracking," 2017 Second IEEE International Conference on Electrical, Computer and Communication Technologies (ICECCT 2017),. Coimbatore, India, pp. 690-696, 2017.

[3] Raspberry Pi, http://www.raspberrypi.org/, September, 2017.

[4] L. Wenxi, C. Antoni, L. Rynson, and M. Dinesh, "Leveraging long-term predictions and onlinelearning in agent-based multiple person tracking," IEEE Transactions on Circuits and Systems for Video Technology, 25.3, pp. 399-410, 2015.

[5] J. Rivera-Rubio, I. Alexiou, and A. A. Bharath, "Appearance-based indoor localization: A comparison of patch desciptor performance," Pattern Recognition Lettrs, Vol. 66, pp. 109-117, 2015.

[6] C. Alejandro, M. Antoni, B. Marc, and V. Jose, "Navigation system for elderly care applications based on wireless sensor networks," Signal Processing Conference (EUSIPCO 2012), Proceedings of the 20th European. IEEE, pp. 210-214, 2012.

[7] K. Komai, M. Fujimoto, Y. Arakawa, H. Suwa, Y. Kashimoto, and K. Yasumoto, "Elderly Prson Monitoring in Day Care Center using Bluettoth Low Energy," 10th International Symposium on Medical Information and Communication Technology (ISMICT 2016), Worcester, MA, USA, pp. 140-144, 2016.

[8] S. Alletto, R. Cucchiara, G. Del Fiore, L. Mainetti, V. Mighali, L. Patrono, and G. Serra, "An Inddor Location-Aware System for an IoT-Based Smart Museum." IEEE Internet of Things Journal, pp. 244-253, 2016.

[9] SIG Bluetooth. Core specication, https://www.bluetooth.com/specifications/bluetooth-core-specification, September, 2017.

[10] J. Beutel, and M. Krasnyanskiy, *Linux bluez howto: Bluetooth proto-col stack for linux*, http://www.tik.ee.ethz.ch/~jbeutel/pub/bluezhowto.pdf, September, 2017.

[11] I. Fette, and A. Melnikov, *The websocket protocol*, https://tools.ietf.org/html/rfc6455, September, 2017.

[12] OpenLayers, https://openlayers.org/, September, 2017.

Indoor Source Localization Using 2D Multi-Sensor Based Spatial Spectrum Fusion Algorithm

Taha Bouras[1], Di He[1], Wenxian Yu[1], Yi Zhang[2]
[1]Shanghai Key Laboratory of Navigation and Location-based Services,
Shanghai Jiao Tong University
Shanghai, P.R. China
E-mail: {tahatox, dihe, wxyu }@sjtu.edu.cn
[2]Huawei Technologies Co. Ltd.
Shanghai, P.R. China
E-mail: aaabear@huawei.com

***Abstract*— In a starving indoor environment where non-line of sight (NLOS) signals are strongly dominant, localization using traditional spatial spectrum estimation techniques easily fails due to low signal to noise ratio (SNR). Accordingly, in this paper, a novel 2-D multi-sensor Spatial Spectrum Fusion (2D-SSF) localization algorithm based on the multiple signal classification (MUSIC) method is proposed. The output data of each uniform rectangular array (URA) at each access point (AP) are first processed to get the noise subspace data. Then, after estimating the corresponding azimuth and elevation angles of each array using the MUSIC approach and finding the position of each point relative to each sensor in the search grid with the help of grid refinement algorithm, the parameters of interest of the target are estimated from a single spectrum that results from fusing all maximum noise subspaces where the position corresponding to the minimum error between the set of angles and every estimated point in the searching area is situated. Different simulation results of the proposed method in terms of RMSE as a function of SNR for various APs LOS/NLOS scenarios, the change in the number of antennas at each AP and the comparison with the MUSIC approach and the 1D localization based spatial spectrum fusion algorithm are carried out. The obtained results prove the significant performance of the proposed 2D-SSF localization algorithm with the strong presence of NLOS signals.**

Keywords—2-D Localization; Multi-Sensor; Spatial Spectrum Estimation Techniques; Data Fusion.

I. INTRODUCTION

In recent decades, the use of multi-sensor data fusion [1] for the purpose of localization has become a fundamental problem in modern signal processing and it has found wide applications in radar, sonar, wireless communications and acoustics [2][3].

In general, the localization of sources using multiple stations based spatial spectrum information at known locations is achieved by first exploiting the spatial information at each base station in order to estimate the direction of arrival (DOA) of the sources by employing an efficient direction finding (DF) estimator algorithm, such as the well-known Multiple signal classification (MUSIC) algorithm [4] .Then, the set of data (DOAs) will be sent to the fusion center where the positions of the sources are determined based on the appropriate approach in the fusion decision center like triangulation (e.g., as used in [5] and [6]) or other techniques that have been proposed in the literature [7].

However, in rush indoor environment, the propagation of the source signal is strongly attenuated by reflection when it hits the surface of an obstacle, which results in the high existence of NLOS signals arriving at the receiver through different paths. This multipath effect is even more severe where a ceiling, equipment, floor, and walls are present. Thus, the performance of the localization methods mentioned before is degraded under such starving environment with low SNR.

To overcome this problem, different methods have been proposed in the literature. In [8], the author proposed the use of the nonlinear PSO optimization algorithm to find the position of the target after the fusion process for a single moving array. A hybrid localization approaches with data fusion, like the employment of TOA/TDOA in [9]. There has also been comprehensive research work centering on fusion frameworks that rely on heterogeneous information, such as the proposed "MapSentinel" tracking system, which performs non-intrusive location sensing based on WiFi access points and ultrasonic sensors [10]. A system that exploits the acoustic properties of the room named as "SoundLoc" in [11] and indoor CO2 concentration based on the sensing by proxy methodology [12].

But, according to many previous types of research that rely on WiFi wireless network based indoor localization, to simplify the research conditions, such as time consumption and computation complexity, the arrays at the receiver sides were considered to be uniform linear array (ULA) geometry, which reduces the accuracy of the localization problem certainly in very low SNR.

In this paper, 2-D multi-sensor Spatial Spectrum Fusion (2D-SSF) localization algorithm based on WIFI signals is used for indoor localization. In the proposed work, the subspace-based MUSIC algorithm is used to estimate the azimuth and elevation angles at each URA array at the receiver side. Then, depending on known search grid dimension, 2D spectrum fusion process at the fusion center is used to estimate the DOAs or the coordinates of the target position.

The remainder of this paper is organized as follows: In Section II, we present the data model and we formulate the main problem. The proposed 2D spatial spectrum fusion algorithm is demonstrated in Section III. Thereafter, in Section IV, different simulation results of the RMSE of the proposed method as a function of SNR are carried out for various APs LOS/NLOS scenarios, the change in the number of antennas at each AP and the comparison with the MUSIC approach and the 1D localization based spatial spectrum fusion algorithm used in [13]. The paper is concluded in Section V.

II. Data Model And Problem Formulation

Consider an indoor environment composed of P Access point (AP) each has URA geometry with M= $N_x \times N_y$ number of antennas impinged by Q multi-path source signal in the far field of the antenna array, see Figure 1. Suppose that the direction of the waves is Φ and Θ. Then, the received signal at the p-th AP, with $p = 1,\dots,P$ is given by:

$$X_p(t) = A_p(\Phi,\Theta)S(t) + N_p(t) \quad (1)$$

Also is equal to

$$X_p(t) = a_p(\Phi_p,\Theta_p) * S_p(t) + \sum_{k=1}^{Q} \gamma_k(t)\ a_p(\Phi_k,\Theta_k)\ S_p(t-\tau_k) + N_p(t) \quad (2)$$

Where; S(t) is the source signal, $\gamma_k(t) = \alpha_k e^{-j2\pi f_c \tau_k}$. α_k, f_c, τ_k, Φ_k, Θ_k, Φ_p, Θ_p are the correlation coefficient, carrier frequency, delay of travel time, azimuth and elevation angles of the k-th multipath signal with k = 1, 2,..., Q, azimuth and elevation angles of the direct signal respectively. N(t) is white Gaussian additive noise with mean 0 and variance σ^2. $a_p(\Phi,\Theta) \in ₵^{M\times P}$ is the steering vector of the URA at each receiver point. We can observe from (2) that the received signal at each array consists of direct path signals and multipath signals. So, the transfer vector corresponding to the LOS signal at the p-th array is equal to:

$$a_p(\Phi_p,\Theta_p) = \left[1\ \ e^{j\frac{2\pi}{\lambda}\Delta_{(p,2)}}\ \ e^{j\frac{2\pi}{\lambda}\Delta_{(p,3)}}\ \dots\dots\dots\ e^{j\frac{2\pi}{\lambda}\Delta_{(P,M-1)}}\right]^T \quad (3)$$

Here, $(.)^T$ denotes the transpose operator, where the inter-element delay $\Delta_{(p,m)}$ is given by:

$$\Delta_{(p,m)} = e^{j\frac{2\pi}{\lambda}(m-1)\, d_x\, \sin(\Theta_p)\cos(\Phi_p)} + e^{j\frac{2\pi}{\lambda}(m-1)\, d_y\, \sin(\Theta_p)\sin(\Phi_p)} \quad (4)$$

In general, the steering matrix corresponding to the direct path signals can be expressed as:

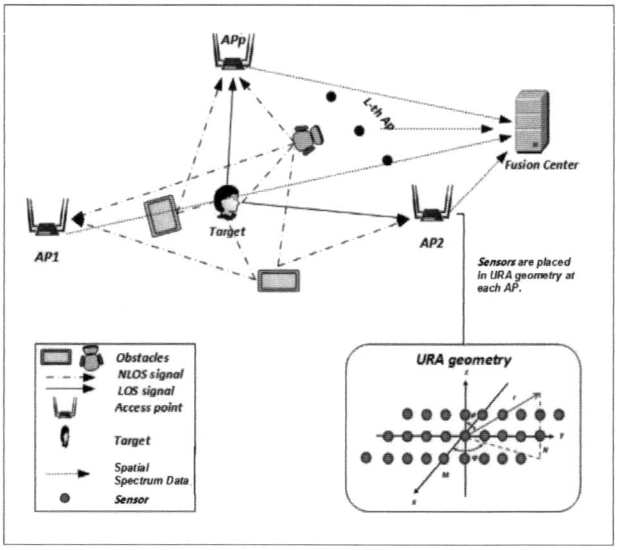

Figure 1. 2D-Multi-sensor spatial spectrum fusion target localization in an indoor environment.

$$A_s(\Phi,\Theta) = [a_1(\Phi_1,\Theta_1)\ a_2(\Phi_2,\Theta_2) \dots\dots\dots\ a_p(\Phi_p,\Theta_p)] \quad (5)$$

However, for simplicity, we can obtain the steering matrix corresponding to the NLOS signals from [14].

Our task is to estimate the position of the target p using the spatial spectrum fusion (SSF) approach starting from estimating the azimuth and elevation of each URA, i.e., two-dimensional search, based on the observations obtained from (2) under an environment mixed with LOS and NLOS signals. It can be briefly demonstrated in Figure 1.

III. Localization Algorithm

A. Spatial spectrum estimation for every array

A.1 Construct the covariance matrix

The first step is to construct the covariance matrix of the received spatial data at each array and then decompose it into signal and noise subspaces. At a certain array p, the covariance matrix of the observed data $X_p(t)$ can be expressed as:

$$R_{X_p} = \frac{1}{L} X_p(t) {X_p}^H(t) \in ₵^{M\times M} \quad (6)$$

$$= U_p \Sigma_p {U_p}^H = [{U_p}^{(s)} {U_p}^{(n)}]\, \Sigma_p [{U_p}^{(s)} {U_p}^{(n)}]^H \quad (7)$$

Here, $(.)^H$ symbolizes to the Hermitian Transpose.

${U_p}^{(s)} \in ₵^{M\times 1}$ denotes the eigenvector spanning the signal subspace.

${U_p}^{(n)} \in ₵^{M\times M-1}$ denotes the eigenvector spanning the noise subspace.

$\Sigma_p \in \mathbb{C}^{M\times M}$ is a diagonal matrix containing the decreasing order of the associated eigenvalues.

A.2 MUSIC algorithm

After obtaining the covariance matrix, DOA based subspace estimation method is used to estimate the spatial spectrum of each array. Here, we use the MUSIC algorithm due to its reliable performance compared to the traditional spatial spectrum estimation algorithms certainly in low SNR [15]. The power spectrum of the MUSIC algorithm is given by:

$$P_p(\Phi, \Theta) = \frac{1}{\text{norm}\,[A^H(\Phi,\Theta)\, U_p^{(n)}]} \quad (8)$$

The used MUSIC algorithm explores the searching area ($-\pi < \Phi < \pi$) and ($0 < \Theta < \pi$) to look around the spectrum peak of (8) where the azimuth and elevation of each URA is located.

B. Spatial spectrum fusion

B.1 Calculate the set of angles of each position p in the search grid

Before starting the data fusion procedure, the fusion center needs to know the position of each point relative to each sensor in the search grid. The search grid is set to vary between $(x_{g_0}, y_{g_0}, z_{g_0})$ and $(x_{g_f}, y_{g_f}, z_{g_f})$. Assuming that the reference AP is placed in the position $G_0(x_0, y_0, z_0)$ where the p-th sensor array coordinates is $G_p(x_p, y_p, z_p)$ proportional to the reference sensor in the search grid. The set of each angle in the whole scanning grid corresponding to each array can be calculated as follows:

for $i=x_{g_0}: x_{g_f}$
for $j=y_{g_0}: y_{g_f}$
for $l=z_{g_0}: z_{g_f}$

$$set\_\Phi_p = \arctan\frac{y_j - y_p}{x_i - x_p} \quad (9)$$

$$set\_\Theta_p = \arccos\frac{z_l - z_p}{\Delta r_p} \quad (10)$$

$$\Delta r_p = \sqrt{(x_i - x_p)^2 + (y_j - y_p)^2 + (z_l - z_p)^2} \quad (11)$$

end
end
end

Where Δr_p is the distance between the p-th sensor and the i-th position of the grid.

B.2 Spectrum Fusion

From (9) and (10), we can observe that the set of angles set_Φ_p and set_Θ_p represents matrices that contain the azimuth and elevation angles for all possible points in the search grid corresponding to the position of each AP.

Now, the target position estimating problem comes down to find the maximum of the spectrum, which is a combination of spatial spectrums of (8) $(P_1(p), P_2(p), \ldots, P_P(p))$, where the position coinciding to the minimum error between each estimated point in the search grid and every angle in the searching area ($-\pi < \rho < \pi$) is situated.

The target position estimation can be expressed by the following formula:

$$p_{target_{est}} = \arg\max_{p}\left\{\arg\min_{p}\left(\sum_{p=1}^{P} P_p\left(P_{err_{\Phi_p}}, P_{err_{\Theta_p}}\right)\right)\right\} \quad (12)$$

$$P_{err_{\Phi_p}} = \text{abs}\left(set_{\Phi_p} - \Phi_\rho\right) \le \varepsilon \quad (13)$$

$$P_{err_{\Theta_p}} = \text{abs}\left(set_{\Theta_p} - \Theta_\rho\right) \le \varepsilon \quad (14)$$

Where $P_{err_{\Phi_p}}$ and $P_{err_{\Theta_p}}$ are the errors between each set position and every azimuth and elevation angles respectively in the searching area. ε is the threshold. The 2D-SSF can be generalized along the lines shown in Figure 2.

1. ***Compute the covariance matrix of the observed spatial output data at each sensor using (6).***
2. ***Decompose (1) into signal and noise subspaces using (7).***
3. ***Use MUSIC algorithm in (8) to get the azimuth and elevation angles of each array.***
4. ***Calculate the set of each position p in the search grid.***
   for $i=x_{g_0}: x_{g_f}$
   for $j=y_{g_0}: y_{g_f}$
   for $l=z_{g_0}: z_{g_f}$
   $set\_\Phi_p =$ ***Use (9)***
   $set\_\Theta_p =$ ***Use (10)***
   with Δr_p ***in (11)***
   end
   end
   end
5. ***Transfer the obtained data to the fusion center and compute the minimum errors between each set position and every azimuth and elevation angles respectively in the searching area using (13) and (14).***
6. ***Get the position of the target using (12).***

Figure 2. The 2D-SSF procedures needed for target positioning.

IV. SIMULATION RESULTS AND DISCUSSION

We consider an indoor environment with dimensions length=20m, width=20m and height=20m contain four APs such that each consists of 4 antenna arrays with half wavelength distance and uniform rectangular geometry is placed inside. The reference sensor is positioned at $A_1(0,0,0)$ whereas the remaining three sensors placed at $A_2(20,0,0)$, $A_3(0,20,0)$ and $A_4(20,20,20)$.The position of the target is P (11, 20, 5) and the number of multipath signals Q= 6. Some obstacles are taken to be placed in the middle of the AP and the target such that no LOS signal exists whereas the others are placed away from the middle. SNR = 5 dB and the sample number is set to be 200 samples. All simulation results obtained using MATLAB R2015a.

Firstly, we consider the case where all APs are able to see the target directly, i.e., the LOS signal between the source signal and each array exists. From Figure 3, the resulting angles (Φ, Θ) of each array are (76.6°, 60.8°), (-3.2°, 23°.4), (-51.8°, 66.4°) and (-0.4°, 120.8°). Compared with the actual angles in Figure 3, the highest error difference between the azimuth ones is in array 2 (about 3 degrees difference) whereas almost 1 degrees error difference in elevation corresponding to array1 and this can improve the additional support of the elevation angle for more target position estimation accuracy during the application of the fusion process.

Figure 4 presents spectrums resulted from the fusion of the spatial spectra of Figure 3. The maximum values of the obtained spectra represent the estimated position of the source signal. From the left side of Figure 4, we can observe that the obtained horizontal coordinates are 10.4 m and 19.4 m while the vertical position (height) of the target is 5.2 m

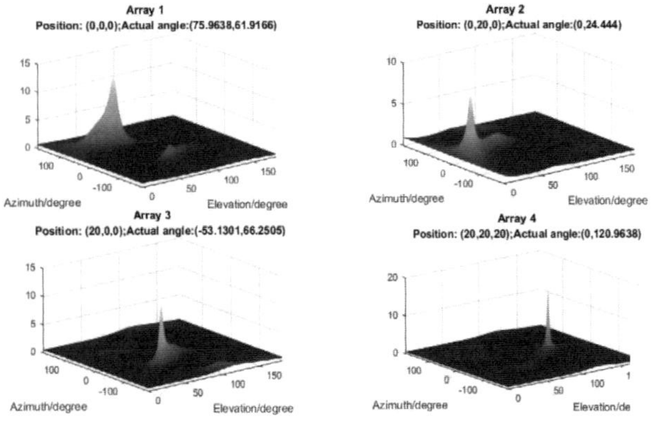

Figure 3. Music spectrums for the four arrays, SNR=5 dB, N=4 antennas.

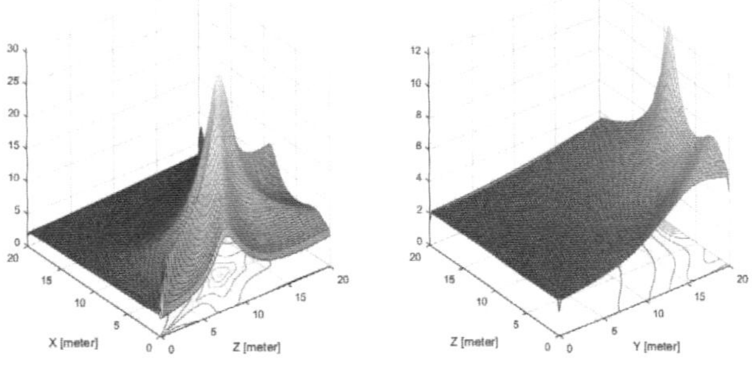

Figure 4. The estimated (x,y,z) coordinates of the target position using the 2D-SSF method. SNR=5 dB, N=4 antennas.

according to the right part of Figure 4. Compared to the actual location of the source (11, 20, and 5) m, the location estimation error is reliable thus can prove the important localization accuracy achievement of the 2D-SSF algorithm certainly in Low SNR.

Now we examine the performance of the 2D-SSF in terms of root mean square error (RMSE) in different LOS and NLOS scenarios (Figure 5). 50 Monte Carlo simulations were carried out. We observe that the RMSE decreases with the increasing number of the LOS APs. For low SNR (-10 dB) the RMSE of the 5 cases varies between 2 and 2.5 meters whereas in high SNR (20 dB) the localization performance improved until 0.1373 m error when the LOS signals can be seen by the whole APS whilst the difference gap between the first and the last case is still reliable (almost 1 meter). When a group of arrays is disorganized with the NLOS signals, the aid of the Aps, which consider the LOS signal is used, we can remark that for the cases of 1AP LOS, 2AP LOS and 3AP LOS with RMSE below than 1 meter and this gives an important point in real applications when a couple of WiFi systems are blocked with massive obstacles, so the placement of the APS should be reliable such that the chance of the LOS signal between the WiFi systems and the user would be dominant.

In order to compare the performance of the 2D-SSF with the traditional approaches, we test the estimation of angles relative to each antenna arrays by using the classical MUSIC algorithm and the 2D-SSF algorithm in terms of RMSE. We consider the case where the target is able to be seen by 2 APs. According to Figure 6, it is obvious that the advocated method outperforms the MUSIC algorithm. From SNR= -10dB to SNR= 20 dB, the RMSE for 2D-SSF decreases slightly and tend to 0 dB in very high SNR while although the SNR is high the MUSIC method cannot give reliable angles estimation for both azimuth and elevation (about 3° error) and this is due to the NLOS environment. Moreover, the error estimation for angles of the 2D-SSF in low SNR (2.5°, 2.1°) is even better than

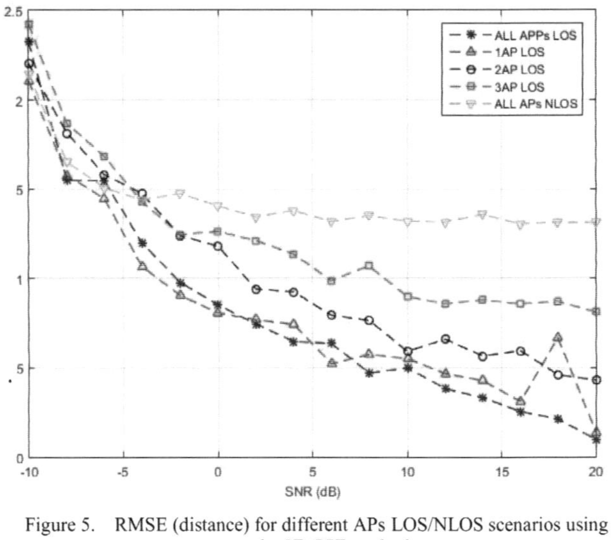

Figure 5. RMSE (distance) for different APs LOS/NLOS scenarios using the 2D-SSF method.

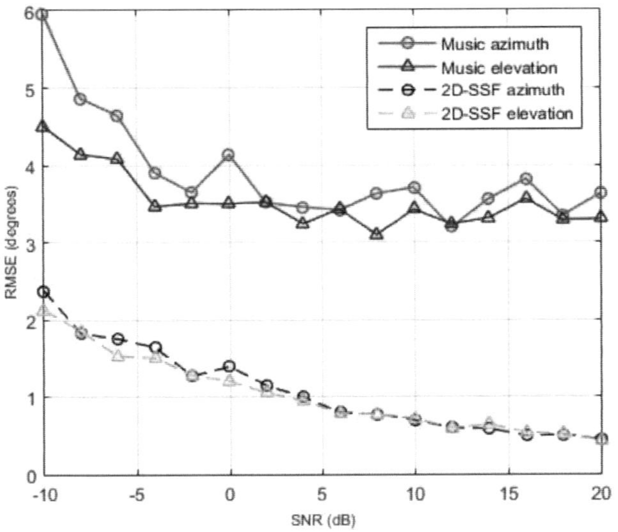

Figure 6. Angles (azimuth and elevation) estimation comparison between MUSIC and the 2D-SSF method.

the estimation of the MUSIC in High SNR (3.4°, 3.1°).

The outperformance of the advocated method is represented in the usage of multi-sensor in addition of that the estimation of the elevation angles of each array that enhance the accuracy of the location of the sensor, hence, the target position.

Here, the performance of the 2D-SSF approach is tested according to the change in the number of antennas at the sensors. The same situation for the target and the sensors is taken as before. It is evident from Figure 7 that the increase in the number of antennas at each AP gives a significant enhancement for the target localization. At SNR=-10 dB there is a considerable decrease in the estimated distance error from 2.3 meters using 4 antennas to 0.7 meters using 16 antennas While the RMSE for using 16 antennas tends to 0 meters at high SNR.

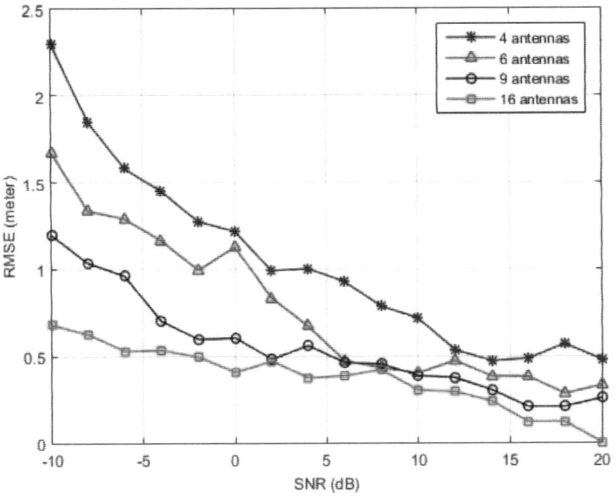

Figure 7. RMSE (distance) for a different number of antennas at each sensor using the 2D-SSF method.

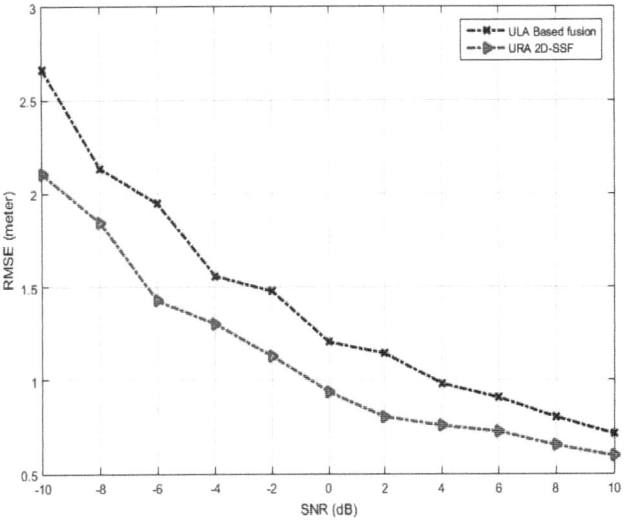

Figure 8. Comparison between ULA based fusion method [13] and the 2D-SSF localization method.

In the final part, the 2D-SSF is compared with the 1-D localization algorithm based fusion method used in [10]. We use the same parameters for the two algorithms during the source location estimation process. According to Figure 8, the change in the geometry of antennas to the 2-D array at each AP results in considerable enhancement of the error difference between the RMSE of the two used algorithms such that in SNR=-10 dB the difference error between the two curves is about 56 centimeters. However, the performance of the two methods attends to be the same as the SNR is higher, obviously, when SNR=10 dB the difference in error reaches 20 centimeters.

V. CONCLUSION

In this paper, 2D multiple sensors based on spatial spectrum fusion estimation algorithm was investigated. Under an indoor environment, the use of multiple sensors with the proposed fusion method in addition of that the change in the geometry of the antennas to URA at each sensor gave a significant improvement in source localization. Simulation results showed that the performance of the 2D-SSF method can be changed according to the used number of antennas at each sensor, the placement of the APs in the monitoring area, and the selected SNR. Moreover, the considerable outperformance of the 2D-SSF compared with traditional and 1-D based source localization methods has been proved.

As future work, the proposed algorithm will be implied to the real environments along with real data and extra massive obstacles, which can lead to the elimination of most LOS signals. Also, the modification of the 2D-SSF might be done by considering the Time of Arrive (TOA) based localization approach for more positioning accuracy.

ACKNOWLEDGMENT

This research work is supported by the Important National Science and Technology Specific Project of China under Grant No. 2016ZX03001022-006, the Shanghai Science and Technology Committee under Grant No. 16DZ1100402, and the National Natural Science Foundation of China under Grant No. 91438113.

REFERENCES

[1] D. L. Hall and J. Llinas, "An introduction to multisensor data fusion," Proceedings of the IEEE, vol. 85, no. 1, pp. 6–23, 1997.

[2] J. Prieto and A. Bahillo, "Adaptive Data Fusion for Wireless Localization in Harsh Environments," IEEE Transactions on Signal Processing. vol. 16, no.04, pp. 1585 - 1596., April 2012.

[3] G. Mirzaei, M. M. Jamali, and J. Ross, "Data Fusion of Acoustics, Infrared, and Marine Radar for Avian Study," IEEE Sensors Journal. vol. 15, no.11, pp. 6625 - 6632., Nov. 2015.

[4] R. O. Schmidt, "Multiple emitter location and signal parameter estimation," IEEE Trans. on Antenna Propagation, vol. 34, no. 3,March 1986, pp. 276-280.

[5] J. Caffery and G. Stuber, "Overview of Radiolocation in CDMA cellular systems," IEEE Commun. Mag., vol. 36, pp. 38–45, Apr.1998.

[6] J. I. Xiu, Y. He, and G. H. Wang, "Constellation of Multi-sensors in Bearing-only Location System," Radar, Sonar and Navigation, IEE Proceedings, Vol. 152, No.3, pp.215-218, 2005.

[7] F. Gustafsson and F. Gunnarsson, "Mobile positioning using wireless networks: Possibilities and fundamental limitations based on available wireless network measurements," IEEE Signal Process. Mag., vol.22, pp 41–53, July 2005.

[8] Z. Huang and J. Wu, "Multi-Array Data Fusion Based Direct Position Determination Algorithm," 2014 Seventh International Symposium on Computational Intelligence and Design.pp.121-124. China. 2014.

[9] R. Reza, "Data fusion for improved TOA/TDOA position determination in wireless systems," Ph.D. dissertation, Virginia Tech., Blacksburg, VA, 2000.

[10] R. Jia, et al., "MapSentinel: Can the Knowledge of Space Use Improve Indoor Tracking Further?, ", Sensors 2016, 16, 472.

[11] R Jia, M. Jin, Z. Chen and C.J. Spanos, "SoundLoc: Accurate Room-level Indoor Localization using Acoustic Signatures," 2015 IEEE International Conference on Automation Science and Engineering (CASE). Gothenburg, Sweden, pp. 186 – 193.

[12] M. Jin, N. Bekiaris-Liberis, K. Weekly, C. Spanos and A. Bayen, "Sensing by Proxy: Occupancy Detection Based on Indoor CO2 Concentration," The 9th International Conference on Mobile Ubiquitous Computing, Systems, Services and Technologies (UBICOMM'15), July 2015, pp. 1-10, ISSN: 2308-4278, ISBN: 978-1-61208-418-3

[13] M. K. Choudhary et al., "DOA Estimation And Localization Using Multi-Base Station Spatial Spectrum Fusion," ION GNSS+, 2017. Manuscript in press.

[14] Mohammad Sajjadieh and Amir Asif, "Uniform Rectangular Time Reversal Arrays: Joint Azimuth And Elevation Estimation," IEEE, 2012, Statistical Signal Processing Workshop (SSP). Ann Arbor, MI, USA, pp. 89-92, 2012.

[15] X. Wang and H. Wang, " Study on Data Fusion Technology in the Field of Spatial Signal Processing," International Conference on Electronics, Communications, and Control (ICECC), Ningbo, China, pp. 4531 – 4533, 2011.

Probabilistic CCRN: Reliability Analysis of Ubiquitous Computing Scenarios Using Probabilistic Model Checking

Reona Minoda, Masakazu Ishihata and Shin-ichi Minato

Graduate School of Information Science and Technology
Hokkaido University
Sapporo, Hokkaido 060–0814, Japan
Email: minoda@meme.hokudai.ac.jp, {ishihata.masakazu, minato}@ist.hokudai.ac.jp

Abstract—**This paper proposes the method of reliability analysis of ubiquitous computing (UC) scenarios. In UC scenarios, various devices communicate with each other through wireless network, and this kind of communications sometimes break due to external interferences. To discuss the reliability in such situation, we introduce the notion of probability into *context catalytic reaction network* (CCRN), which is a description model of UC scenarios. This enables us to conduct quantitative analyses such as considerations of a trade-off between the reliability of UC scenarios and the costs which may be necessary for their implementations. To conduct a reliability analysis of UC scenarios, we use the technique of probabilistic model checking. We also evaluate our method experimentally by conducting a case study using a practical example assuming a museum.**

Keywords–Ubiquitous Computing; Catalytic Reaction Network; Probabilistic Model Checking; Smart Object.

I. INTRODUCTION

Nowadays, we are surrounded with various kinds of devices with computation and communication capabilities and we carry these devices every day. In this paper, we call these devices *"smart objects (SO)"*. SOs include personal computers (PCs), mobile phones, sensor devices, embedded computers and radio frequency identifier (RFID) tags. But we can also treat physical things like foods, medicine bottles and cups as SOs by embedding RFID tags in those. Here, we use the term *federation* to denote the definition and execution of interoperation among resources that accessible either through the Internet or through peer-to-peer ad hoc communication. For example, let us consider that there are a phone, a medicine bottle and food, and RFID tags are embedded in a medicine bottle and food. Imagine that this food and the medicine have a harmful effect when eaten together. If all these things are close to each other, a phone rings to inform a user to *warn not eat them together*. This phenomenon is a federation. Indeed, we can also consider federations related to other SOs and these federation may be involved in each other. We call these federation *"ubiquitous computing application scenarios (UC scenario)"* (see Figure 1).

In our previous works, we showed an approach to verify UC scenarios by proposing context catalytic reaction network (CCRN) and its verification through model checking [1]. We also proposed more efficient method of this kind of verifications through symbolic model checking [2]. These contributions enabled us to verify the property of UC scenario, which is described in formal logic formulation and these verifications

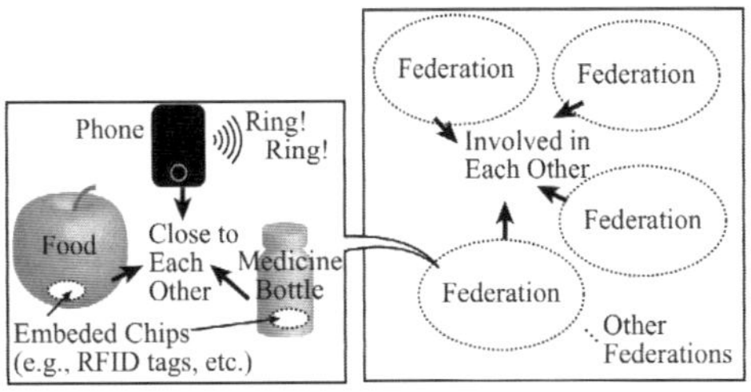

Figure 1. Example of Ubiquitous Computing Application Scenario

are conducted systematically thanks to various model checking verifiers, such as NuSMV2 [3].

However, there are still challenges of our approach. For example, UC scenarios are assumed that SOs typically communicate with each other by the wireless communication. This means that we need to consider these communications sometimes break due to various external causes. For this reason, it is important to discuss this kind of interference formally. In this paper, we show an approach to reliability analysis of UC scenarios by introducing a notion of probability to CCRN, which is a description model of UC scenarios. To analyze this kind of reliability, we use the technique of probabilistic model checking [4].

The rest of this paper is organized as follows. Section 2 introduces related works of our research. Section 3 provides preliminaries of this paper, such as basic definitions and notations including CCRN and probabilistic model checking. Using them, we introduce a notion of probability to CCRN in Section 4. In Section 5, we propose the method of reliability analysis of probabilistic CCRN using probabilistic model checking. Then, we evaluate our approach by conducting the case study assuming a practical scenario in Section 6. Finally, we conclude our contributions in Section 7.

II. RELATED WORKS

In this section, we introduce related works of our work.

A. *Reconfigurable hardware verification for Ubiquitous Systems*

In the field of implementations for ubiquitous systems, Guellouz, et al. use probabilistic model checking to verify the behavior of devices [5]. These devices have reconfigurable function blocks, which is standardized as IEC 61499 and a

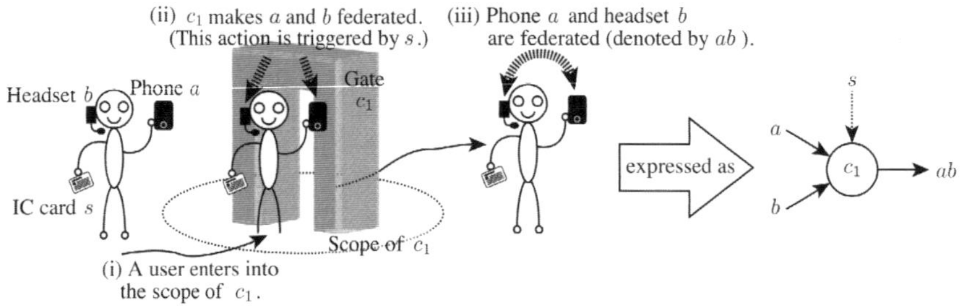

Figure 2. Example of a Catalytic Reaction

part of each blocks behaves probabilistically. Guellouz, et al. analyzed this behavior by using probabilistic model checking.

B. Formal Verification of Cyber Physical Systems

Similarly to ubiquitous computing, a lot of devices, such as sensors measure physical phenomena, such as temperature, humidity, acceleration and so on, while actuators manipulate the physical world, like in automated robots. The combination of an electronic system with a physical process is called cyber physical system (CPS). In the field of CPS, Drechsler and Kühne use *timed automata* [6] as a state transition model to conduct formal verifications of given systems' properties [7].

C. Context Inconsistency Detection

In the field of ambient computing, Xu and Cheung propose a method of context inconsistency detection [8]. This method detects inconsistencies from a series of gathered events, such as "a user entered a room" and "the temperature of room is 30°C" by logical deduction. Unlike a formal verification, this method can be applied only after the system begins to work. Instead, a formal verification can find the failed cases from a given system *in advance*.

III. PRELIMINARIES

In this section, we give definitions and notations which is necessary for this paper.

A. Basic Definitions and Notation

Let X and Y be any two sets, we use $X \cup Y$, $X \cap Y$ and $X \setminus Y$ to denote the union, intersection and difference of X and Y respectively. For a set X, we denote its power set (i.e., all subsets) by 2^X and its cardinality by $|X|$. For a set X, we denote a set of k-elements subsets of X by $\binom{X}{k}$. For a family M of sets (i.e., a set of sets), we denote the union and the intersection of all sets in M by $\bigcup M$ and $\bigcap M$ respectively. Let X be a set, we denote a set of all set partitions of X by $\mathfrak{P}(X)$. For example, given $X = \{1, 2\}$, we have $\mathfrak{P}(X) = \{\{\{1\}, \{2\}\}, \{\{1, 2\}\}\}$.

B. Catalytic Reaction Network

A catalytic reaction network is originally proposed by Stuart Kauffman in the field of biology to analyze protein metabolism [9]. Based on this model, Tanaka applied it to the field of ubiquitous computing as the way to describe an application scenario involving mutually related multiple federations among SOs [10]. In this paper, we mean the latter by the term "catalytic reaction network".

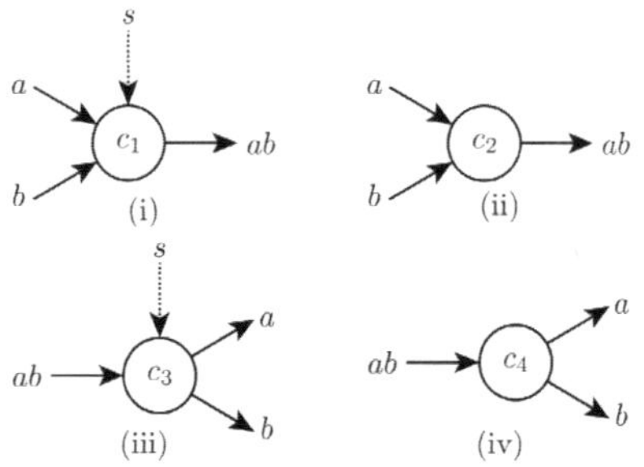

Figure 3. Four Types of a Catalytic Reactions

A catalytic reaction network is a set of catalytic reactions. Each catalytic reaction takes input materials and transforms them into output materials. And each catalytic reaction has a catalyst which is called *context*. It may be also possible to include a catalyst in input materials. We call this kind of catalyst *stimulus*. A catalytic reaction is occurred when all required SOs are in the proximity of each other. We use the term "*scope*" to denote the inside of the proximity area (we assume a range of Wi-Fi radiowave, and so on). The scope of a SO o is represented as a set of SOs which are accessible from the SO o. We assume that only the scopes of contexts are considered instead. In other words, we consider that the catalytic reaction is occurred if all required SOs just enter into the scope of the corresponding context.

Figure 2 shows an example of single catalytic reaction. In this example, there is a gate c_1 regarded as a context and a user has three SOs, i.e., a phone a, a headset b and an IC card s. If the user enters into the scope of c_1, c_1 makes a and b federated. This action is triggered by s. After that, phone a and headset b are federated. We denote federated SOs, such as a and b by a concatenation of a and b, i.e., ab. During this process, c_1 and s work as catalysts. In particular, s is a stimulus in this reaction. We express this reaction as the right hand side diagram of Figure 2.

In catalytic reaction networks, there are four types of catalytic reactions as we show in Figure 3. We categorize these four types of reactions into two groups. One group is the *composition* reaction group (Figure 3 (i) and (ii)), the other group is the *decomposition* reaction group (i.e., Figure 3 (iii) and (iv)). A catalytic reaction of Figure 2 is a type (i) catalytic reaction. We also consider the catalytic reaction without a stimulus, such as Figure 3 (ii). In type (ii), if a user who has SO a and SO b enters into the scope of context c_2,

c_2 makes a and b federated *without a stimulus*. In a similar way, we consider the decomposition reactions, such as Figure 3 (iii) and (iv). In type (iii), if a user who has two SOs that are federated into ab enters into the scope of context c_3, c_3 decomposes these SOs ab into a and b triggered by SO s. Type (iv) is a decomposition reaction without a stimulus.

The output SO of a reaction may promote other reactions as a stimulus or become an input SO of other reactions. In this way, catalytic reactions form a network of reactions.

Now we define these notions, contexts and SOs, formally. Basically, we regard that there are two types of SOs. One is a set of SOs which can federate with other smart objects denoted by O and the other one is a set of SOs which can only promote SOs in O to federate with each other denoted by C. Latter in this paper, SOs $c \in \mathrm{C}$ are called "context" and SOs $o \in \mathrm{O}$ are called just "SO" for convenience. We denote contexts and their corresponding reactions by c_i and r_i respectively.

Next, we define catalytic reactions formally by following definition

Definition 1 (Catalytic Reaction): Let O be a set of SOs, a catalytic reaction r is defined as an action tuple $\langle pre(r), add(r), del(r)\rangle$. Every catalytic reaction r satisfies following conditions:

- $pre(r) \subseteq 2^{\mathrm{O}}$, $add(r) \subseteq 2^{\mathrm{O}}$ and $del(r) \subseteq 2^{\mathrm{O}}$,
- $pre(r)$, $add(r)$ and $del(r)$ are pairwise disjoint sets respectively,
- $del(r) \subseteq pre(r)$, and
- $\bigcup add(r) = \bigcup del(r)$.

$pre(r)$, $add(r)$ and $del(r)$ of catalytic reaction r correspond to the precondition for the reaction application, the addition of federation after the reaction, and the deletion of federation after the reaction respectively. We give some examples of catalytic reactions. Given $\mathrm{O} = \{a, b, s\}$, a catalytic reaction of Figure 3 (i) and (iii) can be defined by $r_1 \triangleq \langle\{\{a\},\{b\},\{s\}\},\{\{a,b\}\},\{\{a\},\{b\}\}\rangle$ and $r_3 \triangleq \langle\{\{a,b\},\{s\}\},\{\{a\},\{b\}\},\{\{a,b\}\}\rangle$ respectively. Note that Definition 1 is more general definition of catalytic reactions compared to four types of catalytic reactions in Figure 2. If we represent only these catalytic reactions by this definition, we just set cardinality constraints of $pre(r)$, $add(r)$ and $del(r)$. If r is a composition reaction (i.e., Figure 2 (i) and (ii)), r should satisfy $|pre(r)| = 2$ or 3, $|add(r)| = 1$ and $|del(r)| = 2$; otherwise, if r is a decomposition reaction (i.e., Figure 2 (iii) and (iv)), r should satisfy $|pre(r)| = 1$ or 2, $|add(r)| = 2$ and $|del(r)| = 1$.

Finally, a catalytic reaction network is defined as follows:

Definition 2 (Catalytic Reaction Network): A catalytic reaction network R is a set of catalytic reactions.

C. Context Catalytic Reaction Network

This section describes a segment graph and a CCRN.

1) Segment Graph: As we discussed in previous section, a catalytic reaction is occurred when required SOs enter into the scope of the corresponding context. To analyze the property of a given catalytic reaction network as a state transition system, it is necessary to formalize the movement of SOs. For example, in Figure 4 (i), there are contexts c_1 and c_2 and these scopes have an *overlap*. A user can walk around the path $\alpha\beta$ shown

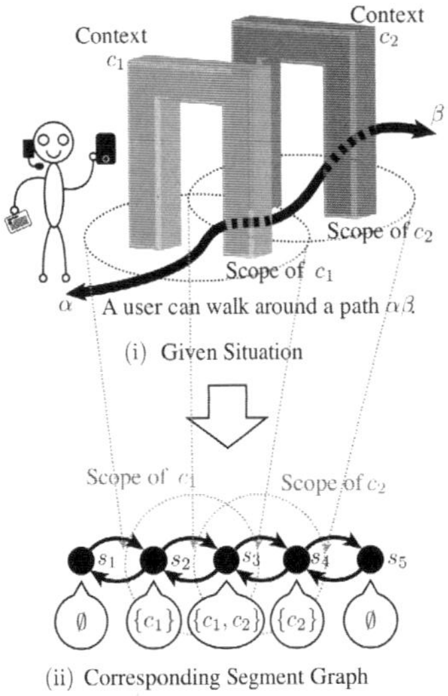

Figure 4. Example of Segment Graph

in Figure 4 (i). This situation can be represented as a segment graph shown in Figure 4 (ii). We consider that the user walk around this segment graph and the user is always located at one of the nodes of this segment graph. Each node of a segment graph has a corresponding set of scopes of contexts. In this way, the given situation like Figure 4 (i) including overlaps of scopes of contexts can be represented as a discrete structure. Now we define a segment graph as follows.

Definition 3 (Segment Graph): Let C be a set of contexts, a segment graph **G** is a tuple $(\mathrm{S}, \mathrm{E}, F)$, where

- S is a finite set of segments,
- $\mathrm{E} \subseteq \mathrm{S} \times \mathrm{S}$ is a set of directed edges between two segments, and
- $F : \mathrm{S} \rightarrow 2^{\mathrm{C}}$ is a function returning scopes of contexts at corresponding segments.

2) Context Catalytic Reaction Network: A context catalytic reaction network (CCRN) is a discrete structure of a situation involving SOs in a catalytic reaction network. A CCRN is defined as a conbination of a segment graph and a catalytic reaction network.

Definition 4 (Context Catalytic Reaction Network): Let O be a set of SOs, a CCRN **C** is a tuple $(\mathrm{R}, \mathbf{G}, f_i, l_0)$, where

- R is a set of catalytic reactions (i.e., CRN),
- **G** is a segment graph $(\mathrm{S}, \mathrm{E}, F)$,
- $f_i \subseteq \mathrm{O}$ is a set of SOs fixed to segment $s_i \in \mathrm{S}$, and
- $l_0 \in \mathrm{S}$ is the initial segment locating mobile SOs (mobile SOs can be represented as $\mathrm{O} \setminus \bigcup f_i$).

D. Model Checking

A model checking is a method to verify a property of a state transition system. It has been often used in various fields, which ranges from electronic-circuit-design verification [11] to secure-network-protocol (e.g., Secure Sockets Layer (SSL) protocol) design verification [12]. In the model checking, it is typically assumed to use a Kripke structure as a state transition system. The property of a Kripke structure is described by a modal logic. There are two kind of commonly used modal logics, such as *linear temporal logic (LTL)* and *computational tree logic (CTL)*. In this paper, we use LTL to describe the property of the Kripke structure.

1) Kripke Structure: Before we look on the detail of a model checking, we give the definition of a Kripke structure [13], which is necessary for a modal logic and a model checking.

Definition 5 (Kripke Structure): Let *AP* be a set of atomic propositions, *a Kripke structrue* M is a tuple (S, I, R, L), where

- S is a finite set of states,
- $I \subseteq S$ is a set of initial states,
- $R \subseteq S \times S$ is a set of transition relation such that R is left-total, i.e., $\forall s \in S,\ \exists s' \in S$ such that $(s, s') \in R$, and
- $L : S \rightarrow 2^{AP}$ is a labeling function.

2) Linear Temporal Logic: Linear temporal logic (LTL) is one of the most well-known modal logic. LTL was first proposed for the formal verification of computer programs by Amir Pnueil in 1977 [14]. First, we give a definition of LTL syntax.

Definition 6 (Linear Temporal Logic Syntax): Let *AP* be a set of atomic propositions, a linear temporal logic formula ϕ is defined by the following syntax recursively.

$$\phi ::= \top \mid \bot \mid p \mid \neg\phi \mid \phi \vee \phi \mid \mathbf{X}\ \phi \mid \mathbf{G}\ \phi \mid \mathbf{F}\ \phi \mid \phi\ \mathbf{U}\ \phi \quad (1)$$

where $p \in AP$.

These right-hand terms denote true, false, p, negation, disjunction, next time, always, eventually and until respectively.

Next, we define a transition path π of a Kripke structure M.

Definition 7 (Transition Path): Let M be a Kripke structure, $\pi = (\pi_0, \pi_1, \pi_2, \dots)$ is a transition path in M if it respects M's transition relation, i.e., $\forall i.(\pi_i, \pi_{i+1}) \in R$. π^i denotes π's ith suffix, i.e., $\pi^i = (\pi_i, \pi_{i+1}, \pi_{i+2}, \dots)$.

Also it can be shown that

$$\begin{aligned}(\pi^i)^j &= (\pi_i, \pi_{i+1}, \pi_{i+2}, \dots)^j \\ &= (\pi_{i+j}, \pi_{i+j+1}, \pi_{i+j+2}, \dots) \\ &= \pi^{i+j}. \end{aligned} \quad (2)$$

Now, we focus on the semantics of linear temporal logic. First, we define the binary satisfaction relation, denoted by $\models$, for LTL formulae. This satisfaction is with respect to a pair - $\langle M, \pi \rangle$, a Kripke structure and a transition path. Then, we enumerate LTL semantics as follows:

- $M, \pi \models \top$ (true is always satisfied)
- $M, \pi \not\models \bot$ (false is never satisfied)
- $(M, \pi \models p)$ iff $(p \in L(\pi_0))$ (atomic propositions are satisfied when they are members of the path's first element's labels)

And there are two LTL semantics of boolean combinations as follows:

- $(M, \pi \models \neg\phi)$ iff $(M, \pi \not\models \phi)$
- $(M, \pi \models \phi \vee \psi)$ iff $[(M, \pi \models \phi) \vee (M, \pi \models \psi)]$

And there are four LTL semantics of temporal operators as follows:

- $(M, \pi \models \mathbf{X}\ \phi)$ iff $(M, \pi^1 \models \phi)$
- $(M, \pi \models \mathbf{F}\ \phi)$ iff $[\exists i.(M, \pi^i \models \phi)]$
- $(M, \pi \models \mathbf{G}\ \phi)$ iff $[\forall i.(M, \pi^i \models \phi)]$
- $(M, \pi \models \phi\ \mathbf{U}\ \psi)$ iff $[(\exists i.(M, \pi^i \models \psi)) \wedge (\forall j < i.(M, \pi^j \models \phi))]$

3) Model Checking Problem: Intuitively saying, a model checking problem is to judge whether a given Kripke structure M satisfies a given property described in a modal logic formula ϕ. A model checking problem is formally stated as follows.

Definition 8 (Model Checking Problem): Given a desired property described by a modal logic formula ϕ (in this paper, we use LTL) and a Kripke structure M, a model checking problem is a decision problem whether the following formula

$$\forall \pi.(M, \pi \models \phi) \quad (3)$$

is satisfied or not. Note that a set $\{\pi \mid (M, \pi \not\models \phi)\}$ is particularly called a set of *counterexamples*.

It is known that a model checking problem can be reduced to a graph search if M has finite states.

There are several implementations of the model checking verifier, such as **S**imple **P**romela **IN**terpreter (SPIN) [15] and **L**abel **T**ransition **S**ystem **A**nalyzer (LTSA) [16].

E. Probabilistic Model Checking

Probabilistic model checking is another method of reliability analysis for given Kripke structure. In original model checking, the reachability between two states of Kripke structure is defined as the existence of the directed edge between these states. Instead, in probabilistic model checking, the reachability between two states of Kripke structure is represented as a probability. This probability of the reachability is normalized with respect to each states as follows

$$\sum_{s', (s, s') \in R} P(s' \mid s) = 1 \text{ for all } s \in S. \quad (4)$$

1) Probabilistic LTL: Probabilistic LTL is extended property description language of LTL for probabilistic model checking. In probabilistic LTL, temporal operators **G** and **F** has an additional bound parameter k denoted by $\mathbf{G}_{\le k}$ and $\mathbf{G}_{\le k}$. These temporal operators have following semantics:

- $(M, \pi \models \mathbf{F}_{\le k}\ \phi)$ iff $[\exists i \le k.(M, \pi^i \models \phi)]$
- $(M, \pi \models \mathbf{G}_{\le k}\ \phi)$ iff $[\forall i \le k.(M, \pi^i \models \phi)]$

To discuss the probability of the transition path, probabilistic LTL also has quantitative operator $\mathbf{P}_{=?}$. Given a LTL property ϕ, $\mathbf{P}_{=?}\ \phi$ evaluates the existence probability of transition paths which satisfies the LTL property ϕ.

2) Probabilistic Model Checking Problem: Intuitively saying, a probabilistic model checking problem evaluates the existence probability of transition paths with length k which satisfies the property ϕ described by probabilistic LTL. This transition assumes discrete-time Markov chain. A probabilistic model checking problem is defined as follows:

Definition 9: Given a Kripke structure M, $\tau_{s,s'} = P(s' \mid s)$, a probabilistic LTL ϕ and a length of bound k, a probabilistic model checking problem evaluates the following probability:

$$\sum_{\forall \pi.(M,\pi \models \phi \wedge |\pi|=k)} \prod_{t=1}^{k} P(\pi_t \mid \pi_{t-1}) \tag{5}$$

One of the most famous implementation of probabilistic model checkers is Probabilistic Symbolic Model Checker (PRISM) [4]. In this paper, we use PRISM to conduct a case study in Section 6.

IV. Probabilistic CCRN

In this section, we propose probabilistic CCRN (P-CCRN), which is the extended model of CCRN by adding a notion of probability. To introduce a notion of probability, we consider two kinds of probability in CCRN. One is the probability of a user behavior, and the other one is the probability of each of catalytic reactions. We denote the probability of users' moving from segment i to segment j by $\tau_{i,j}$ and for all segments $i \in \mathrm{S}$ of a given segment graph, it is satisfied that

$$\sum_{j,(i,j)\in E} \tau_{i,j} = 1 \tag{6}$$

where E is a set of edges in a given segment graph. We denote the probability of the occurrence of catalytic reaction r by $\theta_r = [0, 1]$. By getting them together, we define a probabilistic function P as follows.

Definition 10 (Probabilistic Component): A probabilistic component $\mathbf{P}$ is a tuple $\langle \mathrm{T}, \Theta \rangle$ where $\mathrm{T} = \{\tau_{i,j} \in [0,1] \mid (i,j) \in \mathrm{E}\}$, $\Theta = \{\theta_r \in [0,1] \mid r \in \mathrm{R}\}$, E is a set of edges in a segment graph and R is a set of catalytic reactions.

Definition 11 (Probabilictic CCRN): Let $\mathbf{C}$ and $\mathbf{P}$ be a CCRN and a probabilistic component respectively. A probabilistic CCRN (P-CCRN) is a tuple of $\langle \mathbf{C}, \mathbf{P} \rangle$.

V. Formulation of P-CCRN Reliability Analysis

This section shows a reliability analysis method by using P-CCRN. To do so, we define states of P-CCRN and represent transitions between two states as a probability function. Finally, we propositionize states of P-CCRN to conduct probabilistic model checking.

A. State Representation

Let U be a set of states included in CCRN. Each of states of given CCRN u can be represented as a pair of states of the user's location S_{seg} and states of SOs' federation S_{fed} denoted by $\langle S_{\text{seg}}, S_{\text{fed}} \rangle$ where $S_{\text{seg}} \in \mathrm{S}$ and $S_{\text{fed}} \in \mathfrak{P}(\mathrm{O})$ (i.e., S_{fed} is a partition set of O). We also assume the independence between two events a user behavior and catalytic reactions' success or failure.

B. Transition Representation

A transition (u, u^{next}) between two states are occurred when a user who has SOs moves along with a directed edge in given segment graph. S_{seg} is changed directly when the user moves and S_{fed} is changed by catalytic reactions of corresponding contexts located at the segment that the user aims to go. We define the function of $r_i(S_{\text{fed}})$ to represent applications of catalytic reactions.

Definition 12 (Catalytic Reaction Application): Let r_i and S_{fed} be a catalytic reaction and a state of SOs' federation respectively. $r_i : \mathfrak{P}(\mathrm{O}) \to \mathfrak{P}(\mathrm{O})$ is a function of catalytic reaction application which is a procedure of following update of given S_{fed}:

$$r_i(S_{\text{fed}}) = \begin{cases} S_{\text{fed}} \setminus \mathit{del}(r_i) \cup \mathit{add}(r_i) & \text{if } \mathit{pre}(r) \subseteq S_{\text{fed}} \\ S_{\text{fed}} & \text{otherwise} \end{cases} \tag{7}$$

When the state of CCRN is $\langle S_{\text{seg}}, S_{\text{fed}} \rangle$ and a transition $(\langle S_{\text{seg}}, S_{\text{fed}} \rangle, \langle S_{\text{seg}}^{\text{next}}, S_{\text{fed}}^{\text{next}} \rangle)$ occurs, $\exists S_{\text{seg}}^{\text{next}}.(S_{\text{seg}}, S_{\text{seg}}^{\text{next}}) \in E$ and $\exists r.(r \in R(S_{\text{seg}}^{\text{next}}, S_{\text{fed}}))$ are selected probabilistically where $R(s, \mathrm{A}) = \{r_i \mid c_i \in F(s) \wedge \mathit{pre}(r_i) \subseteq \mathrm{A}\}$.

C. Assigning the probability of a transition between two states

Now we assign the probability of a transition $(\langle S_{\text{seg}}, S_{\text{fed}} \rangle, \langle S_{\text{seg}}^{\text{next}}, S_{\text{fed}}^{\text{next}} \rangle)$ between two states of given probabilistic CCRN. This probability is represented as $P(\langle S_{\text{seg}}^{\text{next}}, S_{\text{fed}}^{\text{next}} \rangle \mid \langle S_{\text{seg}}, S_{\text{fed}} \rangle)$. Using the assumption of the independence between two events a user behavior and catalytic reactions' success or failure, we can rewrite this probability as follows:

$$\begin{aligned} &P(\langle S_{\text{seg}}^{\text{next}}, S_{\text{fed}}^{\text{next}} \rangle \mid \langle S_{\text{seg}}, S_{\text{fed}} \rangle) \\ &\qquad = P(S_{\text{seg}}^{\text{next}} \mid S_{\text{seg}}) P(S_{\text{fed}}^{\text{next}} \mid S_{\text{seg}}^{\text{next}}, S_{\text{fed}}) \end{aligned} \tag{8}$$

$P(S_{\text{seg}}^{\text{next}} \mid S_{\text{seg}})$ can be defined from T directly, namely,

$$P(S_{\text{seg}}^{\text{next}} \mid S_{\text{seg}}) \triangleq \tau_{S_{\text{seg}}, S_{\text{seg}}^{\text{next}}}. \tag{9}$$

On the other hand, $P(S_{\text{fed}}^{\text{next}} \mid S_{\text{seg}}^{\text{next}}, S_{\text{fed}})$ can be defined by several ways. For example, if there are more than one catalytic reaction that can be applied when a user enters into a segment $S_{\text{seg}}^{\text{next}}$ with federated devices S_{fed}, at first, we evaluate the probability of all catalytic reactions independently like we try a coin flip with the number of these reactions of coins and assume that heads are reactions that are applied. In this paper, we give three strategy to deal with this kind of situation.

1) If there are more than one head, we choose one of them uniformly. This represents *mutual exclusion* of concurrent processes among multiple devices.
2) If there are more than one head, we do *not* choose any of these. This assumes that the mutual exclusion does not work and of course this kind of situation should be avoided properly.
3) Let all the catalytic reactions be indexed in order of reaction rate and if there are more than one head, we choose the catalytic reaction with lowest number from them. This represents that fastest catalytic reaction is applied at the highest priority.

In this paper, we use the first strategy to conduct case studies in Section 6. This strategy can be represented as follows:

$$\begin{aligned} &P(S_{\text{fed}}^{\text{next}} \mid S_{\text{seg}}^{\text{next}}, S_{\text{fed}}) = \\ &\begin{cases} \prod_{i \in \mathrm{R}'} (1 - \theta_i) & \text{if } S_{\text{fed}}^{\text{next}} = S_{\text{fed}} \\ \sum_{j=1}^{|\mathrm{R}'|} \sum_{\chi \in X_{ij}} \frac{1}{j} \prod_{k \in \chi} \theta_k \prod_{\ell \in \mathrm{R}' \setminus \chi} (1 - \theta_\ell) & \text{otherwise} \end{cases} \\ &\qquad \text{such that } S_{\text{fed}}^{\text{next}} \setminus S_{\text{fed}} = \mathit{add}(r_i) \text{and } r_i \in \mathrm{R}', \\ &\qquad \text{where } \mathrm{X}_{ij} = \{i\} \cup \binom{\mathrm{R}' \setminus \{i\}}{j-1} \text{ and } \mathrm{R}' = R(S_{\text{seg}}^{\text{next}}, S_{\text{fed}}). \end{aligned} \tag{10}$$

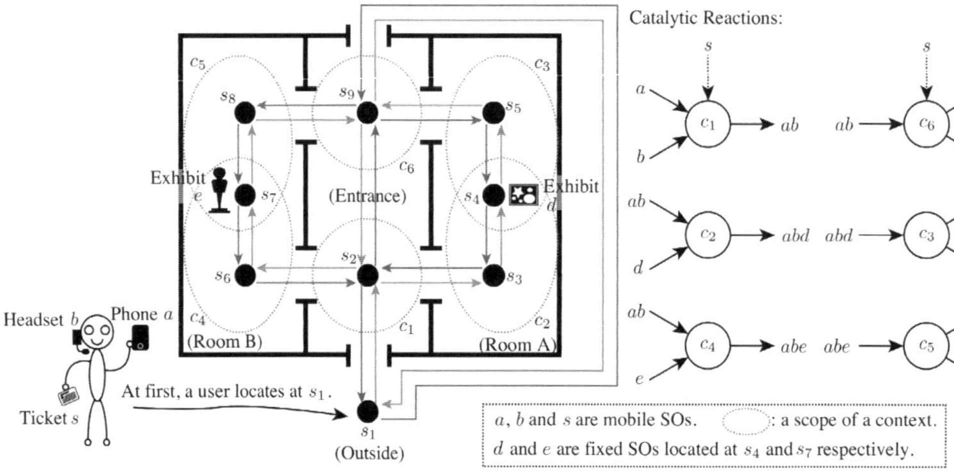

Figure 5. A CCRN assuming a museum

D. Propositionizing

To conduct probabilistic model checking, we assign two kinds of propositions fed($\mathrm{O}' \subseteq \mathrm{O}$) and seg($s \in \mathrm{S}$) to each states of given P-CCRN. Given a state $\langle S_{\text{seg}}, S_{\text{fed}} \rangle$, semantics of these propositions are defined as follows:

- seg($s \in \mathrm{S}$) $\models \top$ iff $s = S_{\text{seg}}$ (a user locates at segment s)
- fed($\mathrm{O}' \subseteq \mathrm{O}$) $\models \top$ iff $\mathrm{O}' \in S_{\text{fed}}$ (a federation O' exists)

VI. Case Study of Reliability Analysis

We have conducted a case study of a reliability analysis of a given P-CCRN, using probabilistic model checking. We assume that a CCRN is given by the designer who intend to design applications of ubiquitous computing. Here we use a CCRN of a museum example as shown in Figure 5. Left hand side and right hand side of this figure represent the segment graph $\mathbf{G}$ and the catalytic reaction network R of this CCRN respectively. In this example, a user enters the entrance of a museum, carrying a phone a, a headset b and a ticket s. Once the user entered the entrance, the phone a and the headset b are federated by a reaction associated with the scope of c_1, which is triggered by the ticket s. Then, the federated SOs ab are worked as a voice guide of the museum. Next, if the user enters into room A, the federated SO ab and an exhibit d are federated by a reaction associated with the scope of c_2. By the federated SO abd, an explanation of the exhibit d can be provided to the user. After this, the user leaves the room A and the federated SO abd is decomposed and becomes ab again by a reaction associated with the scope of c_3. The similar reactions occur in the room B, which is for an explanation of an exhibit e. If the user leaves one of the exhibition rooms and returns to the entrance, the federated SO ab is decomposed before leaving the museum.

Next we assign the probability to the user movement and catalytic reactions. In Figure 5, every directed edges of the segment graph is colored with blue or red. Blue edges assume the regular route of the museum to tour and red edges assume the opposite (i.e., wrong) way. The user can move along with these edges but here we use parameter $\alpha \in [0, 1]$ to decide how frequent he or she tends to go along with the regular route. More precisely, in every segments, the user chooses blue edges with a probability of α, otherwise, he or she chooses red edges with a probability of $1 - \alpha$. Then, if there are more than one edge after he or she chooses color of edge, he or she chooses an one edge uniformly from them. For all $(i, j) \in \mathrm{E}$, we can set $\tau_{i,j}$ as follows:

$$\tau_{i,j} = \begin{cases} \alpha/|\mathrm{BLUE}_i| & \text{if } \tau_{i,j} \text{ is a blue edge} \\ (1-\alpha)/|\mathrm{RED}_i| & \text{if } \tau_{i,j} \text{ is a red edge} \end{cases} \tag{11}$$

where BLUE_i is a set of $\{(i, j) \in \mathrm{E} \mid (i, j) \text{ is a blue edge}\}$ and RED_i is a set of $\{(i, j) \in \mathrm{E} \mid (i, j) \text{ is a red edge}\}$. In regards to catalytic reactions, we assign the same probability $\beta \in [0, 1]$ to occurrences of all catalytic reactions. Namely, we set $\theta_r = \beta$ for all $r \in \mathrm{R}$.

In this configuration, we conducted an experiment of reliability analysis of P-CCRN. We use PRISM to evaluate the probability of following properties with the bound parameter $k = 20$.

$$\phi_1 = \mathbf{P}_{=?}\left[\mathbf{G}_{\leq k}\left(\neg\mathrm{seg}(s_3) \vee \mathrm{fed}(\{a, b, d\})\right)\right] \tag{12}$$

$$\phi_2 = \mathbf{P}_{=?}[\mathbf{F}_{\leq k}((\mathrm{seg}(s_3) \wedge \mathrm{fed}(\{a, b, d\})) \vee (\mathrm{seg}(s_6) \wedge \mathrm{fed}(\{a, b, e\})))] \tag{13}$$

Intuitively, ϕ_1 means that how frequent the user can be always provided the explanation of exhibition d when he or she is at segment s_2 and ϕ_2 means that how frequent the user can be provided the explanation of exhibition d or e even just once when he or she enters the corresponding room of the exhibition.

Figure 6 shows results of these probability evaluation of property ϕ_1 and ϕ_2 by changing parameters α and β from 0 to 1. When α and β are 1, this is the most ideal case. In other words, the user always moves along with the regular route only and catalytic reactions always react when the conditions of them satisfy. In this case, both of properties ϕ_1 and ϕ_2 are satisfied with a probability of 1. However, if α and β are decreased (i.e., the user behaves unpleasantly and catalytic reactions do not fire even if the conditions of them satisfy), probabilities of properties ϕ_1 and ϕ_2 are also decreased. The

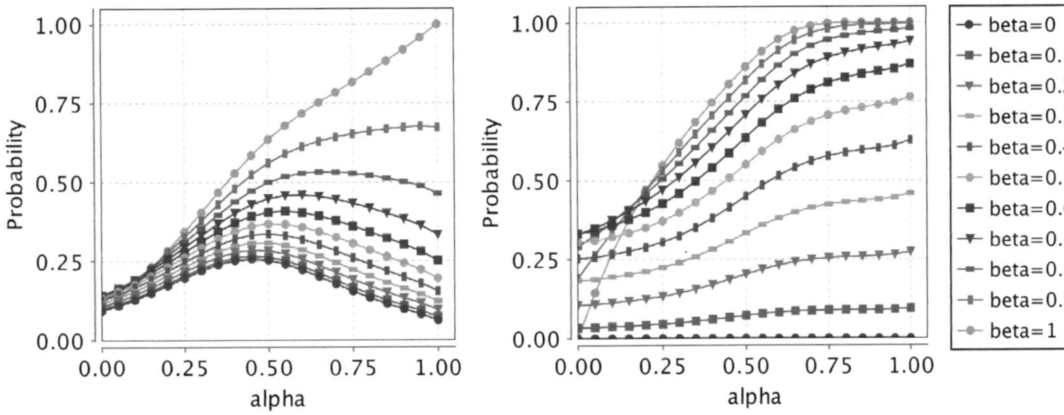

(i) Property ϕ_1 (ii) Property ϕ_2

Figure 6. Results of Experiments

most important aspect of this reliability analysis is that we can evaluate precisely and quantitatively how reliable this kind of UC scenarios are. For a particular example, quantitative evaluation of UC scenarios help us to consider trade-offs between the reliability of UC scenarios and the cost of implementation for the satisfaction of the reliability by changing parameters of probabilities, such as α and β in this case study. In this case, if β is closer to 1, this means we may need more costs for the implementations.

VII. Conclusion

In this paper, we proposed the method of reliability analysis for UC scenarios described by P-CCRN. By our method, we can discuss the reliability of UC scenarios even if these scenarios are in rather practical situation than ideal cases. Reliability analyses are important because these analyses are quantitative, and this means we can discuss about trade-offs between the reliability and the cost for the satisfaction of the reliability. Once we design a UC scenario by P-CCRN, we may actually implement this which usually takes the cost. In that sense, our approach for reliability analysis is not only theoretical but also practical. In future work, we analyze various kinds of UC scenarios assuming more various interferences including possible situations in real places.

Acknowledgment

This work was partly supported by JSPS KAKENHI (S) Grant Number 15H05711.

References

[1] R. Minoda, Y. Tanaka, and S.-i. Minato, "Verifying Scenarios of Proximity-based Federation among Smart Objects through Model Checking," in Proceedings of UBICOMM 2016 The Tenth International Conference on Mobile Ubiquitous Computing, Systems, Services and Technologies, no. c, 2016, pp. 65–71.

[2] R. Minoda and S.-i. Minato, "Efficient Scenario Verification of Proximity-based Federations among Smart Objects through Symbolic Model Checking," in Proceedings of the 7th International Joint Conference on Pervasive and Embedded Computing and Communication Systems (PECCS2017), 2017, pp. 13–21.

[3] A. Cimatti, E. Clarke, and E. Giunchiglia, "Nusmv 2: An opensource tool for symbolic model checking," Computer Aided Verification, vol. 2404, 2002, pp. 359–364.

[4] M. Kwiatkowska, G. Norman, and D. Parker, "PRISM 4.0: Verification of Probabilistic Real-Time Systems," in Proc. 23rd International Conference on Computer Aided Verification (CAV'11), ser. LNCS, G. Gopalakrishnan and S. Qadeer, Eds., vol. 6806. Springer, 2011, pp. 585–591.

[5] S. Guellouz, A. Benzina, M. Khalgui, and G. Frey, "ZiZo : A Complete Tool Chain for the Modeling and Verification of Reconfigurable Function Blocks ZiZo : A Complete Tool Chain for the Modeling and Verification of Reconfigurable Function Blocks," International Conference on Mobile Ubiquitous Computing, Systems, Services and Technologies, no. c, 2016, pp. 144–151.

[6] R. Alur and D. L. Dill, "A theory of timed automata," Theoretical Computer Science, vol. 126, no. 2, apr 1994, pp. 183–235.

[7] R. Drechsler and U. Kühne, Eds., Formal Modeling and Verification of Cyber-Physical Systems. Wiesbaden: Springer Fachmedien Wiesbaden, 2015.

[8] C. Xu and S. C. Cheung, "Inconsistency Detection and Resolution for Context-aware Middleware Support," Proceedings of the 10th European Software Engineering Conference Held Jointly with 13th ACM SIGSOFT International Symposium on Foundations of Software Engineering, 2005, pp. 336–345.

[9] S. Kauffman, Investigations. Oxford New York: Oxford University Press, 2002.

[10] Y. Tanaka, "Proximity-based federation of smart objects: liberating ubiquitous computing from stereotyped application scenarios," in Knowledge-Based and Intelligent Information and Engineering Systems. Springer, 2010, pp. 14–30.

[11] J. R. Burch, E. M. Clarke, K. L. McMillan, and D. L. Dill, "Sequential circuit verification using symbolic model checking," in Proceedings of the 27th ACM/IEEE Design Automation Conference, ser. DAC '90. New York, NY, USA: ACM, 1990, pp. 46–51.

[12] J. C. Mitchell, V. Shmatikov, and U. Stern, "Finite-state Analysis of SSL 3.0," in Proceedings of the 7th Conference on USENIX Security Symposium - Volume 7, ser. SSYM'98. Berkeley, CA, USA: USENIX Association, 1998, p. 16.

[13] S. A. Kripke, "Semantical Analysis of Modal Logic I Normal Modal Propositional Calculi," Zeitschrift für Mathematische Logik und Grundlagen der Mathematik, vol. 9, no. 5-6, 1963, pp. 67–96.

[14] A. Pnueli, "The temporal logic of programs," 18th Annual Symposium on Foundations of Computer Science (sfcs 1977), 1977, pp. 46–57.

[15] G. Holzmann, "The model checker SPIN," IEEE Transactions on Software Engineering, vol. 23, no. 5, may 1997, pp. 279–295.

[16] J. Magee and J. Kramer, Concurrency State Models and Java Programs. New York, New York, USA: John Wiley and Sons, 1999.

Using Brain-Computer Interface and Internet of Things to Improve Healthcare for Wheelchair Users

Ariel Teles*, Maurício Cagy†, Francisco Silva‡, Markus Endler§, Victor Bastos¶ and Silmar Teixeira¶
*Federal Institute of Maranhão, Brazil, Email: ariel.teles@ifma.edu.br
†Federal University of Rio de Janeiro, Brazil, Email: mcagy@peb.ufrj.br
‡Federal University of Maranhão, Brazil, Email: fssilva@lsdi.ufma.br
§Pontifical Catholic University of Rio de Janeiro, Brazil, Email: endler@inf.puc-rio.br
¶Federal University of Piauí, Brazil, Email: {victorhugobastos, silmarteixeira}@ufpi.edu.br

***Abstract*—Brain-to-Thing Communication (BTC) is a type of ubiquitous system that aims to allow the communication from the human brain to smart objects in the Internet of Things (IoT). In this way, brain commands can be used to remotely control sensing and actuation of IoT devices. In this paper, we propose a BTC system for healthcare and show the viability to develop it. We present our BTC system architecture for wheelchair users, an illustrative application example, research challenges in this domain, and we show our current development status and perspectives.**

Keywords–Brain-to-Thing Communication; Internet of Things; Brain-computer Interface.

I. INTRODUCTION

The Internet of Things (IoT) paradigm proposes the expansion of the current Internet infrastructure towards a network with smart objects connected to each other, which not only obtain environmental information, but also interact with the physical world using existing Internet patterns to provide information transparency services, analysis, applications and communications [1]. In this sense, IoT is not related only to interconnection of devices to the Internet, but also with (i) the knowledge acquisition from each smart object and from the physical word around it (i.e., sensing), and (ii) performing actions on the smart object (i.e., actuation).

On the other hand, the Brain-Computer Interface (BCI) technology has been proposed, which is a "communication system that does not depend on the brain's normal output pathways of peripheral nerves and muscles" [2]. A BCI system enables a human to interact with the surrounding environment through brain-generated signals (i.e., brain activity) obtained via ElectroEncephaloGraphy (EEG). BCI systems have normally been proposed to provide communication for people with some type of physical paralysis. Some BCI system examples are neural prostheses, robotic wheelchair [3], and robots in general.

From the union of IoT and BCI systems, we propose a Brain-to-Thing Communication (BTC) system for healthcare. The main idea is to enable a communication from the brain to smart objects (i.e., the "things") for wheelchair users. This will allow actuation and sensing to be performed on smart objects via commands sent by people from their controlled brain activity. In this way, the BTC system can contribute to improve quality of life and reduce intensive care costs for people with some physical or motor problem and who need to use a wheelchair (e.g., paraplegics, patients with severe diseases, such as Amyotrophic Lateral Sclerosis, or people who have suffered from a stroke), providing a mean to enable them to become more independent.

The rest of this paper is organized as follows. Section II presents the initial architecture of our proposed BTC system. Next, Section III exhibits a real illustrative example to show the usage of our proposed system. Section IV gives an overview of the challenges faced by this research. Finally, in Section V, we drive our conclusions.

II. SYSTEM ARCHITECTURE

Figure 1 illustrates the architecture of our proposed BTC system. Initially, signals are obtained in real-time via EEG and sent to the *Recognizer* component, which analyses and recognizes pre-defined patterns. These brain activity patterns represent mental states of the user (e.g., left hand or right hand imagined movements) and are recognized by signal-processing techniques [4]. A non-invasive EEG is a method to register brain activities with electrodes externally distributed along the head of the user. In cases in which it is required to identify only specific patterns (e.g., wink/blink, mouth bite, and muscle artefacts in general, such as hands movements and swallowing), only a few of electrodes are necessary to register signals, such as have been used by commercial and opened wearable devices (e.g., headsets, glasses, and caps as OpenBCI [5]). In this sense, that type of hardware is expected to be used for BTC systems, even if it is required to be adapted or embedded in a wheelchair.

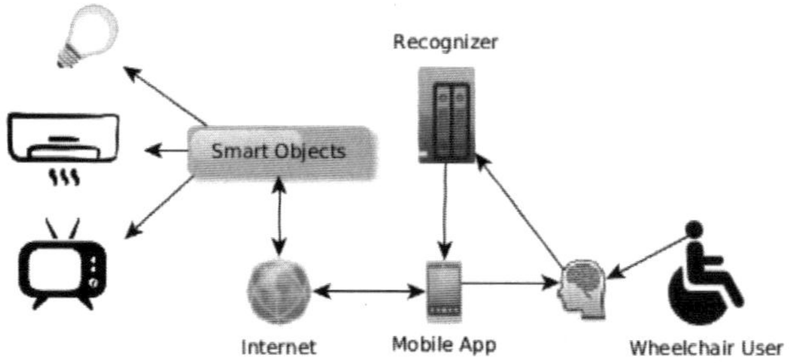

Figure 1. BTC System Architecture.

Recognized brain activity patterns are forwarded to the user's mobile device (e.g., smartphone, tablet) and used as input to an IoT mobile application, which can remotely communicate via Internet protocols with online smart objects, which are connected to the Internet via WiFi. By means of this communication, a brain activity pattern that is recognized by the *Recognizer* component can be used by the user to control smart objects. Therefore, BTC systems provide an alternative communication channel to perform actions and sensing in smart objects via commands sent by users from their controlled brain activities.

BTC Communication differs from IoT systems in general by providing a new communication channel for users, the brain. It differs from traditional BCI systems by proposing the following features:

- Smart environments: smart objects should be spread in the environment with embedded systems running sensing and actuation services (e.g., Raspberry PI [6], Arduino [7], and so on), providing smartness to the place where the wheelchair user lives (i.e., places where the user goes during his/her daily routine);
- Mobility: a wheelchair mobile user can continuously use the system anywhere and anytime, not only where he/she lives, but also during all his/her daily routine activities, remotely sending brain commands via a mobile application to smart objects;
- Transparency for the system: IoT and mobile applications do not know that user inputs are generated by recognized brain activities, because there is a component to recognize brain-generated commands;
- User-aware confirmations: brain commands sent to the mobile device must trigger visual, audio, or vibratory confirmations in the application to allow wheelchair users to know the brain activity patterns recognized by the system. This is specially important because, in some cases, the user may also have some communication problem (e.g., a blind, deaf, or mute person), requiring the user to know if the system correctly identified the command to be sent to a smart object;
- User-aware interfaces: mobile application interfaces should be adapted to allow an appropriate navigation. For example, the mobile application should have a few button options, limited to the number of brain activity patterns that can be recognized, providing a full mapping from all patterns to navigation options.

III. An Illustrative Example

Consider a person called Bob, a patient who lives most of the time in a wheelchair. At the same time, he would like to have a mechanism to control home appliances, because his wife works and thus he lives most of the day alone. By using a BTC system, Bob can turn on/off a lamp, an air conditioner, a television, a hot shower, or a residential security system in his smart home. Moreover, as the brain-to-thing communication is made through a home area network, if Bob is not physically located at his bedroom, he can also send brain commands to remotely control smart objects located there. For example, Bob can obtain the current state of the lamp located in his bedroom, use the mobile application to visualize this information, and act over the lamp, turning it on/off. Therefore, a BTC system is designed to provide resources for people with physical disabilities, mainly wheelchair users, and help them become more independent.

IV. Challenges

Some recent works in literature are going towards BTC systems by proposing initial solutions that show the technical viability to connect the brain with smart objects, such as [8] and [9]. Other recent proposals, such as [10] and [11], develop BTC applications for smart homes combining user inputs from the EEG with other devices (e.g., glass, mouse, keyboard). However, our solution mainly differs from all of them because it is focused on supporting wheelchair users, which have several limitations. This lies the novelty of our idea. In this sense, in addition to using real-time mobile network protocols to avoid delays in the communication among system components, our solution aims to address some non-trivial challenges in this domain:

- Real-time EEG signal processing: EEG signals should be processed and brain activity patterns recognized in real-rime by the *Recognizer* component;
- Good accuracy in recognizing brain activities: the *Recognizer* component should have a high success rate in identifying EEG signal patterns, in order to avoid mistakes. Of course, it is required that wheelchair users have knowledge about the system usage. For this, an initial training phase is needed. This phase is also required to calibrate the system;
- User-oriented mobile application: as previously explained in Section II, mobile application interfaces and confirmations should be developed considering the special needs of wheelchair users (e.g., physical movement and communication restrictions), which is a big challenge from the human-computer interface point of view.

V. Conclusion

We are currently developing the *Recognizer* component in Java. We decided to use this platform because of its rich development framework and wide acceptance. This implementation is integrating a commercial EEG in Brazil with Android mobile devices. The current version of the *Recognizer* component is identifying left and right hand imagined movements. We are also developing the mobile and IoT applications for Android OS and using a pub/sub communication middleware, the *Scalable Data Distribution Layer* (SDDL) [12]. In a second step, we intend to provide our solution regarding the ability of communicating with other people via a chat application. We will evaluate our solution considering as metric the accuracy in recognizing brain activities and also Human-computer interaction aspects, given that users may have different types of limitations. As future research efforts, we plan to develop a EEG wearable device in a cap format with additional resources, such as Global Positioning System and other embedded sensors.

Acknowledgments

The authors would like to thank the Fundação de Amparo à Pesquisa e ao Desenvolvimento Científico e Tecnológico do Maranhão (FAPEMA) for the financial support.

References

[1] J. Gubbi, R. Buyya, S. Marusic, and M. Palaniswami, "Internet of things (iot): A vision, architectural elements, and future directions," Future Generation Computer Systems, vol. 29, no. 7, Sep. 2013, pp. 1645–1660.

[2] Jonathan R. Wolpaw et al., "Brain-computer interface technology: a review of the first international meeting," IEEE Transactions on Rehabilitation Engineering, vol. 8, no. 2, Jun 2000, pp. 164–173.

[3] T. Kaufmann, A. Herweg, and A. Kübler, "Toward brain-computer interface based wheelchair control utilizing tactually-evoked event-related potentials," Journal of NeuroEngineering and Rehabilitation, vol. 11, no. 1, Jan 2014, p. 17.

[4] F. Lotte, A Tutorial on EEG Signal-processing Techniques for Mental-state Recognition in Brain–Computer Interfaces. Springer London, 2014, pp. 133–161.

[5] Openbci. [Online]. Available: http://openbci.com/ [retrieved: November, 2017]

[6] Raspberry pi. [Online]. Available: https://www.raspberrypi.org/ [retrieved: November, 2017]

[7] Arduino. [Online]. Available: https://www.arduino.cc/ [retrieved: November, 2017]

[8] E. Mathe and E. Spyrou, "Connecting a consumer brain-computer interface to an internet-of-things ecosystem," in Proceedings of the 9th ACM International Conference on PErvasive Technologies Related to Assistive Environments, ser. PETRA '16, 2016, pp. 90:1–90:2.

[9] K. Sadeghi, A. Banerjee, J. Sohankar, and S. K. S. Gupta, "Optimization of brain mobile interface applications using iot," in 2016 IEEE 23rd International Conference on High Performance Computing (HiPC), Dec 2016, pp. 32–41.

[10] C. P. Brennan, P. J. McCullagh, L. Galway, and G. Lightbody, "Promoting autonomy in a smart home environment with a smarter interface," in Annual International Conference of the IEEE Engineering in Medicine and Biology Society, 2015.

[11] E. D. Buyser, E. D. Coninck, B. Dhoedt, and P. Simoens, "Exploring the potential of combining smart glasses and consumer-grade eeg/emg headsets for controlling iot appliances in the smart home," in IET International Conference on Technologies for Active and Assisted Living, 2016, pp. 1–6.

[12] L. David, R. Vasconcelos, L. Alves, R. André, and M. Endler, "A dds-based middleware for scalable tracking, communication and collaboration of mobile nodes," Journal of Internet Services and Applications, vol. 4, no. 1, 2013.

Enhancing the Affective Sensitivity of Location Based Services Using Situation-Person-Dependent Semantic Similarity

Antonios Karatzoglou[1,2], Michael Beigl[2]

[1]Robert Bosch GmbH
Corporate Sector Research and Advance Engineering, and
[2]Karlsruhe Institute of Technology
Germany
Email: antonios.karatzoglou@de.bosch.com, antonios.karatzoglou@kit.edu
Email: michael.beigl@kit.edu

***Abstract*—Location prediction plays a steadily growing role in Location Based Services (LBS), as these try to be more proactive and improve in this way the quality of service provided. Although recent location prediction systems go beyond just location data and build upon a wide range of models that describe semantic locations and personal preferences, none of them considers locations from the view of the user. Moreover, none takes into account the variance in people's way of perceiving and understanding concepts (locations in our case) depending on the situation. Minsky referred to this as (cognitive) *frames*. This paper posits that a dynamic semantic-similarity-based clustering of locations can be used for mining such location-specific frames, e.g. the varying meanings that people give to locations over time depending on the situation, their personality and their emotional state. The resulting situation-person-specific frames can in turn be used to enhance the location prediction.**

Keywords*–*LBS; Location Prediction, Ontologies, Dynamic Semantic Similarity, Personality Traits, Emotional State, Personalization, Cognitive Frames.

I. Introduction

Emerging context-aware systems and applications are capable of offering intelligent and personalized services that are tailored to the users and their current environment. Recently, in order for such systems to provide an even better quality of service to the users, developers aim at making them more *proactive* by giving them the ability to take the initiative, instead of just reacting. This is attempted by applying various context prediction techniques. Location represents a particularly important context information type. There exist numerous applications and services by now, so called *Location Based Services (LBS)*, that are premised on the users' current or future location, like location-based advertising and marketing. Social networks experience nowadays a significant upgrade as well through utilizing the current location of their users. In this case these are referred to as *Location-Based Social Networks (LBSNs)*. The location information is provided either manually by the users (e.g. Foursquare [1]) or sensed automatically from the users' personal devices. Furthermore, predictive location awareness can also contribute to a more efficient resource management, e.g. in intelligent navigation and traffic management scenarios or in communication networks.

Location reveals not only the *whereabouts*, but also the *what*, the *when* and eventually the *who* you are. By knowing the location, we humans are able to extract even more information than just the location itself; information that can be used to model and identify behavioral patterns. So, we could, for instance, derive a certain activity (*what*) related to a particular location, or the time of visit (*when*). Moreover, we humans could even draw conclusions regarding the users' temporary mental state and their overall personality profile (*who*) from *knowing their locations* and how they move between them. Vice versa, by knowing all this "metadata" about a person, we could assume to be able to provide an at least rough estimation about her current or future location. Nathan et al. support this theory by interpreting movement as the outcome of the synergy of four components [2]: the internal state of the individual, its motion capacity, its navigation capacity and potential external factors, whereby *internal state* addresses the reason and the motive for the individual to move and visit a certain location, which in turn reflects his/her needs, preferences and personality.

The key phrase here is *knowing the location*. Knowledge is defined as [3]:

> Facts, information and skills acquired through experience or education; the theoretical or practical understanding of a subject

So, each and every type of knowledge acquired by a person refers to the result of personal experience and interpretation. In the special case of location information, this can be interpreted as follows:

> The same place or location has potentially a different meaning to different people

For example, while a guest normally sees in a *restaurant* a place to eat, the same restaurant stands for a working place to the cook working there. Moreover,

> A place may even have many different meanings to the same person depending on the situation and/or her mental and emotional state

People tend to employ *cognitive frames* in order to interpret their experiences [4]. Minsky introduced first in [5] the concept *frame* in the 1970s' as a dynamic structure to be used when *"one encounters a new situation or makes a substantial change in one's view of the present problem"* underpinning our statement. For example, a *company building*, which is usually sensed as a working location, turns into a space of leisure and entertainment during the firm's Christmas party. Similarly, the location *hotel* is usually strongly correlated with a stay over the holidays by a tourist, while it is perceived as a place of work for someone working there as a bellboy or for someone who often visits conferences and/or has business lunches there. Furthermore, a person that enjoys having a drink at the bar of a particular hotel in his hometown (without necessarily being a guest) and a person that makes use of the hotel's Sunday's brunch offer, would associate a hotel on one hand more with night life locations, like a bar or a club, and on the other hand more with a cafe or a restaurant, respectively. A preliminary user study in which we asked 20 people to interpret various locations on their daily routes confirmed the dynamic nature of how people perceive locations. This varying perception of locations could be used to enhance location prediction.

The majority of the existing location prediction systems rely on statistical and machine learning based algorithms in order to estimate the current or predict the future location of a user. These systems recognize and model regularities in the movement patterns of one or more users to provide their estimations. Some use solely recorded trajectories (sequences of locations in form of Global Positioning System (GPS) coordinates or cell IDs and time), while other utilize further information, such as transportation mode and proximity of social contacts among others. However, these systems come with two major drawbacks; first, they are a black box to the user. The users don't really have insight into the estimation mechanism. Second, they work only at that particular regions well, for which they have been trained for. Recently, a new generation of location prediction systems tries to overcome these shortcomings through the use of semantics and so called *semantic trajectories*. The corresponding algorithms yield good results even in regions or cities that users have never visited before and offer (human-understandable) transparency at the same time. Under normal circumstances both approaches are capable of providing good, yet perfectible results. This is principally due to both their incapability of handling irregular human behavior and exceptional situations, as well as to the lack of flexibility and dynamics in their semantic knowledge representation of locations in their models, which makes them incapable of covering the varying perception of locations mentioned before.

We hypothesize that a *dynamic and stochastic semantic-similarity-based clustering* that takes both the person herself, as well as the current situation into consideration when grouping locations, instead of just categorizing them into fixed hierarchies, can lead to capturing the *person-situation-dependent varying perception of locations*, and consequently to a more accurate estimation of the users' intention to visit a certain region or location. Here, *person* refers, on one hand, to the users? preferences and interests, and, on the other hand to their personality traits, while *situation* includes both context information (time, certain event, purpose of visit, activity, etc.) and mental state of the users. Our hypothesis could also be expressed by the following two propositions:

- *Dynamic semantic similarity can be used for mining location-specific (Minsky's) cognitive frames from the user's semantically enriched and ontology-structured context & tracking data,* and
- *A (cognitive) frame-based location prediction yields higher prediction accuracy*

We aim at modeling the variety in people's way of seeing and understanding things (locations in a first case) in order to achieve a higher adaptivity and personalization on the part of the application. After all, what is more personal and human, than the trait of changing our point of view about things, sometimes more and sometimes less, depending on the moods and the events of the day?

This paper is structured as follows. Section II gives a brief summary of the related work. Next, in Section III we describe in detail our approach. Finally Section IV and Section V provide a preliminary evaluation and our conclusions respectively.

II. State of the Art

According to Glassey and Ferguson [6], there exist four representation model types for describing locations: The *geometric*, the *symbolic* the *hybrid* and the *semantic* model that considers the relationship of entities in space among others. Our work concentrates on the *semantic-enhanced location prediction*. Usually, systematic approaches that leverage semantic information for destination prediction base on trajectory mining and analysis, but there exist also other ways for incorporating semantics as we shall see next.

Ying et al. [7] introduced one of the first semantic trajectory mining based approaches, which is based on a Geographic Semantic Information Database (GSID) in order to have the recorded GPS or Cell-ID trajectories semantically enriched. Patterns mined in the resulting trajectory data base are in turn converted into *Semantic Pattern Trees* to finally provide the next place prediction. In [8], they extend their approach by taking temporal information into account as well. Samaan et al. describe buildings and road network elements semantically by using *spatial conceptual maps* in [9]. Furthermore, they utilize a context knowledge base formulated in XML, which contains the users' preferences, schedule, tasks and goals among others, to leverage their system's performance. The underlying algorithm is probabilistic, based on the Dempster-Shafer Theory (DS-Theory). In [10] and [11] they illustrate the same algorithm, only that now, the locations are represented by Cell-IDs assigned by the corresponding cell towers. Ridhawi et al. follow in their work, [12] and [13], a similar direction for improving their indoor tracking and prediction algorithm. Their system uses the Dempster-Shafer Theory as well, but, in contrast with Samaan et al., the knowledge is structured and stored by means of *ontologies*. These include profiles of users, their location history and some activities. Wannous et al. base their framework also on an *ensemble of ontologies*, as well as on a set of *rules* in order to represent and estimate future movement and activity patterns of marine mammals [14]. They defined their rule base with the help of a group of experts and subdivided it into a spatial, a domain-specific and a temporal set of rules, respective each time to the applied ontologies.

Long et al. base their work, [15], on a probabilistic model called Latent Dirichlet Allocation (DLA). DLA is used in text mining and takes the documents' topics into account in order to cluster these accordingly. Long et al. use DLA to extract so called *geographic topics* from the text entered by Foursquare users in their check-ins based on their popularity. By using these geographic topics, their system becomes more adjustable, since in this way, they move away from a static location categorization, like the one provided by Foursquare. Krishnamurthy et al. rely their work on a social network as well [16]. They analyze the Tweets of Twitter [17] users to predict their locations. Specifically, they define a metric (*localness*) to formulate the vicinity of special terms (*local entities*), which appear in Tweets, to particular geographic regions or towns. Various measures including two semantic relatedness measures, the *Jaccard* and the *Tversky Indices* were examined for this purpose. By determining all localness scores between geographic regions and the corresponding local entities in the Tweets of a user, they are finally able to provide an estimation of the location of the users.

Mabroukeh et al. explore a semantic-enhanced method in order to mine Web usage patterns and to be able to predict the next visited Web page at the same time [18]. They use *semantic relatedness* to adjust their probabilistic model accordingly in order to raise the prediction performance. In [19], a *time-dependent semantic similarity measure* is introduced by Zhao et al. for describing the dynamic nature of Web search queries over the time. In addition, they place their trust in a probabilistic similarity measure that reflects the Web queries' frequency distribution.

The person-situation debate addresses the challenging question of what influences the humans' behavior at most; is it their personality or the situation in which they find themselves? While *personality trait theorists* believe that people's behavior is guided by consistent and stable in time traits (habitual patterns of behavior, thought, and emotion [20]), *situationists* argue that people are rather inconsistent in their behavior depending on the situation [21]. Meanwhile, current behavior researchers accept that both of them contribute to a person's behavior [22]. Buss states further that the effect of personality on behavior depends on the situation and vice versa [23]. Numerous works exist, which pursuit and substantiate this subject like Jacquard's [24] and Borkenau's [25]. Therefore, one could easily assume that knowledge of both personality and situation, as well as their interrelation, builds a solid prerequisite to predict one's behavior and intentions. *In this paper, we claim that this fact could be further exploited for raising the location prediction accuracy.* On the other hand, there exists research that goes in the opposite direction as well. Adali et al. and Staiano et al. attempt for instance to infer the personality from the behavior [26] and the social network structure [27], respectively.

All existing location prediction approaches constrain themselves to static location definitions and hierarchies without considering the users' varying perception of locations over time and situation. This leads to non-adaptive and thus perfectible location modelling and prediction algorithms.

III. PROPOSED APPROACH

The location prediction framework that we propose in this paper is illustrated in Fig. 1. Our approach is hybrid and consists of two parts. One part takes over the semantical processing of the input stream (top branch), while the other one takes charge of the actual users' future location prediction (bottom branch).

Recorded data like location and time (e.g., GPS readings), low level activity (e.g., through accelerometer and gyroscope measurements) and biometric data (e.g., pulse, perspiration), together with user-specific high level data retrieved either directly through the users' feedback or indirectly from their calendar, e-mail and social media communication data, are being fed to two separate paths simultaneously (top and bottom branch respectively). On one hand, these are being semantically annotated and stored in our so called Semantically Annotated Database (SADB). The annotation takes place semi-supervised partly by the user (through an Android app running on the smartphone or the smartwatch), partly by utilizing a (geographic) Linked Open Database (LODB), like the OS-Monto [28], and partly through an internal loop considering the existing ontology so far, as well as the similarity analysis taking place in a next step. The annotated data are then used to propagate our Ontology-Suite-based Knowledge Base (OSKB) described in III-A. The reasoner attempts to derive the current mental state and the overall personality of the user from the available data among others and plays therefore a significant role (see III-C) in order to achieve our goal of correlating locations with the users' experience and building that way location-specific cognitive frames. PSSSA is the core component of our approach and refers to the *Person-Situation Semantic Similarity Analysis* component. It is responsible for awarding our approach with a highly personal and human-like dynamic view of locations at anytime. Details about PSSSA can be found in Section III-B. The bottom branch of our framework includes the actual location prediction model. This could be for instance a probabilistic graph, as the Markov model we use at this phase. But other machine learning based prediction models like Artificial Neural Networks (ANNs) are also to be considered and shall be explored in the future. The prediction model is first being trained with the available data. In a next step, the trained model is being optimized through the customization of its (previously learned) parameters by taking the current semantic similarity scores of the locations into account. Section IV provides a brief description of the customization process based on a Markov Chain model. Finally, the customized PSSSA prediction model estimates the users' future location.

A. *Ontology suite*

We propose a modular ontology that consists of following five major ontologies:

1) Spatial ontology
2) Location ontology
3) Activities & Actions ontology
4) Person, Personality & Mood ontology
5) Temporal & Event ontology

The Spatial ontology describes core geospatial concepts and properties, like *building, park, street, etc.* and *close to, near, etc.*, respectively. The Location ontology represents a taxonomy of various location types, like *night life locations, club, bar, restaurant, dinner, fast food restaurant, etc.* The Activities & Actions ontology includes both complex activities, as well as elementary actions of which they are composed. A complex activity represents in our case a high level purpose of visiting a certain location. For instance, the activity *celebrate a birthday* covers the actions *meet friends, meet family, eat, drink, etc.* Person, Personality & Mood ontology profiles the user. This ontology models the user from both a "shallow", as well as a "deeper" point of view and comprises demographic information (*age, sex, profession, etc.*), hobbies and interests up to personality traits (*extroversion, openness, etc.*) and mental states (*emotions, moods, ...*) respectively. In both last two cases, our focus lies on features that can affect the social and particularly the movement behavior of the user. Our personality and mental state models build upon the work of Vidacek-

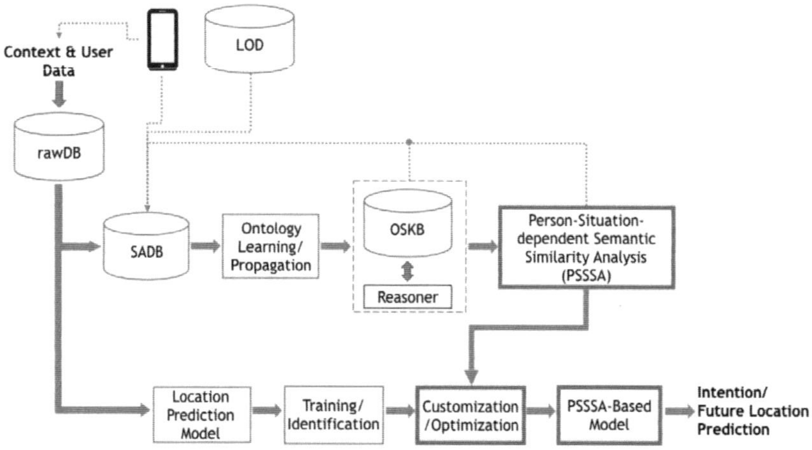

Figure 1. Situation-person-dependent semantic-similarity-based location prediction framework, whereby SADB refers to Semantically Annotated Database, OSKB to Ontology suite Database and PSSSA to Person-Situation Semantic Clustering of Locations respectively.

Hains et al. [29] and Hastings [30] respectively. Finally, the Temporal & Event ontology describes time from a human point of view, considering a human-like time granularity. Beside time in general, a particular attention is paid to the temporal entity event, which refers to special events like *anniversaries, birthdays, public holidays, etc.* that are strongly related to irregular behavior.

The ontology ensemble is instantiated by the users data. For the moment, changes in their lives, like moving to another town or streets, must be stated explicitly by the users. However, we plan to use online pattern mining algorithms to detect such kind of changes in the users' regular movement patterns and update our ontology base automatically.

B. Semantic similarity & probabilistic approach

Our goal is to capture and encapsulate the varying human perception of locations in order to cluster them in a more personalized manner based on the users' current experience. The general idea is to build *location-specific cognitive frames* by tying together situation, purpose of visit, activity, mental state of the user, his/her personality traits and locations using semantic similarity measures. These resulting location-specific frames will engender a dynamic and highly personalized method of modeling and storing location information. Beyond that, the usage of such location-specific frames complies to the Ontology Design Pattern (ODP) method [31], whereby such objects are used to encapsulate complex knowledge and/or to overcome the *n-ary relation* representation issue in the Web Ontology Language (OWL).

There are two different ways of specifying to what degree one term associates with another. On one hand *semantic relatedness* determines the relation between two concepts. On the other hand, *semantic similarity* refers to how similar, how likely two concepts are. For instance, a car is *related* to its driver but rather *similar* to another vehicle like a truck. The Person-Situation Semantic Similarity Analysis attempts to mine dynamic similarities between locations that vary in relation to the current situation, the personality and the mental state of a user. To this end, it mines and makes use of the interconceptual semantic relatedness between the respective locations and other classes/concepts in the ontology suite (like the activities and time). Even locations, which normally do not belong to the same type, can find their way in such situation-person-depended groups. For instance for a user that is jogging in a park, the *park* gets semantically closer to a *gym* than usual. We propose a hybrid and stochastic semantic similarity measure that takes both the topology, as well as the eventual underlying uncertainty into consideration. Thus, our proposed similarity metric consists of the following four parts:

1) *Topological similarity measures* are applied on ontologies and consider on one hand the relations between locations and the type of relation itself (edge-based measures) and on the other hand the surroundings of the locations (node-based measures). Wu & Palmer in [32] propose with the formula (1) an edge-based similarity measure that takes depth into account as well, providing by this means better results. The fact that it is already normalized and can never be zero serves additionally our overall framework because the similarity scores are used to adapt the parameters of the location prediction model. A zero could lead to "broken" inference chains.

$$S_{W\&P} = \frac{2 * depth(LCS(l_1, l_2))}{length(l_1, l_2) + 2 * depth(LCS(l_1, l_2))} \quad (1)$$

   - *LCS*: Least Common Subsumer
   - *depth*: Length from a node up to the root
   - *l1, l2*: 2 locations

   Lin [33], on the other hand introduced a similarity measure based on the information content:

$$S_{Lin} = \frac{2 * logP(LCS(l_1, l_2))}{logP(l_1) + logP(l_2)} \quad (2)$$

   - $-logP(l) = IC(l)$: *Information Content* of location l in the corresponding ontology

2) A particularly important type of similarity measures for our work are the so called *feature-based similarity measures*. These measures define similarity based on the set of common features between two objects (locations in our case). The Jaccard Coefficient, adapted

for our case in (3), is such a measure:

$$S_{Jaccard} = \frac{|l_1 \cap l_2|}{|l_1 \cup l_2|} \quad (3)$$

- $|l_1|$ and $|l_2|$: Feature sets of locations l_1 and l_2 respectively

The features are in our case both user-dependent, such as purpose of visit and correlated emotions (among others), and user-independent, like time of day.

3) At the same time, we plan to treat the available sensor input data as text and the daily semantic enriched trajectories of the user as sentences about locations and project them onto a *vector-space model*. This can help us to learn and to determine non-predefined similarities from the data in an unsupervised manner by analyzing the frequency distribution of locations and their properties in the ontology (statistical similarity). Latent semantic analysis and cosine similarity in combination with term-frequency-inverse document frequency (tf-idf) adjusted to our case would be a solid basis to begin with.

4) Finally, a conditional probabilistic kernel, such as the marginalized kernel from Tsuda [34], will be employed to counteract on one hand the "soft" categorization of locations mentioned in Section I and on the other hand the general underlying uncertainty in humans' behavior. Kernels represent principally the similarity between two objects (in our case locations) and is defined as the dot product in the feature space. Tsuda's kernel employs both visible and hidden information for its calculation.

By fusing the above four types of similarity measures, we expect to overcome the single drawbacks that come when each of them is used alone. In tangible terms, our plan is to implement and evaluate each of them separately first. Then, the best of them will be selected and incorporated into our algorithm. Majority voting and/or a hierarchical decision making process shall be considered and investigated for determining the final similarity score.

C. Social behavior from personality and mental state and vice versa

Our focus rests on the group of personality traits and mental states that correlate stronger with the disposition for changing between locations. There are two directions one can go and we plan to consider both. On one hand, we want to derive movement behavior and consequently locations from them. This is done indirectly by taking them into consideration at the semantic clustering process mentioned in the previous Section. On the other hand, we want to use the available data to infer these automatically in the first place. Here comes axiomatic or rule-based reasoning into play. The rules shall regard all available information and knowledge at the time of the inference process. Two simplified Semantic Web Rule Language (SWRL) [35] rule examples in a human readable syntax are shown below:

$$Person(?p) \wedge hasHighWorkload(?p) \implies hasStress(?p)$$

and

$$Person(?p) \wedge PersonalityTrait(?t) \wedge introversion(?t) \wedge hasPersonalityTrait(?p, ?t) \wedge Situation(?s) \wedge hasCurrentLocation(?p, ?l) \wedge isPArk(?l) \wedge isAlone(?p) \implies hasStress(?p)$$

The second rule describes implicitly the assertion that an introvert person, in contrast to an extrovert one, seeks more probably space and distance when he feels he is stressed, rather than company.

IV. FIRST RESULTS

A first light draft of our ontology suite has already been implemented in OWL2 with Protege [36]. At this stage, it consists of four of the overall five aforementioned major ontologies; the Location, the Person, Personality & Mood, the Activity & Actions and the Temporal & Event ontology. Right now, we use a hybrid semantic similarity metric, which takes both the common features of locations, as well as the topology into account to cluster the available locations and create our corresponding location-specific frames with regard to time, activity, action and/or a certain event. Then, we employ the measured semantic similarity scores to update a 1st Order Markov Chain model by applying the following formula:

$$p(l_{cur})_{i,new} = p(l_{maxSim}) \times Sim + \alpha \times p(l_{cur})_{i,old} \quad (4)$$

- p: Transition probability of the Markov Model
- l_{cur}: Current location
- l_{maxSim}: Most similar location to l_{cur}
- Sim: Semantic similarity score
- α: Offset parameter

Since, to the best of our our knowledge, there is no open dataset containing the semantic information, we need to evaluate our approach, we preliminary tested it on a 5-week long real life dataset, which consists of semantically annotated locations and the respective purpose of visit and activities of 4 users. The data were collected during a user study by using an Android tracking and annotation App we designed. Table I illustrates the performance of our first draft approach compared to the standalone Markov model and the semantic trajectory based approach of Ying discussed in Section II.

TABLE I. EVALUATION TABLE. PSSSA vs. 1st ORDER MARKOV MODEL vs.YING'S APPROACH (min. support=0,01, a=0,2 and b=0,8).

Metrics	ACC	F-measure	Precision	Recall
U1 (1), Markov	0,32	0,46	0,38	0,75
U1(1), PSSSA	0,29	0,42	0,33	0,79
U1 (1), Ying	0,27	0,29	0,29	0,36
U5 (2), Markov	0,23	0,37	0,33	0,56
U5 (2), PSSSA	0,28	0,45	0,40	0,66
U5 (2), Ying	0,2	0,2	0,2	0,53
U2 (3), Markov	0,39	0,55	0,43	0,87
U2 (3), PSSSA	0,37	0,52	0,42	0,87
U2 (3), Ying	0,2	0,2	0,2	0,2
U4 (4), Markov	0,20	0,24	0,23	0,60
U4 (4), PSSSA	0,21	0,24	0,23	0,6 1
U4 (4), Ying	0,0	0,0	0,0	0,0

As we can see, our approach clearly outperforms Ying's framework, which performs extremely weak, especially in the sparse data case. Our approach achieves a f-score of 0.52, the overall second highest score behind the Markov with 0.55. At the same time, it outperforms all other approaches with respect to recall. This reflects the fact that our approach can handle extremely good sparse data sets. However, table I also points out that in two of the cases, the Markov can provide slightly better results than our approach. This can be in part attributed to the similarity threshold we used (0.5%) and in part to the small and unfortunately incomplete semantically annotated data set due to recording inconsistencies during the user study.

V. Conclusions and Future work

This research is centered around the following research question: *Does Semantic Similarity Analysis lead to a more human-like representation of locations? Moreover, does this approach provide us with a solid basis for predicting locations more accurately?* Some first fundamental steps towards answering the above two questions have already been made. Promising preliminary results underpin our hypothesis and point the way to a clearly structured future work to come.

First of all, we plan to refine and finish up our ontology suite. After that, we want to investigate various similarity metrics, such as the marginalized kernel discussed in Section III-B. Then we plan to focus further on the personality-situation debate, because we believe it is a "cherry on the top" feature on the way to reaching personalization and building a preferably human-like Human-Machine Interface. For this purpose we collaborate with a team of psychologists in order to extend our ontological model accordingly. At last, we plan to work on an automated method of propagating our ontology suite with the available data. Various ontology learning methods shall be investigated and tested. Calendar entries, Email content and Reminders or Todo Check List apps shall be used to support this attempt.

References

[1] "Foursquare," 2017. [Online]. Available: https://www.foursquare.com/

[2] R. Nathan et al., "A movement ecology paradigm for unifying organismal movement research," vol. 105, no. 49, 2008, pp. 19 052–19 059.

[3] "Oxford english dictionary," September, 2017. [Online]. Available: https://en.oxforddictionaries.com/definition/knowledge

[4] C. J. Fillmore and C. Baker, "A frames approach to semantic analysis," in The Oxford handbook of linguistic analysis, 2010.

[5] M. Minsky, "A framework for representing knowledge." Cambridge, MA, USA: Massachusetts Institute of Technology, 1974.

[6] R. Glassey and R. Ferguson, "Modeling location for pervasive environments," in 1st UK-UbiNet Workshop, 2003.

[7] J. J.-C. Ying, W.-C. Lee, T.-C. Weng, and V. S. Tseng, "Semantic trajectory mining for location prediction," in Proceedings of the 19th ACM SIGSPATIAL International Conference on Advances in Geographic Information Systems, ser. GIS '11. New York, NY, USA: ACM, 2011, pp. 34–43.

[8] J. J.-C. Ying, W.-C. Lee, and V. S. Tseng, "Mining geographic-temporal-semantic patterns in trajectories for location prediction," vol. 5, no. 1. New York, NY, USA: ACM, Jan. 2014, pp. 2:1–2:33.

[9] N. Samaan and A. Karmouch, "A mobility prediction architecture based on contextual knowledge and spatial conceptual maps," vol. 4, no. 6. Piscataway, NJ, USA: IEEE Educational Activities Department, Nov. 2005, pp. 537–551.

[10] N. Samaan, A. Karmouch, and H. Kheddouci, "Mobility prediction based service location and delivery," in Canadian Conference on Electrical and Computer Engineering 2004 (IEEE Cat. No.04CH37513), vol. 4, May 2004, pp. 2307–2310 Vol.4.

[11] N. Samaan, B. Benmammar, F. Krief, and A. Karmouch, "Prediction-based advanced resource reservation in mobile environments," in Canadian Conference on Electrical and Computer Engineering, 2005., May 2005, pp. 1411–1414.

[12] Y. A. Ridhawi, I. A. Ridhawi, A. Karmouch, and A. Nayak, "A context-aware and location prediction framework for dynamic environments," in 2011 IEEE 7th International Conference on Wireless and Mobile Computing, Networking and Communications (WiMob), Oct 2011, pp. 172–179.

[13] I. A. Ridhawi, M. Aloqaily, A. Karmouch, and N. Agoulmine, "A location-aware user tracking and prediction system," in 2009 Global Information Infrastructure Symposium, June 2009, pp. 1–8.

[14] R. Wannous, J. Malki, A. Bouju, and C. Vincent, "Trajectory ontology inference considering domain and temporal dimensions: Application to marine mammals." Elsevier, 2016.

[15] X. Long, L. Jin, and J. Joshi, "Exploring trajectory-driven local geographic topics in foursquare," in Proceedings of the 2012 ACM Conference on Ubiquitous Computing, ser. UbiComp '12. New York, NY, USA: ACM, 2012, pp. 927–934.

[16] R. Krishnamurthy, P. Kapanipathi, A. P. Sheth, and K. Thirunarayan, "Knowledge enabled approach to predict the location of twitter users," in The Semantic Web. Latest Advances and New Domains: 12th European Semantic Web Conference, ESWC 2015, Portoroz, Slovenia, May 31 – June 4, 2015. Proceedings. Springer International Publishing, 2015, pp. 187–201.

[17] "Twitter," 2017. [Online]. Available: https://www.twitter.com

[18] N. R. Mabroukeh and C. I. Ezeife, "Using domain ontology for semantic web usage mining and next page prediction," in Proceedings of the 18th ACM Conference on Information and Knowledge Management, CIKM 2009, Hong Kong, China, November 2-6, 2009, 2009, pp. 1677–1680.

[19] Q. Zhao et al., "Time-dependent semantic similarity measure of queries using historical click-through data," in Proceedings of the 15th international conference on World Wide Web. ACM, 2006, pp. 543–552.

[20] S. Kassin, "Psychology." Pearson/Prentice Hall, 2004.

[21] D. Funder, "The personality puzzle." W. W. NORTON & Company Incorporated, 2015.

[22] W. Fleeson, "Toward a structure-and process-integrated view of personality: Traits as density distributions of states." vol. 80, no. 6. American Psychological Association, 2001, p. 1011.

[23] A. R. Buss, "The trait-situation controversy and the concept of interaction," vol. 3, no. 2. Sage Publications, 1977, pp. 196–201.

[24] J. J. Jaccard, "Predicting social behavior from personality traits," vol. 7, no. 4. Elsevier, 1974, pp. 358–367.

[25] P. Borkenau, "To predict some of the people more of the time," in Fifty Years of Personality Psychology. Springer US, 1993, pp. 237–249.

[26] S. Adali and J. Golbeck, "Predicting personality with social behavior: a comparative study," vol. 4, no. 1, 2014, p. 159.

[27] J. Staiano, B. Lepri, N. Aharony, F. Pianesi, N. Sebe, and A. Pentland, "Friends don't lie: Inferring personality traits from social network structure," in Proceedings of the 2012 ACM Conference on Ubiquitous Computing. New York, NY, USA: ACM, 2012, pp. 321–330.

[28] M. Codescu, G. Horsinka, O. Kutz, T. Mossakowski, and R. Rau, "Osmonto – an ontology of openstreetmap tags," 2014.

[29] V. V. Hainš, S. Lovrenčić, and V. Kirinić, "Personality model representation using ontology."

[30] J. Hastings, W. Ceusters, B. Smith, and K. Mulligan, "Dispositions and processes in the emotion ontology," in Proceedings of the 2nd International Conference on Biomedical Ontology, 2011, pp. 71–78.

[31] A. Gangemi and V. Presutti, "Ontology design patterns," 2009.

[32] Z. Wu and M. Palmer, "Verbs semantics and lexical selection," in Proceedings of the 32Nd Annual Meeting on Association for Computational Linguistics, ser. ACL '94. Stroudsburg, PA, USA: Association for Computational Linguistics, 1994, pp. 133–138.

[33] D. Lin, "An information-theoretic definition of similarity," in Proceedings of the Fifteenth International Conference on Machine Learning. San Francisco, CA, USA: Morgan Kaufmann Publishers Inc., 1998, pp. 296–304.

[34] K. Tsuda, T. Kin, and K. Asai, "Marginalized kernels for biological sequences," vol. 18, no. 1, 2002, pp. S268–S275.

[35] "Swrl: A semantic web rule language," 2017. [Online]. Available: https://www.w3.org/Submission/SWRL/

[36] "Protege," 2017. [Online]. Available: http://protege.stanford.edu

TPM Framework: a Comprehensive Kit for Exploring Applications with Textile Pressure Mapping Matrix

Bo Zhou*, Jingyuan Cheng‡, Ankur Mawandia*, Yujiang He‡, Zhixin Huang‡, Mathias Sundholm*, Muhammet Yildrim*, Heber Cruz*, Paul Lukowicz*†

*German Research Center for Artificial Intelligence
†TU Kaiserslautern, Germany
‡TU Braunschweig, Germany
bo.zhou@dfki.de, j.cheng@tu-braunschweig.de, ankur.mawandia@dfki.de,
yujiang.he@tu-braunschweig.de, zhixin.huang@tu-braunschweig.de,
mathias.sundholm@dfki.de, muhammet.yildrim@dfki.de,
heber.cruz@dfki.de, paul.lukowicz@dfki.de

***Abstract*—Based on a series of projects with textile pressure mapping matrix (TPM) for ubiquitous and wearable activity recognition in various scenarios, we have accumulated the knowledge and experience to develop an open-access hardware and software framework, which enables a broader education and allows the scientific community to build their own TPM applications. The hardware framework includes all the necessary resources to manufacture the sensing equipment and instructions to build the fabric sensors for an up to 32×32 TPM. The software framework 'Textile-Sandbox' contains ready-to-use tools and modules that support both running experiments and data mining. The framework is evaluated with 10 master students working in 4 groups. 4 applications are developed from scratch and validated within only 40 hours. We present this framework and the evaluated applications in this paper.**

Keywords–Software Framework; Pressure Matrix; Smart Textile; Rapid Prototyping.

I. INTRODUCTION

Textile pressure mapping matrix (TPM) is a sensing modality that measures the planar pressure intensity distribution of the sensing textile, which is related to the people (parts of their body) and analyze a complete modular and miniaturized hardware system, software chains, and data processing and data mining algorithms.

With every new application, we discover:

1) TPM can be a *general sensing modality* for most of the activity recognition applications, as most activities are initiated by interactive force or support surface counter force. Even for contact activities, force can be propagated onto the floor. TPM can also be fixed on-body to measure the muscle activities. Pressure force mapping provides both temporal and spatial information about the activities, very distinct from the dominating sensing modalities, such as inertial measurement units in activity recognition. Its output is similar to a video in the sense of data format and processing methods.
2) Various applications share certain *similar exploration procedures*, as summarized in Fig. 2. The smart fabric produced by Sefar [1] is tailored to fit specific application scenarios [2]. From the hardware perspective, various versions of data acquisition electronics are developed to explore implementation varieties of the scalable modular architecture we proposed in [3]. Different data mining and machine learning methods are also evaluated according to the signal nature of various applications.

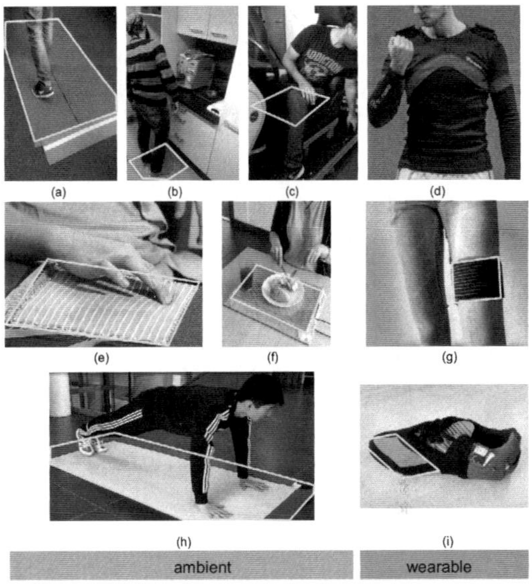

Figure 1. Various applications enabled by textile pressure mapping matrix (TPM)

It has come to a point that certain processes can be generalized in both the hardware and software domain to form a framework, which can greatly reduce time and effort of the idea-to-implementation cycle. Though there are much more application possibilities that can be interesting to be evaluated, we work on developing and improving this open-access framework, that can promote TPM in education and the broader research community, and more developers can be inspired to easily build their own applications.

The major contribution of this paper lies in:

1) We offer the manufacturing resources and firmware builds for the refined data acquisition system.
2) We present Textile-Sandbox, a well documented software framework for application exploration with TPM, including two labeling tools for ground truth annotation and a three-layered Matlab-based data mining tool, which can be both ran by a single click and adjusted in depth.
3) We validated the framework with 10 developers working in small groups, and 4 applications have been prototyped within 40 hours (see Table I). The developers are computer science students with very limited knowledge in the sensing modality and data mining. Therefore, our framework can not only reduce the time and effort spent in new application exploration, but also greatly lower the entry barriers.
4) We open all the code, resources, documentation and ethics templates to the research community [4] [5].

We hope the TPM framework can support more researchers in validating and exploring their own applications with textile pressure sensing matrix.

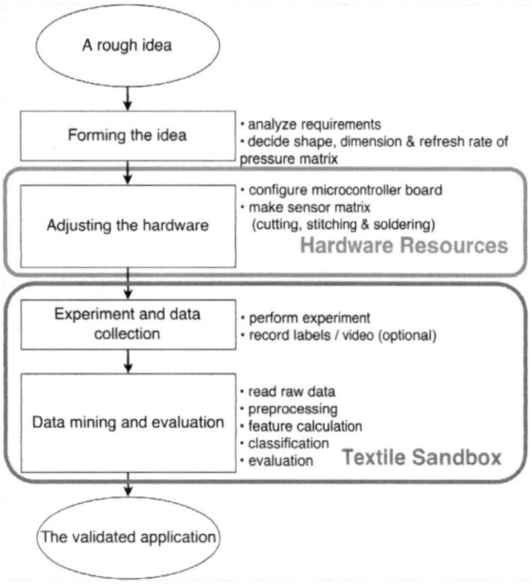

Figure 2. Typical procedures in new application exploration with textile pressure sensing matrix: the "Textile Sandbox" serves as the general framework for data recording and mining

II. Related Work

A. Planar pressure mapping development scene

In ubiquitous computing, planar pressure sensing is used in shoes to analyze gait information [6] [7], on chair/seat to detect user posture [8] [9] or recognize driver's identity [10], on furniture to recognize daily activities of the elderly [11]. A pressure sensing matrix equipped bed can recognize on-bed rehabilitation exercises or monitor sleep posture and stage [12] [13] [14]. Different kinds of pressure sensitive floors have been used for indoor positioning [15] [16], gait and person identification [17] [18] [19] and human computer interaction [20] [21]. Similar to our own previous research, these works focus on creating or enhancing concrete hardware design, on creating data processing algorithms for specific applications. No open-access software framework is available from said works for a broader community to explore their own applications.

There are also a few off-the-shelf pressure sensing matrices. Sensingtex [22] provides a development kit for capturing pressure data using prefabricate hardware serving as seat cover, fitness mat and mattress mat. Tekscan provides both single pressure sensors and sensing matrices, that are used in shoes, mat, seat and bed [23]. Texisense provides a sensor matrix for monitoring walking and seating, accompanied by TexiMonitor-SLT, a custom software for data readout [24]. These commercial products come with fixed hardware, that is, the shape, dimensions, sample rate, etc. are all pre-fixed. Software is provided mainly for data read-out or for feature analysis and only for certain applications. The freedom of adapting these systems to new scenarios is thus greatly limited.

In summary, to the best of our knowledge, there is no existing open-access framework that is based on customizable hardware, and meanwhile provides ready-to-use data acquisition and data mining tools, thus enabling easy and quick exploration of new applications based on pressure sensing matrix. Moreover, our work focuses on textile based pressure mapping, instead of thin film based methods, which is the case with most of the above-mentioned works.

B. Frameworks for ubiquitous computing applications

To ease application exploration in ubiquitous computing, a large number of frameworks were developed. A systematic review on them can be found in Guinea et al.'s work in 2016 [25], based on 132 approaches. Below we name a few, which inspired our Textile-Sandbox.

The iStuff toolkit [26] is composed of multiple physical devices and a supporting software framework, which includes a dynamically configurable intermediary to simplify the mapping of devices to different applications, thus greatly simplifying the exploration of novel interaction techniques in post-desktop era of multiple devices. CRN Toolbox [27] as a modular framework not only allows flexible sensor configuration and sensor data processing, but also provides a graphical configuration editor so that users can intuitively drag modules from library into workspace. It thus enables fast implementation of activity and context recognition systems. The Funf Open Sensing Framework [28] is an extensible sensing and data processing framework for mobile devices, which enables the collection, uploading and configuration of a wide range of data signals accessible via mobile phones. It reduces greatly the app developers' effort through its 3rd-party developer API.

As to smart textile, Buechley built a construction kit consisting of hardware components that can be stitched on garments to create interactive textiles [29]. Interactex [30] serves as a visual, integrated development environment specifically designed for smart textiles, including support on application development, testing and circuit design. Plushbot [31] contains a pattern interface for users to create and trace a plush toy; in the background, the program combines the plush toy pattern with computational pieces, allowing even children to create and customize programmable toys.

In summary, supporting tool-kits and frameworks for ubiquitous computing started to appear around 15 years ago. They all share the common characters of modular design and easy to configure, aim at enabling larger number of developers (specially software developers) to explore their own applications with reduced time, effort and cost. We took these as guidelines while developing our Textile-Sandbox.

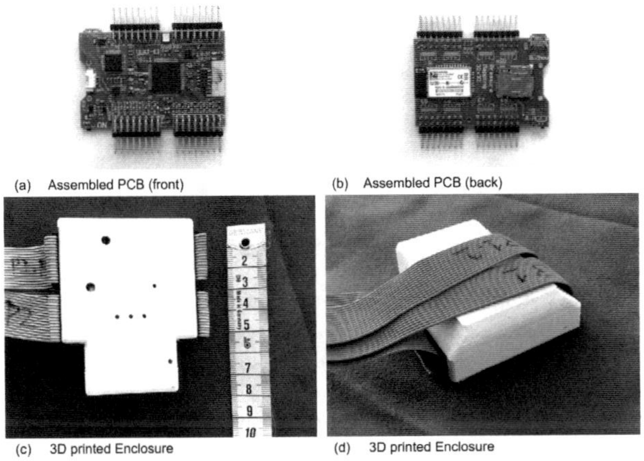

Figure 3. The up-to-date hardware module from the hardware resources

III. TPM APPLICATIONS: THE GENERAL WORKFLOW

The operation principles and detailed hardware designs of our TPM has been presented in [32] [3]. In short, a TPM sensor consists of 3 layers in a sandwich-like structure. The top and bottom layers are made of the same fabric, composed of evenly spaced parallel metallic stripes on a PET fabric substrate. The middle layer is a pressure sensitive semi-conductive fabric. The bottom layer is 90 degree rotated from the top layer. Each cross-section acts as a pressure sensor. The resistances at all cross-sections are turned to voltage by simple voltage-dividers and then turned from analog signal into digital data by ADCs (Analog-to-Digital Converter) scanning through the whole matrix. A complete scan of the matrix results in a pressure mapping imagery. Repeated scans produce a video-like data stream of pressure mapping imagery.

Exploring a application with TPM normally involves 4 steps (Fig. 2):

1) *Forming an idea*: Motivated by a general scenario, first a rough analysis on involved activities shall be carried out and a draft list of the activities shall be defined, then the hardware settings shall be fixed, including: where to put and how to fix the sensor matrix, the dimension and resolution of the matrix, the scanning speed, the electronic placement and cable routing. This step defines the hardware specifications for the next steps.
2) *Adapting the hardware*: Using pre-manufactured electronics, the specific hardware for this application can be made by: 1) tailor the smart fabrics to fit the target surface, 2) connect the sensing fabric to the electronics by careful soldering, 3) prepare the firmware of the electronics (change of scanning ports and speed) 4) fit the hardware into the experiment setting. A small-scaled matrix normally can be made within several hours (see Fig. 4). After this step, raw data can be gathered and visualized using our data acquisition tool in real-time, available at [33].
3) *Experiment and data collection*: Data can be collected by several participants for an abundant amount of repetitions. The ground truth (labels) are generated either at runtime or offline. This step generates the dataset for the next step.
4) *Data mining and evaluation*: The dataset is split into the training set and the testing set. Features are calculated for all the activities and the result is evaluated through n-Fold cross-validation.

IV. HARDWARE RESOURCES

Through the accumulation of our previous works, we have developed a mature hardware system to drive a sensing matrix of up to 32×32 sensing points. The electronics, alone measures at 6×4 cm, are centered around a dsPIC microcontroller, powered by a Li-Po battery with onboard charging and protection circuits. It can be charged with a microUSB (Universal Serial Bus) cable. The data transmission is possible through Bluetooth Classic, USB 2.0 or serial port streaming, or local SD card logging. Several LEDs including a full-color LED (Light-Emitting Diode) provides a rich range of status indication. It also has a 9-axis onboard IMU (Inertial Measurement Unit) for sensor fusion purposes, and optional ESD (Electrostatic Discharge) protection at the smart textile connection ports.

With USB connection, a 32-by-32 sensor matrix can be sampled at 40 frames per second with 12-bit analog resolution, which is limited by the ADC sampling rate. With Bluetooth, the refresh rate is limited to approximately 19.5 frames per second due to the Bluetooth bandwidth (30KB/s). However, as the matrix resolution decreases, the refresh rate can be improved. For example, with USB data transmission, a 16-by-16 matrix can be scanned at 160 frames per second.

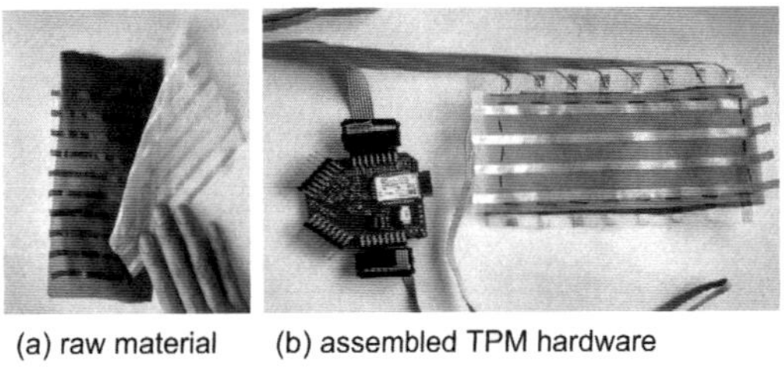

Figure 4. With the instructions in the Textile-Sandbox, developers can easily assemble tailored TPM sensors from raw material

In the open-access resources, the manufacturing files are available together with the micro-controller firmware builds, which streams out data of the full scan of 32 × 32 matrix. The parameters can be easily modified to accommodate different matrix resolutions. The 3D model of an enclosure (22×62×76 mm) for the electronics and the battery is also available. The electronics connects to the smart fabric through 2.54cm-pitch 8×2 headers, which can be clamped onto widely available 1.27cm-pitch ribbon cables. All resources needed to produce a hardware as shown in Figure 3 can be accessed in [4].

V. SOFTWARE FRAMEWORK: TEXTILE-SANDBOX

A. Design Guidelines of the Textile-Sandbox

As our goal is to reduce application exploration effort, and our target users are the computer science students and researchers, who are new to pressure sensing, we identify the following basic requirements on the software framework:

- *Per step support*: Tools should be provided for data recording and data processing/mining. We provide two tools for data labeling, and a Matlab-based data mining tool for feature extraction and classification.
- *Configurable*: Application-specific parameters (matrix size, refresh rate, preprocessing parameters, data path) are configured by an editable .cvs file.
- *Fast kickstart*: Together with the framework, we provide a compact example of labeled dataset and configurations. After downloading the framework, users can execute the whole data processing chain by calling a single function and a few more mouse clicks.
- *Modular design*: We divide our framework into three-layered modules. User can sequentially execute each module and validate its output. The intermediate outcome of former steps are automatically saved, so that the user can resume the data processing from any step.
- *Documented*: An on-line "help" documentation is created, serving as the nexus for resource downloading, tutorials of experiment design, and how to use the labeling tools and data mining tool (open access at [33]).

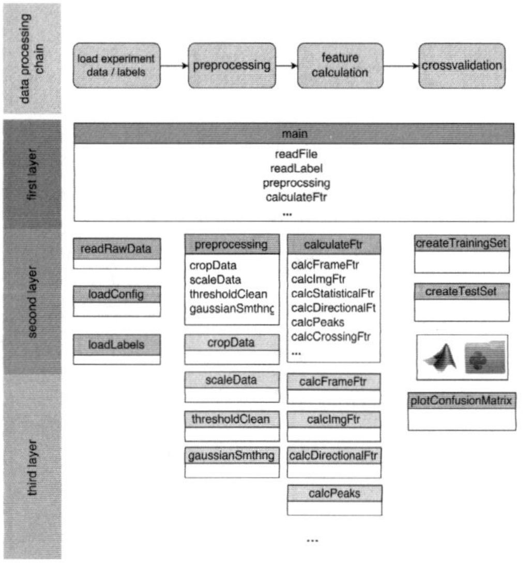

Figure 5. Data processing flow and corresponding design in Textile-Sandbox

B. Data Labeling Tools

As we follow the typical supervised learning method in application exploration, generating accurate labels for recorded data is the base for all data mining tasks afterwards. We developed two labeling tools according to the nature of two types of activities. The first type of activities can be easily controlled by the test subject him/herself to be finished within a predefined period in predefined order. For example, using forefinger to *plot a circle* or to *write "A"* on the pressure mat. The second type of activities shall happen in a more natural way at the speed and the order that the test subject feels comfortable. For example, having a meal contains activities like *eating salad*, *eating bread* and *drinking water*. The test subject however, would most likely want to mix the activities, adapt the duration and sequence of each activity according to his/her own eating habit. We developed a light-weight online labeling tool for the first type and an offline labeling tool for the second (open access at [34]).

C. Data Mining Tool

We followed the general data processing chain in Figure 5 and developed a data mining tool, which allows the user to process the pressure distribution dataset with minimal or no coding. We implemented all the functions in Matlab with self-developed algorithm, except the step "classification", where the Classification Learner app in Matlab [35] is used. The data mining tool is divided into three layers. On the first layer is the main function, which calls the functions on the second layer in a sequence way, so that the end result based on given dataset can be obtained by executing just one function and few clicks. The second layer matches each step in the data processing chain. These functions further call the functions on the third layer, where sub-tasks are performed.

In the data processing chain, first the raw data, the configuration in the .cvs file, and the labels are loaded. The preprocessing step utilizes several methods, such as DC removal, upscaling, filtering to enhance the data quality within each frame (the reasons for applying these methods and the implementations are reported in our former work [32]).

The next step is essential for the final classification performance of every new application. Here the features are extracted from the preprocessed data. We provided 21 basic features, which are generally useful for most of the applications. These features offer an initial classification result, to explore the feasibility of using TPM for the application with little overhead effort. If the user decides to further improve the result, the second layer also supports custom features.

For each event, the 21 basic features are defined as follows:

Statistical features from the time series of frame descriptors (10 features): two descriptors are calculated from each frame: sum of all pixels and the number of pixels after thresholding. From the time series of these two descriptors within the event, the maximum, minimum, mean, number of peaks and number of mean-crossing are calculated.

Pressure center shift (4 features): Three frames from each activity event, the first, the last, and the frame with the highest pixel-sum, are selected. The center of weight [x,y] of these frames are calculated. The difference of [x,y] between the first and the last frame, and between first and the highest pixel-sum frame, are considered as another 4 features.

Image descriptors the average frame (7 features): Each pixel in the average frame is the average of the pixel location within the event period. The 7 Zernike image moments [36] of this frame are calculated as features.

The third layer performs cross-validation using the features from the second layer with the Matlab Classification Learner.

TABLE I. SUMMARY OF THE APPLICATIONS FROM THE 10-PARTICIPANT WORKSHOP

Project	Matrix	Classes	participant × repetitions	Evaluation*	Accuracy
SpyOnMe	32 × 8 2cm pitch	6 [1]	3 × 5	Bagged Trees 8-fold	91%**
Win Your Heart	16 × 16 2cm pitch	6	1 × 10	Random Forest 10-fold	84%
Pressure Password	16 × 16 1cm pitch	5 [3]	2 × 10	SVM 5-fold	76%
Smart Pillow	16 × 16 2cm - 4cm pitches***	5 [4]	3 × 10	Bagged Trees 10-fold	87%

* all projects used the 21 basic features provided by the Textile-Sandbox
** the asymmetric pitch is used to accompany the length of the pillow
[1] typing, writing, sketching with a pen, internet surfing or playing computer games (both mouse and keyboard), idle, and absence.
[2] scratching, hugging, holding the toy's upper part, holding the lower part, beating, pinching and touching with the face (simulating kissing).
[3] five distinct passwords.
[4] 4 sleep positions (supine position, prone position, lying on the left side, lying on the right side) and 1 kneeing posture

This three layered design allows users with varying levels of expertise to benefit from the data mining tool. With the first layer the user can quickly get an impression on the process and check the initial results by running only a few functions plus a few clicks in the Matlab Classification Learner. The user can then get deeper by checking the output of each step on the second layer. As he/she gets more insights, the third layer provides him/her enough freedom to influence the final result with some small changes in the code. The user can then modify the modules even on higher levels. By then the users shall have already gained enough knowledge to develop their own data mining algorithms. Our data mining tool has thus completed its mission in supporting application exploration. From that moment on, it shall serve mainly as a starting point for the user towards the more comprehensive application development.

D. Documentation

A web documentation is created and can be accessed at [33]. It is indexed and can be searched upon, containing: (1) An overview of the application exploration chain; (2) Description of the hardware and operational instructions; (3) Description of the labeling tools; (4) Description of the data mining tool, including detailed description to all the Matlab functions; (5) Links to all source code, tools, introduction powerpoint slides (used in the practicum, details in section VI) and one labeled dataset for an easy start without own data recording and labeling.

VI. APPLICATION EXPLORATION USING TEXTILE-SANDBOX

To evaluate to what degree our Textile-Sandbox can support new application exploration, and to provide computer science students the hands-on experience with hardware and the activity recognition related data processing, we created a workshop for master students majored in Computer Science or System Techniques, where the students develop from scratch their own application. From 10 participants, only 3 had background knowledge on ubiquitous computing through some earlier lectures. Four groups were formed voluntarily. All the groups managed to individually propose and explore one application within only 40 hours (The applications are shown in Fig. 6, detailed time distribution is listed in Table II). All applications are based on general ready-to-use electronics, which are developed by our lab in [37]. It drives one matrix of maximum 32×32 channels and transfers the data via Bluetooth to a mobile phone. The scanning rate is set to 60Hz.

TABLE II. TIME DISTRIBUTION IN APPLICATION EXPLORATION WITH TEXTILE-SANDBOX.

Task	time spent
Introduction lecture	6 hr
Software practice with existing dataset	4 hr
Propose an application	3 hr
Making matrix	4 hr
Data recording and evaluation with Textile-Sandbox	20 hr
Presentation on the explored applications	0.5 hr
Sum	37.5 hr

The motivations of the applications are described below, the physical hardware are shown in Figure 6, and the settings and results are listed in Table I. Since the educational purpose of this workshop is our main focus, the level of innovation and dataset size are limited to only establish a pilot prototype.

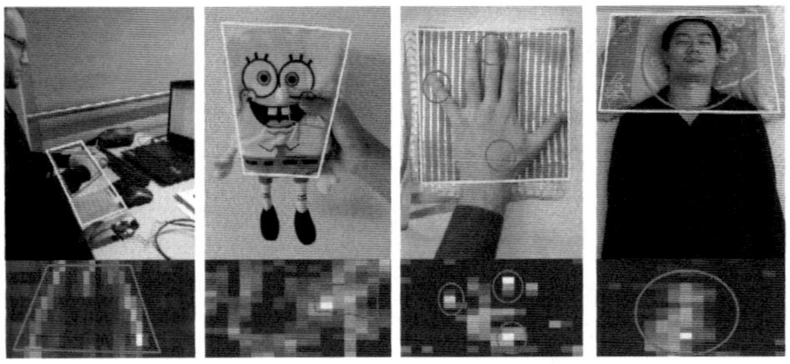

(a)SpyOnMe (b) Win Your Heart (c) Pressure Password (d) Smart Pillow

Figure 6. Applications explored using Textile-Sandbox, along with the representing pressure distribution of one selected activity, (a)SpyOnMe (two arms lying on the table while tying on keyboard), (b)Win Your Heart (grabbing with thumb), (c)Pressure Password (pressing with the middle and the little fingers), (d)Smart Pillow (supine position)

A. SpyOnMe: activity monitoring at workplace

Modern office workplace normally has a similar setting: a work desk, a computer with keyboard and mouse, paper, etc. Detection of typical activities like typing on keyboard, browsing web or away from work can give insights into the person's role, his/her methods and performance at work place. SpyOnMe is proposed, as an non-intrusive method to monitor work space activities based on pressure between forearms and the desk.

TABLE III. FEEDBACK RECEIVED FROM 10 PRACTICUM PARTICIPANTS, SCALED FROM 1 (LOWEST) TO 5 (HIGHEST)

Criteria	avg score	min score
well documented	4.9	4
intutive to use	4.4	3
applicable to multiple scenario	4.3	3
richness of tools	4.1	3
faster application development	4	2

B. *Win Your Heart: a toy for children behavior analysis*

Toys have been widely used, for educational, behavioral training, emotional companion and other purposes. This application aims to enable non-obtrusive monitoring of children's behaviour and their mental status by identifying their interactions with a pressure sensitive toy.

C. *Pressure Password: motionless unlocking*

Pattern or numerical locks are fairly common on mobile devices and keyless entry systems. However, pattern based locks have been shown to be highly insecure as intruders can observe movements and easily crack the pattern [38]. Numerical entry systems, such as in ATM machines have been shown vulnerable to thermal cameras [39]. We explored a motionless password system based on the born shape of palm and length of fingers, and the combination of multiple fingers at different intensity of pressure. All the combinations look the same, making the password hard to copy by observing.

D. *Smart Pillow: sleep position detection*

One third of our life is spent sleeping, which has a high impact also on the other two thirds. A pillow covered with pressure sensing matrix can help monitor the sleep posture and enhance sleep quality.

E. *Developer feedback*

Anonymous questionnaires were given to the ten participants to collect their feedback to the Textile-Sandbox (see Table III). In general, we received a very positive response. Most of the students agree that the framework is easy and intuitive to use, allows them to create and develop applications faster. Eight out of ten students agree that they can independently develop applications with the support from Textile-Sandbox. Two students got inspired to create features suiting their applications. All reported improvement in the understanding of smart textile and its application after developing their own application with Textile Sandbox.

It is suggested to combine the data acquisition app and the online labeling tool into one tool to reduce annotation effort. It is also suggested that more prior applications shall be introduced at the beginning. (We will thus accumulate applications developed within this workshop as example for future students.)

VII. CONCLUSION

We present in this paper our open access framework to explore wearable and ubiquitous applications with textile pressure mapping matrix (TPM), which includes hardware resources and the software framework, Textile-Sandbox. We have explored its application in various activity recognition related domains. To pave its path towards a wider adoption in the research community, we developed the framework to inspire and assist developers new to smart fabric or TPM, but interested in exploring their own applications using this sensing modality. We evaluated this framework with computer science master students, who successfully explored applications proposed by themselves independently within only 40 hours.

In our future work, we plan to keep pushing out hardware and software revisions. A Python port of the software framework is also in the plan. Also, manual mode will be added to the online labeling tool, as suggested by students, so that labels can also be freely generated by the experiment supervisor during the experiment. To further reduce the exploration time and lower the barriers to entry, more features shall be implemented and provided as ready-to-use module. A graphical user interface shall be created, which shows the data processing chain and provides "drag and drop" function for adding and removing modules. We will also look into packaging the functions for using the TPM into APIs that can act as a third-party plugin for other smart textile frameworks, such as Interactex [30]. We are looking forward to further suggestions from the research communities as well.

We believe the TPM hardware sensing platform and the Textile-Sandbox framework, shall free the imagination of a boarder research community, and project another type of light (the gravity and other forces) onto the secrets hidden in human activities and behaviors.

REFERENCES

[1] "Sefar." [Online]. Available: http://www.sefar.com/

[2] S. P. Consortium, "Simpleskin project final report - 4.1.3.1 wp1 textile technologies," Tech. Rep., 2016. [Online]. Available: http://simpleskin.org/downloads/final_report.pdf

[3] B. Zhou, J. Cheng, M. Sundholm, and P. Lukowicz, "From smart clothing to smart table cloth: Design and implementation of a large scale, textile pressure matrix sensor," in ARCS. Springer, 2014, pp. 159–170.

[4] A. Mawandia and J. Cheng, "Textile sandbox: source codes, resources and documentation on-line," http://wearcomlab.com/wcldocumentation/sites.google.com/site/resistivesensingdocumentation/resources.html, last access: Feb. 2017.

[5] S. Doda, M. S. Singh, B. Zhou, and J. Cheng, "Ethics templates for experiments with resistive sensing matrix," http://simpleskin.org/?ethics, last access: Feb. 2017.

[6] L. Shu, T. Hua, Y. Wang, Q. Li, D. D. Feng, and X. Tao, "In-shoe plantar pressure measurement and analysis system based on fabric pressure sensing array," Information Technology in Biomedicine, IEEE Transactions on, vol. 14, no. 3, 2010, pp. 767–775.

[7] W. Xu, M.-C. Huang, N. Amini, J. J. Liu, L. He, and M. Sarrafzadeh, "Smart insole: a wearable system for gait analysis," in Proceedings of the 5th International Conference on PErvasive Technologies Related to Assistive Environments. ACM, 2012, p. 18.

[8] J. Meyer, B. Arnrich, J. Schumm, and G. Tröster, "Design and modeling of a textile pressure sensor for sitting posture classification," Sensors Journal, IEEE, vol. 10, no. 8, 2010, pp. 1391–1398.

[9] W. Xu, M.-C. Huang, N. Amini, L. He, and M. Sarrafzadeh, "ecushion: A textile pressure sensor array design and calibration for sitting posture analysis," Sensors Journal, IEEE, vol. 13, no. 10, 2013, pp. 3926–3934.

[10] X. Xie, B. Zheng, and W. Xue, "Object identification on car seat based on rough sets," in 2011 IEEE 3rd International Conference on Communication Software and Networks, 2011, pp. 157–159.

[11] J.-H. Lim, H. Jang, J. Jang, and S.-J. Park, "Daily activity recognition system for the elderly using pressure sensors," in EMBS 2008. 30th Annual International Conference of the IEEE. IEEE, 2008, pp. 5188–5191.

[12] M.-C. Huang, J. J. Liu, W. Xu, N. Alshurafa, X. Zhang, and M. Sarrafzadeh, "Using pressure map sequences for recognition of on bed rehabilitation exercises," Biomedical and Health Informatics, IEEE Journal of, vol. 18, no. 2, 2014, pp. 411–418.

[13] J. J. Liu, W. Xu, M.-C. Huang, N. Alshurafa, M. Sarrafzadeh, N. Raut, and B. Yadegar, "Sleep posture analysis using a dense pressure sensitive bedsheet," Pervasive and Mobile Computing, vol. 10, 2014, pp. 34–50.

[14] L. Samy, M.-C. Huang, J. J. Liu, W. Xu, and M. Sarrafzadeh, "Unobtrusive sleep stage identification using a pressure-sensitive bed sheet," Sensors Journal, IEEE, vol. 14, no. 7, 2014, pp. 2092–2101.

[15] D. Savio and T. Ludwig, "Smart carpet: A footstep tracking interface," in AINAW'07. 21st International Conference on, vol. 2. IEEE, 2007, pp. 754–760.

[16] Y. Kaddoura, J. King, and A. S. Helal, "Cost-precision tradeoffs in unencumbered floor-based indoor location tracking," in 3rd International Conference on Smart Homes and Health Telematics, Sherbrooke, Québec, Canada, 2005, pp. 75–82.

[17] L. Middleton, A. Buss, A. Bazin, M. S. Nixon et al., "A floor sensor system for gait recognition," in Automatic Identification Advanced Technologies, 2005. Fourth IEEE Workshop on. IEEE, 2005, pp. 171–176.

[18] R. J. Orr and G. D. Abowd, "The smart floor: a mechanism for natural user identification and tracking," in CHI'00 extended abstracts on Human factors in computing systems. ACM, 2000, pp. 275–276.

[19] G. Qian, J. Zhang, and A. Kidané, "People identification using gait via floor pressure sensing and analysis," in Smart sensing and context. Springer, 2008, pp. 83–98.

[20] P. Srinivasan, D. Birchfield, G. Qian, and A. Kidané, "A pressure sensing floor for interactive media applications," in Proceedings of the 2005 ACM SIGCHI International Conference on Advances in computer entertainment technology. ACM, 2005, pp. 278–281.

[21] S. Rangarajan, A. Kidané, G. Qian, and S. Rajko, Design Optimization of Pressure Sensing Floor for Multimodal Human-Computer Interaction. INTECH Open Access Publisher, 2008.

[22] S. Sensing Tex, "Sensing tex smart textiles," http://sensingtex.com/development-kits, last access: Feb. 2017.

[23] Tekscan, "Pressure mapping, force measurement, & tactile sensors — tekscan," https://www.tekscan.com/products-solutions, last access: Feb. 2017.

[24] T. Company, "Texisense textile pressure sensor: Teximat and teximat-slt," http://www.texisense.com/home_en, last access: Feb. 2017.

[25] A. S. Guinea, G. Nain, and Y. Le Traon, "A systematic review on the engineering of software for ubiquitous systems," Journal of Systems and Software, vol. 118, 2016, pp. 251–276.

[26] R. Ballagas, M. Ringel, M. Stone, and J. Borchers, "istuff: a physical user interface toolkit for ubiquitous computing environments," in Proceedings of the SIGCHI conference on Human factors in computing systems. ACM, 2003, pp. 537–544.

[27] D. Bannach, O. Amft, and P. Lukowicz, "Rapid prototyping of activity recognition applications," IEEE Pervasive Computing, vol. 7, no. 2, 2008.

[28] N. Aharony, W. Pan, C. Ip, I. Khayal, and A. Pentland, "Social fmri: Investigating and shaping social mechanisms in the real world," Pervasive and Mobile Computing, vol. 7, no. 6, 2011, pp. 643–659.

[29] L. Buechley, "A construction kit for electronic textiles," in Wearable Computers, 2006 10th IEEE International Symposium on. IEEE, 2006, pp. 83–90.

[30] J. Haladjian, K. Bredies, and B. Brügge, "Interactex: an integrated development environment for smart textiles," in Proceedings of the 2016 ACM International Symposium on Wearable Computers. ACM, 2016, pp. 8–15.

[31] Y. Huang and M. Eisenberg, "Steps toward child-designed interactive stuffed toys," in Proceedings of the 10th International Conference on Interaction Design and Children. ACM, 2011, pp. 165–168.

[32] J. Cheng, M. Sundholm, B. Zhou, M. Hirsch, and P. Lukowicz, "Smart-surface: Large scale textile pressure sensors arrays for activity recognition," Pervasive and Mobile Computing, 2016.

[33] "Textile sandbox." [Online]. Available: http://goo.gl/hiowPc

[34] "Textile sandbox online labeling toll." [Online]. Available: http://wearcomlab.de/resources/exptool

[35] MathWorks, "Matlab classification learner app," https://www.mathworks.com/products/statistics/classification-learner.html, last access: Feb. 2017.

[36] A. Khotanzad and Y. H. Hong, "Invariant image recognition by zernike moments," IEEE Transactions on pattern analysis and machine intelligence, vol. 12, no. 5, 1990, pp. 489–497.

[37] B. Zhou, H. Koerger, M. Wirth, C. Zwick, C. Martindale, H. Cruz, B. Eskofier, and P. Lukowicz, "Smart soccer shoe: monitoring foot-ball interaction with shoe integrated textile pressure sensor matrix," in Proceedings of the 2016 ACM International Symposium on Wearable Computers. ACM, 2016, pp. 64–71.

[38] G. Ye, Z. Tang, D. Fang, X. Chen, K. I. Kim, B. Taylor, and Z. Wang, "Cracking android pattern lock in five attempts," 2017.

[39] K. Mowery, S. Meiklejohn, and S. Savage, "Heat of the moment: characterizing the efficacy of thermal camera-based attacks," in Proceedings of the 5th USENIX conference on Offensive technologies. USENIX Association, 2011, pp. 6–6.

Estimation of Relative Offset and Drift for Synchronization of Local Clocks in Wireless Sensor Networks

Ayako Arao and Hiroaki Higaki
Department of Robotics and Mechatronics,
Tokyo Denki University, Japan
Email: {arao,hig}@higlab.net

***Abstract*—In wireless sensor networks, each wireless sensor node records events that occurred in its observation area with their observation time. Each wireless sensor node possesses its own local clock whose drift and offset are generally different from the others. In addition, it is difficult for the wireless sensor nodes to adjust drifts and offsets of their local clocks since transmission delay of messages between neighbor wireless sensor nodes are difficult to estimate due to Carrier Sense Multiple Access with Collision Avoidance (CSMA/CA) and Request to Send/Clear to Send (RTS/CTS) control for collision avoidance. Thus, it is difficult to achieve orders and intervals among events observed by different wireless sensor nodes. Moreover, even if multiple wireless sensor nodes observe the same event, their recorded observation times might be different and two observation records for the same event by two wireless sensor nodes are not always recognized as the records for the same event. Based on an assumption that observation areas of neighbor wireless sensor nodes are overlapped, by using observation records of the commonly observed events by neighbor wireless sensor nodes, this paper proposes a novel method to estimate the relative drift and offset between local clocks of the neighbor wireless sensor nodes. Here, each sensor node only detects the occurrences of events and cannot achieve the locations where the events occur. Hence, commonly observed events between neighbor wireless sensor nodes are required to be detected. Our proposed method applies a heuristic that multiple observation records in neighbor wireless sensor nodes whose intervals are the same are estimated to be commonly observed events.**

***Keywords*–Wireless Sensor Networks; Observation Time; Local Clock Synchronization; Relative Drift Estimation; Relative Offset Estimation.**

I. INTRODUCTION

A wireless sensor network consists of a great number of wireless sensor nodes with their sensor modules for achieving environmental data and wireless communication modules for transmission of data messages containing the environmental data to one of stationary sink nodes by using wireless multi-hop communication based on wireless ad-hoc communication. Each wireless sensor node possesses its local clock and the sensor node records observed events with the clock value at that time. Since the wireless sensor nodes work autonomously and their local clocks have individual differences, it is almost impossible for the local clocks in the wireless sensor nodes to be completely synchronized [4]. Especially due to individual differences in their crystal oscillators, incremented clock values in the same time duration are generally different one by one and networks with numerous number of nodes with their local clocks should be designed and managed on the assumption of the asynchronous local clocks [8]. Similar to [10], this paper assumes that a local clock value $C_i(t)$ of a wireless sensor node S_i is represented with its offset O_i and drift dt_i/dt as $C_i(t) = (dt_i/dt)t + O_i$. Since each local clock of S_i has its own offset and drift, it is expected that a clock value difference $|C_i(t) - C_j(t)|$ between local clocks of S_i and S_j is required to be kept small by a certain clock synchronization procedure with a certain short interval. In addition, local clock values recorded when a wireless sensor node observes events are also required to be corrected according to the clock synchronization procedure.

In environments where Global Positioning System (GPS) or wave clocks are not available, relative offset and drift between two local clocks of wireless sensor nodes are required to be estimated. Various conventional methods for clock synchronization in wired networks have been proposed. Here, control messages carrying local clock values are exchanged among wired nodes and transmission delay for the messages are estimated for clock synchronization as in Figure 1. However, in wireless networks, due to collision avoidance methods such as CSMA/CA and RTS/CTS [1] control in wireless Local Area Network (LAN) protocols, dispersion of transmission delay of the control messages carrying local clock values is large and it becomes difficult to achieve precise synchronization of local clocks based on estimation of relative offset and drift between the local clocks of neighbor wireless sensor nodes. Hence, this paper proposes a novel clock synchronization method without control message transmissions with local clock values whose transmission delay is difficult to estimate. Our proposed method is based on the fact that observation areas of neighbor wireless sensor nodes are usually overlapped and events which occurs in the overlapped area are observed by the wireless sensor nodes simultaneously.

In Section 2, we review related works. In Section 3, we propose our clock synchronization method based on records of observed events in neighbor wireless sensor nodes. Its performance is evaluated in simulation experiments and the results are discussed in Section 4. Finally, we conclude in Section 5.

II. RELATED WORKS

The problem of synchronization among local clocks in a network has been discussed and various synchronization methods have been proposed. The most fundamental approach to solve the problem is the algorithm discussed in [2]. Here, between two computers, local clock value request and reply control messages are exchanged where these control messages carry local clock values of sender computers (Figure 1). However, since the receiver computer cannot achieve its local clock values when the received control message is transmitted, the transmission delay of the received control message is required to be estimated. Therefore, the methods for clock synchronization by exchange of local clock values require more precise estimation of transmission delay of control messages.

Even with variation of transmission delay of control messages, it may be practically applicable for proposed methods to wired networks whose variation of transmission delay is not so large.

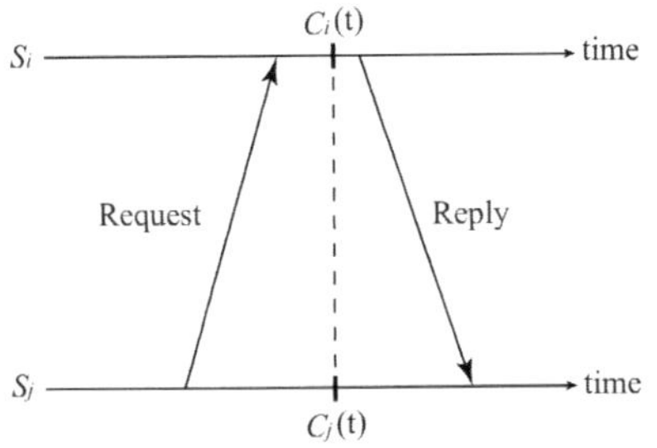

Figure 1. Clock Synchronization by Exchange of Control Messages with Local Clock Values.

For synchronization of local clocks of wireless nodes in wireless ad-hoc networks, Reference-Broadcast Synchronization (RBS) [3], Flooding Time Synchronization Protocol (FTSP) [5] and Timing-sync Protocol for Sensor Networks (TSPN) [7] have been proposed. All these methods are based on the transmissions of control messages carrying local clock values as discussed before. Hence, for achieving highly precise synchronization among local clocks in wireless nodes, more precise estimation of transmission delay of control messages carrying local clock values are required. However, due to collision avoidance methods such as CSMA/CA and RTS/CTS control, it becomes much more difficult to estimate transmission delay of control messages for clock synchronization. The backoff timer for collision avoidance in CSMA/CA introduces unpredictable waiting time for data message transmissions and RTS/CTS control for avoiding collisions due to the hidden terminal problem requires much longer suspension of data message transmission procedure causing much higher unpredictability of total transmission delay as shown in Figure 2.

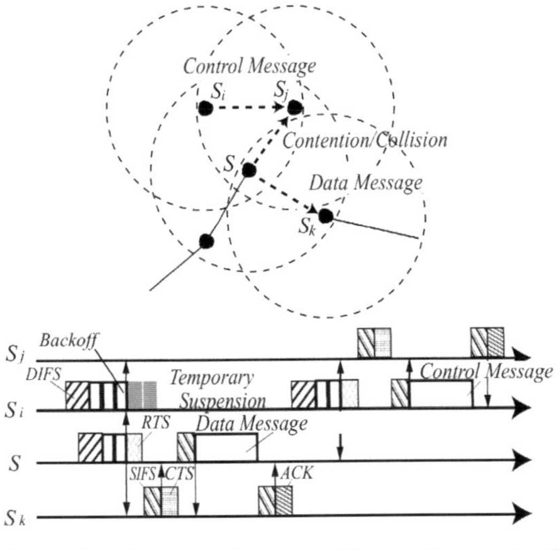

Figure 2. Unpredictable Transmission Delay of Control Messages for Clock Synchronization in Wireless Ad-Hoc Networks.

Especially in wireless sensor networks, high congestions of sensor data messages around the stationary wireless sink nodes are unavoidable so that prediction of transmission delay of control messages becomes difficult or almost impossible. In addition, burst traffic of data messages caused by some critical events also makes difficult to estimate transmission delay of control messages. In order to solve this problem, another approach without transmissions of control messages to which current local clock values are piggybacked are required to be considered.

III. PROPOSAL

A. *Commonly Observed Events*

Each wireless sensor node consists of a sensor module which detects events that occurred within its observation area and a wireless communication module which transmits/receives wireless signals from/to its neighbor wireless nodes within its wireless signal transition area. A wireless sensor node S_i which detects an occurrence of an event within its observation area records kinds of the events with some additional related attributes including the clock value $C_i(t)$ of its local clock at the instance t when S_i observes the event. For simplicity, this paper assumes that each event is detected by all the wireless sensor nodes whose observation areas include the location of the event at that instance, i.e. without any observation delay. In reality, each sensor device requires its specific response time for an event observation and the effect of the delay is discussed in our future work. In addition, all events are assumed to be the same kind. Hence, in accordance with the event observation records by a wireless sensor node S_i, a sequence $ESeq_i := |C_i(t_0), C_i(t_1), \ldots, C_i(t_{N_i})\rangle$ of the clock values at the instances when S_i observes the events is induced. Here, $C_i(t_j)$ is the value of the local clock of S_i at the instance t_j when S_i observes an occurrence of an event $e_i(t_j)$ in its observation area. On the other hand, each wireless sensor node S_i communicates with its neighbor wireless sensor nodes within its wireless signal transmission area. Thus, it is possible for S_i to exchange its clock value sequence $ESeq_i$ at occurrences of locally observed events with its neighbor wireless sensor nodes.

Generally, the observation area of a wireless sensor node is included in its wireless signal transmission area. In addition, in a wireless sensor network, an observation area where all the event occurred are surely observed and recorded by at least one wireless sensor node is required to be covered by observation areas of multiple wireless sensor nodes as shown in Figure 3 [6] [9]. Hence, observation areas of neighbor wireless sensor nodes usually overlap and the wireless sensor nodes whose observation area overlap can communicate directly by using wireless ad-hoc communication.

Suppose the case where observation areas of wireless sensor nodes S_i and S_j overlap as shown in Figure 4. As mentioned, S_i and S_j can communicate directly by wireless ad-hoc communication since they are included in their wireless transmission areas one another. Here, all the events occurred in the overlapped observation area are observed by both S_i and S_j and recorded with clock values of their own local clocks. These events are called *commonly observed events* of S_i and S_j. The other events, i.e. events observed by only one of S_i and S_j, are called *solely observed events*.

[Commonly/Solely Observed Events]

An event which occurs at a certain instance t in an overlapped area of observation areas OA_i and OA_j of wireless sensor nodes S_i and S_j respectively and is observed and recorded with local clock values $C_i(t)$ and $C_j(t)$ into clock value sequences $ESeq_i$ and $Eseq_j$ by S_i and S_j respectively is called a commonly observed event of S_i and S_j. On the other hand, an event which occurs at a certain instance t in an area included by OA_i and excluded by OA_j and is observed and recorded with a clock value $C_i(t)$ into only a clock value sequence $ESeq_i$ by S_i is called a solely observed event of S_i against S_j. □

Each wireless sensor node S_i assumes to observe all the events occur within an observation area OA_i of S_i. As various widely available sensor modules, S_i only identifies the occurrence of the events and gets the clock values of its local clock at the instance of the occurrence of the events; however, it cannot identify the precise locations of the events in its observation area. Hence, it is impossible for S_i to identify whether an observed event is a commonly observed event with a neighbor wireless sensor node S_j or a solely observed event against S_j. Even though clock values at an instance when an event occurs are recorded by wireless sensor nodes which observe the event, since clock values $C_i(t)$ and $C_j(t)$ of wireless sensor nodes S_i and S_j at any instance t are generally different, it is impossible for a wireless sensor node to identify its commonly observed events with a specified neighbor wireless sensor nodes only by comparison of local clock values in their clock value sequences as shown in Figure 4. Since clock values $C_i(t)$ and $C_j(t)$ of S_i and S_j for a commonly observed event at an instance t are different and it is impossible to identify commonly observed events of S_i and S_j only by simply comparing the sequences of clock values.

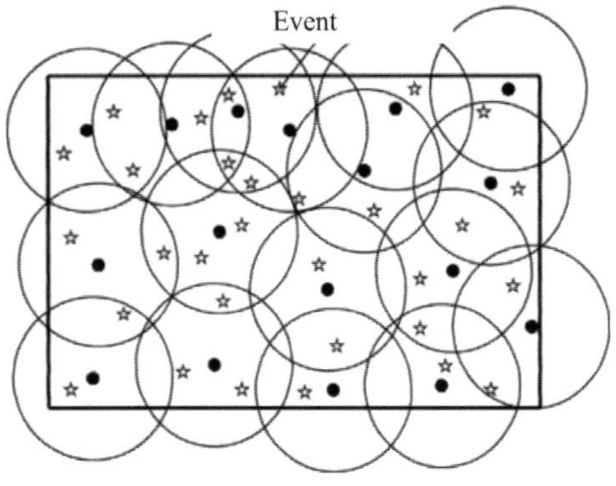

Figure 3. Whole Coverage of Observation Area by Overlap Observation Areas of All Sensor Nodes.

B. Relative Offset Estimation

By using commonly observed events defined in the previous subsection, this paper proposes a method to estimate a relative drift $dt_j/dt_i = (dt_j/dt)/(dt_i/dt)$ and a relative offset $O_j - O_i$ under an assumption that local clock values $C_i(t)$ and $C_j(t)$ of wireless sensor nodes S_i and S_j are given as $C_i(t) = (dt_i/dt)t + O_i$ and $C_j(t) = (dt_j/dt)t + O_j$, respectively. This subsection discusses a method to estimate only a relative offset where a relative drift is assumed to be

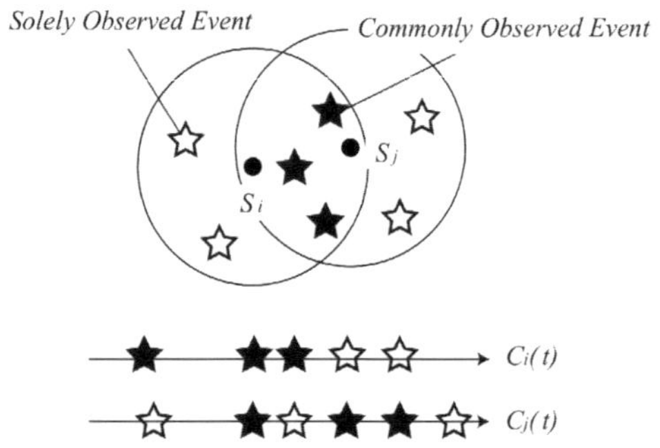

Figure 4. Local Clock Values of Observation Time in S_i and S_j.

1. The method to estimate both a relative drift and a relative offset is discussed in the next subsection.

In case that a relative drift of $C_i(t)$ and $C_j(t)$ is 1, i.e. $dt_j/dt_i = 1$, $C_j(t) - C_i(t) = O_j - O_i$, i.e. a difference between clock values at any instance equals to their relative offset. Hence, if one of pairs of clock values of commonly observed events is identified, the difference between the clock values is their relative offset. However, it is difficult to identify a pair of clock values of a commonly observed event from local clock value sequences of neighbor wireless sensor node. This is because, as discussed in the previous section, even if wireless sensor nodes S_i and S_j observe the same event, i.e. their commonly observed event, at an instance t, their local clock values $C_i(t)$ and $C_j(t)$ at t are usually different, i.e. $C_i(t) \neq C_j(t)$. In addition, even if the instances t and t' of solely observed events observed by S_i and S_j respectively are different, i.e. $t \neq t'$, their local clock values $C_i(t)$ and $C_j(t')$ might be the same, i.e. $C_i(t) = C_j(t')$. Hence, the simple comparison between individual clock values $C_i(t)$ and $C_j(t')$ recorded in sequences $ESeq_i$ and $ESeq_j$ of local clock values of S_i and S_j does not result in correct estimation of the relative offset between their local clocks.

In order to solve this problem, this paper proposes a novel method to estimate the relative offset and drift between the local clocks of neighbor wireless sensor nodes by using multiple pairs of clock values recorded in the sequences of local clock values. As discussed, a clock value sequence $ESeq_i$ of local clock values of a wireless sensor node S_i when it observes events in its observation area OA_i includes local clock values of commonly observed events with its neighbor wireless node S_j. Though local clock values of S_j for the same commonly observed events are surely included in a clock value sequence $ESeq_j$ of local clock values of S_j when it observes them, it is impossible to detect the commonly observed events by simple comparison of local clock values in $ESeq_i$ and $ESeq_j$. However, since the commonly observed events, i.e. events which occurs in the overlapped area of observation areas OA_i and OA_i of S_i and S_j, are observed at the same instance t by S_i and S_j even though $C_i(t)$ and $C_j(t)$ may be different, intervals between the same pair of commonly observed events in S_i and S_j are the same. That is, suppose that clock values of S_i and S_j when they observe two commonly observed events occur at instances t and t' are $C_i(t)$, $C_i(t')$, $C_j(t)$, $C_j(t')$, respectively. Even if $C_i(t) \neq C_j(t)$ and $C_i(t') \neq C_j(t')$,

$C_i(t') - C_i(t) = C_j(t') - C_j(t)$ is surely satisfied.

Since both locations where events occur and intervals between successive events contain a certain randomness, i.e. a certain unpredictability, this paper introduces a heuristic based on a reversed proposition of the above one into estimation of commonly observed events. Thus, if there exist local clock values $C_i(t_1)$ and $C_i(t_2)$ in $ESeq_i$ of S_i and $C_j(t_3)$ and $C_j(t_4)$ in $ESeq_j$ of S_j and $C_i(t_2) - C_i(t_1) = C_j(t_4) - C_j(t_3)$ is satisfied though $C_i(t_1) \neq C_j(t_3)$ and $C_i(t_2) \neq C_j(t_4)$, it is highly possible for S_i and S_j to have been observed two same events, i.e. there are two commonly observed events occurred at $t_1 = t_3$ and $t_2 = t_4$ respectively in the overlapped area of their observation areas. Needless to say, it might be possible for solely observed events whose recorded clock values are $C_i(t_1)$, $C_i(t_2)$, $C_j(t_3)$ and $C_j(t_4)$ to satisfy $C_i(t_2) - C_i(t_1) = C_j(t_4) - C_j(t_3)$ on accident. Hence, our heuristic method regards the possible relative offset that provides the maximum number of estimated commonly observed events which satisfies the above condition as an estimated relative offset.

[Estimation of Relative Offset]

Let $ESeq_i$ and $ESeq_j$ be sequences of local clock values $C_i(t)$ and $C_j(t)$ at instances when wireless sensor nodes S_i and S_j observe events. An estimated relative offset is what provides the maximum number of estimated commonly observed events where the transformed clock values with the estimated relative offset are the same. That is, with the estimated relative offset O, if the number of pairs of local clock values satisfying $C_i(t) + O = C_j(t')$ where $C_i(t) \in ESeq_i$ and $C_j(t') \in ESeq_j$ is the maximum for all possible relative offsets, O is regarded as the estimated relative offset for S_i and S_j. □

For example, Figure 5(a) shows two sequences of local clock values $ESeq_i$ and $ESeq_j$. Figures 5(b), 5(c) and 5(d) show the results of parallel translation of $ESeq_j$ with possible relative offsets, i.e. where a pair of a local clock value $C_i(t)$ and a transformed local clock value with a possible relative offset $C_j(t') + O$ become the same value. There are 1, 2 and 3 estimated commonly observed events with the same transformed local clock values. If the maximum number of estimated commonly observed events is 3, the relative offset in Figure 5(c) is the estimation result in our method.

Now, we design an algorithm for estimation of a relative offset based on the heuristics. Here, for every pair of local clock values $C_i(t^i_k)$ and $C_j(t^j_l)$ in $ESeq_i$ and $ESeq_j$ of S_i and S_j respectively, it is assumed that these local clock values represent those at a certain commonly observed event, that is the difference $O = C_j(t^j_l) - C_i(t^i_k)$ is regarded as the estimated relative offset of the local clocks of S_i and S_j, and the number of estimated commonly observed events where $C_j(t^i_{l'}) = C_i(t^i_{k'}) + O$ is satisfied is counted. Here, the possible related offset is between the maximum $C_i(t^i_{N_i}) - C_j(t^j_0)$ and the minimum $C_i(t^i_0) - C_j(t^j_{N_j})$ and the algorithm counts the estimated commonly observed events for every possible relative offset in this range. If there is a certain upper limit of relative offset between the local clocks of S_i and S_j, it is possible for the proposed algorithm to work with this limitation to reduce the time duration required for the proposed algorithm.

[Relative Offset Estimation Algorithm]

1) Initialize the maximum number of estimated commonly observed events of wireless sensor nodes S_i and S_j as 0 by $MCO_{iv} := 0$.
2) A temporary relative offset and the number of estimated commonly observed events are initialized as $Soff_{iv} := C_i(t^i_{N_i}) - C_j(t^j_0)$ and $CO_{ij} := 0$.
3) For each local clock value $C_i(t^i_k) \in ESeq_i = |C_i(t^i_0), C_i(t^i_1), \ldots, C_i(t^i_{N_i})\rangle$, search events $C_j(t^j_l) \in ESeq_j = |C_j(t^j_0), C_j(t^j_1), \ldots, C_j(t^j_{N_j})\rangle$ satisfying $C_i(t^i_k) = C_j(t^j_l) + Soff_{ij}$ and increments CO_{ij}.
4) If $CO_{ij} \geq MCO_{ij}$, $MCO_{ij} := CO_{ij}$ and an estimated relate offset $Eoff_{ij} := Soff_{ij}$.
5) If $Soff_{ij} = C_j(t^j_{N_j}) - C_i(t^i_0)$, jump to step 8).
6) Search a relative offset update $Uoff_{ij} := \min(C_j(t^j_l) + Soff_{ij} - C_i(t^i_k))$ where $C_j(t^j_l) + Soff_{ij} - C_i(t^i_k) > 0$.
7) $Soff_{ij} := Soff_{ij} - Uoff_{ij}$ and $CO_{ij} := 0$. Then, jump to step 3).
8) Return $Eoff_{ij}$ as the required estimated relative offset and the algorithm terminates. □

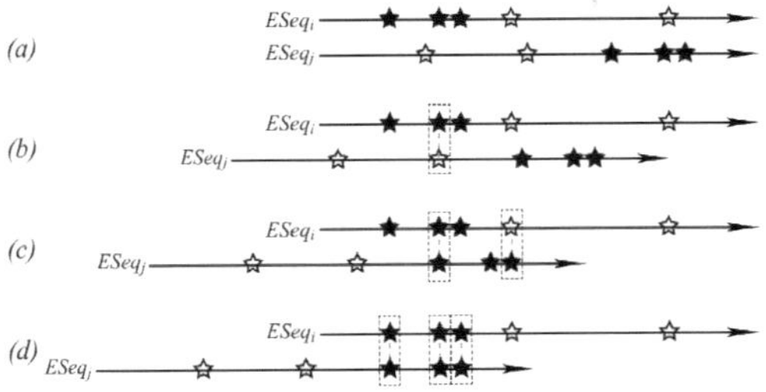

Figure 5. Estimation of Relative Offset.

C. Relative Drift Estimation

This subsection proposes an extended algorithm for estimation of both the relative offset and the relative drift for recorded local clock values in two neighbor wireless sensor nodes whose observation areas overlap. Figure 6 shows the overview of our proposed method. Same as the method proposed in the previous subsection which supports only the cases with 1 relative drift, the number of estimated commonly observed events between local clock value sequences $ESeq_i$ and $ESeq_j$ for every possible relative offset $C_i(t^i_k) - C_j(t^j_l)$. In addition, for estimation of the relative drift, another pair of local clock values $C_i(t^i_{k'}) \in ESeq_i$ and $C_j(t^j_{l'}) \in ESeq_j$ ($k \neq k'$ and $l \neq l'$) is needed. Here, an estimated relative drift is $(C_i(t^i_{k'}) - C_i(t^i_k))/(C_j(t^j_{l'}) - C_j(t^j_l))$. After applying the transformation of local clock values with the estimated relative offset and the estimated relative drift, the number of estimated commonly observed events whose local clock values are the same is evaluated. Same as the previous subsection, according to a heuristic that the correct pair of relative offset and relative drift provides the maximum number of estimated commonly observed events, our proposed method estimate them. In order to apply our proposed method, for neighbor wireless sensor nodes to estimate relative offset and drifts to transform the local clock values for synchronization, there should be more than 3 commonly observed events. Hence, enough observation period to record local clock values are required.

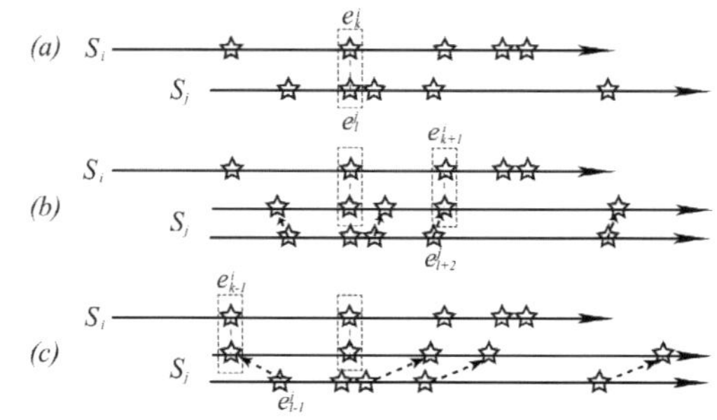

Figure 6. Estimation of Relative Drift..

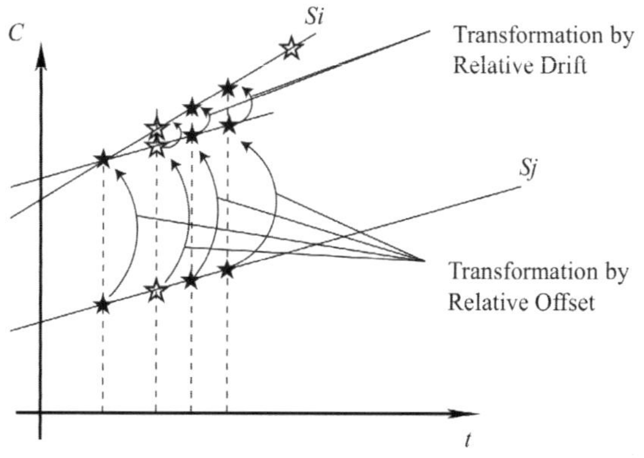

Figure 7. Estimation of Commonly Observed Events by Offset and Drift Estimation (Correct).

Figure 7 shows a case of correct estimation of commonly observed events with correct estimation of a relative drift dt_j/dt_i and a relative offset $O_j - O_i$. Here, pairs of local clock values $C_i(t^i_1)$ and $C_j(t^j_1)$, $C_i(t^i_2)$ and $C_i(t^j_3)$, and $C_i(t^i_3)$ and $C_j(t^j_4)$ are those for commonly observed events, i.e., $t^i_1 = t^j_1$, $t^i_2 = t^j_3$ and $t^i_3 = t^j_4$, respectively, and the rest $C_i(t^i_4)$ and $C_j(t^j_2)$ are local clock values for solely observed events in S_i and S_j, respectively. By consideration that $C_i(t^i_1)$ and $C_j(t^j_1)$ are local clock values in S_i and S_j when a commonly observed events of S_i and S_j occurs, the relative offset is estimated as $O_j - O_i = C_j(t^j_1) - C_i(t^i_1)$ and the line representing the local clock value in S_j is parallelly displaced as the points representing the local clock values $C_i(t^i_1)$ and $C_j(t^j_1)$ of the commonly observed event are overlapped. Then, by consideration that $C_i(t^i_2)$ and $C_j(t^j_3)$ are local clock values in S_i and S_j when a commonly observed events of S_i and S_j occurs, the relative drift is estimated as $dt_j/dt_i = (C_j(t^j_3) - C_j(t^j_1))/(C_i(t^i_2) - C_i(t^i_1))$ and the line representing the local clock value in S_j is rotated around the point representing the local clock value $C_i(t^i_1)$ as the points representing the local clock values $C_i(t^i_2)$ and $C_j(t^j_3)$ of the commonly observed event are overlapped. Now, the lines representing the local clock values of S_i and S_j are overlapped and all the commonly observed events including that for $C_i(t^i_3)$ and $C_j(t^j_4)$ are correctly estimated.

On the other hand, Figures 8 and 9 show the cases when estimation of relative drift and/or offset is incorrect and estimation of commonly observed events is also incorrect as a result. In Figure 8, same as in Figure 7, $C_i(t^i_1)$ and $C_j(t^j_1)$ are considered to be local clock values in S_i and S_j when a commonly observed events of S_i and S_j occurs, and the relative offset is correctly estimated as $O_j - O_i = C_j(t^j_1) - C_i(t^i_1)$ and the line representing the local clock value in S_j is parallelly displaced as the points representing the local clock values $C_i(t^i_1)$ and $C_j(t^j_1)$ of the commonly observed event are overlapped. However, by incorrect consideration that $C_i(t^i_2)$ and $C_j(t^j_4)$ are local clock values in S_i and S_j when a commonly observed events of S_i and S_j occurs, the relative drift is incorrectly estimated as $dt_j/dt_i = (C_j(t^j_4) - C_j(t^j_1))/(C_i(t^i_2) - C_j(t^i_1))$ and the line representing the local clock value in S_j is rotated around the point representing the local clock value $C_i(t^i_1)$ as the points representing the local clock value $C_j(t^j_4)$ has the same C value (virtual axis) as $C_i(t^i_2)$. Here, pairs of points on the two lines representing the local clock values in S_i and S_j with the same C value (vertical axis) correspond to a commonly observed event of S_i and S_j. However, in Figure 8, though pairs of $C_i(t^i_2)$ and $C_j(t^j_3)$, and $C_i(t^i_3)$ and $C_j(t^j_4)$ are those of local clock values for commonly observed events, their C values are not the same, i.e., these pairs of local clock values are not estimated to be those for commonly observed events.

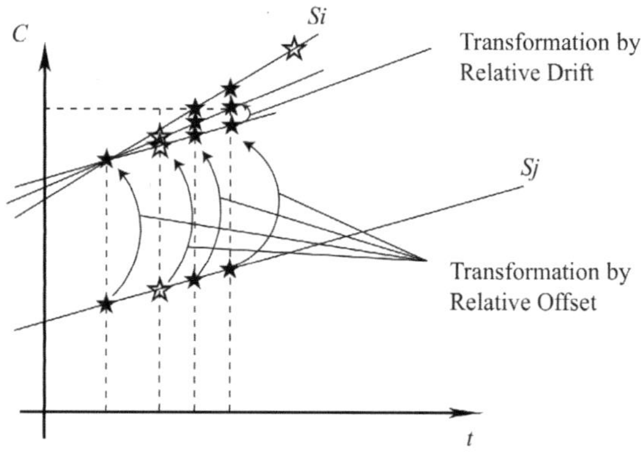

Figure 8. Estimation of Commonly Observed Events by Offset and Drift Estimation (Incorrect Drift).

Moreover, in Figure 9, both relative offset and drift are incorrectly estimated. Here, $C_i(t^i_1)$ and $C_j(t^j_2)$ which is local clock value in S_j when its solely observed event occurs are considered to be local clock values in S_i and S_j when a commonly observed event of S_i and S_j occurs. A relative offset is incorrectly estimated as $O_j - O_i = C_j(t^j_2) - C_i(t^i_1)$ and the line representing the local clock value in S_i is parallelly displaced as the points representing the local clock values $C_i(t^i_1)$ and $C_j(t^j_2)$ have the same C value (vertical axis). Then, $C_i(t^i_2)$ and $C_j(t^j_4)$ are considered to be local clock values of the commonly observed event of S_i and S_j, that is, the relative drift is also incorrectly estimated as $De_j/dt_i = (C_j(t^j_4) - C_j(t^j_1))/(C_i(t^i_2) - C_i(t^i_1))$, and the line representing the local clock value in S_j is rotated around the point representing $C_j(t_1^j)$ which has already displaced from the original position as the points representing the local clock value $C_j(t_4^j)$ has the same C value (vertical axis) as $C_i(t_2^i)$. Here, pairs of points on the two lines representing the local clock values in S_i and S_j with the same C value (vertical axis) correspond to a commonly observed event of S_i and S_j. In Figure 9, no correct pairs of local clock values in S_i and S_j are estimated to be those of commonly observed events and two pairs of local clock values in S_i and S_j are incorrectly estimated to be those of commonly observed events.

As shown in these three examples in Figures 7, 8 and 9, the number of estimated commonly observed events with incorrect estimation of relative offset and drift is usually smaller than that with correct estimation of them. It may be possible for pairs of local clock values of different events to be estimated as those of commonly observed events since the transformed C values are coincidentally the same. However, since the probability of such coincidental cases is low, the proposed heuristic that the correct relative drift and offset provides the maximum number of estimated commonly observed events is almost always applicable.

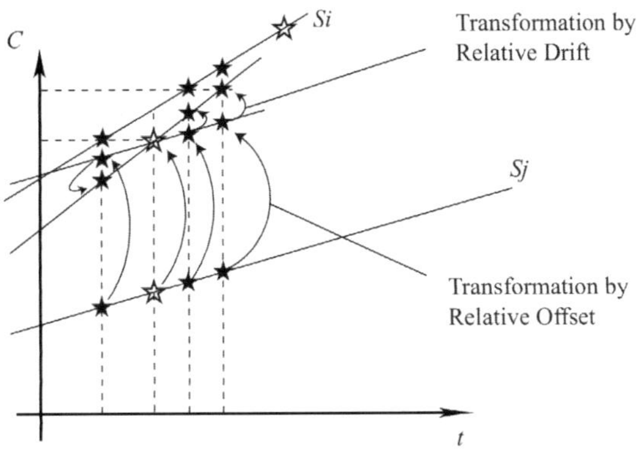

Figure 9. Estimation of Commonly Observed Events by Offset and Drift Estimation (Incorrect Offset and Drift).

[Relative Offset and Draft Estimation Algorithm]

1) Initialize the maximum number of estimated commonly observed events of wireless sensor nodes S_i and S_j as 0 by $MCO_{iv} := 0$.
2) A temporary relative offset is initialized as $Soff_{iv} := C_i(t^i_{N_i}) - C_j(t^j_0)$.
3) For every possible temporary relative drift $Sdri_{iv} := (C_i(t^i_{k'}) - C_i(t^i_k))/(C_j(t^j_{l'}) - C_j(t^j_l)) > 0$, apply the following steps 4), 5) and 6).
4) The number of estimated commonly observed events is initialized as $CO_{ij} := 0$.
5) For each local clock value $C_i(t^i_k) \in ESeq_i = |C_i(t^i_0), C_i(t^i_1), \dots, C_i(t^i_{N_i})\rangle$, search events $C_j(t^j_l) \in ESeq_j = |C_j(t^j_0), C_j(t^j_1), \dots, C_j(t^j_{N_j})\rangle$ satisfying $(C_i(t^i_{k''}) - C_i(t^i_k))/(C_j(t^j_{l''}) - C_j(t^j_l)) = Sdri_{ij}$ and increments CO_{ij}.
6) If $CO_{ij} \geq MCO_{ij}$, $MCO_{ij} := CO_{ij}$, an estimated relate offset $Eoff_{ij} := Soff_{ij}$ and an estimated relative drift $Edri_{ij} := Sdri_{ij}$.
7) If $Soff_{ij} = C_j(t^j_{N_j}) - C_i(t^i_0)$, jump to step 10).
8) Search a relative offset update $Uoff_{ij} := \min(C_j(t^j_l) + Soff_{ij} - C_i(t^i_k))$ where $C_j(t^j_l) + Soff_{ij} - C_i(t^i_k) > 0$.
9) $Soff_{ij} := Soff_{ij} - Uoff_{ij}$ and $CO_{ij} := 0$. Then, jump to step 3).
10) Return $Eoff_{ij}$ and $Edri_{ij}$ as the required estimated relative offset and the required estimated relative drift and the algorithm terminates. □

Figure 6 shows an example. According to the method proposed in the previous subsection, a pair of local clock values $C_i(t^i_k)$ and $C_j(t^j_l)$ is assumed to be for a possible commonly observed events. In addition, another pair of local clock values are also assumed to be for another possible commonly observed events and all the local clock values are transformed according to parallel translation. Then, the number of estimated commonly observed events with the same transformed local clock values are assigned is counted and the relative offset and drift that provide the maximum number of estimated commonly observed events is regarded as the correct ones.

IV. EVALUATION

Precision of our proposed method depends on the number of commonly observed events of neighbor wireless sensor nodes. Form this point of view, this section evaluates the performance of our proposed method by simulation experiments. Suppose two stationary wireless sensor nodes with 10m observation ranges are located with their distance 0.5–19.5m. Locations of events and intervals of two successive events are randomly determined according to unique distribution and exponential distribution, respectively. That is, events occur according to Position arrivals. With various event density, the ratio of correct estimation of commonly observed events, i.e. the ratio of correct estimation of relative offset and drift of their local clocks, is evaluated.

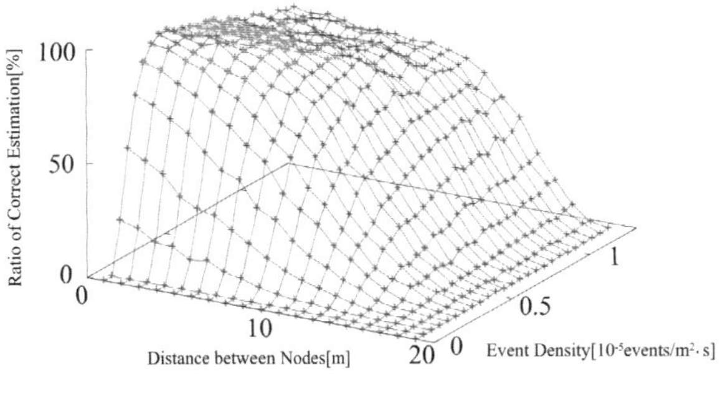

Figure 10. Ratio of Correct Estimation of Commonly Observed Events.

Figure 10 shows the simulation results. Red points represent correct estimation ratio higher than 99%, green points represent correct estimation ratio higher than 90%, and bule points represent others. Except for cases with extremely low event density and with extremely narrow overlapped observation area, our proposed method provides high correct estimation ratio. The performance is independent of the wireless transmission traffic of sensor data messages, e.g. around stationary wireless sink nodes, which is the most important advantage against the conventional method in which precise estimation of transmission delay of control messages are required.

V. Conclusion

This paper has proposed a novel clock synchronization method for wireless sensor networks. Different from the conventional methods by exchanging control messages with current local clock values and by estimation of transmission delay of the control messages, the proposed method estimates the relative offset and drift between two local clocks of neighbor wireless sensor nodes based on records of local clock values of event observations and estimation of commonly observed events of them. This paper has also designed estimation algorithms of relative offset and drift and evaluated their performance.

References

[1] "Wireless LAN Medium Access Control (MAC) and Physical Layer (PHY) Specifications," Standard IEEE 802.11 (2016).

[2] Cristian, F., "Progabilistic Clock Synchronization," Distributed Computing, *Springer*, vol. 3, no. 3, pp. 146–158 (1989).

[3] Jeremy, E., Lewis, G. and Deborah, E., "Fine-Grained Network Time Synchronization using Reference Broadcasts," Proceedings of the 5uh Symposium on Operating Systems Design and Implementation, pp. 147–163 (2002).

[4] Kopetz, H. and Ochsenreiter, W., "Clock Synchronization in Distributed Real-Time Systems," ICE Transactions on Computers, vol. C-36, no. 8, pp. 933–940 (1987).

[5] Miklos, M., Branislav, K. and Kayla, S., "The Flooding Time Synchronization Protcol," Proceedings of the 2AD International Conference on Embedded Networked Sensor Systems, pp. 39–49 (2004).

[6] Qu, Y., and Georgakopoulos, S.V., "A Distributed Area Coverage Algorithm for Maintenance of Randomly Distributed Sensors with Adjustable Sensing Range," ICE Global Communications Conference, pp. 286–291 (2013).

[7] Saurabh, G., Ram, K. and Mani, B.S., "Timing-Sync Protocol for Sensor Networks," Proceedings of the 1st International Conferenceon Embedded Networked Sensor Systems, pp. 138–149 (2003).

[8] Tanenbaum, A.S. and Steen, M., "Distributed Systems Principles and Paradigms," *Prentice Hall* (2002).

[9] Tuba, E., Tuba, M., and Simian, D., "Wireless Sensor Network Coverage Problem Using Modified Fireworks Algorithm," Wireless Communications and Mobile Computing Conference, pp. 696–701 (2016).

[10] Wu, Y-C., Chaudhari, Q. and Serpedin, E., "Clock Synchronization of Wireless Sensor Networks," ICE Signal Processing Magazine, vol. 28, no. 1, pp. 124–138 (2011).

A Quantitative Study on Live Virtual Machines Migration in Virtualized Computing Environment

Marcela Tassyany Galdino Santos, Edlane de Oliveira Gusmão Alves, Anderson F. B. F. da Costa
Federal Institute of Paraíba (IFPB)
Campina Grande, Brazil
e-mail: marcelatassyany@ieee.org, edlaneoliveira@ieee.org, anderson@ifpb.edu.br

Abstract—**The live virtual machines migration is a widely used technique in cloud computing environments because it is not necessary to stop services hosted on the migrated virtual machines. This paper aims to conduct an experimental and quantitative study on the migration of virtual machines through the evaluation of different scenarios. For this, a fully virtualized computing environment was implemented with the purpose of performing experiments that allow to analyze the influence of the live migration process in the performance of the services offered by the virtual machines migrated. The following metrics were evaluated: number of requests per second, server response time, throughput, latency and total migration time. Benchmarks ab- Apache Benchmark and YCSB-Yahoo! Cloud Serving Benchmark were used to generate the workload for the Web services and Database (Cassandra), respectively. The results obtained revealed that during the migration period, the services considered presented a reduction in their performance, but although there is a decrease, the service is not interrupted, thus complying with the principles of live migration.**

Keywords - virtualization; virtual machines; live migration; xen.

I. INTRODUCTION

The current scenario of globalization has generated the need for organizations, in general, to seek a flexible Information Technology (IT) infrastructure [1]. In this scenario, virtualization appears as a central element in datacenters environments, as it allows the optimization of idle resources, thus reducing costs with equipment and energy, optimizing the use of physical space, as well as enabling rapid alteration of the computing infrastructure and the portability of computational systems.

It is possible to define virtualization as a layer of software that allows partitioning a computational system from a physical machine into independent virtual machines that simulate different systems [2]. One of the great advantages of virtualization is to enable servers consolidation by allowing a host to host more than one independent virtual server, following the "one server per service" philosophy while reducing the waste of computing resources, as well as the costs of implementation and maintenance of the infrastructure [3].

There are situations where virtual machines need to be reallocated, such as in hardware maintenance cases. For this, a technique called virtual machines migration is used. Two types of migration can be performed and are commonly referenced in the literature, namely, Stop-and-Copy and Live Migration. This last approach allows the Virtual Machines (VM) to be migrated from the source host to the destination without interruption of the service execution, from the user perspective [4].

The live migration can be further subdivided into: pre-copy and post-copy. In the pre-copy approach, while the virtual machine is kept running at the source, all the memory pages that are at the source are transferred to the destination host. If there is a modification of some page during the transfer process, then it needs to be re-copied [5]. Hypervisor Xen works using this approach. In post-copy, initially the virtual machine is suspended at the source. Subsequently, information regarding its minimum state is transferred to the destination host. Then, the process of transferring the pages of memories is started. If a page that has not been transferred is requested from the destination host, a network fault will be generated, and this fault will be forwarded to the source that responds by transferring the requested page [7].

Therefore, realizing that the correct management and planning of the entire physical and virtual infrastructure of the computational environments influence the performance of the different running applications, and in view of the insufficient work that takes into account the occurrence of simultaneous migrations. This article aims to conduct an experimental study on migration of virtual machines in real time. Will be analyzed the influence of this in the performance of the Web and Database (DB) services from the perspective of the client of the application. The following scenarios were considered: Without Migration, With Migration and Simultaneous Migrations.

The paper is organized as follows: Section 2 presents the related works. In Section 3, we expose the methodology used to perform the experiments by describing the configuration of the virtualized environment implemented, in addition to the materials, scenarios and metrics used. Data analysis is in Section 4. Then, in Section 5, we conclude this paper and discuss futures works.

II. RELATED WORKS

Several works seek to optimize the location of Virtual Machines (VMs) among the physical resources available in datacenters [8][9]. These studies address the optimization of the available physical resources, aiming at saving resources, updating hardware, saving energy, among others.

In [10] and [11], it is possible to find the comparison of performances between different hypervisors. The most commonly used benchmarking strategy applies to a series of benchmark software that tests the most diverse system devices such as input / output, memory, network, processor, and so on. None of the cited works realizes performance evaluation by observing a specific application running in VM.

Alkmim *et al.* [12] considered the performance analysis of VM resources (memory, processing and file system - share VM image) before and during the migration process. Their results showed that the file system transfer rate was reduced by 55% during the migration period and its latency increased considerably.

In [4], a comparative evaluation was performed between stop and copy and pre-copy migrations using metrics such as total migration time, downtime, response time, and demand flow. Their results showed that stop-and-copy had five times more downtime than the pre-copy approach. However, the latter presented higher values in total migration time and response time. However, it did not show unavailability of the service, as in stop-and-copy.

Ye et al. in [13], carried a performance analysis using metrics such as downtime and total migration time, considering simultaneous migrations. It also evaluated resource reservation techniques for migration. However, no metrics were used to assess the migration impact from the user's perspective of the application.

Elsaid et al. in [14] developed an empirical model of single and multiple migration performance analyses to be used in estimating migration overhead. However, only factors related to CPU (Central Processing Unit) processing, transmission rate and dirty pages, for example, are considered and not the influence of the type of workload and the impact that the migration process can cause on the service offered in the migrated VM.

Bezerra et al. [15] conducted a preliminary statistical study evaluating the performance under the perspective of the user of the application, considering the scenarios With Migration and Without Migration to real and virtual environments. The results showed that there is a reduction of performance in the occurrence of migration, and that for virtual environments this reduction is more accentuated. However, scenarios with simultaneous migrations were not considered in this work.

III. METHODOLOGY

A. Xen

Xen is an open source virtual machine monitor (or hypervisor), which uses the para-virtualization concept by default [5]. In addition, it performs all the management, control and sharing of the resources of the hosts where the VMs will be dynamically allocated [3]. In addition to providing live migration support, it is modular, allows scalability, robustness and adequate security even for large and critical environments.

According to [16] and [17], Citrix, Microsoft and VMware, are the companies that have the best solutions in this market. Considering live migration, Xen is the most used solution [18]. Of the companies contributing to the Xen Project, we can mention: Alibaba / Aliyun [19], AWS [20], AMD [21], Citrix [22], Google [23], Intel [24], Oracle [25], Rackspace [26] and Verizon [27]. In this sense, it is possible to verify that Xen is commonly adopted, so it was the solution chosen for the experimentation environment implemented in this work.

B. Fully virtualized experimental environment

Figure 1 illustrates the fully virtualized environment configured on an actual machine of 16GB with RAM (Random Access Memory), Intel Dual Core 1066 MHz and 500GB of disk. Four VMs have been configured using the VMware Workstation Player: Xen1, Xen2, Client, and NFS (Network File System).

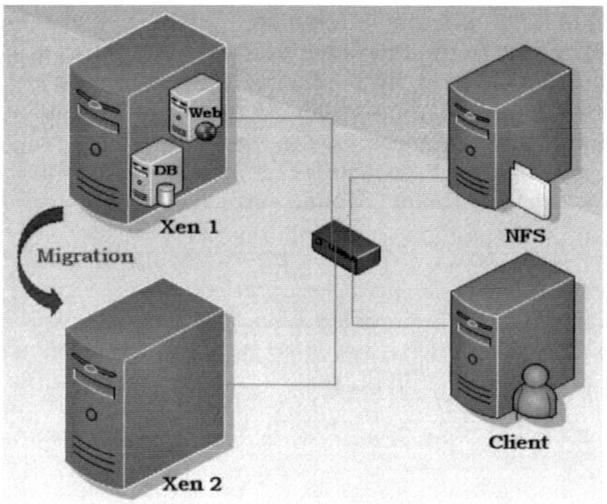

Figure 1. Fully virtualized experimental environment

Xen1 and Xen2 are the source and destination machines in the migration process. They are both virtualized with the Xen hypervisor. That way, Xen1 and Xen2 are responsible for hosting the Web Server and DB-Server machines, as well as their respective applications.

The Web-Server and DB-Server VMs are the instances that will be migrated and host the Apache Web HTTP services, as well as the Apache Cassandra™ Database server, respectively.

The VM Client is the element responsible for generating the workload for the VMs Web Server and DB-Server, using the benchmarks ab- Apache Benchmark [28] and YCSB - Yahoo! Cloud Serving Benchmark [29], respectively.

The Network File System (NFS) is the VM responsible for sharing the virtual machines' images and virtual disks involved in the migration process. The existence of this element is one of the requirements of the Xen hypervisor.

Table I shows the hardware and operating system configurations of all machines that make up the fully virtualized experimentation environment. One caveat to be made is that all network traffic is established through a LAN (Local Area Network) Fast Ethernet network.

TABLE I. MEMORY, DISK, AND SOFTWARE CONFIGURATIONS OF THE VMS CREATED IN THE DEPLOYED ENVIRONMENT

Virtual Machines	Memory	Disk	Operating System
Client	1 GB	25 GB	Ubuntu 14.04
Xen 1	6 GB	40 GB	Ubuntu 14.04
Xen 2	6 GB	40 GB	Ubuntu 14.04
DB-Server	1 GB	10 GB	Ubuntu Server 14.04
Web-Server	1 GB	10 GB	Ubuntu Server 14.04
Storage NFS	1 GB	50 GB	Ubuntu 14.04

Some contexts and metrics were considered and collected during the experiments in the environment implemented in this work.

C. *Scenarios and metrics*

Experiments were carried out in order to individually evaluate the Web and Database Services. For both cases, three scenarios were considered and thirty samples were collected for analysis in each of the experiments.

As specified in Section III B, the workload generated for both the Web service and the database service was performed through the Benchmarks ab and YCSB, respectively. For both, we simulated the existence of 10 Clients making requests simultaneously. For YCSB, the number of operations and records were set to 200000. For Apache, the number of requests was set to 1000000.

For both cases, three scenarios were considered:

- Without Migration: This scenario was implemented with the purpose of observing the influence of the workload generated by the Client to the VM-Server, without considering the migration occurrence.
- With Migration - No Load: In this scenario, the influence of the workload generated by the Client is observed during the VM-Server migration. The total migration time was analyzed in this scenario.
- With Migration: The VM-Server receives the Client's workload while it is being migrated.
- Simultaneous Migration: For this scenario, two VMs with the same service are migrated concurrently while receiving the Client workload.

Some metrics have been evaluated for the Web Service, considering all scenarios described above. These metrics are the following:

- Number of requests per second: Corresponds to the number of requests served by the server in one second.
- Transfer rate: It used to measure the ratio of the amount of data that is transferred in a second between the Client and the Web server
- Server Response Time (SRT): Corresponds to the time in milliseconds that the server takes to respond to a request.

For the database service, some other metrics were also considered. These metrics are the following:

- Throughput (operations per second): Matches the number of operations that are performed on the database in one second.
- Read Latency (nanoseconds): This metric is the average time between the request and response of a read operation.
- Update Latency (nanoseconds): Similar to Read Latency, this metric refers to the average time between the request and response of an update operation.

For both services, the Total Migration Time (TMT) was also evaluated. The TMT is the time between the start of the migration, the transfer of all memory pages (registers states, CPUs, network interfaces, etc.) until the moment the VM is executed at the destination. For each experiment, thirty repetitions were performed.

IV. RESULTS AND ANALYSIS

To analyze the influence of the migration on the Web service and the Database service, the scenarios: No Migration, With migration, and Simultaneous Migration were considered for all metrics. For the evaluation of the total migration time the scenario With Migration - Without Load, was also considered, as described in section III B.

Thirty samples were collected during each run of the experiments. From this, the measurements used to better represent the dataset were: the mean, the standard deviation and the median.

A. *Web service*

Tables II and III, respectively, show the Number of Requests per Second and the Transfer Rate, considering the scenarios Without Migration, With Migration and Simultaneous Migration.

TABLE II. NUMBER OF REQUESTS PER SECOND FOR SCENARIOS: WITHOUT MIGRATION, WITH MIGRATION AND SIMULTANEOUS MIGRATION

Number of requests per second	Without Migration	With Migration	Simultaneous Migration
Average	676,35	555,58	524,97
Medium	677,29	556,84	518,58
Standard deviation	9,66	6,21	33,5

Considering the Web service, as shown in Tables II and III, in relation to the Number of Requests per Second and the Transfer Rate, a performance reduction of 17.85% was observed in the scenario With Migration and 22.38% for Simultaneous Migrations, comparing both with the Without Migration scenario.

TABLE III. SCENARIO TRANSFER RATE: WITHOUT MIGRATION, WITH MIGRATION AND SIMULTANEOUS MIGRATION

Transfer Rate (Bytes / second)	Without Migration	With Migration	Simultaneous Migration
Average	539,63	443,28	418,85
Medium	540,38	444,28	413,75
Standard deviation	7,71	4,95	26,74

Comparing the scenarios With Migration and Simultaneous Migration with regard still to the Number of Requests per Second and the Transfer Rate, a small reduction was observed which indicates that equivalent performances may occur. Although the decrease shown is not so evident, it is possible to observe that the TMT for the simultaneous migration was considerably higher, as shown in Table IV. This suggests that although the values for the referred metrics did not show such a significant reduction, the migration time increased significantly between these two scenarios.

Table IV also displays the TTM for the case where the migrated VM receives no load from the Client. With this it is possible to observe that the presence of workload implies an increase in the total time of migration. This is because under these circumstances, the memory pages are constantly being modified and it is necessary to resend them to the destination (as is typical of the pre-copy migration), thus increasing the time for the migration process to end.

TABLE IV. TOTAL MIGRATION TIME FOR THE SCENARIOS: WITH MIGRATION-NO LOAD, WITH MIGRATION, AND SIMULTANEOUS MIGRATION

TMT	With Migration - No Load	With Migration	Simultaneous Migration
Average	104,43	267,88	652,09
Medium	106,78	267,62	649,63
Standard deviation	4,26	9,53	0,57

Table V shows the Server Response Time for each of the scenarios considered.

TABLE V. SERVER RESPONSE TIME FOR SCENARIOS: WITHOUT MIGRATION, WITH MIGRATION AND SIMULTANEOUS MIGRATION

Server Response Time	Without Migration	With Migration	Simultaneous Migration
Average	8,46	9	9,93
Medium	8	9	10
Standard deviation	0,51	0	0,36

It is possible to observe that the presence of migration resulted in an increase in the SRT, which increases in the case of of Simultaneous Migrations.

B. Database service

For the Database service, Throughput presented a reduction of 39.16% for the scenario With Migration and 45.42% when considering Simultaneous Migrations, as shown in Table VI.

TABLE VI. THROUGHPUT FOR THE SCENARIOS:WITHOUT MIGRATION, WITH MIGRATION AND SIMULTANEOUS MIGRATION

Throughput (operations / second)	Without Migration	With Migration	Simultaneous Migration
Average	277,12	168,59	151,27
Medium	275,98	167,62	159,56
Standard deviation	51,47	13,41	35,64

As shown in Tables VII and VIII, it was observed that there is an increase of Latency in the presence of migration.

TABLE VII. AVERAGE READ LATENCY FOR SCENARIOS: WITHOUT MIGRATION, WITH MIGRATION AND SIMULTANEOUS MIGRATION

Average Latency - READ (ns)	Without Migration	With Migration	Simultaneous Migration
Average	46,08	73,16	100,40
Medium	44,28	69,77	84,20
Standard deviation	13,38	11,69	43,77

Compared to the Without Migration scenario, the latency for read operations showed an increase of 37% for the scenario With Migration and 54.1% for the scenario with Simultaneous Migration. Latency in Update operations showed an increase of 33.04% and 28.41%, for the same scenarios, respectively.

TABLE VIII. LATENCY AVERAGE UPDATE FOR THE SCENARIOS: WITHOUT MIGRATION, WITH MIGRATION AND SIMULTANEOUS MIGRATION

Average latency - UPDATE (ns)	Without Migration	With Migration	Simultaneous Migration
Average	27,97	41,76	39,07
Medium	28,11	44,72	39,72
Standard deviation	2,22	9,98	6,47

We note that there was a reduction in the performance related to the metrics evaluated for Simultaneous Migrations, when compared to the scenario With Migration. However, the results indicate that equivalent performances can occur.

TABLE IX. TOTAL MIGRATION TIME FOR SCENARIOS: WITHOUT MIGRATION, WITH MIGRATION AND SIMULTANEOUS MIGRATION

TMT	Without Migration - No Load	With Migration	Simultaneous Migration
Average	104,43	352,18	699,06
Medium	106,78	7,18	44,14
Standard deviation	4,26	350,19	706,918

It was also observed that the total migration time increased significantly, growing approximately twice in the occurrence of simultaneous migrations, as shown in Table IX.

V. CONCLUSION

Migration is an important technique commonly used in cloud computing environments. This article presented a study carried out with the objective of evaluating the influence of the migration in the services offered by the migrated machines.

Through the experiments, it was possible to verify that the migration of virtual machines generates an impact on the performance of the services offered to the users. It was also observed that in scenarios with multiple migrations the impact generated was small in relation to the metrics analyzed compared to the scenario with a single migration.

In future works, we intended to evaluate other metrics, implement other configurations, as well as to consider and evaluate the results obtained in a concrete context of a real environment.

Finally, it is worth mentioning that in the experiments network failures or requests were not observed, which allows to conclude that, although there is a downtime corresponding to the period in which the VM is interrupted at the origin and put into execution at the destination, this time is so minimal that it does not entail a failure in the services offered, thus achieving the goal of online migration that does not interrupt, from the user's point of view, the services during the process.

REFERENCES

[1] M. Veras, Virtualização: Central Component of the Datacenter. Preface Marco Américo D. Antonio. Editora Brasport: Rio de Janeiro, Brasil, 2011.

[2] A. Cassimiri, Virtualization: Basic Principles and Applications. Em: Escola Regional de Alto Desempenho - ERAD, Caxias do Sul, 2009.

[3] S. Citrix, Inc. Xenserver Open Source Virtualization. XenServer. Available in: <http://xenserver.org/>. Access on 15 de Sep 2016.

[4] V. M. Deborah, M. S. José, G. G. Danielo, "Analysis of the Impact of Migration of Virtual Machines on Virtualized Computational Environment". XXIX Simpósio Brasileiro de Redes de Computadores e Sistemas Distribuídos, Campo Grande, MS, 2011.

[5] C. Clark, et al, "Live Migration of Virtual Machines". in NSDI'05: 2nd Symposium on Networked Systems Design Implementation, 2005.

[6] Xen, Xen Project. Available in: <https://www.xenproject.org/>. Access on Oct 31 2017.

[7] M. G. Bezerra, Automated Resource Management System for Virtualized Environments. Federal University of Rio de Janeiro. Polytechnic School: Department of Electronics and Computation, Rio de Janeiro, 2013.

[8] S Chaisiri, B. S. Lee, D. Niyato, "Optimal virtual machine placement across multiple cloud providers". Services Computing Conference, APSCC. IEEE Asia-Pacific, 2009.

[9] M. Tsugawa, P. Riteau, A. Matsunaga, J. Fortes, "User-level virtual networking mechanisms to support virtual machine migration over multiple clouds". The 2nd IEEE International Workshop on Management of Emerging Networks and Services (IEEE MENS), 2010.

[10] L. Jack, et al, "Performance overhead among three hypervisors: An experimental study using hadoop benchmarks". IEEE International Congress on BigData Congress, 2013.

[11] P. V. V. Reddy, "Performance Evaluation of Hypervisors in the Private Cloud based on System Information using SIGAR Framework and for System Workloads using Passmark". International Journal of Advanced Science and Technology, Vol. 70, pp. 17-32, 2014.

[12] G. P. E. U. Alkmim, "A low cost solution for Virtual Machine Migration". XXIX Congress of the Brazilian Computer Society. Bento Gonçalves, 2009.

[13] K. Ye, X. Jiang, D. Huang, "Live Migration of Multiple Virtual Machines with Resource Reservation in Cloud Computing Environments". IEEE 4th International Conference on Cloud Computing, 2011.

[14] M. E. Elsaid, "Multiple Virtual Machines Live Migration Performance Modelling VMware vMotion based Study". IEEE International Conference on Cloud Engineering, 2016.

[15] P. Bezerra, G. Martins, C. Rocha, R. Gomes, F. Cavalcante, "Evaluating VM Live Migration Overhead With Xen Hypervisor". 15th International Conference WWW/Internet. Alemanha, 2016.

[16] P. L. Silva, Use of VMware ESX virtualization technology to improve the utilization of hardware resources and increase performance in datacenters. Monograph (Technologist in computer science to business management) - the East Zone Technology College, São Paulo, 2009.

[17] N. Ruest, Virtualization, a begginer´s guide. New York: McGraw Hill Publications. New York, 2009.

[18] P. Padalla, X. Zhu, Z. Wang, S. Singhal, K.G. Shin, Performance evaluation of virtualization technologies for server consolidation. HP Labs Tec. Report, 2007.

[19] Alibaba, Alibaba Cloud. Available in: <https://www.alibabacloud.com>. Access on Oct 31, 2017.

[20] AWS, Amazon Web Services Cloud. Available in: <aws.amazon.com/>. Access on Oct 31, 2017.

[21] AMD, Advanced Micro Devices. Available in: <www.amd.com/pt/home>. Access on Oct 31, 2017.

[22] Citrix, Citrix Systems. Available in: <https://www.citrix.com.br/>. Access on Oct 31, 2017.

[23] Google. Available in: <https://www.google.com>. Access on Oct 31, 2017.

[24] Intel Corporation. Available in:<https://www.intel.com>. Access on Oct 31, 2017.

[25] Oracle. Available in:<https://www.oracle.com/>. Access on Oct 31, 2017.

[26] Rackspace. Available in:< https://www.rackspace.com/>. Access on Oct 31, 2017.

[27] Verizon. Available in:< https://www.verizon.com/>. Access on Oct 31, 2017.

[28] Apache, The Apache Software Foundation. Available in: <https://httpd.apache.org/docs/2.4/programs/ab.html>. Access on Sep 15, 2016.

[29] YCSB, Yahoo! Cloud Serving Benchmark. Available in: <https://github.com/brianfrankcooper/YCSB/wiki>. Access on Sep 15, 2016.

Management of Forest Fires Using IoT Devices

Josué Toledo-Castro, Iván Santos-González, Candelaria Hernández-Goya, Pino Caballero-Gil

Department of Computer Engineering and Systems. University of La Laguna
La Laguna, Tenerife, Spain
Email: [alu0100763492, jsantosg, mchgoya, pcaballe]@ull.edu.es

Abstract—**Effectiveness and response time in emergency situations management are key factors that directly influence the number of victims. The analysis of environmental conditions in real time (such as weather events and polluting gases) could provide relevant data on the environment that could help prevent or detect an emergency situation. Nowadays, IoT (Internet of Things) devices and sensors allow the monitoring of different environmental variables, such as temperature, humidity, pressure and concentrations of pollutant gases, such as carbon monoxide and carbon dioxide. Radical changes and combinations of these variables could indicate the occurrence of adverse weather events that could cause a natural disaster, such as a forest fire. Thus, the developed system integrates IoT devices and sensors that can perform a real time control of different atmospheric variables and polluting gases, in order to activate alerts when pollution levels increase excessively or when detecting certain conditions that are considered to be possible factors for causing adverse climatic events. These events can favour the occurrence of fires and other emergency situations. Particular attention has been paid to the communication security among IoT devices, Web service and mobile devices. Moreover, a secure data transmission protocol, a block cipher algorithm and a secure authentication scheme have been implemented.**

Keywords–IoT; sensors; emergency situations management; weather events; forest fires; atmospheric pollutions.

I. INTRODUCTION

Nowadays, emergency situations involve huge losses, both material and personal. Adverse natural events and atmospheric pollution caused by human activities become disasters when they exceed a limit of normality and cause damages to the ecosystems and various diseases for the population. The effects of these events can be amplified due to poor planning of resources, such as lack of security or control steps, emergency plans and alert systems that can increase the options for predicting their occurrence or controlling their progress once they have occurred.

The existence and combination of certain atmospheric conditions in addition to unusual and excessive presence of pollutant gases (carbon monoxide and carbon dioxide) can anticipate the occurrence of an increasingly frequent natural disaster: forest fires. Generally, these kinds of events usually result in serious emergency situations that cause the need of mobilization of different emergency management agencies and services.

The land topography, different types of vegetation in the area and weather conditions are the main factors that affect forest fires generation and progress. The control and monitoring of atmospheric variables (temperature, relative humidity and atmospheric pressure) in addition to the concentration levels of certain pollutant gases (such as CO2 and CO) can favour the detection of fire generation and the monitoring of their progress.In this sense, some factors (excessive temperature increase, relative humidity decrease or dioxide and monoxide levels increase) could be important indicators to detect fire emergence or its proximity. It is important to name "the rule of 30" [1], which is based on three relevant factors associated with the forest fires detection: temperature values above 30°C, humidity values below 30% and wind speed values above 30 Km/h in the same area. The use of this rule as forest fires prevention standard can contribute to determine which areas have a high probability of fires occurrence, in order to enable the deployment of preventive mechanisms and action protocols that could favour the environmental conservation.

Thus, an information system has been developed that integrates IoT devices and sensors which are able to register atmospheric variables, such as temperature, humidity and pressure in addition to pollutant gases, such as CO2 and CO (which are very important in the air quality measurement). These gases can affect people's health and are emitted during forest fires excessively as result of combustion of huge amounts of biomass. Furthermore, this system is responsible of realising a real time management of alerts that could be activated according to the latest events as well as realising the coordination of operations required between emergency teams situated in affected area and the emergency services platform.

In Section 2, we present the state of art and the preliminaries about the general topic that is addressed. Then, the proposed system is explained in Section 3. The developed system is explained in detail in Section 4 and the system security is detailed in Section 5. Finally, Section 6 contains some brief conclusions and future research lines.

II. PRELIMINARES

In the field of IoT applications for the control of forest fires, several kinds of systems can be used for the warning, prevention and monitoring of these natural disasters. For example, this is the case of the application Forest Fire Danger Meter [2] available for Android. It stands out mainly because it is a calculator to find the fire hazard according to the classification of McArthur Forest Fire Danger Index [3], taking as reference the following parameters: temperature, relative humidity, wind speed, dryness factor, vegetation and pending.

In the same field, Incendios CyL [4] beta application is under development. Although it currently only provides data for the province of Soria, this application has as its fundamental objective to realize a meteorological forecast which indicates in which recreational areas tourists are allowed to make a fire, prohibitions and recommendations of how to act in nature, etc.

Another important element in the area of emergency situations and forest fires management is how Geographic Information Systems (GIS) [5] have become very relevant in the forest fires prevention and control. GIS allows real time access to data in the area, creating strategies to evacuate affected people, performing simulations, establishing health care points and redefining transport routes depending on the affected areas among other aspects. In fact, this system has been used recently by organizations such as the Civil Guard during the work of extinguishing the last fire in La Palma Island in 2016 and in other cases, such as a Portugal forest fire in 2017 [6].

Similarly, Senticnel [7] fire detection system (NTForest company) uses sensors and IoT technology to collect information on humidity, temperature and other environmental factors that could allow to predict the evolution of this type of natural disasters and encourage their extinction.

Due to the importance of natural disasters and emergency situations management, multiple projects and IoT applications exist. The system Find&Rescue [8] offers a global online vision of emergency teams through a specific device carried by each emergency team member. Several IoT applications are based on the deployment from helicopters [9] of different kinds of sensors, which could register environmental data: temperature, gases, etc. In the MERIS project, a real time application allows accessing the information of the status of recoverable victims through devices and sensors that control vital signs [10]. The management of emergency tactics is done using sensor technologies, such as liDAR and the Esphera platform: helicopter tracking through a 3D environment, integration of video from different resources and others aspects [11]. iSafety is a comprehensive emergency management system, which allows the integration of smart sensors and other applications to realize a real time emergency situation control [12].

Taking into account the previous applications, the proposed system in this paper offers new improvements, such as the use of innovative IoT technologies and a data treatment focused on the prevention, detection, activation of alarms and management of operations for the extinction of fires. A system with secure communications has been configured that allows the monitoring of different variables of the environment and the processing and visualization of the information registered in real time guaranteeing the access for all users through diverse platforms.

III. PROPOSED SYSTEM

The developed system is based on a sensor network and distributed wireless IoT devices able to obtain data from the environment and process it in real time. The main goal is to provide information to the systems responsible for the management and strategic planning in emergency situations generated mainly due to forest fires. In this sense, the system consists of gathering data of magnitudes and atmospheric variables that determine the meteorological conditions and the presence of polluting gases in each zone to transform it into useful information that could be visualized through interactive elements (maps, graphs, statistics and gauges) (Figure 1).

Atmospheric variables and pollutant gases control and monitoring can favour forest fires prevention in different ways. Firstly, it helps to prevent and determine possible risk areas for forest fires. Taking into account values collected by IoT devices and "the rule of 30", temperature measurements that exceed 30°C and humidity values below 30% in a same zone could implicate a preventive management process through alerts activation. The main reason is the existence of meteorological conditions that are favorable to forest fires generation. In addition to these factors, the pressure value is relevant in the field of early detection of periods of storms or anticyclones that can improve or aggravate the weather conditions in case of fire. Secondly, the control and monitoring of atmospheric variables and pollutant gases can also favour the early forest fires detection (when values and measurements provided by the IoT devices imply unusual meteorological conditions in the area, such as an abrupt rise of temperature values, decrease of humidity in the area or periods of anticyclone). In addition, an excessive increase of the CO_2 and CO concentrations could indicate an evidence of biomass combustion. Thirdly, the control and monitoring of atmospheric variables and pollutant gases can also favour the control of the forest fires progress. The monitoring of the commented variables in the surroundings of the burned zone allows to control the fire progress through detection of progressive increases of temperature, humidity, and CO_2 or CO concentrations. In this way, it is possible to realize a real time management of the area occupied by forest fire.

The developed information system is composed of three important parts: IoT devices, Web services and mobile application.

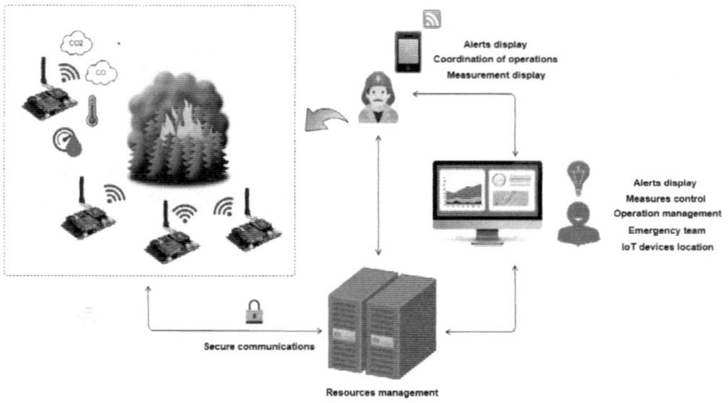

Figure 1. Operation of the system

A. *IoT devices*

Every IoT device distributed in the environment communicates wirelessly through 4G with the Web service, which is the responsible for storing and processing all data. So, these devices have integrated 3 different sensors that are able to interact with the environment and collect multiple variables: temperature, humidity, atmospheric pressure and pollutant gases, such as carbon monoxide and carbon dioxide (indicators of air quality). In addition, they are based on Arduino and are composed of a motherboard that is assembled with a 4G module to send the collected data. Other hardware elements are also necessary to integrate the multiple sensors that allow to register the atmospheric variables. The use of a 4G module allows registering the location of each distributed device guaranteeing their visualization and representation through interactive maps.

Once the IoT device is in the environment, the atmospheric variables and the pollutant gases of the area where it is located are captured. Besides, it is necessary to add some other device parameters: battery level, latitude and longitude (to manage their locations from the Web service) and International Mobile station Equipment Identity (IMEI) parameter that allows them to be uniquely identified in the system (Figure 2).

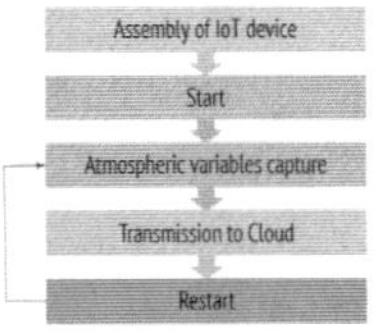

Figure 2. IoT devices functions

Temperature, humidity and pressure measurements have been registered by a same digital sensor. Regarding the temperature, the operational range is situated between -40°C and +85°C. In the case of humidity, the measurement range of relative humidity is 0 - 100%, taking into account the temperature values. Regarding atmospheric pressure, measures are situated between 30 - 110 kPa, based on the sensor sensing capacity. Furthermore, CO2 and CO data have been collected using 2 other different sensors. In the case of carbon monoxide gas, the measurement range limits the registration of data between 30 - 1000 particles per million (ppm) every second. Finally, the CO2 sensor can register values from 350 ppm to 10000 ppm.

Overall, measurement values change depending on each monitored zone and other factors, such as altitude, typical climate or the presence of human activities (car pollution, industries, etc.). For example, taking into account CO2 and CO gases, some tests developed have evidenced that measurements are decreaser at outdoor areas than at indoor areas or cities. While in forests the sensors register values around 8 ppm (CO) and 350 ppm (CO2), these results are usually higher in cities or indoor areas (CO2 and CO concentrations above 400 ppm and 10 ppm, respectively). The increase of the concentrations of these gases is much more evident from the burning of biomass in forest fires.

B. Web service

Once all the required data is available, the information is sent to the Web service that manages the resources. In this sense, it is responsible for database management of the entire information system: new measurements, users and active IoT devices. In addition, the Web service stores measures and manages their visualization through graphs and other interactive elements (graphs, indicators, gauges, etc.) that allow the interpretation of meteorological conditions and contamination levels of each registered area by users.

Other functionalities of the Web service could be to synchronize all system information among all users in real time by connecting IoT devices, mobile devices and the Web application. However, the data synchronization process needs information that system obtains by a continuous monitoring of new measurements. This aspect allows to activate alerts depending on whether registered values represent a potential hazard for forest fire generation or other emergency situations. In this case, notifications will be sent to the active users through the mobile application. In addition to these notifications, new information about activated alerts and the state of variables (temperature, humidity, etc.) will be updated in the Web application.

The Web service has been configured to allow bidirectional real time communication based on events through any platform or browser. Websockets [13] are used in order to satisfy this requirement. So, the server will send data to the connected users without the need of making client requests. When new data is processed (new measurements, activation of alerts, new IoT devices, etc.), the server transmits it to all listening sockets, so the information accessed by users is updated automatically. This advantage offered by this technology avoids the need to manually update the application to see new changes. Continuous availability of updated information is an essential requirement for prevention, detection and extinction of forest fires or other emergency situations.

The system configuration is exposed to users through automatic updating of graphs and gauges, interactive maps or updating information that is associated with the state of each monitored environmental variable.

Every security failure or unusual system event is stored in database for future security audits. This data is sent in real time thanks to the use of sockets to the system administrator who can display this information through a special management interface. In addition to having access to registered failures, the administrator can also add new IoT devices, changes their configuration parameters and changes variable atmospheric limits depending on the weather conditions of each zone. Only the role of the administrator has the specific privileges to perform these operations and to see this type of information.

C. Mobile application

Finally, an Android mobile application has been developed with the objective of representing locations of IoT devices, measures and averages for each variable monitored through graphs that users could interpret easily. Moreover, this application is responsible for synchronizing notifications and activated alerts that have been sent from the server (when a measure registered recently represented a potential hazard for the generation of an emergency situation). In the application, the authenticated users can interact with a map that represents locations of IoT devices through latitude and longitude parameters and markers. When one of them clicks on a marker, a new interface will be displayed showing all available information about the device selected: location, description, level of the battery in addition to all registered measures of each monitored variable in that day (Figure 3). Users can also access a bar chart that represents the real time averages of measurements for each atmospheric variable or pollutant gases.

However, another important element is the alert control panel. This section is used for representing all notifications and alerts activated from the server when a measurement involves a danger for forest fires generation. Each notification received informs the users about the exact zone associated with the danger, the variable and a description to identify which alert level has been increased. This functionality has been configured through the cloud messaging Firebase services and an identification token that the server needs to identify each mobile device when it's necessary to notify and synchronize a new alert. Only notifications or alerts that are associated

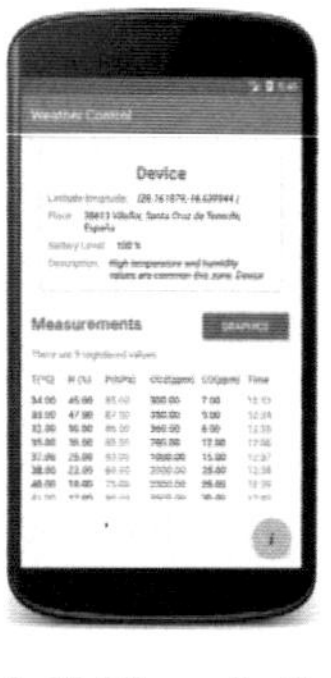

Figure 3. Mobile application view

with the mobile device location can be received. In addition, notifications are controlled by a time period. In this sense, a same alert that repeats constantly will not be sent from the server to the same mobile device until 10 minutes have passed since last notification was sent. This rule was set to avoid overloading the application.

Finally, this mobile application has been considered especially useful for emergency teams located in affected areas when forest fires or emergency situations are active. For that, it has also an operational panel integrated to show all actions and required operations for fire extinction.

D. Alerts management

One of the features of the developed information system is the introduction of an alarm management component that is activated every time when a new measurement arrives at the server. To this end, the system verifies if the value associated with each monitored variable (temperature, humidity, CO2, etc.) represents a potential danger that indicates the proximity of an adverse weather event that could favour the occurrence of a forest fire or another type of emergency situation.

For this reason, some reference limits and ranges have been defined for each atmospheric variable and pollutant gas. So, when a new measurement does not increase these limits, the value is considered as normal or stable, in addition to the fact that it does not indicate any danger or the need to activate any alerts. There are three main alert levels associated with these ranges or limits (Table I).

TABLE I. VARIABLE ALERTS MANAGEMENT

Variable	*Alert: level 3*	*Alert: level 2*	*Alert: level 1*
Temperature	>= 30°C	>= 37°C	>= 40°C
Humidity	<= 30 %	<= 20 %	<= 10 %
CO2	>= 350 ppm	>= 2000 ppm	>= 5000 ppm
CO	>= 10 ppm	>= 25 ppm	>= 50 ppm

In the case of temperatures, all values above 30°C have been considered as reference to activate a level 3 alert taking into account "the rule of 30" that considers zones characterized by temperatures above 30°C and humidity values below 30 % as risk areas for forest fires. Temperatures below this limit are situated in a normal range and are not considered a risk factor to activate any type of alert. An increase of the registered measurements above 37°C means that environmental conditions have aggravated, so a level 2 alert is established. Finally, temperatures above 40°C imply potentially dangerous meteorological values for the activation of forest fires. In these cases, a level 1 alert is activated.

Humidity values considered normal and beneficial to the health of people are between 40 % and 60 %. Taking into account "the rule of 30" again, measures below 30 % involves the activation of a level 3 alert. Most radical values below 20 % and 30 % imply the generation of a level 2 and level 1 alerts, respectively. Atmospheric conditions favour forest fires generation when relative humidity percent is lower especially if temperature alerts have been established in the same area at the same time. Values close to 0 % and 100 % are harmful to the health of people, because they can complicate physiological processes, such as sweating or elimination of fluids. For these reasons, activation of level 3, 2 and 1 alert has been considered in the same way when the server receives measures of 70 %, 80 % and 90 % relative humidity, respectively.

In the case of atmospheric pressure, control of its variations is so relevant for detecting of storms and anticyclones that could improve or aggravate forest fires generation conditions and their advance. Activation of alerts for this variable has been configured taking into account the occurrence of abrupt pressure changes [14]: excessive rises of 1 mb/h in a period of 6 hours (evidence of the proximity of strong winds) and excessive drops of 1 mb/h in a period of 6 hours too (evidence of the storm generation).

Other very important elements for early forest fire detection are the air pollutant gases, such as CO2 and CO. These chemicals are emitted during forest fire disasters and they can cause serious health issues for people. In this sense, excessive rises of their concentrations are relevant factors at the time of considering forest fire activation in a certain zone.

Carbon monoxide is fixed in the hemoglobin of blood and impedes the transport of oxygen. It can cause death in people when its value is too high. The limit value considered in a time of 8 hours is around 10 ppm [15], so it is the reference for activating a level 3 alert. Taking into account IoT devices are distributed in forest areas mainly (where air quality is better) and some studies of CO measures emitted in forest fires [16], level 2 alert is activated since 25 ppm values and level 1 alert for CO concentrations above 50 ppm.

Regarding CO2, the activation of level 3 alert has been considered at 350 ppm, taking into account multiple results that establish this value as the limit to be considered to prevent the worsening of the climate change [17]. From this value, other studies propose the establishment of 2000 ppm as reference for level 2 alert activation and CO2 measures over 5000 ppm for level 1 alert. With level 2, some health problems could be experimented (headaches, drowsiness, nausea, tachycardias, etc.). Besides, oxygen privation could occur for level 1 alert [18].

Each new measurement of each atmospheric variable or pollutant gas is analyzed taking into account thresholds associated with these alert levels. Depending on each monitored zone, these limits can change because of the weather conditions and environment. For these reasons, an interface of system management has been configured in the Web service to manage alert levels and their graphical representation.

In agreement with common European criteria [19], each level of alert is associated with a specific color. The color code is used to indicate visually the state and range of values in which each registered measurement is situated. This code in addition to the graphic interface components allow for a quick interpretation when a measurement value of an atmospheric variable or pollutant gas is normal or dangerous.

- Green color indicates all measurements that do not favour certain dangerous weather conditions for forest fires generation. So, alerts are not activated.
- Yellow color. There is no meteorological risk for the general population. However, measurements could mean that there is some danger for some specific activities or locations. It is associated with a level 3 alert.
- Orange color. It includes important and unusual meteorological risks. These weather conditions may be dangerous for common activities. It is associated with a level 2 alert.
- Red color. Extreme weather risks. All unusual and very intense meteorological events that usually involve dangerous situations for population. It is the riskiest alert, so this color refers to level 1 alert.

Since the server checks if an alert has been detected, the next step is to register it in the system and to transmit in real time the new data to all connected users through notifications (for the mobile app) or update special information panels (for the Web application). The creation of a new alert implies the declaration of some attributes, such as alert level (3, 2 or 1), IoT device, variable values that have activated the alert, a description, and the alert activation date.

E. Data visualization

In the Web service, the visualization of information and resources are mainly focused on four aspects: geolocation of IoT devices that are available, new registered measurements, atmospheric variables and pollution levels (through the devices on each zone), activated alarms in the server (when some of the processed values are out of the normal range for each monitored variable) and the management of emergency teams that are situated in the zone affected by the forest fire. Every new registered measurement by an IoT device can be represented in the Web service through different types of graphics and gauges. Furthermore, there are two different modules to represent them depending on the registration time.

To represent these values from the environment, some elements, such as charts and gauges, have been configured. Firstly, the Web service interface shows to users independent line graphs to represent (through dotted lines) variable values registered by devices for each atmospheric variable or pollutant gas. In addition, bar diagrams are used to make real time comparisons between different magnitude groups: a group for atmospheric variables (temperature, humidity and atmospheric pressure) and another group for pollution gases (CO2 and CO). Other important graphic element are gauges. They are used to represent only the latest value available from each variable monitored from the environment. Line graphs and gauges are organized together in a way to show all data associated with magnitude measurements. Finally, there is an alert control panel that indicates to users the real time state of each magnitude or variable registered in the monitored environment. Every time that new values are collected by the server from IoT devices, this panel updates and changes its information.

Each linear graph is formed by a dotted line that shows each measurement of the corresponding atmospheric variable, so users can interpret their variations visually. Updating these graphs occurs automatically each time a new value is registered in the system. Moreover, users can group measurements taking into account different time periods through a control button panel at the top left of the graph. In addition to these aspects, each graph has got colored bands as background to represent different ranges of values and limits that are defined depending on each atmospheric variable. Colours have been used taking into account the same color code that was explained in the previous section: green color (normal values), yellow color (level 3 alert), orange color (level 2 alert) and red color (level 1 alert). So, users have access to the exact value of the measurement (through the dotted line), the time that measure was registered and the range of values in which it was situated, in addition to which level alert was activated (Figure 4).

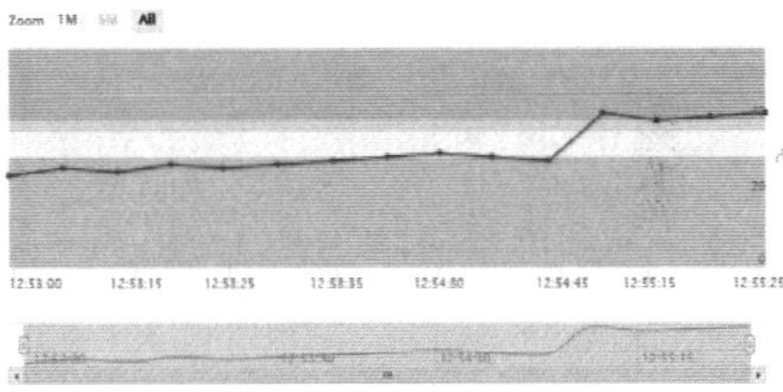

Figure 4. Temperature linear graphic

Other graph components have been developed, as follows:

- A special and interactive map that changes typical markers to colored circles depending on the average of all registered measurements on each zone, taking into account the same color codes and the defined limits or alert levels for each atmospheric variable.
- Another interactive map that manages the emergency teams location when a forest fire has been activated.
- A graph comparison module that allows to make comparisons and simultaneous reviews of the measurements registered by different IoT devices.

IV. SECURITY

System security has been divided in two different fields: IoT devices confidentiality and secure authentication.

Firstly, before sending each measurement registered through 4G by the sensors of distributed devices, data values (temperature, humidity, latitude, longitude, IMEI, etc.) are ciphered through the use of AES 128 key bits algorithm [20]. Moreover, Cipher Block Chaining (CBC) mode has been used so each block of plaintext is XORed with the previous ciphertext block before being cyphered. In this way, each ciphered block depends on all plaintext blocks processed up to that point. In addition to CBC mode, Zero padding has been used so the padding system is based on null characters. When data reaches the cloud server, it is deciphered using the same algorithm. Then, IoT device identification is verified by IMEI parameter and data measurements are processed and stored in the database if verification is correct.

Secondly, secure authentication has been developed through Open Web Application Security Project (OWASP) guidelines verification [21] in order to protect the system against different attacks.

In this sense, each specified standard guideline has been verified in order to guarantee a secure authentication process. In particular, the following aspects have been considered. It is a requirement that all authentication processes are to be performed exclusively on the server. Besides, authentication tokens have been used, avoiding the use of cookies to save user information. In this way, users are authenticated and each HTTP request is accompanied by a token in the header from that moment. This token is configured through a ciphered signature only available in the server. This technique allows adding more security to the authentication system and avoiding Cross-Site Request Forgery (CSFR) [22] attacks. Also HTTPS has been used for the transport of credentials. The encryption of authentication keys allows to use external services to the application as Google Maps API. Finally, we have included the registration of possible attacks to the system and the addition of metadata for future security audits.

V. Conclusion

The proposal presented in this paper describes a new information system that has been developed taking into account innovative technologies, IoT devices and the use of sensors with the aim of helping to improve the management of emergencies. Specifically, devices based on Arduino have been used. During the development of this solution, multiple challenges, such as the use of data transmission protocols (4G), interaction with hardware devices, integration of sensors and the transformation of registered data into useful information for the visualization of users have been solved. Furthermore, the integration of different technologies (mobile devices, Web service and IoT devices), the synchronization of all system data among different platforms (new alerts, measurements, etc.) and more considerations have been done.

Given the importance of confidentiality and authenticity, the system has been provided with security services. Specifically, OWASP guidelines and AES CBC encryption have been applied. This proposal is a work in progress, so several lines of work are still open. First, we will try to incorporate new sensors in the system that allow to control new environment variables, in order to improve prevention, detection and management of emergency situations. Secondly, we will try to increase interaction possibilities with emergency teams and workforce that are situated in the zone affected by forest fire, in order to gather more data as multimedia real time information. Finally, we will try to introduce and combine more layers and content types in the system for improving development of action protocols and forest fires extinction.

Acknowledgment

Research supported by Binter-Sistemas grant and the Spanish Ministry of Economy and Competitiveness, the European FEDER Fund, and the CajaCanarias Foundation, under Projects TEC2014-54110-R, RTC-2014-1648-8, MTM2015-69138-REDT, TESIS- 2015010106 and DIG02-INSITU.

References

[1] J. Lecina-Diaz, A. Alvarez, and J. Retana, "Extreme fire severity patterns in topographic, convective and wind-driven historical wildfires of mediterranean pine forests," PloS one, vol. 9, no. 1, 2014, p. e85127.

[2] "Forest Fire Danger Meter app," 2015, URL: https://www.greenappsandweb.com/noticias/4-apps-para-luchar-contra-los-incendios-forestales/ [accessed: 2017-07-24].

[3] L. Sanabria, X. Qin, J. Li, R. Cechet, and C. Lucas, "Spatial interpolation of mcarthur's forest fire danger index across australia: observational study," Environmental modelling & software, vol. 50, 2013, pp. 37–50.

[4] "Incendios CyL Application," 2016, URL: https://play.google.com/store/apps/details?id=com.cesefor.Incendios [accessed: 2017-07-10].

[5] M. Sánchez, A. Fernández, P. Illera, and L. Ponferrada, "Los sistemas de información geográfica en la gestión forestal," in Teledetección. Avances y Aplicaciones. VIII Congreso Nacional de Teledetección. Albacete, España, 1999, pp. 96–99.

[6] "GIS, a tool in the fight against fire," 2017, URL: https://esriblog.wordpress.com/2017/07/04/el-gis-una-herramienta-en-la-lucha-contra-el-fuego/ [accessed: 2017-07-12].

[7] "Senticnel System," 2017, URL: https://www.senticnel.com/ [accessed: 2017-07-12].

[8] "Telematic management of emergency teams," 2017, URL: http://iotparaemergencias.com/HTML/index-equipos_en.php [accessed: 2017-07-10].

[9] "Rain of sensors to manage catastrophes," 2008, URL: http://www.agenciasinc.es/Noticias/Lluvia-de-sensores-para-gestionar-catastrofes [accessed: 2017-07-07].

[10] A. Abril, J. Portilla, and T. Riesgo, "Monitorización de emergencia de víctimas de catástrofes. proyecto meris," Cuadernos Internacionales de Tecnología para el Desarrollo Humano, 2007, núm. 6, 2007.

[11] O. F. Price and C. E. Gordon, "The potential for lidar technology to map fire fuel hazard over large areas of australian forest," Journal of environmental management, vol. 181, 2016, pp. 663–673.

[12] "iSafety system ," 2017, URL: http://www.digitalavmagazine.com/2013/-04/10/indra-integra-en-isafety-su-solucion-global-de-gestion-de-emergencias-para-smart-cities/ [accessed: 2017-07-20].

[13] V. Wang, F. Salim, and P. Moskovits, "The websocket protocol," in The Definitive Guide to HTML5 WebSocket. Springer, 2013, pp. 33–60.

[14] "Atmospheric pressure variations ," 2017, URL: http://lasrutasdemoskys.blogspot.com.es/2017/03/la-presion-atmosferica.html?m=1 [accessed: 2017-07-21].

[15] "CO concentration limits for the health of people ," 2000, URL: http://http://eur-lex.europa.eu/legal-content/ES/TXT/PDF/?uri=CELEX:32000L0069&from=ES [accessed: 2017-07-20].

[16] B. Carballo Leyenda, J. A. Rodríguez-Marroyo, J. López-Satué, C. Ávila Ordás, R. Pernía Cubillo, and J. G. Villa Vicente, "Exposición al monóxido de carbono del personal especialista en extinción de incendios forestales," Revista Española de Salud Pública, vol. 84, no. 6, 2010, pp. 799–807.

[17] "350 ppm for CO2 concentrations ," 2015, URL: http://www.tecnozono.com/350ppm [accessed: 2017-07-15].

[18] G. R. Van der Werf, D. C. Morton, R. S. DeFries, J. G. Olivier, P. S. Kasibhatla, R. B. Jackson, G. J. Collatz, and J. T. Randerson, "Co2 emissions from forest loss," Nature geoscience, vol. 2, no. 11, 2009, pp. 737–738.

[19] "Alerts interpretation by code of colors ," 2017, URL: http://www.aemet.es/es/eltiempo/prediccion/avisos/ayuda [accessed: 2017-07-18].

[20] J. Daemen and V. Rijmen, "Rijndael, the advanced encryption standard," Dr. Dobb's Journal, vol. 26, no. 3, 2001, pp. 137–139.

[21] D. Fox, "Open web application security project," Datenschutz und Datensicherheit-DuD, vol. 30, no. 10, 2006, pp. 636–636.

[22] A. Barth, C. Jackson, and J. C. Mitchell, "Robust defenses for cross-site request forgery," in Proceedings of the 15th ACM conference on Computer and communications security. ACM, 2008, pp. 75–88.

ASUT : Advanced Software Update for Things

Juhyun Choi

Samsung Electronics and
Sungkyunkwan University
Suwon, South Korea
Email: honest.choi@samsung.com

Changue Jung, Ikjun Yeom and Younghoon Kim

Sungkyunkwan University
Suwon, South Korea
Email: {ckjung1987, ijyeom, kyhoon}@gmail.com

***Abstract*—Due to severe competition among manufacturers, timely firmware updates have become one of the most important issues. The constantly increasing number of things connected to the Web leads to high traffic contention in shared networks that causes poor service quality. In this paper, we propose an efficient software update system for smart things. The burden of downloading updates is offloaded to an always-on in-home hub. This delegation achieves not only avoidance of contention, but also the decrease of unnecessary transfer requests. Updates are transferred to the registered smart things without harming active service traffic. To achieve these goals, we implement a transport scheme based on Quick User Datagram Protocol (UDP) Internet Connections (QUIC) protocol that is known as emerging transport layer for Hypertext Transfer Protocol (HTTP). Our experimental results show that the proposed scheme is completely backed off with the existence of active service traffic and quickly completes the transfers when no others are active.**

Keywords–protocol; transport; software update.

I. INTRODUCTION

Recently, the rapid growth of smart things enforces manufacturers to be in a hurry when releasing their products. As a result, flawed software is often shipped and on-time software updates become one of the most urgent and important issues among manufacturers and service providers. Although both online and offline updates are possible, updates through the Internet occupy a dominant portion thanks to the development of network infrastructure and easier user scenarios for deploying them. A naive server-client communication model is commonly used for updating things, and updating scenarios can be categorized in two distinctive ones. In the first category, downloading firmware and/or applying it occurs when the things are in standby mode. Timely firmware updates for things, however, become hard to be achieved in this scenario due to efforts for reducing standby power based on this report [1]. So, not-in-use things would be unplugged and updating in the standby mode would not be realized. In the second scenario, things are updated only when they are in-use. Downloading and updating are initiated when users actually use the things. Regarding large sizes of firmware, however, it makes updating procedures unreliable due to unpredictable users' on-off patterns. Partial firmware updating is one alternative, but it is not considered as a realistic option because of its high implementation complexity. In case of always-on small things, keeping a connection for updating is a burden because of insufficient processing power. Also, in the view of service quality with shared network, numerous Hypertext Transfer Protocol (HTTP) requests congest the network. This contention causes a fluctuation in request latency.

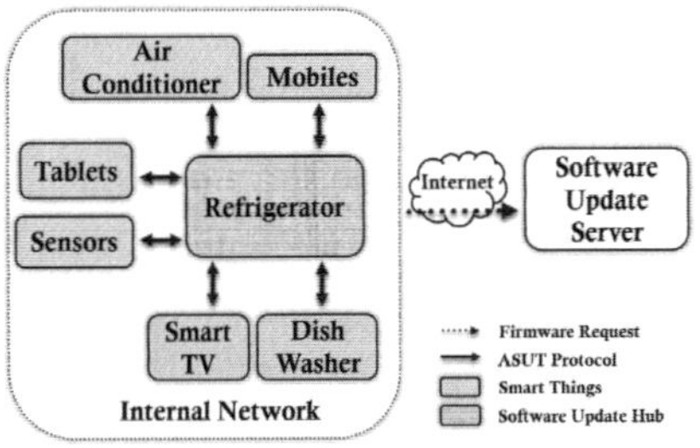

Figure 1. Overall ASUT Architecture

In this paper, we consider an alternate efficient firmware updating system for smart things. In our proposed scheme, an always-on thing (a refrigerator in this paper) is exploited as a software update hub onto which smart things can offload their firmware downloading. Once the hub completes downloading firmware, it starts updating things. As mentioned above, the size of firmware becomes large and transferring it with conventional transport protocols may cause severe contention between things' traffic and firmware transfer. Under the assumption that in-home network is separated from the Internet, a new transport protocol is proposed to mitigate this contention. The proposed protocol achieves high transfer rate in idle network and uses a quick backoff algorithm not to harm the users' quality of network usage. Another advantage of our proposed scheme is that stored firmware can be reused when identical things reside in shared network. This aspect not only enhances firmware accessibility but also lowers update servers' loads which suffer from repeated update requests.

The rest of this paper is structured as follows. In Section 2, we illustrate the design of our proposed scheme. Section 3 shows the result of the proof-of-concept tests. Finally, in Section 4, the conclusion of our work is described.

II. ASUT DESIGN

In perspective of network, a network software update can be treated as one large file transfer that needs high reliability. But, the conventional network update scheme has no way to consider the firmware transfer in a special manner. To transfer firmware efficiently with less damage to active services, we designed a system as described in Figure 1, and named it Advanced Software Update for Things (ASUT).

ASUT is an advanced network update system for smart things. ASUT offloads firmware downloading to the dedicated hub residing in home and efficiently distributes it to internal devices without degrading the network quality of running services. All firmware requests are delegated to the software

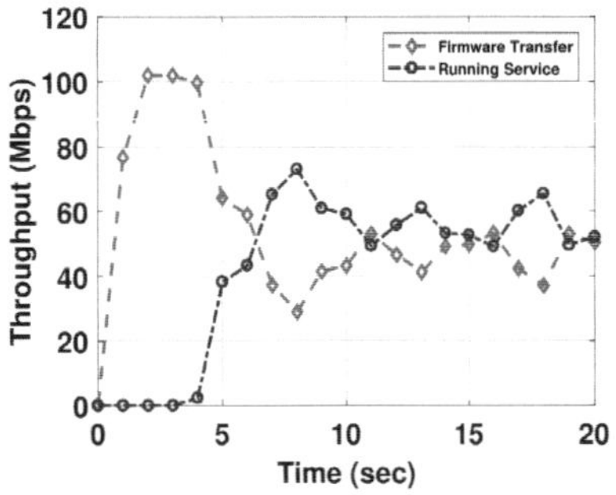

Figure 2. Contention Simulation in Conventional Network

update hub, which has to be an always-on thing, normally a refrigerator. To avoid congestion, firmware downloading is postponed until the network is idle. This centralization achieves not only high utilization of bandwidth, but the decrease of redundant transfers from identical things. For the distribution of downloaded firmware, we modified Quick User Datagram Protocol (UDP) Internet Connections (QUIC) [2] protocol. In order to steer the aggressiveness of the transfer, we utilize the combination of the number of the virtual connections and pacing mechanism [3]. The number of virtual connections implies the aggressiveness of a flow, and we manipulate it to control the aggressiveness in a coarse-grained manner. Setting a larger number of virtual connections empowers aggressiveness to the flow. So, our protocol dynamically adjusts it based on the number of packet loss.

To manage aggressiveness in a fine-grained manner, pacing is employed. Pacing is aware of the time intervals between two consecutive packet-send-events, and it determines when to send a next packet. We exploit pacing to make ASUT to be conservative when there are other active flows in the same network. Otherwise, ASUT should utilize maximum bandwidth. Specifically, we let the pacing rate increase after a large number of successful packet transfers (slow increase) and we let it decrease sharply with only a few packet losses (fast backoff). These features are designed to achieve the maximum throughput in idle conditions, while staying at a minimum during contention.

III. Preliminary Evaluation

In this section, we will show the result of proof-of-concept tests to verify the ASUT transport algorithm. The test is conducted in a dumbbell topology that employs a bottleneck link featuring 100Mbps and a queue size of bandwidth delay product. Our server and client implementation are based on proto-quic [4], and Ubuntu 14.04 distribution is installed on nodes. One server mimics the software update hub in the test, and the other one acts as contending running services.

Figure 2 shows how the conventional firmware transfer competes with an existing service flow. As soon as the transfer starts, the existing flow immediately yields the bandwidth. This implies existing HTTP requests are delivered with high latency. And, if the active traffic is for video streaming, this bandwidth sharing may lower streaming bitrate or cause the distortion of video streaming, which severely spoils user experience.

The test in Figure 3 illustrates the effect of ASUT. Once the network is dominated by the running service, the transport protocol of ASUT operates to maintain the minimum bandwidth as shown in Figure 3(a). If packet losses are detected frequently, ASUT decreases the pacing rate that contributes to decrease

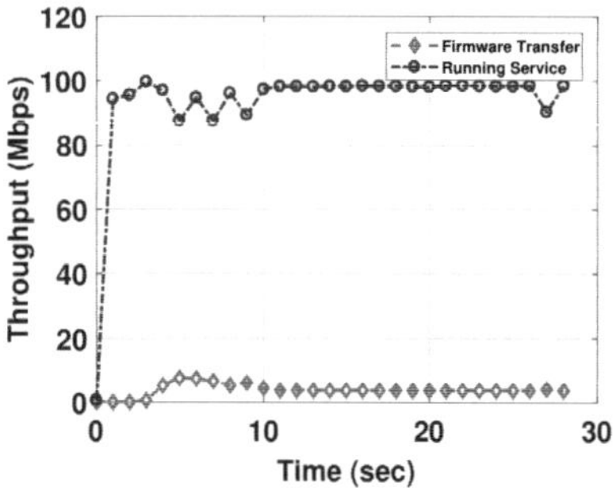

(a) Less Damages in Contention with ASUT

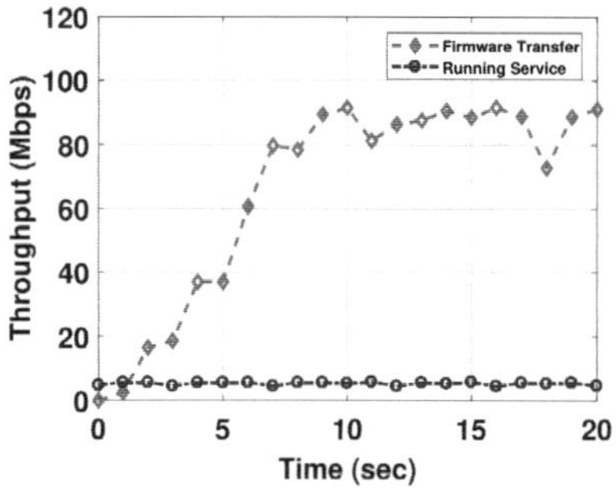

(b) Efficient Transfer in Idle Network with ASUT

Figure 3. Contention with ASUT

the bandwidth. On the other hand, the maximum bandwidth is achieved in idle network as shown in Figure 3(b). Once the flow maintains high pacing rate without the packet losses, ASUT accelerates the flow by the increase of the number of virtual connections.

IV. Conclusion

We proposed an efficient and reliable software update system for smart things, named ASUT. In ASUT, jobs for downloading software updates are offloaded to an in-home hub and those updates are transferred to things without harming other active HTTP traffic. A transport protocol, designed based on QUIC, achieves quick transfer between the hub and devices with no harm to other protocols or services. Our ASUT helps both network utilization and service quality in a flood of smart things. For the future works, we have plans to precisely design the communication protocol and implement ASUT on real devices.

Acknowledgment

This work was supported by National Research Foundation (NRF) of Korea grant funded by the Korea government (MSIP) (NRF-2016R1E1A1A01943474 and NRF-2016R1C1B1011682).

References

[1] Harrington et al., "Standby energy: Building a coherent international policy frameworkmoving to the next level," Stockholm: European Council for an Energy Efficient Economy, 2007.

[2] R. Hamilton, J. Iyengar, I. Swett, and A. Wilk, "Quic: A udp-based secure and reliable transport for http/2," IETF, draft-tsvwg-quic-protocol-02, 2016.

[3] A. Aggarwal, S. Savage, and T. Anderson, "Understanding the performance of tcp pacing," in INFOCOM 2000. Nineteenth Annual Joint Conference of the IEEE Computer and Communications Societies. Proceedings. IEEE, vol. 3. IEEE, 2000, pp. 1157–1165.

[4] [Online]. Available: https://github.com/google/proto-quic [retrieved: October, 2017]

Towards Remote Control of Mobile Robots to Help Dependent People

Yvon Autret, Jean Vareille, David Espes, Valérie Marc and Philippe Le Parc
Université Européenne de Bretagne, Université de Brest
Laboratoire en Sciences et Techniques de l'Information (Lab-STICC UMR CNRS 6285)
France
Email: {yvon.autret, jean.vareille, david.espes, valerie.marc, philippe.le-parc}@univ-brest.fr

Abstract—**In this paper, we focus on a Web-controlled mobile robot for home monitoring, in the context of Ambient Assisted Living. The key point is low-cost and the robot is built from standard components. We use a few sensors to allow the robot to estimate its position, its direction and the obstacles in front of it. An Ultra Wide Band system is used to estimate the position of the robot. A distant user controls the robot by using a map in the user interface. The result is a small robot that can be used inside or outside the house.**

Keywords-Home monitoring; Web control; UWB positioning.

I. Introduction

In 1898, Nikola Tesla demonstrated a remote-controlled boat [1]. It was based on the radioconduction discovered by French physicist Edouard Branly in 1890. One century later, the emergence of the Web technology provided new opportunities. The first Web controlled robot was developed at the University of Western Australia by Kenneth Taylor in 1995 [2]. At the beginning of the 2000's, Web development has led to the emergence of Service Robotics [3].

However, Web-controlled robots have rather remained unused until now, especially for Ambient Assisted Living (AAL) applications. A typical application consists of helping persons with diminishing mental or physical ability to stay at home as long as possible. When picking up the phone becomes too difficult, a mobile robot usable as a phone could be useful. In the same way, care helpers or relatives cannot spend all their time with a person. Devices that would be able to monitor what is going on in a house, and send the information to the care helpers could be of great interest. Cameras could be installed in every room. Such systems exist but they are not really acceptable because they are too intrusive. Thus, we think that a mobile robot could be more easily accepted. The robot can look like an animal. It can move in the house, and only one camera is required in the house. If the camera is considered too intrusive, it can be replaced by a lidar to analyze movements in the house.

Such robots are easy to build at affordable cost. Some of them are even commercially available. However, almost nobody uses them in real-world environments, such as AAL. The Romo example is typical [4]. The robot was launched in 2012 by the Romotive company. It is a mobile robot that uses a smartphone to control the motors. It can be remotely controlled from anywhere by using the smartphone connectivity. As soon as 2013, one Romotive co-founder wanted to move in the direction of making a robot that could solve real-world problems. After years of aimless decisions, Romotive's Website was shut down in 2016. Beyond disputes that have led Romotive to its fall, one key point appears. It is possible to build and sell toy robots, but nobody knows whether it is possible to build and sell at affordable prices, robots that can be used in the real world, especially in an AAL environment. In this paper, we will ask why. We will review the main criteria required to make an AAL mobile robot truly usable.

A. The cost

The cost must be kept as low as possible because it will probably be used by elderly people who often have tight budgets. It is inconceivable to rent a satellite channel to control the robot. In the same way, it is neither possible to use components, such as those found in military weapons, for example a €50000 inertial unit. From our point of view, the cost of an AAL robot should not exceed €1000. The price of a TV or a high-tech smartphone is also a good estimate.

B. Performance of the network

When a command is sent to a robot through a network, if an acknowledgment is received back in less than 200 ms, there is no perceptible lag between the triggering of the action and the visual result [5]. A guaranteed 200 ms round-trip-time (RTT) allows secured remote command of mechanical devices. In the case of AAL robots, a 300-500 ms RTT remains acceptable if the speed of the robot is low (1 km/h). When the RTT is beyond 500 ms, the operator feels something uncertain.

C. Security of the system

If a server is installed on or near the robot, it can cause serious security problems in the house. A server is never 100% secure. Even if techniques, such as traffic analysis are implemented, and if a problem is detected, who will handle the problem? It is not the role of the robot users.

If there is a wireless connection between a server and the robot, the radiations may cross the limit of the house and they can be captured and modified from the outside. Data will have to be encrypted but it may not be sufficient.

D. Security of the persons and resilience

If there is a failure, the robot may become dangerous. It may go anywhere in the house and hurt people. In any case, the speed of the robot must remain low. The robot should not exceed 1 km/h to avoid frightening the inhabitants. The resilience of the system is also very important. The robot must be able to work despite total or partial failure of one or more components. For example, if the network performance decreases, the robot should automatically reduce its speed. When a fault is detected, the robot must be able to restart, and eventually go to a fallback position. An accurate positioning system must be available.

E. User interface

The user interface must be designed for a semi-autonomous robot. When only using video feedback, controlling the robot is not easy. If images are not sent to the distant user for a while, the robot control may quickly get lost. The user interface must give accurate information about the robot, its position and its environment. The information must be redundant.

F. Positioning

Estimating the robot position is a key point. If the estimated position is not accurate, the whole system will collapse. The user interface will display wrong information, and the robot will be dangerous. Most of the previous criteria depend on the estimation of the robot position.

In this paper, Section II presents the proposed robotic system. We will show how the previous criteria have been taken into account. Section III presents the user interface. The results are shown in Section IV. The paper finishes by a conclusion and perspectives.

II. DESIGNING A HOME ROBOT FOR AN AAL ENVIRONMENT

A. The mechanical base

We use a very simple experimental mechanical base (Figure 1). There are four wheels mounted on gear motors and a wooden plate. An Arduino and a motor shield control the motors two by two. The motor shield is a 2x2A. It is based on a L298P chip. This means that the robot will slide slightly on the floor when turning. This choice reduces the cost but it will make the robot more difficult to locate. In the future, it might be necessary to have independent wheel control. The gearmotors rotate at a maximum of 84 revolutions per minute. The 120 mm wheels allow a maximum speed of 1.9 km/h. The motor torque is 1,0 kg.cm and the total mass of the robot can reach about 3 kg. This mechanical base is very reliable, especially if brushless motors are used.

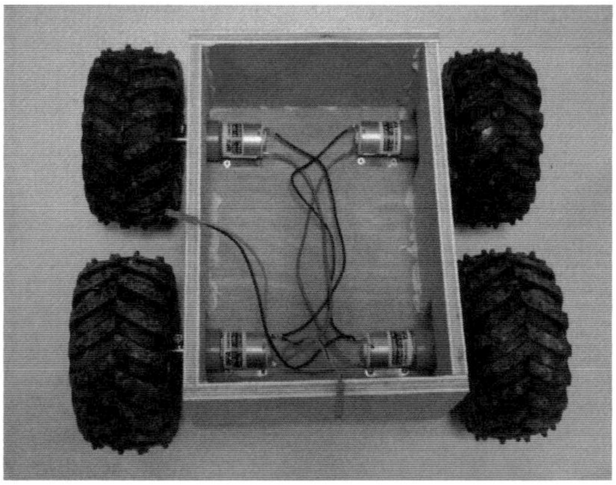

Figure 1. The mechanical base

B. The proposed architecture

If the mobile robot is in a house and the user in a different place, we have no choice but the Web to allow remote control. Another solution would increase the total cost too much. The remaining question is whether a thin client is preferred to a fat client. We have chosen a thin client for security reasons. A fat client would have been more powerful but the risk of security breach would have been higher. When using a thin client, we use a standard Web browser and rely on its security. The Web browser communicates with a Tomcat Web server that is fairly secure. The HTTP(S) protocol is used.

Figure 2. The proposed architecture

The architecture is shown in Figure 2. The distant user uses a Web browser to reach an Internet Box in the house, and next the Web server through an Ethernet cable. This ensures that there will be no wireless problems from the Box to the Web server.

Between the Web server and the robot we use a wireless Ultra Wide Band network (UWB) [6]. It will give us positioning capabilities.

The system works as follow. The Tomcat Web server is running on a computer that can be a Raspberry PI 2 or any other computer. A second server is running on the computer. The Tomcat server communicates with the second server by the mean of sockets. The second server rejects all communications except those coming from the Tomcat server. It is used to handle an Arduino connected to the computer. The Arduino has to manage an UWB communication with the robot. Thus, 128 bytes packets can be sent from the Web server to the mobile robot. When the robot is too far from the computer, UWB relays are required. Depending on the environment, relays must be added every 5 to 30 meters. UWB is managed by a Pozyx shield. Sending one hundred bytes from an Arduino UNO to the mobile robot and receiving a response of one hundred bytes takes 75 ms when using the I2C bus on the Arduino.

C. The sensors

As defined above, a distant user could make the robot move by using basics commands, such as forward, backward, right or left. If video is available, a remote control is possible.

A webcam is available on the robot. It is managed by a Raspberry PI 2. It is a light solution to stream videos over an IP-based network. The webcam is independant from the robot. The Tomcat Web server catches the video and sends it to the distant user when required. Thus, the webcam is not directly accessible from the outside. Only the Tomcat Web server can be accessed from the outside and security is kept relatively high because distant users must be identified in order to get the video images.

However, if the mobile robot is used by caregivers who do not know the house very well, video feedback is not sufficient because the experience shows that users are quickly lost. Moreover, estimation of the position of obstacles is not easy with video only. Thus, we have two main problems, estimating the obstacle positions, and estimating the robot position in the house.

Estimating the obstacle positions can be done by using a laser telemeter (Lidar) [7]. Such devices are available since several years. However their price can easily reach €2000. We rather use a €150 Lidar-lite that can measure distances in only one direction. To scan a 180 degree field in front of the robot, we mount the Lidar-lite on a servo motor.

To make the robot go forward and follow a direction, we also use a 9-axis accelerometer/magnetometer. Experiments have shown that for our problem, a Kalman filter is required. Without the Kalman filter, the magnetometer produces many wrong values. Using an extended Kalman filter does not seem to be necessary until now. We use a €30 CMPS11 tilt compensated compass module from Robot-Electronics [8]. The module includes a processor to compute a Kalman filter. It processes the raw values produced by the gyroscope, the accelerometer and the magnetometer. The compass output is pitch, roll and heading. To give correct results, the compass must be at 30 cm above the gear motors. Only heading will be used in our case. We will use that value to make the robot follow a direction. The distance traveled by the robot could also be computed from the accelerometer data, but the errors would accumulate and the position of the robot would be incertain. We will rather use UWB to determine the distance traveled by the robot.

D. Estimating the robot position

Estimating the absolute robot position is now possible, thanks to UWB. One of the main features of UWB signals is their potential for accurate position location and ranging. UWB technologies are often described as the next generation of real time location positioning systems. Due to their fine time resolution, UWB receivers are able to accurately estimate the time of arrival (ToA) of a transmitted UWB signal. This implies that the distance between an UWB transmitter and an UWB receiver can be precisely determined.

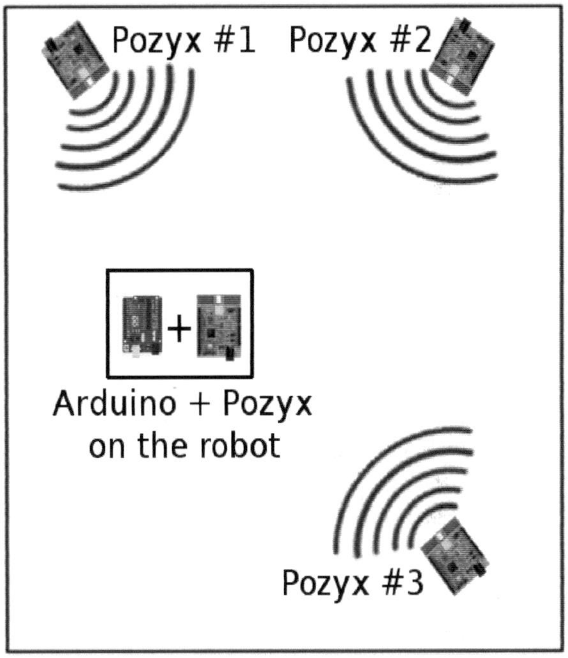

Figure 3. The positioning system

This feature of high localization accuracy makes the UWB an attractive technology for diverse ranging and indoor localization applications. It really allows 10-30 cm accuracy in ranging and promises the realization of low-power and low-cost communication systems [6].

We already have one UWB Pozyx module on the robot to ensure communication with the Web server. Three other modules will be added in the house to allow positioning. We will use the trilateration technique to estimate the position of the robot. Three Pozyx modules are positioned in the house (Figure 3).

The Arduino on the robot is connected to a Pozyx. It computes the distance from the robot to the three other Pozyxs. When the signal received from the reference nodes is noisy, the system is non-linear and cannot be solved. An estimation method has to be used. To get a satisfying approximated position of the mobile robot, we use the Newton-Raphson method [9]. This method attempts to find a solution in the non-linear least squares sense. The main idea of the Newton-Raphson algorithm is to use multiple iterations to find a final position based on an initial guess (for example, the center of the room), that would fit into a specific margin of error.

The first results of our experiments show that distance values are not constant due to multipath components. Hence, the precision of our system is about 30-50 centimeters. Such a precision is sufficient to know where the robot is in a room, but insufficient to pass through a door or something narrow.

Figure 4. A part of the robot (compass and webcam not shown)

After the addition of sensors and UWB positioning, the mobile robot architecture is as follows. The robot includes several sensors that are managed by two Arduinos communicating through a 9600 baud serial link. The first Arduino manages the motors, the Lidar-lite laser telemeter, and the compass. It is able to make the robot move, stop if there is an obstacle, and follow a direction. It communicates with a second Arduino that estimates the robot position. The second Arduino periodically sends the estimated position to the first one. It can also send orders, such as stop, change the heading, or move forward in the current direction over a certain distance. To estimate its position, the second Arduino computes the distance between itself and the Pozyx modules. To compute the position, the Arduino sends the measured distances to the distant computer that processes the Newton-Raphson algorithm. Results are obtained faster if the computer has efficient floating point capabilities.

A part of the obtained robot is shown in Figure 4. A single LiPo 3s battery powers the robot. DC-DC converters are used to power the two Arduinos. One Arduino manages both the Lidar and the compass, another Arduino manages the Pozyx modules.

The robot is now able to estimate its position by using UWB Pozyxs. It is also able to communicate with a remote server installed in the house, to detect obstacles by using a Lidar-lite, and to follow a direction by using a compass. We must now propose a user interface to make all those features available to a distant user.

III. The user interface

A. *Using a map*

The main item of the user interface will be a map. We will try to show the robot moving on the map in real time. To build the map, we have chosen to extend an available solution: OpenStreetMap [10]. In France, most of the buildings, including the individual houses, are shown by OpenStreetMap. Thus, we can use these basics plans that show the edges of the buildings. We will superimpose a detailed plan on the basic OpenStreetMap plan. To build the detailed plan, we provide a tool that allows to draw on the basic OpenStreeMap. It is implemented by using the OpenLayers V3 (or V4) standard library [11]. Details such as furniture or door openings can be shown. The direction of the exterior walls relative to magnetic north is shown by OpenStreetMap, and all other elements can be placed on the map accordingly (Figure 5). More sophisticated solutions, such as Lidar analysis have not been experiment yet to automatically produce maps. Although limited, the current solution is easy to use and makes it easy to produce a relatively detailed plan.

When zoomed in, a room of a house can be seen in full screen. The robot position is shown by the letter "R". The direction of the robot is shown by the direction of the letter. For example, if the letter is inverted on the map, the robot goes south.

To make positioning work, we must hang three Pozyxs on the walls. Our algorithm requires that they must be at the same height which can be different from that of the robot. In order to simplify configuration, the three Pozyxs must form a right angle triangle (Figure 6). Thus, in the user interface, there is something to indicate the position of the #1 Pozyx (P1), the position of the #2 Pozyx (P2), the distance between the #1 and #2 Pozyx (P1-P2), and the distance between #1 and #3 (P1-P3). The system deduces the position of the Pozyx #3 and there is no need to indicate directly its position. Pozyx configuration is very easy because walls of a house are very often perpendicular. The distant user must click twice on the map, the first click to indicate where the #1 Pozyx will be positioned, the second one to indicate where the #2 Pozyx will be positioned. Using a perpendicular axis for the Newton-Raphson algorithm we use in position estimation, can lead to problems because zero divisions can occur. In fact, experiments have shown that it is not a problem. If one position estimation can not be computed, the next one almost always can be computed. Even if the robot is stopped, the Pozyxs continuously produce distance values.

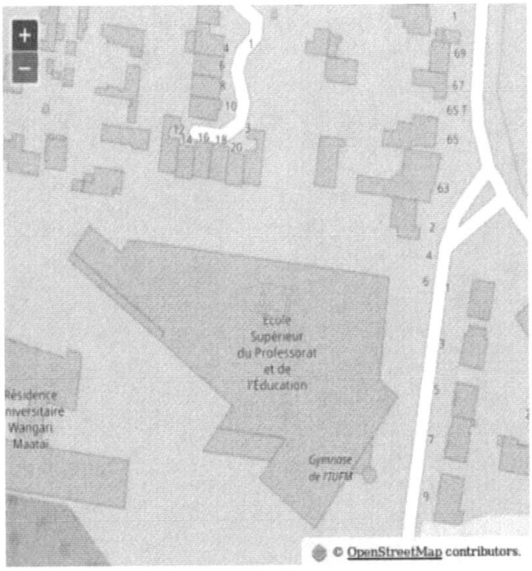

Figure 5. Example of OpenStreetMap plan with overlay

As soon as the Pozyxs are configured in the user interface, the robot position is displayed. The user interface shows the estimated distances between the robot and the Pozyxs by means of three circles. Those circles were used for debug at the beginning. We keep them in the user interface because they show a living system. The circles oscillate slightly continuously and the distant user can see if the system is working or not, and if there is no network problem. As seen above, the robot position is shown by the letter "R". It should be at the intersection of the three circles.

The implementation has been done by using Javascript [12], Ajax [13], jQuery[14] and OpenLayers V3 [11]. An Ajax request is sent to the Tomcat Web server, the position is computed as seen above, and the result is sent back to the distant user, and shown on the user interface. As soon as the result is available, another Ajax request is sent and another position estimation expected. We have measured a round trip time (RTT) close to 500 ms when the distant user is in the same town as the robot. It takes about 100 ms to compute a distance from one Pozyx to another. As there are three distances to compute, we have a 300 ms duration. The results must furthermore be sent to the Tomcat Web server, and we have a RTT close to 500 ms to communicate between the distant user and the robot.

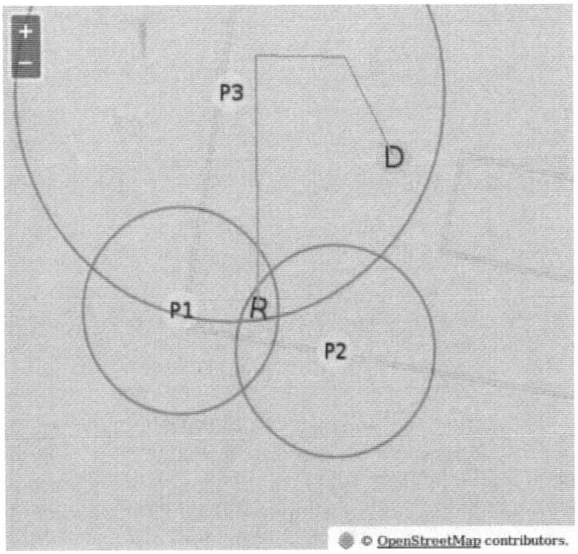

Figure 6. The user interface map

The RTT is also used on the robot. When the RTT increases, the robot automatically reduces its speed, or stops, or goes to a fallback position. Thus, if the robot does not receive commands from the Tomcat Web server, it stops.

B. *Making the robot move*

To make the robot move, the distant user must indicate a destination position on the map by clicking once or more. In Figure 6, there is an orange stroke that can be split into three segments. To draw such a stroke, the distant user must click three times. The last click corresponds to the desired robot destination.

To make the robot reach that destination, the user interface will automatically send a set of commands to the robot. The three segments will be processed one by one, as follows:

- Computation of the direction of the segment (almost north for the first segment in Figure 6)
- Alignment of the robot in that direction
- Computation of the segment length
- Sending a command to the robot to make it move by the desired distance in the current direction
- Stopping the robot for two seconds to have a better robot position estimation
- Verification of the current position of the robot and adjustment (adjustment can be automatic or performed by the distant user)

We finally obtain a system that allows semi-automatic robot remote control. In addition to the map, the distant user has a control panel to monitor the robot (Figure 7).

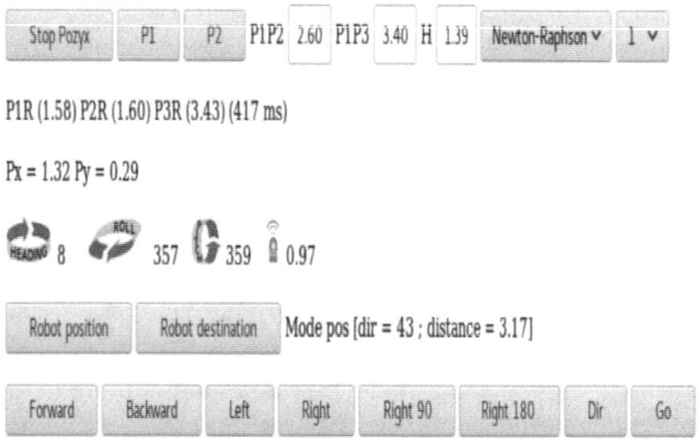

Figure 7. Elements of the user interface

The current user interface is experimental. It shows the distances measured from the Pozyxs (P1R, P2R, and P3R), the Round Trip Time (417 ms in Figure 7), the position of the robot on the orthogonal axis defined by P1, P2 and P3 (1.32 m from P1 on the X-axis defined by P1-P2, 0.29 m from P1 on the Y-axis defined by P1-P3).

The user interface also shows the heading of the robot in degrees (8 degrees, almost north, in Figure 7), and also the unused pitch and roll values. The distance from the closest obstacle to the robot is also shown (0.97 m in Figure 7). There is also a set of buttons to define a new robot destination and make the robot move.

In the next section, we will show the results and review the criteria exposed in the introduction.

IV. Results

A. The total cost

In the introduction, we said that the total cost should not exceed €1000. If there were no Pozyx, the total cost would be lower. The mechanical base costs about €100, the Lidar-lite about €200 [15], the compass about €30 [8], and the webcam about €100 including Raspberry PI 2 (Figure 8). We must still add the price of a computer that supports the Tomcat web server (from €50 to €500 depending on the model). We reach a maximum €900 total cost, Pozyx excluded.

One Pozyx is about €150 [16] and we need at least five. However, we think that it is not a problem. The very first Pozyxs were sold by the end of 2015 and the price will probably fall. The Decawave DW1000 chip used on the Pozyx module costs about one euro. The DWM1000 version that includes an antenna is now sold per unit for €30. We can expect UWB boards much cheaper in the near future. If a €50 UWB board was available, the cost criteria would be met.

Figure 8. The experimental robot

B. Performance of the external network

We have been testing Web performance for a decade. Tests have been done from Brest (France) to Auckland (New-Zealand). It is the longest distance possible in the world. Results are shown in Figure 9.

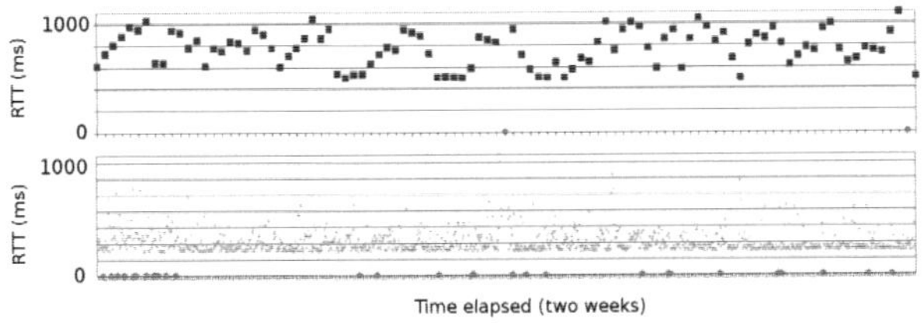

Figure 9. Web performance 2005-2015

The top diagram shows the measures taken in 2005 overs two weeks (horizontal axis in Figure 9). We have measured the Round Trip Time (RTT) between two computers, one located at the University of Brest (France) the other at the University of Auckland (NZ). We have obtained values from 495 to 1093 ms (vertical axis in top diagram in Figure 9). The average RTT is 768 ms. Exactly ten years later, the average RTT is 415 ms and most values are close to this average (bottom diagram in Figure 9). The minimum was 295 ms. The measures were performed between one Wi-Fi connected computer, located in a hotel in Auckland (NZ), and another computer located at the University of Brest (France).

This means that the Web can be used for remote control all over the world. However, we still have numerous RTT values greater than 500 ms. A RTT prediction system would be of great interest.

In fact, the problem comes from the local UWB network. The positioning process is very slow because communication between a Pozyx and an Arduino UNO is slow. One reason seems to be the use of the I2C Arduino bus. The Decawave chip on the Pozyx board uses the SPI bus (Serial Peripheral Interface Bus). The SPI bus must be converted to an I2C bus. Faster Arduinos or equivalent could improve communications. Direct connections to the Decawave chip by using the SPI bus could also produce improvements. That remains to be tested.

C. *Security of the system*

The security of the system is that of a distant user communicating with a remote Tomcat Web server through the encrypted HTTPS protocol.

The weakness is again in the local UWB network. Future studies will focus on the security of the local UWB network.

D. *Security of the persons and resilience*

The robot is able to detect any problem on the network and stop if required. Its low speed should make it safe for people. Experiments have shown the positioning system is accurate in the range between 30 and 50 cm. Perfect positioning is not available but it seems sufficient in a current AAL environment. The main remaining problem is door crossing. A better use of the Lidar could be the solution.

Moreover, we have no automatic charging dock yet. This is another key point that needs to be addressed. We assume that reliable standard charging docks will be available soon.

E. *User interface*

On the user interface, we can follow the robot on a map. As first experiments have shown that the Pozyx positioning system seems to be reliable, we have a control system based on standard components, such as OpenStreetMap. The time required to configure the system and make it work is very short.

F. *Positioning*

Even if the 30-50 cm obtained precision does not allow to make the robot go everywhere in house, it allows the robot to follow predefined paths. These paths must only be carefully chosen because the Pozyx signal may be easily stopped. The signal is very weak (about -40 dBm) and has shown to be very sensitive to metal obstacles, even if they are small.

V. Conclusion

The aim of this paper was to present a mobile home robot that could be helpful for old and/or dependent persons, and easily used by caregivers or relatives. Proposing a low cost solution, using high tech components, promoting simplicity were some of the key ideas that conducted this project.

This has been achieved by the use of a positioning system based on UWB Pozyx modules. Combined to a map in the user interface, it seems to be a promising technique.

However, several key points must be improved. Our knowledge of the security of such a system is very weak and must be improved. The accuracy of the positioning system must be also be improved to allow at least door crossing.

References

[1] Nikola Tesla. [Online]. Available from: https://en.wikipedia.org/wiki/Nikola_Tesla 2017.07.03

[2] K. Taylor and J. Trevelyan, "A telerobot on the world wide web," 1995 National Conference of the Australian Robot Association, 1995 July 5-7.

[3] "Robots With Their Heads in the Clouds," IEEE Spectrum, March 2011.

[4] Why Romotive shut down. [Online]. Available from: http://www.simplebotics.com/2016/02/the-rise-and-fall-of-robot-startup-romotive.html 2017.07.03

[5] F. De Natale and S. Pupolin, "Multimedia Communications," Springer Science & Business Media, 2012.

[6] U. Mengali, "Receiver architectures and ranging algorithms for UWB sensor networks," 2012. [Online]. Available from: http://www.iet.unipi.it/dottinformazione/Formazione/OffForm2011/Mengali/SoloTesto.html 2017.07.03

[7] Lidar. [Online]. Available from: https://en.wikipedia.org/wiki/Lidar 2017.07.03

[8] CMPS11 - Tilt Compensated Compass Module. [Online]. Available from: https://www.robot-electronics.co.uk/htm/cmps11doc.htm 2017.07.03

[9] D. Espes, A. Daher, Y. Autret, E. Radoi, and P. Le Parc, "Ultra-wideband positioning for assistance robots for elderly," 10th IASTED (SPPRA 2013), Feb. 2013, Austria.

[10] OpenStreetMap. [Online]. Available from: https://en.wikipedia.org/wiki/OpenStreetMap 2017.07.03

[11] OpenLayers. [Online]. Available from: https://openlayers.org 2017.07.03

[12] Javascript. [Online]. Available from: https://en.wikipedia.org/wiki/JavaScript 2017.07.03

[13] Ajax. [Online]. Available from: https://en.wikipedia.org/wiki/Ajax_(programming) 2017.07.03

[14] jQuery. [Online]. Available from: http://jquery.com 2017.07.03

[15] LIDAR-Lite V3. [Online]. Available from: https://www.sparkfun.com/products/14032 2017.07.03

[16] Pozyx. [Online]. Available from: https://www.pozyx.io 2017.07.03

MQTT-based Translation System for IoT Interoperability in oneM2M Architecture

Jiwoo Park, Geonwoo Kim and Kwangsue Chung
Department of Electronics and Communications Engineering
Kwangwoon University, Seoul, Korea
e-mail: {jwpark, gwkim}@cclab.kw.ac.kr, kchung@kw.ac.kr

***Abstract*—The key challenge for the future Internet of Things (IoT) is interoperability between IoT systems and platforms. To support the interconnection and interoperability between heterogeneous IoT systems and services, open-source Application Programming Interfaces (APIs) is one of the key features of common software platforms for IoT devices, gateways, and servers. The oneM2M standard is a global initiative led jointly by major standards organizations in order to standardize a common platform for globally-applicable and access-independent IoT services. In this paper, we present the design and open-source implementation of an IoT translator that enables heterogeneous IoT devices to be interoperable in oneM2M architecture. The translation system abstracts basic functionalities from IoT devices and interconnects them within oneM2M platform through MQTT, which is a publish/subscribe messaging protocol for the lightweight M2M communication. The implementation has been validated in a real test case and proved the interoperability by testing tools.**

Keywords-Internet of Things; interoperability; oneM2M; MQTT.

I. Introduction

The Internet of Things (IoT) is a large and heterogeneous collection of networks, protocols, devices, systems, services, solutions, and users. Advances in low cost processors have been a key enabler of intelligent automation devices. IoT takes the next step of networking these devices, resulting in intelligent environments. With the heterogeneity of independent platforms, a numerous of protocols have been developed. Many of the protocols will never be known as they are proprietary. But even within standardized protocols, there is a large variety to choose from. They are the result of evolving requirements and technology, leading to a highly dynamic ecosystem of co-existing protocols unable to work with each other. Interoperability in such an ecosystem is a major challenge, and yet it is a crucial aspect of successful IoT. However, many issues are still open in this domain, and the interest has constantly increased in the recent years both in the research and industrial communities [1].

One of the critical points for IoT deployment is the interoperability between devices and applications across multiple architectures, platforms and networking technologies. As a matter of facts, the proliferation of competing communication protocols and data representations across the device ecosystem makes it difficult for smart things to be easily integrated and cooperate with each other in a common IoT network. Several IoT horizontal platforms are being developed to overcome this issue; such platforms aim at abstracting from the complexity of the hardware and the networking sub-systems, so as to give smart things the ability to automatically discover and communicate with each other, and dynamically join and leave IoT proximal networks. Examples of open-source frameworks currently being developed by industries are the AllJoyn platform developed by the AllSeen Alliance [2], IoTivity, sponsored by the Open Connectivity Foundation (OCF) [3], and Google's Thread [4] and Weave [5]. Standard platforms are also being specified like, e.g., oneM2M [6], while many others have been developed as a result of research projects (e.g., EU FIWARE [7] and BETaaS [8]).

There exist many relatively mature IoT communication protocols, such as HTTP, Constrained Application Protocol (CoAP) [9] and Message Queueing Telemetry Transport (MQTT) [10], that may be already applied to pre-existing successful IoT implementations and are not supported for the future IoT framework. Replacing or updating IoT devices to integrate them in such frameworks is not always a feasible option due to device cost and other technical limitations. In these cases, a middleware that behaves like a translator between the pre-existing IoT platforms is therefore more appropriate in order to address interoperability challenges.

In this paper, we present the design and open-source implementation of a translation system that enables non-oneM2M devices to be compatible with oneM2M systems. The contribution of this paper covers the mapping of both IoT resources into oneM2M entities, and MQTT messages into oneM2M interface. The implementation of the translation system is validated in a real test case, and proved to properly work in a transparent manner.

The rest of the paper is organized as follows. Some relevant related work is described in Section II. In Section III, the design and architecture of the proposed system is presented while Section IV illustrates some implementation results. Finally, Section V offers concluding remarks.

II. Related Work

Without standards, IoT systems and services would be developed independently for different vertical domains, causing high fragmentation problems and increasing the overall cost for development and maintenance. In order to mitigate the fragmented IoT ecosystem, several industry/international standards organizations have come together and published standard specifications on IoT systems.

A. oneM2M Standard

The oneM2M global initiative has made an effort to standardize a common service layer platform for globally-applicable and access-independent M2M/IoT services. Swetina et al. summarized well the oneM2M standardization activities [11]. The oneM2M first collected various compelling use cases from a wide range of vertical business domains. After that, it formulated requirements for the oneM2M common service layer and then designed the system architecture. The main goal of oneM2M is to define a globally agreed M2M service platform by consolidating currently isolated M2M service layer standards activities. The oneM2M standard is organized into five technical working groups focusing on M2M requirements, system architecture, protocols, security, and management, abstraction and semantics. The oneM2M standard adopted a RESTful architecture, thus all services are represented as resources to provide the defined functions.

Fig. 1 presents the oneM2M reference architecture model. Considering a configuration scenario where oneM2M systems are deployed, the oneM2M architecture divides M2M/IoT environments into two domains (infrastructure and field domain) and defines four types of nodes, which reside in each domain: Infrastructure Node (IN), Middle Node (MN), Application Service Node (ASN), and Application Dedicated Node (ADN). Furthermore, the oneM2M architecture is based on a layered model, which comprises the application layer, the common service layer, and the underlying network service layer, each of which is represented as an entity in the oneM2M system. The Application Entity (AE) represents application services located in a device, gateway, or server. The Common Service Entity (CSE) stands for an instantiation of a set of Common Service Functions (CSFs) that can be used by applications and other CSEs. CSFs includes registration, security, application, service, data and device management, etc.

B. AllJoyn Framework

AllJoyn is an open source IoT software framework developed under the guide of the AllSeen Alliance consortium [12]. Its role is to handle the complexities of discovering nearby IoT devices, creating sessions between them, and communicating securely. AllJoyn can run on multiple platforms and it supports multiple language bindings and transports, so that devices and applications from different manufacturers, running on different operating systems, written with different language bindings have a common way to interact to each other. The basic element of the framework is the AllJoyn bus, which enables the exchange of marshaled messages around the distributed system. AllJoyn provides its own bus based on the D-Bus Wire protocol, an Inter-Process Communication (IPC) and Remote Procedure Call (RPC) mechanism, and extends it to support distributed devices.

The AllJoyn network comprises AllJoyn Routers, which deliver messages within the network, and AllJoyn Applications, which include the application code and the AllJoyn Core Library. Applications implement and advertise one or more service objects, each of which exposes its functionality through AllJoyn interfaces. The framework enables client applications to discover service objects advertised on the network, and then to invoke methods and properties, or to receive signals, provided by the interfaces. A consumer application invokes methods through a proxy object, which is a local representation of a remote service object.

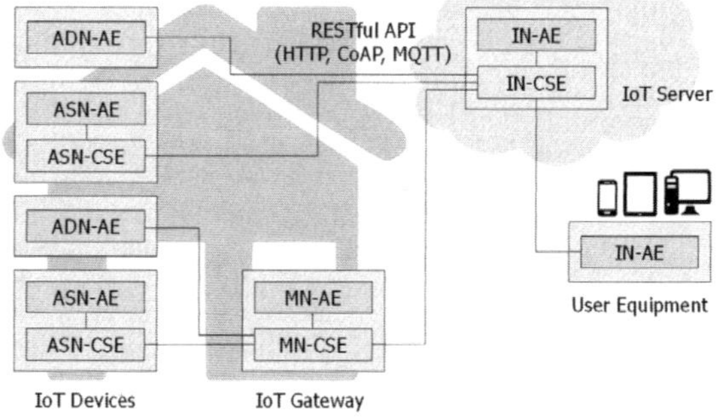

Figure 1. oneM2M reference architecture.

C. MQTT

MQTT stands for message queuing telemetry transport. Unlike CoAP, TCP, UDP, it is used because MQTT specializes in low-bandwidth, high-latency environments; it is an ideal protocol for M2M communication. Basically, there are three components in MQTT: publisher, subscriber and broker. Here, the process of receiving and publishing the data is very much secure and accurate. Whenever the user wants to check or go through any data it sends the request to broker and upon receiving the request it sends to the publisher, it responds to the requests and sends the data that is requested by the subscriber and hence publishes the data, in overall process the communication is secure and up to the topic of interest. MQTT broker acts like a filter allowing only those data, which are requested thereby saving the flow of ambiguous data.

III. PROPOSED MQTT-BASED TRANSLATION SYSTEM

Middleware is a common approach to addressing interoperability. We developed a translation system as a middleware in the oneM2M platform in order to interwork with the non-oneM2M devices.

A. System Overview

The interaction between heterogeneous IoT systems ensured by a translation middleware should be done in a transparent manner, so that an application can communicate with any devices in the foreign system as if those devices were based on the same technology. Therefore, the design of the translation system primarily involves how to map the communication interface to a resource-oriented system based on oneM2M. The translation middleware also entails mapping both IoT resources into oneM2M entities, and MQTT messages into oneM2M interface.

Fig. 2 shows the concept of the translation system. The proposed system consists of things, a translation middleware, a server, a validation tool and a user device. Things include

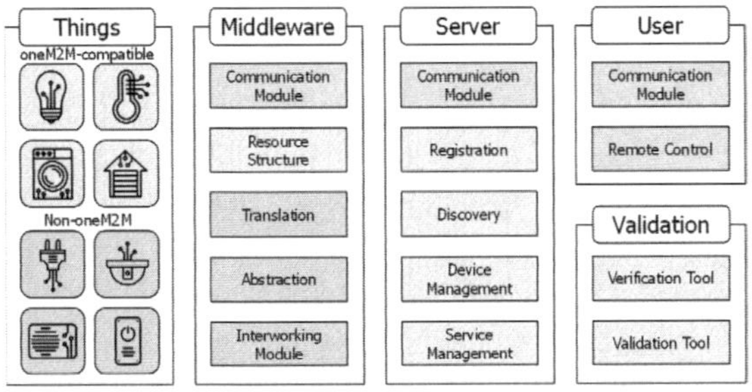

Figure 2. Concept of the proposed translation system.

oneM2M-compatible devices and commercial IoT products that are not compatible with oneM2M but support open-source APIs and libraries. The translation middleware is basically working as a MN-CSE to communicate with oneM2M devices. For supporting non-oneM2M devices, the interworking module is developed in the middleware using open-source libraries supported by each IoT service platform. The middleware abstracts data from connected non-oneM2M things and translates their functionality to the oneM2M-based resource structure. The server provides high-level features to users; for example, registration and device management. To verify and validate the translation function, the proposed system runs several test tools for interoperability.

B. Design of MQTT-based Translation System

Since the oneM2M architecture adopted the Resource-Oriented Architecture (ROA) model, the services and data that oneM2M system supports are managed as a resource information model. With the ROA concept, resources in the ROA are uniquely addressed by the Uniform Resource Identifier (URI), and the interactions with the resources are supported by the basic four operations: create, retrieve, update, and delete. The oneM2M system manages its resources as a hierarchical structure as shown in Fig. 3. Starting from the root of CSEBase, resources are created as child resources, which represent services and data in the oneM2M system. When accessing the resource, the address of the resource should be represented as a hierarchical address that looks like the resource structure. For example, considering the CONT1 resource, its address with which it can be accessed is CSEBase/CSE1/AE1/CONT1. Additionally, oneM2M specifies a service layer protocol and its protocol binding with underlying delivery protocols including HTTP, CoAP and MQTT.

The oneM2M standards are developed for creating globally-applicable, access-independent IoT applications, but there exists a huge number of non-oneM2M systems already deployed across multiple domains. To interwork with the non-oneM2M systems, the proposed translation system provides non-oneM2M reference points and remapping the related data model into the oneM2M-defined data model, which are eventually exposed to other oneM2M systems. When translating data models, a full semantic interworking between two data models would be possible with the help of the related protocol interworking, but otherwise, the encoded non-oneM2M data and command messages will be packaged into a list of oneM2M containers. Consequently, the oneM2M applications need to know the protocol rules of the non-oneM2M systems to decode and understand the content within the containers.

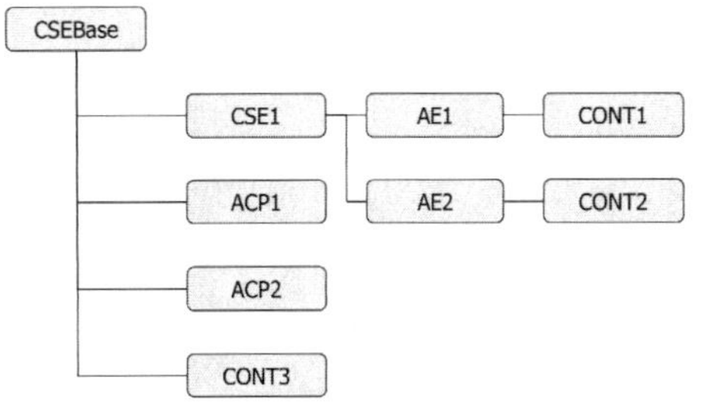

Figure 3. oneM2M-based resource structure.

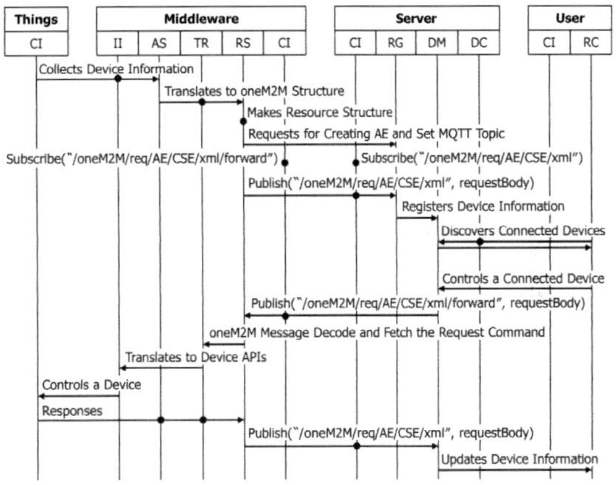

Figure 4. Sequence diagram of the MQTT-based translation system.

Fig. 4 shows a sequence diagram of the MQTT-based translation system. First, the middleware searches for IoT devices through the Interworking Interface (II) module. After searching for devices, the Abstraction (AS) module collects device information and extracts features and functions from it. The Translation (TR) module translates its functionality to the oneM2M Resource Structure (RS). The Communication Interface (CI) modules in the middleware and the server subscribe a specific topic for the MQTT communication. When the server receives a resource structure from the RS module, the Device Management (DM) module first registers newly added devices through a Registration (RG) module. Users find IoT devices connected to the home network by requesting a device list from the Discovery (DC) module. Once users get the device list from the server, users can control IoT devices by using a Remote Control (RC) module. The control messages are translated to the corresponding device APIs in the TR module. After performing users' command, it needs to update the device status. Updating process is performed in a similar way to the registration step as we described above.

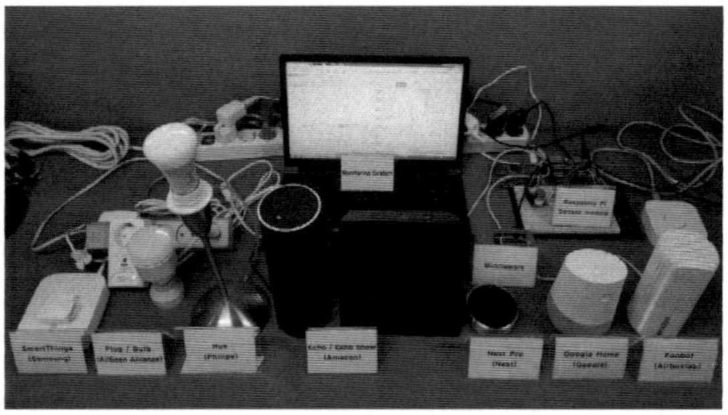

Figure 5. Configuration of the test environment.

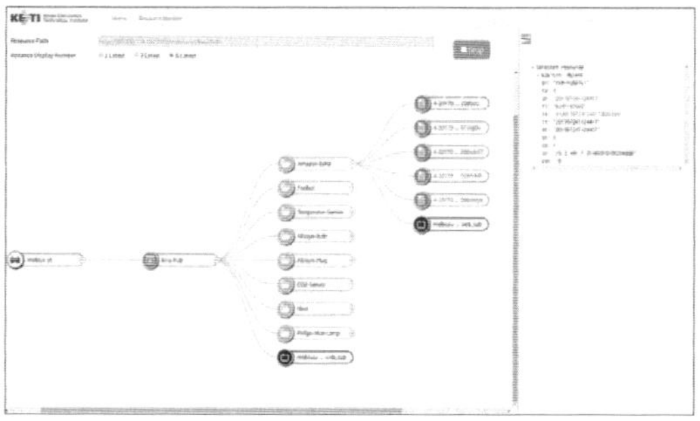

Figure 6. oneM2M resource discovery using a monitoring tool.

IV. IMPLEMENTATION RESULTS

We conduct the implementation of the proposed system in a real environment. The test case is set up with a translation middleware, an IoT server and commercial IoT products, as shown in Fig. 5. The proposed system is built on oneM2M platforms, Mobius [13] and &Cube [14]. The translation middleware is implemented on a Raspberry Pi 3, which is s a credit-card sized single-board computer. The server runs an open-source MQTT broker, Mosquitto [15], on a Linux PC to interconnect with the middleware and users. We start with interworking AllJoyn-enabled devices, such as smart light bulbs and smart plugs. Then, we support various types of IoT products, e.g., thermostat, air quality monitor, smart home appliances.

To validate interoperability between IoT devices, we use a web-based resource monitoring tool supported from the oneM2M organization. When we access the server using the monitoring tool, the oneM2M-based resource structure is presented in a graphical form as shown in Fig. 6. If the translation system works correctly, the resource of non-oneM2M devices will be listed with oneM2M-compatible devices. We have shown that all the devices connected to the middleware works well in a real test case and can access their resources by using the oneM2M monitoring tool.

V. CONCLUSION

In this paper, we presented the design and implementation of a translation system that allows non-oneM2M devices to be accessible in oneM2M systems. On the device side, each device is connected to the middleware in order to advertise its resources and functions. The translation middleware provides an oneM2M-based hierarchical structure for each of these resources, which is exchanged with the IoT server. The IoT server is implemented as part of the translation system to provide high-level IoT functions for users. The implementation has been extensively tested in a real test case, and is built on open-source libraries. Currently, the proposed system supports a few commercial IoT services but the interoperability with oneM2M systems is fully tested.

For future work, we plan to support other commercial IoT solutions, especially sensor/actuation-type devices and voice-activated services. We also plan to modify the proposed system in order to satisfy the oneM2M release 2 specification.

ACKNOWLEDGMENT

This work was supported by Institute for Information & communications Technology Promotion (IITP) grant funded by the Korea government (MSIT). (No.2017-0-00167, Development of Human Implicit/Explicit Intention Recognition Technologies for Autonomous Human-Things Interaction)

REFERENCES

[1] J. A. Stankovic, "Research directions for the Internet of Things," *IEEE Internet of Things Journal*, vol. 1, no. 1, pp. 3–9, Feb. 2014.

[2] The AllSeen Alliance. [Online]. Available: https:// allseenalliance.org

[3] IoTivity. [Online]. Available: https://www.iotivity.org

[4] Thread. [Online]. Available: http://threadgroup.org

[5] Weave. [Online]. Available: https://developers.google.com/ weave

[6] oneM2M - Standards for M2M and the Internet of Things. [Online]. Available: http://www.onem2m.org

[7] The FIWARE Catalogue. [Online]. Available: https:// catalogue.fiware.org

[8] C. Vallati et al., "BETaaS: A platform for development and execution of machine-to-machine applications in the internet of things," *Wireless Personal Communications*, vol. 87, no. 3, pp. 1071–1091, May 2015.

[9] Z. Shelby, K. Hartke, and C. Bormann, "The Constrained Application Protocol (CoAP)," *RFC 7252*, Jun. 2014. [Online]. Available: https://tools.ietf.org/html/rfc7252

[10] "Information technology – Message Queuing Telemetry Transport (MQTT) v3.1.1," *ISO/IEC 20922:2016*, Jun. 2016.

[11] J. Swetina, G. Lu, P. Jacobs, F. Ennesser, and J. Song, "Toward a standardized common M2M service layer platform: Introduction to oneM2M," *IEEE Wireless Communications*, vol. 21, no. 3, pp. 20-26, Jun. 2014.

[12] The AllJoyn Core Framework. [Online]. Available: https:// allseenalliance.org/framework/documentation

[13] J. Kim, S. Choi, J. Yun, and J. Lee, "Towards the oneM2M standards for building IoT ecosystem: Analysis, implementation and lessons," *Peer-to-Peer Networking and Applications*, pp. 1-13, Sep. 2016.

[14] J. Yun, I. Ahn, N. Sung, and J. Kim, "A device software platform for consumer electronics based on the Internet of Things," *IEEE Transactions on Consumer Electronics*, vol. 61, no. 4, pp. 564-571, Nov. 2015.

[15] Mosquitto. [Online]. Available: https://mosquitto.org

High-performance Wireless Sensor Node Design for Water Pipeline Monitoring

Fatma Karray, Mohamed W. Jmal, Mohamed Abid

Digital Research Center of Sfax
Computer and Embedded System laboratory
National Engineering School of Sfax
Sfax, Tunisia
Email: fatma.karray@enis.tn, mohamedwassim.jmal@enis.rnu.tn, Mohamed.Abid@enis.rnu.tn

***Abstract*—Water utilities owners are facing critical challenges in repairing and maintaining pipeline infrastructure. Leakages in water pipeline infrastructure cost millions of dollars every year. The need for a reliable, continuous and efficient system for pipeline monitoring becomes crucial. Wireless Sensor Network (WSN) is a very promising technology to detect leaks in an autonomous way. In this paper, we present a WSN system for water pipeline monitoring. A wireless sensor node based on Zynq System on Chip is developed and simulated. A leak detection algorithm based on Kalman filter is also implemented and accelerated using the Zynq platform. The experimental results show that the usage of high-performance platforms is suitable only if the power management techniques are employed or for video applications.**

Keywords–Wireless sensor network; Water pipeline monitoring; Leak detection; node design; Zynq platform; Kalman Filter.

I. Introduction

With the rapid evolution of embedded systems, Wireless Sensor Networks (WSNs) have invaded our daily life in the last years. One of the most important applications of WSNs is Water Pipeline Monitoring (WPM). In fact, a large amount of water is wasted daily due to leakages in pipelines. This is aggravated by the lack of automatic systems [1]. Hence, WSN could play a primordial role in such application by decreasing the human intervention and providing continuous monitoring. WSN is composed of a large number of nodes that are widely deployed to inspect physical phenomena (pipeline leakages in our case) in a cooperative way.

The node, which is the main component of the network, integrates four units: sensing unit, treatment unit, communication unit and power unit [2]. The node is generally powered by a battery, which makes the node power considered as a major constraint. The main goal of the node design is to preserve energy consumption and extend the lifetime of the battery. Therefore, the majority of nodes used for WSN are based in general on "limited resources" microcontrollers (MCUs), which make some processing tasks difficult or impossible in some cases [3].

An investigation on high-performance platforms becomes essential. In that line, we aim in this paper to design a robust WPM system using WSN. For this purpose, we propose a leak detection algorithm using a modified Kalman filter (KF) for accurate inspection. Moreover, we suggest a wireless sensor node platform based on a high-performance Zync system on chip (SoC).

The paper is organized as follows: In section II, we review the leak detection methods existing in the literature. Section III also reviews the WSN node platforms used for WPM from MCUs to FPGAs (Field-Programmable Gate Array). In section IV, we detail our proposal in terms of leak detection algorithm and wireless sensor node platform. Section V shows and discusses the experimental results. We finish this work with conclusion and perspectives in section VI.

II. Leak Detection Methods

Pipeline infrastructure could be threaten by several factors. This, in fact, affects the fresh water quality in pipes. It begets also economical losses and countless damages such as leaks, obstruction, corrosion, etc [4]. In this context, preserving the pipeline infrastructure is crucial. This could be accomplished by using and automating pipeline inspection. In this work, we are interested in leak detection methods.

Plenty of leak detection techniques exist in the literature [5]. These methods depend on the instrument used or the inspected physical parameter. The shared principle of these techniques is the exploitation of the pipeline material's physical properties and/or the water flow's characteristics to detect damages and abnormalities. From these methods, we could cite:

A. Visual Inspection Techniques

These methods are the oldest ones that employ video or image sensors to inspect leaks in pipes. Depending on the instrument used for inspection, many techniques are proposed for this method like the laser scan and the Closed-Circuit Television (CCTV) inspection [4]. The CCTV technique is composed of a robot with a camera traveling inside the pipe to inspect the pipe. We should mention that the visual methods are not based on the same idea. Laser scan technique employs laser and could be used inside or outside the pipeline. Pulse-based, phase-based and triangulation are techniques based on scanning [4]. Visual inspection techniques are used in WSNs by attaching Charge-Coupled Device (CCD) or CMOS image sensors to the computing unit in the sensor node. The captured images and/or videos are streamed to the base station for analysis [6].

B. Acoustic Techniques

Several acoustic techniques exist for leak detection. These techniques are widely used, especially for small leaks. They are non-destructive. In WSN, some sensors are used such as hydrophones, piezoelectric sensor, accelerometers and vibration sensor and deployed inside and/or outside the pipeline. The principle of this technique is the detection of acoustic waves or noise caused by escaped liquid when a leak occurs. This escaped liquid flows turbulently and causes acoustic signals [7]. For instance, the authors in [8] propose a leak detection method for pressurized pipeline using acoustic emissions. Another work [9] exploits acoustic signals to inspect leaks in underground pipes. The authors in [10] tested the feasibility of acoustic emission for pressurized pipe using R15a acoustic sensor. The acoustic signals are very weak and operate in noisy environments. Almost all the time, the distinction of these signals is very difficult. Pre-amplifiers as well as filters are required to avoid noise. This technique is not very adequate for underground pipes due to the deployment difficulties [11].

C. *Ultrasound Techniques*

The ultrasound techniques are based on ultrasound waves detection. These waves are in general of mechanical vibrations. They propagate along the pipe and are reflected then. This allows leaks detection and measuring pipeline wall thickness. The ultrasonic sensors could be used inside or outside the pipe. Many ultrasound techniques exist, such as discrete ultrasound, immersion testing, straight beam, phased array, etc [12]. The guided wave technique could be defined as ultrasound wave traveling in delimited pipes. For this reason, this technique is widely used for an economical and easy inspection [13]. The authors in [14] prove the effectiveness of ultrasonic guided waves for high temperature pipes. Jeffrey et al. propose a pipeline monitoring system that exploits ultrasound guided waves for corrosion detection. The sensors are placed outside of pipeline [15]. Another work suggests a modular WSN system to monitor the pipeline wall thickness using the ultrasound method [16]. Despite the effectiveness of the ultrasound techniques, they should be employed jointly with other technique to enhance the accuracy of the detection and avoid false alarms. Moreover, these techniques suffer from high power consumption.

D. *Electromagnetic Techniques*

The electromagnetic methods are based on the principle of measuring variations in the electrical properties of a subsurface. From the electromagnetic methods used for leak detection in water pipelines, we could mention: Ground-penetrating radar (GPR), Magnetic flux leakage (MFL), Ultra-wideband (UWB) pulsed radar system (P-Scan) [4].

E. *Computational Pipeline Monitoring (CPM) Techniques*

CPM methods exploit internal pipeline parameters like pressure, flow, temperature with algorithmic tools to monitor and detect leaks. The data is collected using pressure sensors or other sensors and then analyzed mathematically or statistically to provide an alarm. From the CPM techniques, we can cite the Mass Balance and the Real Time Transient Modelling (RTTM) [17]. The Mass Balance method is based on mass conservation. The leak in such method is detected when the difference between the upstream and the downstream flow exceeds a given threshold. Although this method is simple, cost effective and easy, it suffers from false detection [18]. RTTM analyzes the pipeline hydraulic behavior to predict the existence of leaks. It is based on the resolution of momentum calculations and numerous flow equations to detect and also localize leaks. The main drawback of this method is the computational complexity [19].

CPM methods are exploited in WSN. The use of WSN enhances the accuracy and the autonomy of such system. WSN is considered as a hybrid method that combines different kinds of sensors and algorithms to get precise, easy and early information about the leak. From the WSN projects, PipeNet [20] is a well-known project that adopts acoustic, pressure and vibration sensors for leak detection and localization. The sensor node is based on Intel mote. MISE-PIPE [21] employs soil properties, pressure and acoustic sensors. Furthermore, SmartPipe [22] uses soil properties and pressure sensors for underground pipeline inspection and monitoring. These two methods are coupled to improve the system accuracy. WSN seems a promising leak detection and localization tool. It enhances the performance by improving algorithms or combining methods by using more than one kind of sensors. However, there is no attention given to architecture of nodes [3]. Almost all WSN platforms for pipeline monitoring are based on simple MCUs. In the following, node platforms used for WPM are presented.

III. WSN Node Platforms for Water Pipeline Monitoring

Some researches on pipeline monitoring focus on improving the leak detection techniques. Others are working on the placement and replacement of nodes while some others try to improve the network communication especially for underground pipelines. Insignificant interest is devoted to the nodes architecture and design. A typical WSN node consists mainly of a processor, a radio transceiver, memories, an antenna, sensors and a battery. Commercial motes based on MCUs are the most used in WPM applications. Other technologies and platforms are not widely investigated. Few works describing alternatives to MCUs such as DSPs, ASICs (Application-specific integrated circuit) and FPGAs for WPM are presented.

A. *Nodes based on MCU*

MCU is an integrated circuit that includes a microprocessor, memories and input/output peripherals. It is characterized by its low cost and its low power consumption. For this reason, it is exploited in many WSN projects like [3][20][21][23][22], etc. In fact, advances in MCU technology allow easy and low cost implementations. It permits also data processing. The MCU allows also to manage the communication and the power consumption of the node. Various WSN projects that employ MCUs exist in the literature [24].

For example, PipeNet [20] is a WPM project that allows leaks detection and localization. Many signal processing algorithms have been implemented such as WT, cross-correlation algorithm, pattern recognition algorithms and other algorithms. The sensor node is based on Intel mote, which consists of an ARM7 core, a 64KB RAM, a 512 KB Flash, and a Bluetooth communication.

PipeProbe [25] is designed for pipeline monitoring. The PipeProbe node has a hydro molecule form. It consists of a EcoMote and a MS5541C pressure sensor, nRF24E1 transceiver, an antenna, a 32 KB external EEPROM, a flex-PCB expansion port and a battery.

SPAMMS [6] is another WSN system for WPM. It is an autonomous and cost effective system for leak control, localization and maintenance of the pipeline by using static and mobile sensors and a robot. Different kinds of sensors are used like CCD, chemical, pressure and sonar sensors. This high number of sensors leads to high processing requirements. The sensor node is composed of MiCA1 mote (mobile sensor), an EM4001 ISO RFID system and a robot agent. Mica1 is a mote that contains a ATMega103 MCU, a 4 Kb of RAM, a 512 Kb of EEPROM and a 128 Kb of Flash memory.

SmartPipe [22] is also a WSN for underground pipeline monitoring. It is a non-invasive solution that employs force sensitive resistor sensors and sol proprieties sensors. The sensor node contains a PIC16LF1827 MCU, an eRA400TRS radio transceiver, two temperature sensors and one FSR based pressure sensor.

Another work, TriopusNet [23] is a mobile WSN for pipeline monitoring. The node encompasses a Kmote, a spherical case, a motor, a MS5541C pressure sensor and gyro-scope sensor. The Kmote is composed of a MSP430 MCU and a CC2420 transceiver. This work aims to automatically place or replace failed nodes using a replacement algorithm.

MCUs are widely exploited in WPM application thanks to their low cost, their low power and their flexibility. However, they have some drawbacks such as the limited processing capabilities and the small memory size. Other alternatives to MCUs are cited in this paper.

B. Sensor nodes based on DSP

General purpose processors are not usually adequate for some specific applications like Fourier transforms, filtering, signal processing and image processing algorithms. The DSP (Digital Signal Processor) is a microprocessor optimized for real time digital signal processing applications. It allows high speed streaming and processing data thanks to its specific architecture comparing MCUs. Despite the advantages of DSPs, only few implementations are dedicated for WSN-WPM application. For instance, the authors in [26] suggest an implementation on DSP of a leak detection algorithm based on FFT correlation of sound sensor data for underground pipeline monitoring. Zhang et al. employ a DSP to process acoustic signals with correlation function for leak detection [27].

DSPs are efficient for signal processing algorithms. However, they are power consuming processors. That is why, they are not largely used for WSN-WPM application.

C. Sensor Nodes based on FPGA/ASIC

ASIC/FPGA technologies are not broadly used for node design in monitoring applications. To the best of our knowledge, few works use FPGA or ASIC directly or indirectly. The sensor node, suggested in [20], is composed of a OEM piezoresistive silicon sensor. This sensor includes an ASIC compensation-based technology, which allows to achieve an accuracy better than 0.2%. FPGA is used, in general, as prototyping platform to achieve faster calculation of complex applications. It offers hardware and software high speed and flexibility. Moreover, the price and the performance is more favorable than an ASIC [28]. It permits also system reconfiguration after a field deployment [29]. For instance, the authors in [27] propose a FPGA system for data acquisition. This FPGA is employed as co-processor with a DSP for leak detection and localization using acoustic sensors. The system is composed of a FPGA, DSP, acoustic sensors, a LCD, a wireless module and an ADC. Another work suggests a leak detection method based on magnetic flux for pipeline inspection. The node prototype is implemented on Altera Cyclone FPGA [30].

The design of a sensor node based on ASIC or FPGA for the WPM application could offer an efficient and a flexible system. However, it can also result in high power consumption. Hence, saving energy and power consumption is a crucial issue for WSN nodes design. Moreover, many challenges should be satisfied for WSN-WPM. In fact, it is crucial to find a trade-off between the energy, the performance, the small size, the low cost, the time-to-market and the security [31]. For this purpose, we aim to design an efficient sensor node using a high performance platform and a reliable algorithm.

IV. Proposed Leak Detection System using WSN

WSNs face several challenges in WPM applications [32] in terms of reliable inspection, external analyses, a non-real time processing and high false alarm rates. Therefore, a novel WSN system that gets over the limitation of this technique and enhances the performance of the sensor node is essential. For this purpose, a novel KF leak detection method has been implemented and accelerated using Zynq platform.

A. Leak detection algorithm

KF is a recursive data processing algorithm proposed by Kalman in 1960 [33]. It is largely explored in WSNs due to its low requirements of memory, its low complexity and its ability to predict data. We implement a modified KF to filter noise and to detect and locate leaks. Various works that use KF exist for WPM application. For example, the authors in [34] suggest a linear KF for detecting leaks using the hydraulic measurements and the linearity of data within one week. The authors in [35] propose an Extended KF for pipeline monitoring. Torres [36] has employed an extended KF and a set of observers to detect and locate leaks in water pipes. To the best of our knowledge, this work is the first that explores KF for WSN and WPM at the same time. Our approach is applied to long distance above ground pressurized pipelines. We detail briefly the algorithm steps [33]. The KF is based on two steps: the prediction and the correction. In the first step, the estimated state x, which is a vector of the pressure and the flow in this case, at time k is elaborated from the updated state at k-1. In the first step, the prediction of the current state and the covariance matrix is given by:

$$\hat{x}_k^- = A.\hat{x}_{k-1} + B.u_k \tag{1}$$

where A is the transition matrix, B is the transition matrix of inputs; u_k is the input vector;

$$P_k^- = A.P_{k-1}.A^T + Q_k \tag{2}$$

The second step is the correction step. This step aims to get an improved estimate by incorporating new measurements into the predicted estimate using the Kalman gain (K_k).

$$K_k = P_k^-.H^T.(H.P_k^-.H^T + R_k)^{-1} \tag{3}$$

$$\hat{x}_k = \hat{x}_k^- + K_k(z_k - H\hat{x}_k^-) \tag{4}$$

$$P_k = (I - K_k H)P_k^- \tag{5}$$

KF estimates pressure and flow variations caused by leaks using the innovation variation. When the variation exceeds a threshold, this indicates the existence of leaks.

B. *Sensor nodes design and SW/HW implementation*

After implementing the algorithm, we need to focus on improving the performance of the node. We should mention again that little interest is given to the sensor node architecture in WPM applications. For this purpose, testing and evaluating a high performance platform is essential. A high-performance sensor node allows in-node processing, real time and quick response. It provides also satisfaction of the application's requirements. It decreases the human intervention and facilitates pipeline monitoring.

1) Node design and implementation: A SoC technology has been chosen for this work. It is an innovative platform that allows to perform complex computational tasks, to reuse Intellectual Properties (IPs) and to miniaturize devices by integrating the greater part of the components in a single chip [1]. In this context, we implement a SoC using Zybo board.

This board is built around the Xilinx Zynq-7000 family; the Z-7010. The Z-7010 incorporates a dual core ARM Cortex-A9 processor and Xilinx programmable logic equivalent to Artix-7 FPGA in a single device. It includes also a DDR3 memory controller with 8 DMA channels, an Advanced Microcontroller Bus Architecture (AMBA) Interconnect and I/O peripherals (USB (Universal Serial Bus), SPI (Serial Peripheral Interface), UART(Universal Asynchronous Receiver Transmitter), I2C(Inter-Integrated Circuit), etc). The Programmable logic block consists of 4,400 logic slices, 240 KB of block RAM, 80 DSP slices, Internal clock speeds exceeding 450MHz, analog-to-digital converter (XADC), etc. The first basic built architecture contains the ARM Cortex-A9 processor, an AXI GPIO, a memory controller and the AXI interconnect, as shown in Figure 1.

2) Leak Detection Algorithm Implementation: The application detailed in the subsection IV-A is implemented in C. We introduce also a new function Prodmatrix, which affects the matrix multiplication. Hence, the steps of the algorithm will include the following function:

- Xestimate, Pestimate and Prodmatrix for the prediction step.
- KGain, Xupdate, Pupdate and Prodmatrix for the correction step.
- other code for the leak calculation.

The application and the hardware are performed using Vivado 14.4 and the Software Development Kit (SDK) provided by Xilinx. In fact, after generating the bit stream of the design, the project is exported in the SDK to run the leak detection algorithm and to program the board. SDK offers also the possibility of application profiling as it integrates the GNU gprof. The GNU gprof is composed of the gcc compiler and the gprof. In fact, profiling allows the application's performance analysis. The goal of this task is to select the complex function (in the algorithm), which is the most time consuming for hardware implementation. This part is very important since it requires a careful selection of the right function needed to be transformed into a hardware accelerator to speed up the application and to enhance the performance of the system. However, this is not always possible as it depends on many other parameters. Hence, a compromise between time, energy and area is crucial. Profiling has provided us statistics about the execution time and the number of calls. After profiling the leak detection algorithm a gmon.out file is generated.

Table I gives the execution time of each function in the leak detection algorithm for one iteration. The Prodmatrix is the most time consuming function in the algorithm. It is characterized also by a high number of call. Thus, we choose to implement it into hardware.

TABLE I. Execution Time of the Algorithm functions

Function	Cycles	Time
Xestimate	159	0.35
Pestimate	860	0.75
Xupdate	180	0.5
Pupdate	566	1.25
KGain	249	0.75
Prodmatrix	522	1.75

C. *Hardware Accelerator Implementation*

Hardware acceleration is used to make some tasks more efficient than in software implementation and to speed up the execution time of the system. Two methods are adopted to implement the Prodmatrix hardware module: with Vivado High-Level Synthesis (HLS) and manually. Vivado HLS is a tool provided by Xilinx to accelerate the creation of IPs. It allows to rapidly transform a C code to a RTL description. It permits also resource allocation and partitioning and IP module generation. We have used also Pragma directives to optimize the hardware IP like INTERFACE directive, as shown in Figure 4.

The hardware accelerator aims to speed up the execution time by transforming a software function or algorithm executed by the processor into a hardware block attached in our case to the "AXI-lite" bus. In this step, the choice of the connection mode and the register number is necessary. The register number depends on the Input/Output number of the accelerator. Then, the Prodmatrix hardware accelerator appears in the IP catalog to be integrated with the architecture, as shown in Figure 2. The bitstream is then generated and exported to the SDK to test the accelerator results. After that, we implement the all KF into a hardware block, as given in Figure 3.

The two accelerators are generated manually (VHDL programming) and with Vivado HLS. The different results of the implementations will be detailed in the next section.

V. RESULTS AND DISCUSSION

In this section, we compare the results to decide the best architectural design selection. The metrics that we have used are time, power and space. As explained before, the Zybo board is used to perform the previous implementations. All the results are given for one iteration.

A. *Execution Time*

The execution time is essential to test the efficiency of the application. It influences also the power consumption of the node. It is evaluated using profiling technique in the all cases,

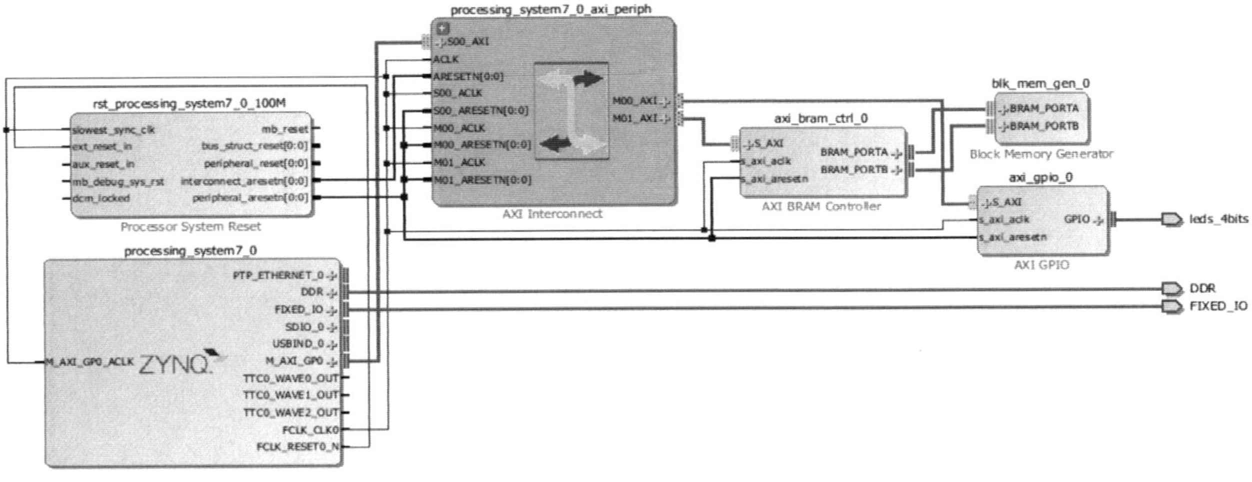

Figure 1. Proposed Sensor Node Implementation

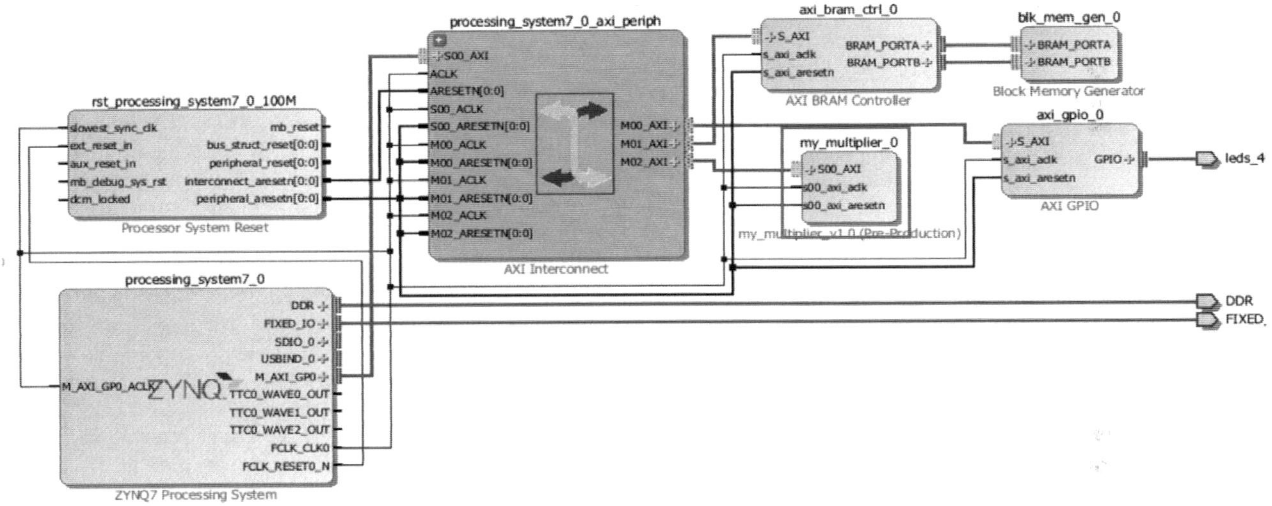

Figure 2. Hardware Acceleration and Integration of the Prodmatrix

```
double kalman_filter(double A[2][2],double H[1][2],double R,
{
#pragma HLS INTERFACE s_axilite port=return bundle=CTRL_BUS
#pragma HLS INTERFACE s_axilite port=innova bundle=CTRL_BUS
#pragma HLS INTERFACE bram port=HH
#pragma HLS INTERFACE bram port=AA
#pragma HLS INTERFACE bram port=id
#pragma HLS INTERFACE bram port=X_estimat
#pragma HLS INTERFACE bram port=X_updat
#pragma HLS INTERFACE bram port=P_estimate
#pragma HLS INTERFACE bram port=P_update
#pragma HLS INTERFACE s_axilite port=e bundle=CTRL_BUS
#pragma HLS INTERFACE bram port=Q
#pragma HLS INTERFACE s_axilite port=R bundle=CTRL_BUS
#pragma HLS INTERFACE bram port=H
#pragma HLS INTERFACE bram port=A
```

Figure 4. Pragma directives

as shown in the Figure 5. In the software implementation, the execution time is very low compared to the hardware accelerator, which is slightly abnormal. However, this could be explained by the high frequency of the processor and the difference of frequencies between the processor and the FPGA. Another reason is the usage of AXI-lite. The AXI4-Stream could maybe enhance the results.

B. Resource Utilization

Resources utilization is an important metric in SoC design. In fact, optimal resources allow optimal area, which could save energy and miniaturize node platform. We present the resources of all five implementations. Table II shows the different area occupancy including the look up tables (LUTs), Random Access Memory blocks (BRAMs), Flip Flops (FF) and Digital Signal Processing (DSP) blocks in the programmable device. These values are calculated using Vivado tool. The implementations of Vivado HLS are not optimal, a lot of resources are used. These implementations exploit DSP blocks more than other implementations.

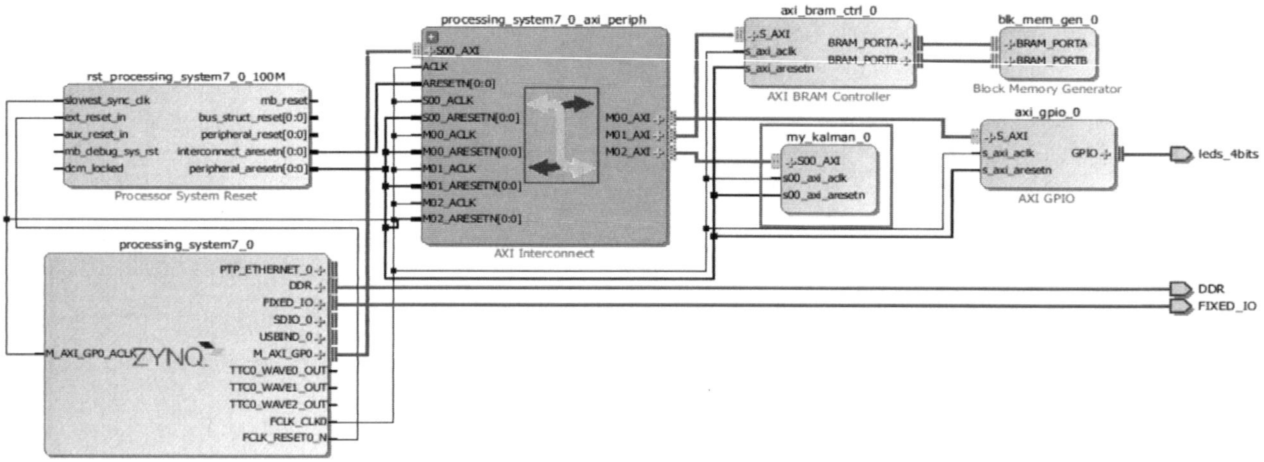

Figure 3. Hardware Acceleration and Integration of the KF

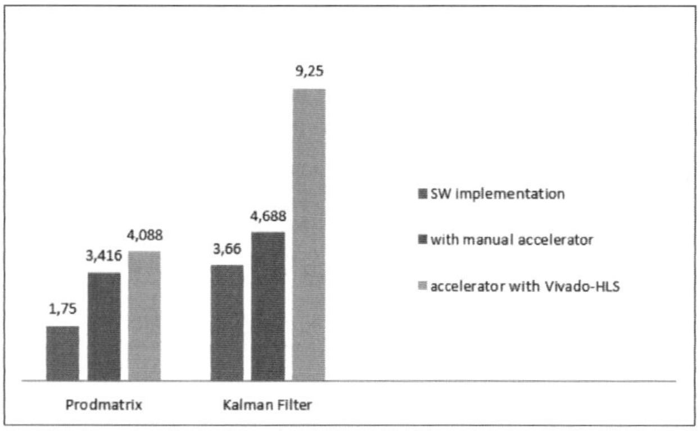

Figure 5. Execution Time of different implementations (μs)

TABLE II. Resource utilization (%)

Resources	SW	Prodmatrix		Kalman Filter	
		M	Vivado HLS	M	Vivado HLS
LUT	8.4	13.84	16.33	17.9	72.99
BRAM	26.67	3.3	10	3.33	50
FF	14.78	7.32	9.05	9.01	40.47
DSP48	0	10	17.5	0	62.5

C. Power Consumption

The power consumption of the node is a crucial criterion. In this work, we measured the power consumption of the five architectures using Vivado power report. This report details the static and the dynamic powers related to intrinsic leakage, design, inputs data patterns, etc. The total on-chip power for the software implementation was 1.484 W while the power of the Prodmatrix HW accelerator is 1.487 W for the manual implementation and 1.485 W for the Vivado HLS implementation. KF HW accelerator has as power consumption 1.726 W with manual implementation and about 2 W for the Vivado HLS implementation. As we remark, the power consumption is very high in all implementations. This again is related to the high frequency and performance of the cortex-A9 processor.

VI. CONCLUSION

We have detailed in this paper a WSN node platform design for water pipeline monitoring. A leak detection algorithm based on KF is implemented and accelerated using Zybo board. Five designs have been implemented for the node and compared using Xilinx Electronic Design Automation tools. The evaluation is based on three metrics: the execution time, the resource utilization, and the power consumption.

The results were not promising. This is due to several factors. First of all, the frequency of the processor is very high. In general, a high frequency processor will result in a high power dissipation. Moreover, the difference of frequency between the processor (650Mhz) and the programmable logic block (450Mhz) may decrease the performance of the accelerators and the communication between these two components. Furthermore, the usage of AXI-lite was also not very promising. In fact, this bus is characterized by its small logic footprint, a light-weight and single transaction memory mapped interface. We note also that the built accelerator using Vivado HLS is not optimized compared to the manual accelerator.

As future work, to reduce the power consumption of the node, many techniques should be implemented. On one hand, we could adjust the frequency of the processor and decrease it to meet the frequency of the FPGA and to save power. Moreover, the AXI4-Stream with the usage of a Direct Memory Access (DMA) may enhance the performance and accelerated the data reading. In fact, the AXI4-Stream offers a high-speed streaming data. On the other hand, the usage of power management techniques like wake up receiver, dynamic voltage and frequency scaling will be explored in the future. Finally, other processors with moderate frequency and features like ARM cortex M3 will be investigated.

ACKNOWLEDGMENT

The authors would like to thank the King Abdulaziz City for Science and Technology (KACST), which supports this work under a research grant (project no. 35/1012).

They would like to thank also Mrs. Mariem Chabbouh and Dr. Mouna Baklouti for their effort.

REFERENCES

[1] A. M. Obeid, F. Karray, M. W. Jmal, M. Abid, and M. S. BenSaleh, "Towards realisation of wireless sensor network-based water pipeline monitoring systems: a comprehensive review of techniques and platforms," IET science, measurement & technology, vol. 7, 2016.

[2] F. Karray, M. Jmal, M. Abid, M. S. BenSaleh, and A. M. Obeid, "A review on wireless sensor node architectures," in Reconfigurable and Communication-Centric Systems-on-Chip (ReCoSoC), 2014 9th International Symposium on. IEEE, 2014, pp. 1–8.

[3] F. Karray, A. Garcia-Ortiz, M. W. Jmal, A. M. Obeid, and M. Abid, "Earnpipe: A testbed for smart water pipeline monitoring using wireless sensor network," Procedia Computer Science, vol. 96, 2016, pp. 285–294.

[4] Z. Liu and Y. Kleiner, "State of the art review of inspection technologies for condition assessment of water pipes," Measurement, vol. 46, no. 1, 2013, pp. 1–15.

[5] R. Li, H. Huang, K. Xin, and T. Tao, "A review of methods for burst/leakage detection and location in water distribution systems," Water Science and Technology: Water Supply, vol. 15, no. 3, 2015, pp. 429–441.

[6] J.-H. Kim, G. Sharma, N. Boudriga, and S. S. Iyengar, "Spamms: A sensor-based pipeline autonomous monitoring and maintenance system." COMSNETS, vol. 10, 2010, pp. 118–127.

[7] M. Ahadi and M. S. Bakhtiar, "Leak detection in water-filled plastic pipes through the application of tuned wavelet transforms to acoustic emission signals," Applied Acoustics, vol. 71, no. 7, 2010, pp. 634–639.

[8] D. Ozevin and J. Harding, "Novel leak localization in pressurized pipeline networks using acoustic emission and geometric connectivity," International Journal of Pressure Vessels and Piping, vol. 92, 2012, pp. 63–69.

[9] C. Qi and D. Que, "Design of pipeline leakage point location system and simulation of related algorithm," in Information and Automation (ICIA), 2013 IEEE International Conference on. IEEE, 2013, pp. 92–96.

[10] A. Mostafapour and S. Davoudi, "Analysis of leakage in high pressure pipe using acoustic emission method," Applied Acoustics, vol. 74, no. 3, 2013, pp. 335–342.

[11] K. Anupama, N. Kamdar, S. K. Kamalampet, D. Vyas, S. Sahu, and S. Shah, "A wireless sensor network based pipeline monitoring system," in Signal Processing and Integrated Networks (SPIN), 2014 International Conference on. IEEE, 2014, pp. 412–419.

[12] A. Santos and M. Younis, "A sensor network for non-intrusive and efficient leak detection in long pipelines," in Wireless Days (WD), 2011 IFIP. IEEE, 2011, pp. 1–6.

[13] J. L. Rose, J. Mu, and Y. Cho, "Recent advances on guided waves in pipe inspection," in Proceedings of the 17th World Conference on Non-Destructive Testing, Shanghai, China, 2008, pp. 25–28.

[14] L. Schubert, B. Weihnacht, T. Klesse, and B. Frankenstein, "Monitoring of high temperature steel pipes by ultrasonic waveguide solutions," in Ultrasonics Symposium (IUS), 2012 IEEE International. IEEE, 2012, pp. 2758–2761.

[15] J. D. Bergman, S. J. Lee, H. Chung, and I. Li, "Real-time active pipeline integrity detection (rapid) system for corrosion detection and quantification," in EWSHM-7th European Workshop on Structural Health Monitoring, 2014.

[16] A. El Kouche, H. Hassanein, and K. Obaia, "Monitoring the reliability of industrial equipment using wireless sensor networks," in Wireless Communications and Mobile Computing Conference (IWCMC), 2012 8th International. IEEE, 2012, pp. 88–93.

[17] J. Xu, Z. Nie, F. Shan, J. Li, Y. Luo, Q. Yuan, and H. Chen, "Leak detection methods overview and summary," in ICPTT 2012: Better Pipeline Infrastructure for a Better Life, 2013, pp. 1034–1050.

[18] J. Doorhy, "Real-time pipeline leak detection and location using volume balancing," Pipeline Gas J, vol. 238, no. 2, 2011, pp. 65–67.

[19] A. F. Colombo, P. Lee, and B. W. Karney, "A selective literature review of transient-based leak detection methods," Journal of Hydro-environment Research, vol. 2, no. 4, 2009, pp. 212–227.

[20] I. Stoianov, L. Nachman, S. Madden, T. Tokmouline, and M. Csail, "Pipenet: A wireless sensor network for pipeline monitoring," in Information Processing in Sensor Networks, 2007. IPSN 2007. 6th International Symposium on. IEEE, 2007, pp. 264–273.

[21] Z. Sun, P. Wang, M. C. Vuran, M. A. Al-Rodhaan, A. M. Al-Dhelaan, and I. F. Akyildiz, "Mise-pipe: Magnetic induction-based wireless sensor networks for underground pipeline monitoring," Ad Hoc Networks, vol. 9, no. 3, 2011, pp. 218–227.

[22] A. M. Sadeghioon, N. Metje, D. N. Chapman, and C. J. Anthony, "Smartpipes: Smart wireless sensor networks for leak detection in water pipelines," Journal of Sensor and Actuator Networks, vol. 3, no. 1, 2014, pp. 64–78.

[23] T. T.-T. Lai, W.-J. Chen, K.-H. Li, P. Huang, and H.-H. Chu, "Triopusnet: Automating wireless sensor network deployment and replacement in pipeline monitoring," in Proceedings of the 11th international conference on Information Processing in Sensor Networks. ACM, 2012, pp. 61–72.

[24] F. Karray, W. M. Jmal, M. Abid, D. Houssaini, A. M. Obeid, S. M. Qasim, and M. S. BenSaleh, "Architecture of wireless sensor nodes for water monitoring applications: From microcontroller-based system to soc solutions," in Environmental Instrumentation and Measurements (IMEKO), 2014 5th IMEKO TC19 Symposium on, 2014, pp. 20–24.

[25] Y.-C. Chang, T.-T. Lai, H.-H. Chu, and P. Huang, "Pipeprobe: Mapping spatial layout of indoor water pipelines," in Mobile Data Management: Systems, Services and Middleware, 2009. MDM'09. Tenth International Conference on. IEEE, 2009, pp. 391–392.

[26] G. Gaizi and Y. Zongzuo, "Design and implementation of leak detector using dsp based on correlation calculation," in Future Computer and Communication (ICFCC), 2010 2nd International Conference on, vol. 1. IEEE, 2010, pp. V1–492.

[27] L. Zhang, Y. Wu, L. Guo, and P. Cai, "Design and implementation of leak acoustic signal correlator for water pipelines," Inf. Technol. J, vol. 12, 2013, pp. 2195–2200.

[28] K. Yifan and J. Peng, "Development of data video base station in water environment monitoring oriented wireless sensor networks," in Embedded Software and Systems Symposia, 2008. ICESS Symposia'08. International Conference on. IEEE, 2008, pp. 281–286.

[29] Y. E. Krasteva, J. Portilla, E. de la Torre, and T. Riesgo, "Embedded runtime reconfigurable nodes for wireless sensor networks applications," IEEE Sensors Journal, vol. 11, no. 9, 2011, pp. 1800–1810.

[30] J.-j. XIN, S.-l. HUANG, L.-l. LIU, and W. ZHAO, "Design of super multi-channel and high-speed data acquisition system based on fpga [j]," Electrical Measurement & Instrumentation, vol. 10, 2008, pp. 34–36.

[31] S. Kumar, C. R. Krishna, and A. Solanki, "A survey on security architecture and key management systems in a wireless sensor network," International Journal of Computer Science and Network Security (IJCSNS), vol. 17, no. 4, 2017, p. 263.

[32] A. Lay-Ekuakille, G. Griffo, and P. Vergallo, "Robust algorithm based on decimated padè approximant technique for processing sensor data in leak detection in waterworks," IET Science, Measurement & Technology, vol. 7, no. 5, 2013, pp. 256–264.

[33] R. E. Kalman, "A new approach to linear filtering and prediction problems," Journal of basic Engineering, vol. 82, no. 1, 1960, pp. 35–45.

[34] G. Ye and R. A. Fenner, "Kalman filtering of hydraulic measurements for burst detection in water distribution systems," Journal of pipeline systems engineering and practice, vol. 2, no. 1, 2010, pp. 14–22.

[35] A. Benkherouf and A. Allidina, "Leak detection and location in gas pipelines," in IEE Proceedings D (Control Theory and Applications), vol. 135. IET, 1988, pp. 142–148.

[36] L. Torres, "Location of leaks in pipelines using parameter identification tools," arXiv preprint arXiv:1406.5437, 2014.

An Extensible Edge Computing Architecture: Definition, Requirements and Enablers

Volkan Gezer and Jumyung Um and Martin Ruskowski
Innovative Factory Systems (IFS)
German Research Center for Artificial Intelligence (DFKI)
Kaiserslautern, Germany
Emails: {name.surname}@dfki.de

***Abstract*—Cloud computing is highly being used for several years for various purposes. From daily tasks, such as reading e-mails, watching videos to the factory automation and device control, it changed where the data is being processed and how it is accessed. However, increasing number of connected devices brings problems, such as low Quality of Service (QoS) due to infrastructure resources and high latency because of the bandwidth limitations. The current tendency to solve the problems that the Cloud computing has is performing the computations as close as possible to the device. This paradigm is called Edge Computing. There are several proposed architectures for the Edge Computing, but there is no an accepted standard by the community or the industry. Besides, there is not a common agreement on how the Edge Computing architecture physically looks like. In this paper, we describe the Edge Computing, explain how its architecture looks like, its requirements, and enablers. We also define the major features that one Edge Server should support.**

Keywords–Edge computing; requirements; enablers; Fog computing.

I. INTRODUCTION

With the increased tendency towards Internet of Things (IoT), number of connected devices to the Internet are increasing day by day. In 1992, the connected devices count was around one million which went up to 500 million in 2003 with increased usage of notebooks. Later, IoT became even more popular and made three billions of devices connected. In 2012, with the inclusion of wearable devices this number went high as 8.7 billion. In 2013, this number was 11.2 billion thanks to connected home appliances and in 2014, 14.4 billion with smart grids. The numbers increased in the upcoming years due to involvement of small personal objects, such as toothbrushes, traffic lights, and table watches. Finally, even door levers are expected to be part of smart objects in 2020 [1].

Connected devices are expected to be around 50 billion by 2020 [1][2]. This number is high as the Cyber-Physical Systems (CPS) and more intelligent components being used even for simple tasks. Using different standards, a single infrastructure to keep the system reliable is becoming even more complex, causing difficult and costly maintenance. Relying on a single information technology (IT) infrastructure can also increase the downtime of communication which disrupts the service leading to non-productive time. The bandwidth for communication is also becoming a problem to transmit that amount of data.

Cloud Computing [3] is an emerging technology which allows machines/people to access the data ubiquitously. It enables on-demand sharing of available computing and storage resource among its users which could be either human or machine, or even both. Today, it is even possible for a simple device to share its status or get information over Internet with millions of users. In Cloud Computing, the communication between the device and the infrastructure which provides the service is direct, without involvement of other tiers. However, increased usage of Cloud increases latency and the load on the server and on the network. Having billions of devices and processing the data produced by each of them is a troublesome task for centralized systems [4]. Figure 1 shows some examples for Cloud Computing, such as E-Mail services, Cloud Storage systems, Video hosting web sites, etc.

A layer is a logical organisation of set of services, devices, or software with the same/similar specific functionality, mainly defined for abstraction of tasks. A tier is, however, a physical deployment of layers for scalability, security and to balance performance [5].

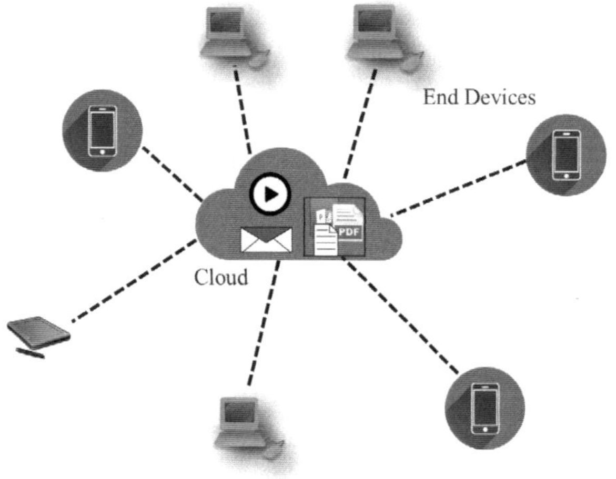

Figure 1. Some of daily usage examples of Cloud Computing, such as e-mails, music/video streaming, and data storage.

Edge Computing is a recent paradigm, which moves computing application and services from centralized units into the logical extremes or at the closest locations to the source and provides data processing power there. It adds an additional tier between the Cloud and the end-devices as depicted in Figure 2. Increase in Edge nodes within a location will reduce the number of devices connected to a single Cloud and eliminate the problems of the Cloud Computing. Examples to Edge Computing can be listed as Smart Cities, Machine to Machine communication, Security Systems, Augmented Reality, Wearable Health Care Systems, Connected Cars, and Intelligent Transportation. For example, a plane produces gigabytes of data per second [6], which cannot be handled by a single base infrastructure due to bandwidth limitations. Another example is a Formula One car which produces approximately 1.2 GB/s data [7] that requires gathering, analysis, and acting in-time to stay competitive in the race [8]. Edge Computing is believed to solve these issues by aggregating and pre-processing the data in Edge, before transmitting to the Cloud or even deciding the next steps on the Edge.

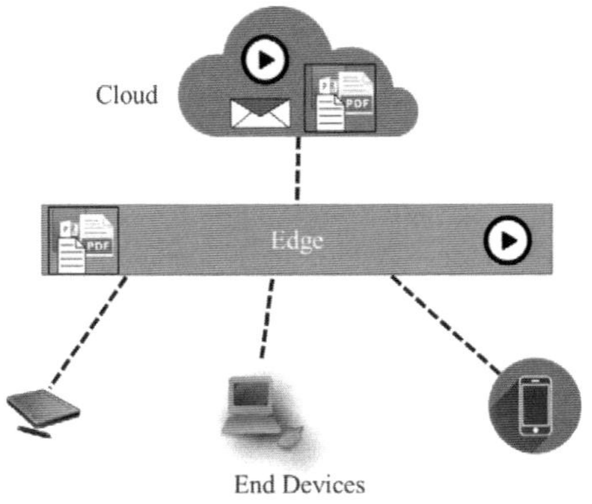

Figure 2. A simplified version of communication using Edge Computing.

Both Edge Computing and Cloud Computing are part of Internet of Things (IoT) and allow accessibility of the data ubiquitously. To build an architecture, the issues on the current Cloud or IoT systems must be identified, requirements must be specified, enabling technologies must be listed, and then a concept must be given. Later, the concept can be implemented in an architecture, validated, and evaluated.

This paper presents an ongoing work on Edge Computing with its clear description. It also explains its requirements and enablers to solve the introduced issues because of high usage of Cloud and IoT.

The paper is structured as follows. In Section II, a short overview on related work in Edge Computing domain is given. In Section III, the concept of Edge Computing is explained. Later, in Section IV, its requirements, and in Section V, enablers are explained. In Section VI, the major functionalities of the proposed architecture is explained. The paper is concluded in Section VII with the future work.

II. RELATED WORK

Although usage of the term "Edge Computing" is recent, there are already several proposed architectures available, each considering different aspects to meet the requirements of the Edge Computing. Below, some of the existing proposed architectures will be discussed.

The architecture proposed by IBM considers the requirements for autonomy and self-sufficiency of production sites. The architecture is three-layered to balance the workload between the Edge, the Plant, and the Enterprise. The challenges of the architecture are listed as productivity gains for high throughput, failure prevention for reliable system and high product quality, and flexibility while hiding the complexity and allowing reconfiguration without a lot of effort [9].

Another reference architecture is proposed by OpenFog Consortium [10]. This architecture names the core principles as pillars. Pillars group requirements within their scope. These pillars are Security, Scalability, Openness, Autonomy, Agility, and Programmability. OpenFog Reference Architecture is proposed by covering industrial use cases.

Another recent initiative to build a common platform for Industrial IoT Edge Computing is EdgeX Foundry [11]. It was launched by Linux Foundation and initial contribution made by Dell. However, similar to OpenFog Consortium, it is also open for new memberships. EdgeX Foundry is a vendor-neutral open source software platform that interacts at the Edge of the network. It defines its requirements in architectural tenets as follows: platform agnostic in terms of hardware and operating system, flexible in terms of replacability, augmentability, or scalability up and down, capable in storing or forwarding data, intelligent to deal with latency, bandwidth, and storage issues, secure, and easily manageable. A similar framework called Liota is being developed by VMware and it also aims at easy to use, install, and modify. Secondarily, it targets for a general, modular and enterprise-level quality. This framework is also open source and governed by VMware [12].

The aim in this research is not simply to build another architecture, but to analyse the existing architectures and consider industrial requirements to make up a generic reference architecture which is vendor-independent and extensible. The architecture is also able to execute real-time tasks. To the best of our knowledge, this is not considered in any of the aforementioned reference architectures.

III. CONCEPT

One of the main goals of Edge Computing is to reduce latency and to keep the Quality of Service (QoS) as high as possible. As seen in Figure 1, in Cloud Computing, the Cloud infrastructure communicates with the end-devices directly. Edge Computing intends to solve the issues of Cloud Computing or IoT by adding an additional tier between the IoT devices and back-end infrastructure for computing and communication purposes. As depicted in Figure 3, this tier also has intermediate components for the first gathering, analysis, computation of the data. These intermediate components are called *Edge Servers*. Several architecture types for IoT-enabled applications are proposed [13]. In this paper, a three-tier architecture is used.

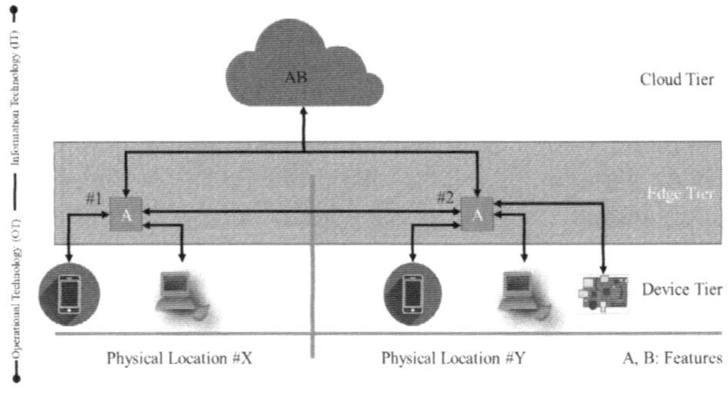

Figure 3. Edge Computing is an additional tier between Cloud and the Devices. The Edge Servers can be in the same or different physical locations.

As seen in Figure 3, the proposed architecture for Edge

Computing consists of *Cloud Tier*, *Edge Tier*, and *Device Tier*. In the Device Tier, there are end-user devices. The green blocks in the Edge Tier are Edge Servers. These servers gather, aggregate, analyse, and process the data before offloading them to the Cloud Tier. The end-devices can be in the same location, or in different physical locations as depicted in the figure. When an end-device needs to communicate with the Cloud, first, the request is sent to the Edge Server which is at the closest location. Then, if the Edge Server is capable of completing the task by itself, it automatically handles the data and responds to the end-device with the result. If not, the data is offloaded to another server in the same tier provided that it exists. Otherwise, the data is offloaded to the Cloud. The decision process is made by considering available resources in other available servers in the same network, physical distance, and time requirements.

Assume that the Cloud provides functionalities A and B. When one of the devices in *Physical Location X* intends to do task *B*, first the data is passed to the server #1. Since this server is not capable of performing this task, it passes the data either to the Cloud. As Cloud is capable of performing task B, the data is processed here and sent back to the originating end-device. The challenge here is to decide on functionalities in the Edge Tier by keeping the costs at minimum and the QoS at maximum. However, deciding on the count and available resources of Edge Servers are also big challenges and big trade-offs. There are several aspects to consider before passing the data to the Cloud. For example, if a device located at Y needs task A to be done, and if the Edge Server #2 is busy with servicing other two connected devices, another trade-off will be existent. In this case, the server #2 needs to offload the task either onto server #1 or the Cloud. However, depending on the urgency of the task, the server #2 needs to calculate a function to decide on the best recipient of the data. According to this, the function should consider the priority of the task, resource utilization of the servers, computing cost for the task, and the physical distance or distance cost of the servers that is going to be used.

IV. Requirements

Edge Computing is a paradigm which uses Cloud Computing technologies and gives more responsibilities to the Edge tier. These responsibilities are namely, computing offload, data caching/storage, data processing, service distribution, IoT management, security, and privacy protection [4].

Without limiting the Cloud Computing features, Edge Computing needs to have the following requirements, some of which are also defined for Cloud Computing [14][15]:

1) Interoperability: Servers in Edge Computing can connect with various devices and other servers. In Cloud Computing, IoT allows countless number of devices to communicate with humans or each other. This creates a big market for manufacturers of these devices. For this reason, there is the issue of interoperability with connected device using different communication protocols. Advanced Message Queuing Protocol (AMQP), Message Queue Telemetry Transport (MQTT), and TCP/IP are widely used and should supported by Edge Computing. Using a widely-used and widely-known standard will remove the technology and language barriers, increasing interoperability among the devices.

2) Scalability: Similar to Cloud services, Edge Computing will also need to be adapted for the size of its users and sensors. First deployment enables small number of users and devices while few Edge Servers should handle higher number. Additional deployment of Edge Servers is costly and small number of Edge Servers is desirable in terms of economical aspects. For this reason, high scalability is also mandatory.

3) Extensibility: Computing technology is developing rapidly. After 2-3 years of deployment, clock speeds, memory size and program size increase, too. Easy deployment of new services and new devices with small effort is required for essential goal of Edge Computing. New functions and devices should be integrated without (re)configuration of the Edge network. Therefore, the system should allow extensibility with hardware and software components.

4) Abstraction: For the seamless control and communication, the abstraction of each Edge Node and group of nodes is required. Moreover, abstraction helps the topology of an Edge network to be flexible and reconfigurable. Fundamentally, an Edge node is located between device tier and Cloud tier. In other words, an Edge tier is a border between Information Technology (IT) and Operational Technology (OT). This tier can consist of one or more Edge nodes and groups. In this case, one Edge node of the group can share tasks or nodes in the group can be prioritized. Utilization of Application Programming Interfaces (APIs) in abstraction is useful to provide backward compatibility for the new functionalities or big changes in the architecture.

5) Time sensitiveness: Below OT, the operations may be near-real-time or real-time. Edge Computing is expected to solve time issues which Cloud computing cannot guarantee. Unlike Cloud Computing, physically close distance is one strength of reliable and fast communication without worrying about traffic problem. Video streaming service is one of expected applications of Edge Computing. It is required for real-timeness of the service provision. In addition, time-sensitiveness adds big benefits to providers of reactive services, such as location-based advertisements and user-status based guide systems.

6) Security & Privacy: Using Cloud Computing services has a trade-off for enterprises like manufacturing and high-tech companies because there is a concern about the leakage of high knowledge and business activities outside their own organization. Edge Computing is a way to secure data contents, which is different from firewall which only controls external access into the network. It is also important to isolate the data by preventing access from even non-authorized users.

7) Reliability: Edge Servers provide real-time or non-real-time control for the devices. Real-time tasks may be vital which involve human safety. Therefore, it is vital to have a reliable system which reacts when it is needed and how it is needed. The physical reliability requirements for Edge servers providing services is similar to Cloud Computing. Harsh environments, such as factories and construction yards, require water-proof ceiling, fanless computers and dust-proof system. In power plant, magnetic shield is equipped by sensor gateways.

8) Intelligence: Multi-sensor generates tremendous amount of data and uploads into Cloud, directly. It causes network congestion and heavy load on the Cloud server. Edge Computing supports first and second filtering of these data by converting into higher level of data contents. Data filtering is implemented by rule-based engines or machine learning algorithms. In the case of multi-camera system like security systems, Edge Computing supports image processing, computer vision and enables object detection before transferring the data into the Cloud. Another example is predicting the failure or abnormalities in a production line by analysing the sensor data and taking the precautions for prevention or informing the user. These kinds of intelligent functions are necessary for Edge Computing.

9) Power: Unexpected shutdown or blackout is the cause of breakdown of Edge Server. Uninterruptible power supply (UPS) is required to give an ample amount of time to protect the electronic units and data storage in case of an unexpected shutdown due to power outage.

V. ENABLERS

Edge Computing uses wide range of technologies and brings them together. Within this domain, Edge Computing utilizes many technologies, such as wireless sensor networks (WSN), mobile data acquisition, mobile signature analysis, Fog/Grid Computing, distributed data operations, remote Cloud services, etc. Additionally, it combines the following protocols and terms:

1) 5G communication: It is the fifth generation wireless system which aims at higher capacity, lower power consumption, and lower latency compared to the previous generations. Due to increased amount of data between the data, 5G is expected to solve traffic issues which arose with the increased number of connected devices.

2) PLC protocols: Object Linking and Embedding for Process Control Unified Architecture (OPC-UA) is a protocol developed for industrial automation. Due to its openness and robustness, it is widely used by industries in the area of oil and gas, pharmaceutical, robotics, and manufacturing.

3) Message queue broker: MQTT and TCP/IP are popular message protocols of smart sensors and IoT devices. Supporting these message brokers, Edge Computing increases the device count that it connects. For the problem of MQTT security, AMQP is useful in the communication with Cloud Computing server.

4) Event processor: After messages of IoT arrive in the Edge server, event processor analyses those messages and creates semantic events using pre-defined rules. EsperNet, Apache Spark, and Flink are some examples for this enabler.

5) Virtualisation: Cloud services are deployed as virtual machines on a Cloud server or clusters. Using virtual machines allow running multiple instances of operating systems (OS) on the same server.

6) Hypervisor: As well as virtual machine, performance evaluation and data handling are required and realized by hypervisor to control virtual machines in the host computer.

7) OpenStack: Managing multiple resources could be challenging. OpenStack is a Cloud operating system that helps control of pools of computing and storage resources at ease through a control panel and monitoring tools.

8) AI platform: Rule-based engine and Machine learning platform supports data analysis in local level. As stated in Section IV, this is quite important to reach one of the goals of Edge Computing which is to gather, analyse, and perform the first filtering of the data.

9) Hyperledger: Blockchain technology is currently used for highly sensitive areas, such as digital currencies like BitCoin. It is also considered as useful for the data protection in Cloud Computing. By using this technology, secure data can be shared with external persons and servers with high security.

10)Docker: Virtual machines work with installation of operating systems. Unlike virtual machines, Docker is a Container as a Service (CaaS) which can use a single shared operating system and run software in isolated environment. It only requires the libraries of the software which makes it a lightweight system without worrying about where the software is deployed.

VI. ARCHITECTURE DESIGN

Edge Computing adds an additional tier between the Cloud and IoT devices for computing and communication. The data produced by the devices themselves are not directly sent to the Cloud or back-end infrastructure, but initial computing is performed on this tier. Considering the number of connected devices and the data they produced, this tier is used to aggregate, analyse, and process the data before sending it into the upper layer, the infrastructure.

Figure 4 depicts the proposed core functionalities for an Edge Server.

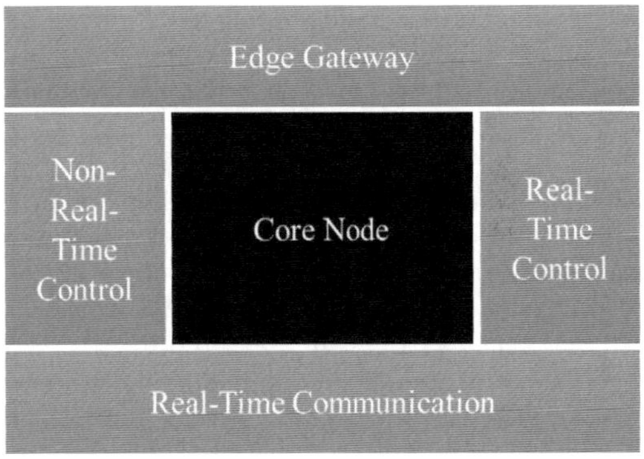

Figure 4. View of the proposed extensible Edge server architecture with its major functionalities, where green blocks extend the functionalities for the blue core node.

The proposed Edge Server architecture is to be designed modular and should provide functionalities for real-time and non-real-time control, as well as real-time communication. Core node runs on an operating system and tracks resources and makes decisions on where to execute a task. In the proposed architecture, addition of a new hardware or software modules enable new functionalities and improve the usability of the server. For example, in the case that machine learning algorithms are desired to be executed on the server, connecting a dedicated artificial intelligence (AI) module with dedicated Graphics Processing Unit (GPU) should require none to minimal configuration to be active.

As mentioned in Section IV, scalability is quite important to accomplish the tasks. In the scope of scalability, one server is expected to be aware of its neighbouring servers along with their functionalities. Using the previous example, in case an AI module is connected to one server, other servers are informed with this functionality and they can utilize this server more often for AI-related tasks. The decision, of course, depends on the conditions required by the task, such as deadline.

VII. Conclusion and Future Work

Edge Computing is a recent term which moves the services from the Cloud to the device as close as possible. It is a borderline between the Cloud and the device tier. Although the Cloud Computing has brought many advantages in the previous years, increased number in the connected devices raised some issues, such as latency and low QoS problems. Edge Computing is believed to solve these issues by analysing the issues and considering the requirements of real world use cases.

This paper showed an ongoing work on how *Edge Computing* physically looks like together with its requirements and enablers. It also explained the basics on how the communication between the end-devices and Edge servers are expected to be.

There are already several existing proposed architectures in the domain of Edge Computing, such as EdgeX Foundry, Liota, and OpenFog Reference Architecture. Although they are also extensible and they allow inter-connectivity, they do not talk about the real-timeliness of the architectures. This work will be focusing on real-time computing and communication for the given tasks. Of course, it will also be available for non-real-time tasks. The work is being developed by considering the real-world use cases of the industrial partners. The validation will be performed with these use cases and the comparison with the legacy systems will be made.

In the future, internal software and hardware components for the Edge Server will be decided. Later, they will be simulated as an initial work for the architecture design. Next, the software components will be individually implemented in the simulation environment. By analysing the simulator results, a hardware benchmarking will be performed and a hardware will be chosen to be used as the Edge Server solution. The final task will be to realize the components by deploying them on the chosen hardware.

Acknowledgment

This research was funded in part by the H2020 program of European Union, project number (project FAR-EDGE). The responsibility for this publication lies with the authors. The project details can be found under project website at: `http://www.far-edge.eu`

References

[1] NCTA, "The Growth of The Internet of Things," Infographic, May 2014, [retrieved: Sep 2017]. [Online]. Available: https://www.ncta.com/platform/industry-news/infographic-the-growth-of-the-internet-of-things/

[2] D. Evans, "The Internet of Things - Cisco," Cisco, White Paper, April 2011, [retrieved: Sep 2017]. [Online]. Available: https://www.cisco.com/c/dam/en_us/about/ac79/docs/innov/IoT_IBSG_0411FINAL.pdf

[3] M. Peter and G. Timothy, "The nist definition of cloud computing," in National Institute of Standards and Technology Technical report, September 2011.

[4] W. Shi, J. Cao, Q. Zhang, Y. Li, and L. Xu, "Edge Computing: Vision and Challenges," IEEE Internet of Things Journal, vol. 3, no. 5, October 2016, pp. 637–646.

[5] R. Lhotka, "Should all apps be n-tier?" Blog, 2005, [retrieved: Sep 2017]. [Online]. Available: http://www.lhotka.net/weblog/ShouldAllAppsBeNtier.aspx

[6] S. Higginbotham, "Sensor Networks Top Social Networks for Big Data," Article, 2010, [retrieved: Sep 2017]. [Online]. Available: https://gigaom.com/2010/09/13/sensor-networks-top-social-networks-for-big-data-2/

[7] T. Valich, "Big Data In Planes: New P&W Gtf Engine Telemetry To Generate 10GB/s," Article, 2015, [retrieved: Sep 2017]. [Online]. Available: https://vrworld.com/2015/05/08/big-data-in-planes-new-pw-gtf-engine-telemetry-to-generate-10gbs/

[8] F. Bi, "How Formula One Teams Are Using Big Data To Get The Inside Edge," Article, 2017, [retrieved: Sep 2017]. [Online]. Available: https://www.forbes.com/sites/frankbi/2014/11/13/how-formula-one-teams-are-using-big-data-to-get-the-inside-edge/

[9] I. C. A. Center, "IBM: Internet of Things," Cloud Garage Method, 2017, [retrieved: Sep 2017]. [Online]. Available: https://www.ibm.com/devops/method/content/architecture/iotArchitecture/industrie_40

[10] "OpenFog Consortium Reference Architecture," Website, 2017, [retrieved: Sep 2017]. [Online]. Available: https://www.openfogconsortium.org/ra/

[11] "EdgeX Foundry Architectural Tenets," EdgeX Foundry Wiki, 2017, [retrieved: Sep 2017]. [Online]. Available: https://wiki.edgexfoundry.org/display/FA/Introduction+to+EdgeX+Foundry

[12] "VMware Introduces Liota," Website, 2017, [retrieved: Sep 2017]. [Online]. Available: https://www.vmware.com/radius/vmware-introduces-liota-iot-developers-dream/

[13] A. Al-Fuqaha, M. Guizani, M. Mohammadi, M. Aledhari, and M. Ayyash, "Internet of things: A survey on enabling technologies, protocols, and applications," IEEE Communications Surveys Tutorials, vol. 17, no. 4, 2015, pp. 2347–2376.

[14] G. Orsini, D. Bade, and W. Lamersdorf, "Context-Aware Computation Offloading for Mobile Cloud Computing: Requirements Analysis, Survey and Design Guideline," Procedia Computer Science, vol. 56(1), December 2015, pp. 10–17.

[15] J. Shamsi, M. A. Khojaye, and M. A. Qasmi, "Data-intensive cloud computing: Requirements, expectations, challenges, and solutions," Journal of Grid Computing, vol. 11, no. 2, Jun 2013, pp. 281–310.

GeSCo: Introducing an Edge Layer Between Cloud MES and Shop-Floor in Decentralized Manufacturing

Badarinath Katti
TU Kaiserslautern
Kaiserslautern, Germany
email:katti@rhrk.uni-kl.de

Michael Schweitzer
SAP SE
Walldorf, Germany
email:Michael.Schweitzer@sap.com

Christiane Plociennik
DFKI GmbH
Kaiserslautern, Germany
email:Christiane.Plociennik@dfki.de

***Abstract*—Decentralized manufacturing is an active research topic in current smart and open integrated factories, and is probably also the future state of practice in both the process and manufacturing industries. The Manufacturing Execution System (MES) is a comprehensive automation software solution that coordinates all the responsibilities of modern production systems. However, the MES solution is essentially designed as a centralized manufacturing control unit, which goes against the principle of the decentralized manufacturing paradigm. When operated as a cloud based solution, the MES faces another big challenge: connectivity and network latency. This paper addresses the problem of network latency experienced when the Cloud MES (CMES) is in charge of production control by introducing an edge layer near the shop-floor. In other words, the CMES delegates the responsibility of manufacturing control to this edge layer which consequently facilitates decentralization in manufacturing.**

Keywords–Decentralized Manufacturing; Edge Computing; Cloud MES; Generic Shop-Floor Connector.

I. Introduction

Traditionally, the production was conceived to be a top-down approach comprising of different layers such as Enterprise Resource Planning (ERP) [1], MES, Supervisory Control And Data Acquisition (SCADA) [2] and shop-floor (see Figure 1 left). However, with the advent of low-cost and smart sensors, the MES can directly coordinate with the plant machines. The trend of moving towards standardized communication protocols on all layers of the automation pyramid is fostering the development of circumvention of the vendor-specific SCADA layer as illustrated in Figure 1. In centralized manufacturing, a

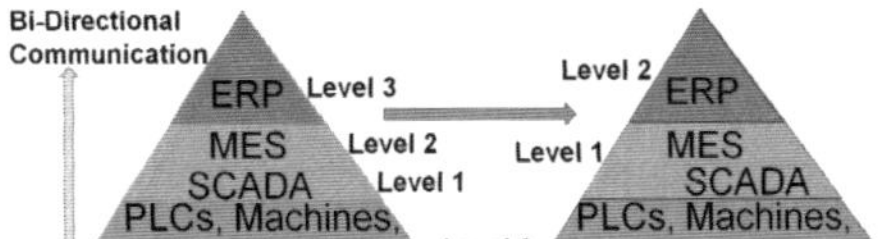

Figure 1: Evolution of classical Automation Pyramid.

central entity is responsible for the system planning aimed at the optimization of the objectives of an entire organization [3]. Centralized systems are often complex in design and hence inflexible in cases of unexpected events and product customizations [3]. Decentralized manufacturing systems are based on distributed control in which the local decision-making bodies react to conditions of the shop-floor at real time. Centralized systems have slower response times since they employ complex algorithms and analyze more data. However, the solution quality of decentralized systems may be lower since they are based on local information. Furthermore, they require more communication effort. In terms of robustness, decentralized systems perform better: The failure of the machines at the lower level of the automation pyramid does not cause the whole system to fail. In a typical centralized system, a failure of central entity can cause the catastrophic failure of the entire system [4]. These arguments support the adoption of decentralized control in manufacturing.

The IEC 62264-3:2016 standard [5] divides the entire MES activities into four functional areas namely production, maintenance, quality and inventory management. This paper focuses on the production management aspect of MES. The MES is inherently difficult to own, maintain and evolve owing to the tight coupling of IT infrastructure to the manufacturing operations [6]. In the interest of protection of investment, a detailed feasibility evaluation is necessary as the selection of MES generally results in long term relationship with the MES vendor. Therefore, a recent trend is to move MES to the cloud. Cloud MES (CMES) can quickly adapt to the newer innovative technologies and offer significant cost benefits to the manufacturer. The generic set of functionalities provided by CMES are richer than on-premise counterparts [7]. Another main benefit of the CMES is that it requires nearly no IT resource investment [1] and hence, lowers the IT barriers to innovation in manufacturing processes [7]. The CMES helps face the challenge of peak production demand without additional investment on on-premise resources [8]. Since the cloud servers are run as per the necessity, licenses can be increased or decreased accordingly. However, when the MES shifts from on-premise to cloud, it faces the challenge of the remote resource management and production control. Since modern industries increasingly make decisions by coordinating with business systems, it results in higher network load and latency. To tackle this problem, we propose to introduce an edge layer called *Generic Shop-Floor Connector (GeSCo)* between CMES and shop-floor that caches the routing details and other production related data and hence supports the decentralization in manufacturing. The outline of the paper is as follows: Section II lists related work. Section III highlights the problem of network latency in the context of high speed manufacturing. Section IV introduces an edge layer that acts as production control delegate to tackle the network latency and lists the challenges faced by the edge layer. Section V presents a system architecture that addresses these challenges. Section VI presents implementation details based on the proposed system design and some simulation results. Section VII provides the conclusion and an outlook on the future work.

II. Related Work

1) Edge Analytics and Decentralized Manufacturing: Edge computing is in practice since two decades and is also known by other names such as fog computing, mobile edge computing, cloudlets and cyber foraging [9]. Edge analytics applied to the domain of manufacturing addresses the problem of network latency and enables to take decisions at runtime in production and thus, can adopt to changes in the Production Order (PO) within short time. [10] proposes decentralized work-in-progress manufacturing control that serves as an alternative to the centralized manufacturing systems. The RFID-enabled MES was introduced for mass-customization in manufacturing that faced challenges of manual and paper-based data collection, production plans and schedules [11]. However, the assumption was that machines in the factory shop-floor are at best partially connected and the decision-making rests entirely on employees on the shop-floor. Agent-based manufacturing [6] and holonic manufacturing [12] introduced the concept of artificial intelligence in manufacturing with an aim to respond promptly and correctly to changes in PO. [13] professes the idea of edge datacenters that process the data on behalf of IoT devices and delegate to the cloud only when more complex analysis is required. [14] proposes a Centralized Scheduling System (CSS) and decentralized MES, where the latter follows a fixed global schedule and turns to CSS in case of perturbation. [15] discusses the autonomous MES that generates alternative schedules when given schedule is infeasible. However, [16] argues that localization of decision-making with an obligation to decentralize has the risk of losing the global vision of the network. [17][18] argue that even though the decentralization of manufacturing is the norm in the future, there are cases where a centralized entity is obligatory to overwrite the lower level decisions, e.g., in the event of redefinition of production processes at higher levels of automation pyramid. [19] also contends that the absence of a central decision-making body necessitates continuous harmonization of objectives among the agents leading to high coordinative complexity. Therefore, there is a renewed interest in incorporating centralized production control concepts to manufacturing.

2) Cloud Manufacturing: There have been several works, for example [20][21], in the domain of cloud manufacturing, that combine the emerging advanced technologies, such as cloud computing, virtualization, internet of things and service oriented architecture. The potentials and relationships among cloud computing, internet of things and cloud manufacturing is investigated in [7]. [22][23] illustrate the concept of centrally managed CMES, but its application area is distributed manufacturing which is outside the purview of this paper. In general, the focus has shifted from centralized manufacturing systems - and MES in particular - to the decentralized paradigm of manufacturing. This research paper is novel in the aspect that it focuses on the adaptation of CMES, which is traditionally linked to the centralized paradigm, to the context of decentralized manufacturing. In other words, it attempts to retain a degree of centralized aspects of manufacturing to strike the right balance.

III. CMES Use Case and Network Latency

During production execution, the shop-floor constantly seeks information from MES. The work stations at the shop-floor request MES for routing details at every stage of the production. Each work station collects the operation, Bill Of Materials (BOM), machine parameters and other resource configuration details. Once this information is collected the machine is instructed on how to proceed with that step of the production process. Once that step of the production is completed, the work station informs MES the same along with the generated results. The MES then processes the results and accordingly sets the next operation of the production. This process continues until all the planned operations are executed to manufacture the planned component. During exceptional cases if the need arises, the routing path is changed, as instructed by MES, to accommodate the exceptional situations. For example, the work in progress is diverted to rework station if the concerns regarding the quality of the products are raised.

The communication between MES and shop-floor takes place over WAN, which means that the transmission delay is not bounded [24]. When moving from MES to CMES, network latency becomes an even bigger challenge as the geographical distance and, consequently, the number of intermittent routers increase. Hence, direct client and server communication between the CMES and shop-floor over WAN encounters network latency due to a variety of factors such as nodal processing delay, queueing delay, transmission delay, propagation delay and packet loss, and thus affect the throughput of the network. These delays are explained in the context of Figure 2. The data packets are sent from source to destination via routers r_1 and r_2. Each router has an incoming queue and an outbound link to each of the connected routers. The packet arriving at a router goes through the queue and the router determines the outbound link after examination of the packet header. An incoming data packet is immediately bound to outbound link if the router queue is empty and there are no packets being sent on the outbound link at the time. If the router queue is non-empty or the corresponding outbound link is busy, the incoming packet joins the router queue. This causes a delay which is known as Processing delay d_{proc} and is the key component of network delay. The node also checks for bit level errors in the packet arising while transmitting from the previous node. After this nodal processing, the router directs the packet to a queue that precedes the outbound link. The

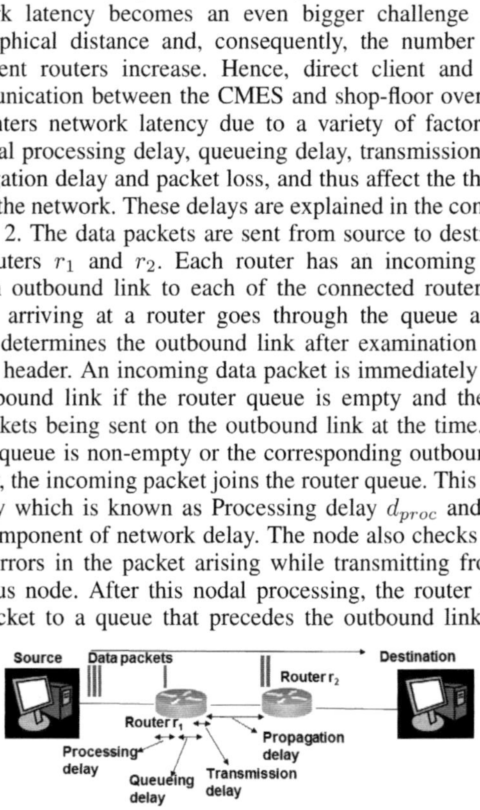

Figure 2: Illustration of network delays.

time a packet spends in the queue while earlier packets are transmitted at the node is called queueing delay d_{queue}. The incoming packet experiences zero queueing delay when the router queue is empty and no other packet is being transmitted by the router. Alternatively, the incoming packet experiences a queueing delay in direct accordance with the length of the router queue. The router transmits the data at a rate known as transmission rate R. When the data packets arrive for a sustained period at a given router at a rate more than its transmission rate, these data packets will queue in at the router. The ratio of $(A * B)/R$, called network traffic intensity, plays an important role in determining the queueing delay, where A denotes the average number of packets that arrive at the router queue per unit time and B is the average number of bits in each of these packets. The qualitative dependence of average queueing delay on the network traffic intensity is demonstrated in Figure 3. It can be observed from Figure 3 that as the

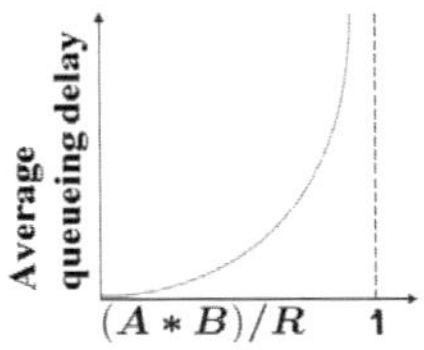

Figure 3: Dependence of average d_{queue} on traffic intensity [25].

traffic intensity tends to 1, the average queueing delay grows exponentially. When the packet arrival rate is greater than router transmission rate, the size of packet queue grows at the router. However, this cannot continue indefinitely due to the finite capacity of the router queue. Therefore, the router drops the packet when it finds no place at its queue. Such a dropped packet is lost and this phenomenon is called Packet loss. At this juncture, the client that transmitted the packet to the network core expecting the delivery acknowledgement from the server re-transmits the packet after waiting for a specified amount of time. This reduces the throughput of the network connection. The router takes a finite time to transfer the bits of a data packet onto the outbound link. This time is known as transmission delay d_{trans} and mathematically, it is defined as B/R. The packet on the outbound link propagates to the next node in a time known as the propagation delay. If l is the length of the physical link and v is the propagation speed of the data packet in the physical link, the propagation delay d_{prop} is then given by l/v. The total nodal delay d_{nodal} is then given by,

$$d_{nodal} = d_{proc} + d_{queue} + d_{trans} + d_{prop} \quad [26] \qquad (1)$$

If there are N number of similar routers between the source and destination spaced apart at equal distances, then the end-to-end delay $d_{end-to-end}$ is measured as,

$$d_{end-to-end} = N*(d_{proc}+d_{trans}+d_{prop})+\sum_{n=1}^{N} d_{queue_n} \quad (2)$$

where the last part of the above equation is sum of the queueing delays experienced at each of the routers. The network delays are directly proportional to the distance and consequently, the number of intermittent routers, between the client and the server. In practice, with the exception of d_{proc}, which is on the order of microseconds, all other above-mentioned delays are on the order of milliseconds [26][25]. It is not possible to accurately determine the latency between two fixed points since the data packets encapsulated at the network layer of OSI model need to pass through several proprietary routers of the internet before reaching the destination. Each of these routers has unpredictable traffic which is dependent on variety of factors and hence, the network latency is a function of internet traffic that undergoes random fluctuation for the same bandwidth and infrastructure. Therefore, instead of imposing the hard real-time constraints, the practical unit of measurement should be average time for the network latency. The virtualization principle of cloud computing that can be applied at different levels such as computer hardware, operating system, storage and network also introduces its own series of packet delays and causes further performance degradation. The Figure 4 illustrates this situation where there are three operations - welding, color spraying and quality check, that are required to be performed to produce the planned component. In the state of the art industries, the work stations constantly

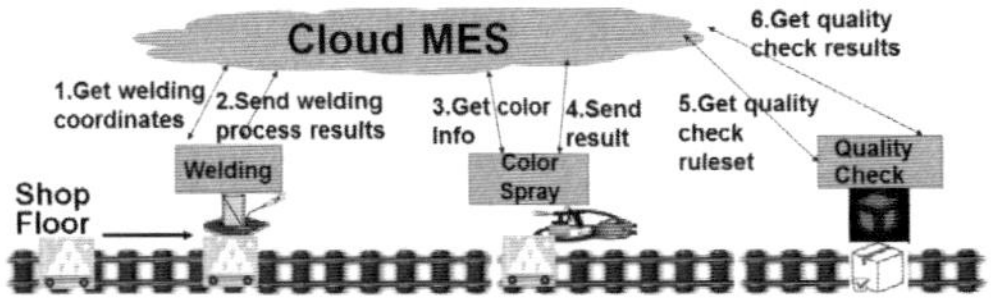

Figure 4: CMES - Shop floor connectivity in production.

communicate with CMES to seek process parameters, recipe, machine configuration values and push the results during production control. The problem of network latency which is encountered each time the request is created to fetch the next operation details from CMES does not auger well in high speed manufacturing scenarios. In addition, although cloud providers claim near 100% availability, there is an average non-availability of 7.884 hours per year [27]. Such network outages are not acceptable in the event of manufacturing a priority order.

IV. Introducing an Edge Layer

As explained in Section III, the network latency is directly proportional to the geographic distance. The MES in cloud is not guaranteed to be close to the site of production. Hence, caching the production control data in proximity to the shop-floor can reduce the problem of network latency. To this end, this research paper proposes introducing an edge layer called *Generic Shop-Floor Connector (GeSCo)* between CMES and shop-floor.

GeSCos are close to, but not tightly coupled to the shop-floor. They control the production processes and collect the data to and from the shop-floor and enterprise software. GeSCos also help in enabling the 'plug and work' feature of today's smart factory, since they can connect to wide variety of industry specific data sources of diverse manufacturers, such as OPC UA, classical OPC and http based web services. Due to the physical proximity of GeSCos and shop-floor, the data communication latency is short as data packets need not cross multiple routers. GeSCos also alleviate the problem of latency introduced by the virtualization layer of cloud infrastructure explained in Section III. Furthermore, the caching strategy facilitates the implementation of *decentralization* of the production execution. In its basic conception, the GeSCo is a web

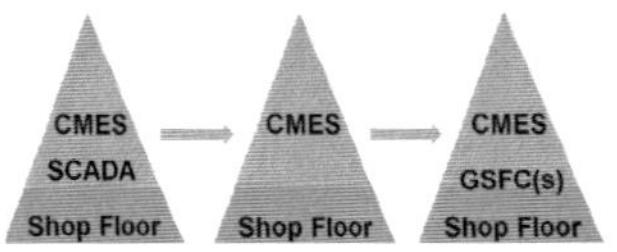

Figure 5: Evolution of CMES - Shop Floor Connectivity.

service framework that collaborates with enterprise software and diverse industrial data sources to execute a PO by performing division of labor in the shop-floor under the supervision of CMES, i.e., it distributes the production operations to resources on the shop floor based on the production recipe at run-time. The introduction of GeSCo in the shop-floor is not to take over the role of SCADA. It should just serve as a thin client to CMES server. Based on these arguments, the CMES and the shop-floor communication evolution can be illustrated as in Figure 5.

After the production control data is cached, the intention is to reduce the communication between the GeSCo and CMES as far as possible. Several exceptional situations may arise in the shop-floor while the GeSCo is in control of the production execution. The GeSCo should either resolve or find an alternative course of actions to the prevailing exceptional situations. The objective of this exercise is the successful completion of the production execution. The CMES should support this goal by sending meaningful data at the right time.

A. Challenges of Integration of GeSCo: A Survey

The GeSCo should assume the role of the CMES after the PO is transferred to its cache. The transfer of production control to the GeSCo is smooth under normal circumstances when the production encounters no problems. However, the system should be designed such that it should be robust against production fluctuations and should mitigate or solve the problems that may arise under exceptional circumstances.

In order to determine which responsibilities such a system must fulfill, several experts in the field of manufacturing were asked to prioritize the challenges for GeSCo during the execution of shop orders. The results of this survey are, in descending order of their weighted average:

1) Determination of next routing step since business rules that govern the routing decisions are present in the CMES
2) Semantic translation of data arriving from CMES to technology and business agnostic solution such as GeSCo
3) Adaptation in GeSCo in the event of change of the data model in centralized CMES
4) Determination of the suitable resources to perform the current operation
5) Routing-path substitution in the event of machine breakdown [6]
6) Dealing with the change of the PO [6]
7) Handling the POs of high priority [6]
8) Course of action in the event of quality defects
9) Course of action in the event of unavailability of raw materials
10) Distributed manufacturing where components are being manufactured at different sites

V. Proposed System Architecture

The solution architecture should be designed taking into account the challenges mentioned in Section IV-A. It should enable the CMES to exercise control over the production process while at the same time ensuring a smooth integration of the GeSCo for providing flexibility in exceptional cases. Hence, the architecture should incorporate both centralized and decentralized aspects.

A. Design of CMES

This section describes the proposed set of building blocks and services that are required in the CMES. The overall architecture is depicted in Figure 7.

1) Production Planning System: This application layer enables the human production planner to plan the production sequence in a generic way. To this end, it has different maintenance user interfaces that help define the plant and product definition, operation planning and production execution aspects. This master data facilitates the design of BOM and the shop-floor routing for a product variant. This unit also enables the human to create and release the PO to the shop-floor.

2) Manufacturing Resource Model and Servitization: Remote resource sharing and management is a challenge to CMES since it is geographically separated from the shop-floor. The resource virtualization is the key idea behind building the cloud services in the context of manufacturing. The resource model is the transformation of a real manufacturing resource to a virtual or logical resource. Each manufacturing resource is modeled formally with a set of inputs and outputs according to its main functionality. The functional and non-functional capabilities of the resource can be semantically modeled. The model is then subjected to real-to-virtual mapping methods to map to a logical resource as illustrated in Figure 6. The virtual

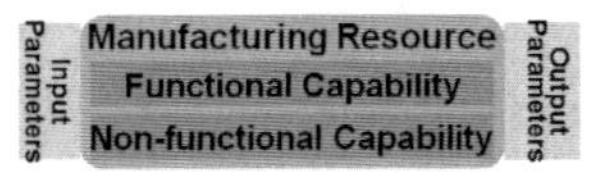

Figure 6: Resource Virtualization.

resource servitization is the transformation of abstract concepts of capabilities provided by these resources into formal services that are understandable by the cloud platform. This process involves several aspects such as definition of the service model, message model, ports and protocols. The service model includes the template for the service offered by cloud platform. The reception of inputs and generation of outputs of the service is defined in the message modeling process. The port modeling involves the definition of functional operation port used to accomplish the operation target. The protocol binding specifies the different protocols that are supported by the service.

This service interface of resource enables GeSCo to store the resource relevant data in resource model, which is resource digital twin. The GeSCo collects the machine data from resource periodically and pushes it to CMES resource model, which is required for real time resource monitoring and calculate the equipment effectiveness. The data is also archived and the aggregated historical data is fed to the predictive analytics tool to find the insights into the resource behavior.

3) Dispatcher: The PO created and released by the production planner is transferred from the CMES to the shop-floor by the dispatcher. The logic of transferring the priority order(s) is pre-loaded into the dispatcher. The parameters that expedite the release and subsequent transfer to the shop-floor are production end date, priority customer, and inventory and manufacturing resource availability. The GeSCo, introduced in this paper, is a technology and business agnostic solution. Therefore, the dispatcher should send the unambiguous data, for example, a collaborative product definition and operations semantic model to the GeSCo. The GeSCo translates this information to its compatible data model for further processing.

4) Data mining and predictive analytics: Instead of relying on human expertise alone, there is an increasing inclination towards aggregating and processing a large amount of data at the shop-floor, which in turn enables to train better models for classification, clustering and prediction. This component analyzes the current and past semi-structured or unstructured data and extracts useful patterns and transfers this knowledge to GeSCo. This knowledge of past experience is then helpful for GeSCo to take run-time decisions that solve or mitigate the problems arising in the shop-floor during production. This information is also helpful to achieve optimization of the production processes in the shop-floor.

5) Information systems: This constituent stores the product genealogy including complete work instructions, components and phantom assemblies, operation flow and routing, manufacturing resources and work centers employed, bill of materials, activities on the shop-floor, rework instructions and the discrepancies. This is realized using the Digital Object Memory (DOMe) [28] which maintains all the information about a product instance over its production lifecycle, where each product is identified and tracked using RFID tag that contains the unique shop-floor control number. Since DOMe is centrally accessible to all the involved entities of production, it enables production coordination among these entities, compilation of the historic manufacturing report, quality investigations and process improvements.

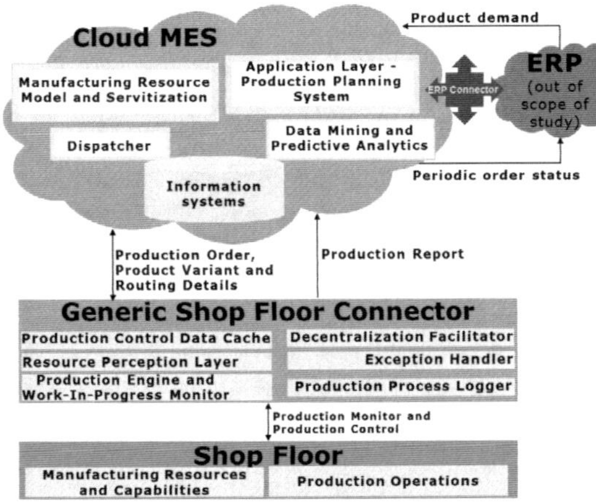

Figure 7: Integration of GeSCo with CMES.

B. Design of GeSCo

The GeSCo should consist of the following components with dedicated responsibilities (see also Figure 7):

1) Manufacturing Resource Perception Layer: To achieve harmonization among various manufacturing resources, they need to be coupled together. The perception layer undertakes this responsibility of loose coupling of different resources on the shop-floor. The different manufacturing resources at the site also register themselves to this layer. The registration can take place either with the resource meta-data or the resource endpoint that permits the perception layer to browse the resource data structures to extract the meta-data of the resource. This data is transferred to decentralization facilitator component which enables it to take decisions at run-time. The perception layer should support the standard industrial communication protocols, such as OPC UA, classic OPC and HTTP based data sources. These IoT protocols are employed to perceive different manufacturing resources with an intent to enable intelligent identification, detection, communication, tracking, monitoring and management. The effectiveness of this exercise hinges on the ability of this layer to extract the key information from the real resources.

2) Production Control Data Cache: This component stores the data delivered by the CMES. It contains the blueprint of the production execution on the shop-floor, which is the detailed routing information in the case of discrete manufacturing. Various entities of GeSCo such as decentralization facilitator and production engine base their decisions and actions on this cached production execution data. This unit is designed to address the first three challenges listed in Section IV-A.

3) Decentralization Facilitator: This entity enables the decentralization in the manufacturing by coordinating with various manufacturing resources and CMES, and thus helps address the challenge of determining the suitable resources for a particular operation. The layer maintains the virtual resource pool consisting of a collection of virtual manufacturing resources. It is used in run-time classification of resources that aids in on-demand resource capability matching. The virtual resource management helps GeSCo identify capabilities intelligently by semantic searching of suitable services and the manufacturing resources on the shop-floor to meet the production requirement.

4) Exception Handler: This block of the GeSCo is accountable for overcoming any shortcomings that arise in the production environment. These shortcomings are explained in Section IV-A, numbering from 5 to 9. The exception handler either attempts to find alternate course of action by local coordination or seeks further instructions from the centralized entity which has global picture of the system.

5) Production Engine and Work-In-Progress Monitor: The production engine is the heart of the GeSCo that collaborates with all the other components of GeSCo to achieve the end goal of successful completion of the PO. It fetches the PO information and routing details from the production control data cache and delegates the responsibility of matching the manufacturing resources for the given operation to the decentralization facilitator. After the decision-making process, the production engine delegates the job to the perception layer that assigns the operation to the real resources after the necessary configuration. The PO is put on hold in the event of non-availability of default and alternate resources, and is only resumed after the required resource registers to the perception layer. To ensure the production is running as expected, it is necessary to monitor run-time status and respond to changes. In case of changes and exceptions, this layer coordinates with decentralization facilitator and exception handler to solve or mitigate the contingency. The production engine also has the intelligence to recognize the situations where GeSCo cannot take the optimal decision based on local information. In such scenarios, it seeks the master data, the singular source of truth, stored in centralized CMES.

6) Production Process Logger: This component uploads the variety of knowledge it gathers during the production onto the CMES. This unstructured data is subjected to analysis and an effort is made by CMES to find patterns and transform it into a structured data. This knowledge in turn can be channeled as a feedback to the closed loop system in order to optimize the production in the long run.

VI. IMPLEMENTATION

In order to evaluate the above mentioned findings, the author simulated the shop-floor behavior by implementing the prototype of the architecture shown in the Figure 7. A CMES was developed that mocks the real CMES in the context of production planning and execution. The SAP Plant Connectivity (SAP-PCo) [29], which is a framework of set of services and management tools was chosen to act as GeSCo. During the research, the PCo was architecturally enhanced to cache the production control and routing data, which is also known as Enhanced Method Processing (EMP). A web server was designed inside a SAP-PCo agent instance and its operations were hooked on to the Dynamically Linked Libraries (DLLs) embedded with the production control logic. The shop-floor is simulated via a series of Raspberry Pi3 units that act as resources that receive the control instructions from the PCo during production. For the purpose of this simulation, the CMES was geographically separated by approximately 1000km from the GeSCo and mock resource work station deployments to reproduce the typical network latency, where as the GeSCo and resource work stations were deployed on the same Local Area Network (LAN). A production process without exceptions was simulated to address the challenges 1 and 4 from Section IV-A with different product types of lot size 1, where production routing contained operations that were distributed to resources in a random manner. Two POs with 5 and 3 operations respectively in their routing plan were created in CMES in order to measure the network latency encountered during the production execution. The latency times were measured in the SOAP UI tool [30]. Tables I and II provide the simulation results w.r.t. the network latency encountered by POs without and with GeSCo, respectively. The total latency encountered by the PO showed a marked decrease in simulation with the edge layer. The research concept was also implemented in the open integrated factory that SAP along with other partners showcased in *Hannover Industrial Fair - 2017*, which verifies the assumption that the result of simulations is valid under real manufacturing conditions.

TABLE I: SIMULATION RESULTS WITHOUT GeSCo

Number of Operations in PO	5	3
Client - Server Entities	Resource - CMES	Resource - CMES
Network Latency Per Call	~400 ms	~400 ms
Client-Server calls	10	6
Total Network Latency suffered by PO	~4000 ms	~2400 ms

TABLE II: SIMULATION RESULTS WITH GeSCo

Number of Operations in PO	5		3	
Client - Server Entities	GeSCo-CMES	GeSCo-Resource	GeSCo-CMES	GeSCo-Resource
Network Latency Per Call	~400 ms	~30 ms	~400 ms	~30 ms
Client-Server calls	2	10	2	6
Total Network Latency	~800 ms	~300 ms	~800 ms	~180 ms
Total Network Latency suffered by PO	~1100 ms		~980 ms	

VII. CONCLUSION AND FUTURE WORK

This paper argues that the CMES is better suited in changing production environments than traditional MES solutions. To overcome the problem of network latency associated with CMES and also achieve decentralization in manufacturing, an edge layer called GeSCo is introduced and a comprehensive architecture is designed to integrate this edge layer with the CMES. Future work includes further refinement in realization of decentralization, development of semantic data model for GeSCo, research on the extent of caching under given conditions and handling of priority orders.

ACKNOWLEDGMENT

This work was supported by a doctoral grant from SAP SE. A patent, with ID 62/566551, on the research of this paper has been filed in USA with the authors as the inventors.

REFERENCES

[1] A. Lenart, *ERP in the Cloud – Benefits and Challenges*. Springer Berlin Heidelberg, 2011, pp. 39–50.

[2] D. Wu, M. J. Greer *et al.*, "Cloud manufacturing: Strategic vision and state-of-the-art," *Journal of Manufacturing Systems*, pp. 564–579, 2013.

[3] G. Saharidis, Y. Dallery *et al.*, "Centralized versus decentralized production planning," *RAIRO-Oper.Res., 2006*, vol. 40, no. 2, p. 113128.

[4] C. Anderson and J. Bartholdi, "Centralized vs Decentralized control in manufacturing: lessons from social insects," in *Complexity and Complex Systems in Industry,2000*, pp. 92–105.

[5] "IEC 62264-3:2016," URL: https://www.iso.org/standard/67480.html [accessed: 2017-10-17].

[6] P. Leitao, "Agent-based distributed manufacturing control: A state-of-the-art survey," in *Engineering Applications of Artificial Intelligence, 2009*, pp. 979–991.

[7] S. Marston, Z. Li *et al.*, "Cloud computing, The business perspective," in *Decision Support Systems, 51, 2011*, pp. 176–189.

[8] T. Wood, A. Gerber *et al.*, "The case for enterprise-ready virtual private clouds," in *Proceedings of the HotCloud 2009.*

[9] T. Luana, L. Gao, Z. Li *et al.*, "Fog computing: Focusing on mobile users at the edge, 2015," *CoRR*, vol. abs/1502.01815.

[10] H.Loedding, K.W.Yu *et al.*, "Decentralized wip-oriented manufacturing control," *Production Planning & Control, 2003*, pp. 42–54.

[11] R. Zhong, Q.Y.Dai *et al.*, "Rfid-enabled real-time manufacturing execution system for mass-customization production," *Robotics and Computer-Integrated Manufacturing, 2013*, pp. 283–292.

[12] A. W. Colombo and R. Neubert, "An Agent-Based Intelligent Control Platform for Industrial Holonic Manufacturing Systems," 2006.

[13] D. Georgakopoulos, P. Jayaraman *et al.*, "Internet of things and edge cloud computing roadmap for manufacturing, 2016," pp. 66–73.

[14] C. Pach, T. Berger *et al.*, "Orca-fms: a dynamic architecture for the optimized and reactive control of flexible manufacturing scheduling," *Computers in Industry, 2013*, pp. 706 – 720, 2014.

[15] P. Valckenaers, H. V. Brussel *et al.*, "Schedule execution in autonomic manufacturing execution systems," *Journal of Manufacturing Systems, 2007*, vol. 26, no. 2, pp. 75–84.

[16] B. Montreuil, J.-M. Frayret *et al.*, "A strategic framework for networked manufacturing," *Computers in Industry, 2000*, vol. 42, pp. 299 – 317.

[17] M. Marquesa, C. Agostinho *et al.*, "Decentralized decision support for intelligent manufacturing in Industry," *JAISE, 2017*, pp. 299–313.

[18] B.Hubanks, *Self-organizing military logistics*. Cambridge,Mass., 1998.

[19] D. Mourtzis and M. Doukas, "Decentralized manufacturing systems review:challenges and outlook," *Logistics Research,2012*, pp. 113–121.

[20] D. Wu, M. J. Greer *et al.*, "Cloud manufacturing: Strategic vision and state-of-the-art," *Journal of Manufacturing Systems, 2013*, vol. 32, no. 4, pp. 564–579.

[21] F. Tao, Y. Cheng *et al.*, "Cciot-cmfg: Cloud computing and internet of things-based cloud manufacturing service system," *IEEE Transactions on Industrial Informatics, 2014*, vol. 10, no. 2, pp. 1435–1442.

[22] P. Helo, M. Suorsa *et al.*, "Toward a cloud-based manufacturing execution system for distributed manufacturing," *Computers in Industry, 2014*, vol. 65, no. 4, pp. 646 – 656.

[23] L. Zhang, H. Guo *et al.*, "Flexible management of resource service composition in cloud manufacturing," in *International Conference on Industrial Engineering and Engineering Management, 2010.*

[24] "CISCO Wiki," URL: https://docwiki.cisco.com/wiki/Introduction_to_WLAN_Technologies [accessed: 2017-10-17].

[25] J. Kurose and K. Ross, *Computer Networking: A Top-Down Approach.* New York: Addison-Wesley. p. 35-42., 2013.

[26] N. Weng and T. Wolf, "Characterizing Network Processing Delay," 2004.

[27] C. Cerin *et al.*, "Downtime Statistics of Current Cloud Solutions," 2014.

[28] J. Haupert, "Domeman : Repraesentation, verwaltung und nutzung von digitalen objektgedaechtnissen," Ph.D. dissertation, 2013.

[29] "SAP PCo," URL: http://help.sap.com/pco [accessed: 2017-10-17].

[30] "SOAP UI," URL: https://www.soapui.org/ [accessed: 2017-10-17].

Combining Edge Computing and Blockchains for Flexibility and Performance in Industrial Automation

Mauro Isaja
Research & Development
Engineering Ingegneria Informatica SpA (ENG)
Rome, Italy
e-mail: mauro.isaja@eng.it

John Soldatos
IoT Group
Athens Information Technology (AIT)
Maroussi, Greece
e-mail: jsol@ait.gr

Volkan Gezer
Innovative Factory Systems (IFS)
German Research Center for Artificial Intelligence (DFKI)
Kaiserslautern, Germany
e-mail: Volkan.Gezer@dfki.de

Abstract — **The advent of Industry 4.0 has given rise to the introduction of new industrial automation architectures that emphasize the use of digital technologies. In this paper, we introduce a novel reference architecture (RA) for industrial automation, which leverages the benefits of edge computing, while using blockchain technologies for flexible, scalable and reliable configuration and orchestration of automation workflows and distributed data analytics. The presented RA is unique in blending the merits of blockchains and edge computing, while being compliant with emerging standards for industrial automation, such as RAMI4.0 and the RA of the Industrial Internet-Consortium.**

Keywords-Factory automation; edge computing; blockchain; RAMI4.0; IIRA; Industry4.0.

I. INTRODUCTION

The vision of future manufacturing foresees flexible and hyper-efficient plants that will enable manufacturers to support the transition from conventional "made-to-stock" production models, to the emerging customized ones such as "made-to-order", "configure-to-order" and "engineering-to-order". Flexibility in automation is a key prerequisite to supporting the latter production models, as it facilitates manufacturers to change automation configurations and rapidly adopt new automation technologies, as a means of supporting variation in production without any essential increase in production costs.

In order to support flexibility in automation, the industrial automation community has been exploring options for the virtualization of the automation pyramid, as part of the transformation of mainstream centralized automation models (like ISA-95) to more distributed ones. Several research and development initiatives have introduced decentralized factory automation solutions based on technologies like intelligent agents [1] [2] and Service Oriented Architectures (SOA) [3] [4]. These initiatives produced proof-of-concept implementations that highlighted the benefits of decentralized automation in terms of flexibility. However, they are still not being widely deployed in manufacturing plants, mainly due to that the cost-benefit ratio of such solutions is perceived as unfavourable. Nevertheless, the vision of decentralizing the factory automation pyramid is still alive, as this virtualization can potentially make production systems more flexible and agile, increase product quality and reduce cost.

With the advent of the fourth industrial revolution (Industry 4.0) and the Industrial Internet of Things (IIoT), decentralization is being revisited in the light of the integration of Cyber-Physical Systems (CPS) with cloud computing infrastructures. Therefore, several cloud-based applications are deployed and used in factories, which leverage the capacity and scalability of the cloud while fostering supply chain collaboration and virtual manufacturing chains. Early implementations have also revealed the limitations of the cloud in terms of efficient bandwidth usage and its ability to support real-time operations, including operations close to the field.

More recently, the edge computing paradigm has been explored in order to alleviate the limitations of cloud-centric architectures. Edge computing architectures move some part of the system's overall computing power from the cloud to its edge nodes, i.e., on the field or in close proximity to it –as a means of [5], [6]:

- Saving bandwidth and storage, as edge nodes can filter data streams from the field in order to get rid of information without value for industrial automation.
- Enabling low-latency and proximity processing, since information can be processed close to the field.
- Providing enhanced scalability, through supporting decentralized storage and processing that scales better than cloud processing.
- Supporting shopfloor isolation and privacy-friendliness, since edge nodes at the shopfloor are isolated from the rest of the network.

These benefits make edge computing suitable for specific classes of use cases in factories, including:

- Large scale distributed applications, typically applications that involve multiple plants or factories, which process streams from numerous devices at scale.
- Near-real-time applications, which analyse data close to the field or even control Cyber-Physical Systems such as smart machines and industrial robots.

As a result, the application of edge computing to factory automation is extremely promising, since it empowers decentralization in a way that still supports real-time interactions and scalable analytics. It's therefore no accident that there are ongoing efforts to provide edge computing implementations for industrial automation in general and factory automation in particular. Furthermore, reference architectures for IIoT and industrial automation exist, which highlight the importance of edge computing for compliant implementations. In this article, we present a reference architecture (RA) for factory automation based on edge computing, which has been specified as part of the H2020 FAR-EDGE project [11]. The FAR-EDGE RA and associated compliant implementations comprise some unique features and capabilities, which differentiate them from other on-going implementations of edge computing for factory automation. Most of these unique features concern the exploitation of Distributed Ledger Technology (DLT, today commonly referred to as "blockchain") as a means of representing automation and data analytics processes based on Smart Contracts. These can be dynamically configured, stored securely and executed in a distributed way, enabling flexibility and scalability in factory automation processes.

The paper is structured as follows: Section 2, following this introduction, presents state-of-the-art specifications and implementations of the edge computing paradigm for factory automation. It also positions FAR-EDGE against them. Section 3 introduces the FAR-EDGE RA, from a functional and structural perspective. Section 4 illustrates a number of automation use cases and the way in which they can be supported by FAR-EDGE compliant systems. Finally, Section 5 concludes the paper.

II. Related Work

Acknowledging the benefits of edge computing for industrial automation, standards development organizations (SDOs) have specified relevant reference architectures, while industrial organizations are already working towards providing tangible edge computing implementations.

SDOs such as the OpenFog Consortium and the Industrial Internet Consortium (IIC) have produced Reference Architectures. The RA of the OpenFog Consortium prescribes a high-level architecture for internet of things systems, which covers industrial IoT use cases. On the other hand, the RA of the IIC [7] outlines the structuring principles of systems for industrial applications. The IIC RA is not limited to edge computing, but rather based on edge computing principles in terms of its implementation. It addresses a wide range of industrial use cases in multiple sectors, including factory automation. These RAs have been recently released and their reference implementations are still in their early stages.

A reference implementation of the IIC RA's edge computing functionalities for factory automation is provided as part of IIC's edge intelligence testbed [8]. This testbed provides a proof-of-concept implementation of edge computing functionalities on the shopfloor. The focus of the testbed is on configurable edge computing environments, which enable the development and testing of leading edge systems and algorithms for edge analytics. Moreover, Dell-EMC has recently announced the EdgeX Foundry framework [9], which is a vendor-neutral open source project hosted by the Linux Foundation that builds a common open framework for IIoT edge computing. The framework is influenced by the above-listed reference architectures and is expected to be released in 2017. Other vendors are also incorporating support for edge devices and edge gateways in their cloud platforms.

FAR-EDGE is uniquely positioned in the landscape of edge computing solutions for factory automation. In particular, the FAR-EDGE architecture is aligned to the IIC RA, while exploiting concepts from other RAs and standards such as the OpenFog RA and RAMI 4.0 (Reference Architecture Model Industry 4.0) [10]. However, FAR-EDGE explores pathways and offers functionalities that are not addressed by other specification and reference implementations. In particular, it researches the applicability of disruptive key enabling technologies like DLT and Smart Contracts in factory automation. DLT, while being well understood and thoroughly tested in mission-critical areas like digital currencies (e.g., Bitcoin), have never been applied before to industrial systems. FAR-EDGE aims at demonstrating how a pool of specific Ledger Services built on a generic DLT platform can enable decentralized factory automation in an effective, reliable, scalable and secure way. Ledger Services will be responsible for sharing process state and enforcing business rules across the computing nodes of a distributed system, thus permitting virtual automation and analytics processes that span multiple nodes – or, from a bottom-up perspective, autonomous nodes that cooperate to a common goal. This is the project's unique contribution, which sets it apart from similar efforts worldwide.

III. FAR-EDGE RA Oveview

The FAR-EDGE RA is the conceptual framework that drives the design and the implementation of the project's automation platform based on edge computing and DLT technologies. As an RA, its first goal is communication, i.e. providing a terse representation of concepts, roles, structure and behaviour of the system under analysis for the sake of dissemination and ecosystem-building. Its second goal concerns reuse: exploiting best practices and lessons learned in similar contexts by the global community of system architects.

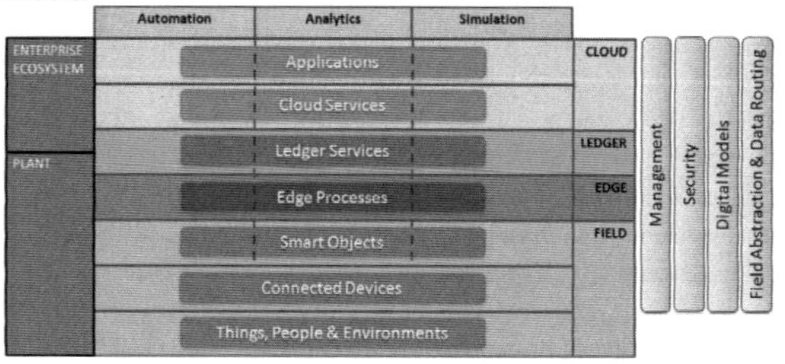

Figure 1. Overview of the FAR-EDGE RA

The FAR-EDGE RA is aligned to IIC's RA concepts and described from two architectural viewpoints: the functional viewpoint and the structural viewpoint, as outlined in following paragraphs.

An overall architecture representation that includes all elements is provided in Figure 1.

A. *Functional Viewpoint*

According to the FAR-EDGE RA, the functionality of a factory automation platform can be decomposed into three high-level Functional Domains - Automation, Analytics and Simulation – and four Crosscutting (XC) Functions – Management, Security, Digital Models and Field Abstraction & Data Routing. To better clarify the scope of such topics, we have tried to map them to similar IIRA concepts. Functional Domains and XC Functions are orthogonal to structural Tiers: the implementation of a given functionality may – but is not required to – span multiple Tiers, so that in the overall architecture representation Functional Domains appear as vertical lanes drawn across horizontal layers. In Figure 2, the relationship between Functional Domains, their users and the factory environment is highlighted by arrows showing the flow of data and of control.

Automation Domain: The FAR-EDGE Automation domain includes functionalities supporting automated control and automated configuration of physical production processes. While the meaning of "control" in this context is straightforward, "configuration" is worth a few additional words. Automated configuration is the enabler of plug-and-play factory equipment (better known as plug-and-produce), which in turn is a key technology for mass-customization, as it allows a faster and less expensive adjustments of the production process. The Automation domain requires a bidirectional monitoring/control communication channel with the Field, typically with low bandwidth but very strict timing requirements (tight control loop). In some advanced scenarios, Automation is controlled – to some extent – by the results of Analytics and/or Simulation. The Automation domain partially maps to the Control domain of the IIRA.

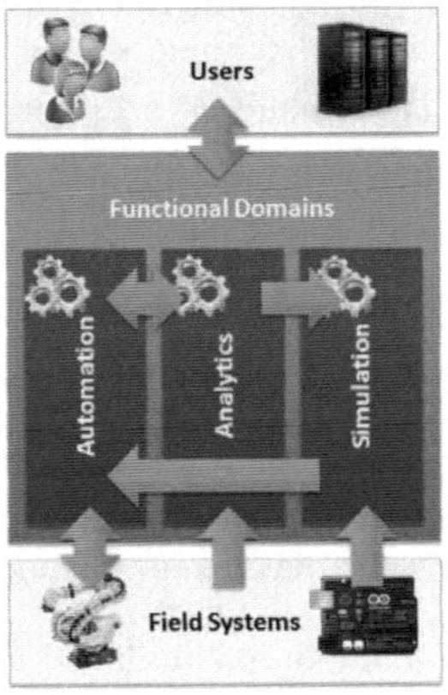

Figure 2. FAR-EDGE RA Functional Domains

Analytics Domain: The FAR-EDGE Analytics domain includes functionalities for gathering and processing Field data for a better understanding of production processes, i.e. a factory-focused business intelligence. This typically requires a high-bandwidth Field communication channel, as the volume of information that needs to be transferred in a given time unit may be substantial. On the other hand, channel latency tends to be less critical than in the Automation scenario. The Analytics domain provides intelligence to its users, but these are not necessarily limited to humans or vertical applications (e.g., a predictive maintenance solution): the Automation and Simulation domains, if properly configured, can both make direct use of the outcome of data analysis algorithms. In the case of Automation, the behaviour of a workflow might change in response to changes detected in the controlled process – e.g., a process drift caused by the progressive wear of machinery or by the quality of assembly components being lower than usual. In the case of Simulation, data analysis can be used to update the parameters of a digital model (as illustrated in the following section). The Analytics domain matches perfectly the Information domain of the IIRA, except that the latter is receiving data from the Field through the mediation of Control functionalities.

Simulation Domain: The FAR-EDGE Simulation domain includes functionalities for simulating the behaviour of physical production processes for the purpose of optimization or of testing what/if scenarios at minimal cost and risk and without any impact of regular shop activities. Simulation requires digital models of plants and processes to be in-sync with the real world objects they represent. As the real world is subject to change, models should reflect those changes. For instance, the model of a machine assumes a given value of electric power / energy consumption, but the actual values will diverge as the real machine wears down. To detect this gap and correct the model accordingly, raw data from the Field (direct) or complex analysis algorithms (from Analytics) can be used.

Crosscutting Functions: Crosscutting Functions address common specific concerns. Their implementation affects several Functional Domains and Tiers. They include.

- **Management**: Low-level functions for monitoring and commissioning/decommissioning of individual system modules..
- **Security**: Functions securing the system against the unruly behaviour of its user and of connected systems. These include digital identity management and authentication, access control policy management and enforcement, communication and data encryption.
- **Digital Models**: Functions for the management of digital models and their synchronization with the real-world entities they represent. Digital modes are a shared asset, as they may be used as the basis for automated configuration, simulation and field abstraction – e.g., semantic interoperability of heterogeneous field systems.
- **Field Abstraction & Data Routing**: Functions that ensure the connectivity of business logic (FAR-EDGE RA Functional Domains) to the Field, abstracting away the technical details – like device discovery and communication protocols. Data routing refers to the capability of establishing direct producer-consumer channels on demand, optimized for unidirectional massive data streaming – e.g., for feeding Analytics.

B. *Structural Viewpoint*

The FAR-EDGE RA uses two classes of concepts for describing the structure of a system: Scopes and Tiers.

Scopes are very simple and straightforward: they define a coarse mapping of system elements to either the factory - Plant Scope - or the broader world of corporate IT - Enterprise Ecosystem Scope. Examples of elements in Plant Scope are machinery, Field devices, workstations, SCADA and MES systems, and any software running in the factory data centre. The Enterprise Ecosystem Scope comprises ERP and PLM systems and any application or service shared across multiple factories or even companies – e.g., supply chain members.

Tiers are a more detailed and technical-oriented classification of deployment concerns. They can be easily mapped to scopes, but they provide more insight into the relationship between system components. This kind of classification is quite similar to OpenFog RA deployment viewpoint, except for the fact that FAR-EDGE Tiers are industry-oriented while OpenFog ones are not. FAR-EDGE Tiers are one of the most innovative traits of its RA, and are described in following paragraphs.

The Field Tier is the bottom layer of the FAR-EDGE RA and is populated by Edge Nodes (EN), i.e. any kind of device that is connected to the digital world on one side and to the real world to the other. ENs can have embedded intelligence (e.g., a smart machine) or not (e.g., a sensor or actuator). The FAR-EDGE RA honours this difference: Smart Objects are ENs with on board computing capabilities, Connected Devices are those without. The Smart Object is where local control logic runs: it's a semi-autonomous entity that does not need to interact frequently with the upper layers of the system. As shown in Figure 3. ENs is actually located over field devices.

The Field is also populated by entities of the real world, i.e., those physical elements of production processes that are not directly connected to the network, and as such are not considered as ENs: Things, People and Environments. These are represented in the digital world by some kind of EN wrapper. For instance, room temperature (Environment) is measured by an IoT sensor (Connected Device), the proximity of a worker (People) to a physical checkpoint location is published by an RFID wearable and detected by an RFID Gate (Connected Device), while a conveyor belt (Thing) is operated by a PLC (Smart Object).

The Field Tier is in Plant Scope. Individual ENs are connected to the digital world in the upper Tiers either directly by means of the shopfloor's LAN, or indirectly through some special-purpose local network (e.g., WSN) that is bridged to the former. From the RAMI 4.0 perspective, the FAR-EDGE Field Tier corresponds to the Field Device and Control Device levels on the Hierarchy axis (IEC-62264/IEC-61512), while the entities there contained are positioned across the Asset and Integration Layers.

The Edge Tier is the core of the FAR-EDGE RA. It hosts those parts of Functional Domains and XC Functions that can leverage the edge computing model, i.e., software designed to run on multiple, distributed computing nodes placed close to the field, which may include resource constrained nodes. The Edge Tier is populated by Edge Gateways (EG): computing devices that act as a digital world gateway to the real world of the Field. These machines are typically more powerful than the average intelligent EN (e.g., blade servers) and are connected to a fast LAN. Strategically positioned close to physical systems, the EG can execute Edge Processes: time- and bandwidth-critical functionality having local scope. For instance, the orchestration of a complex physical process that is monitored and operated by a number of sensors, actuators (Connected Devices) and embedded controllers (Smart Objects); or the real-time analysis of a huge volume of live data that is streamed from a nearby Field source.

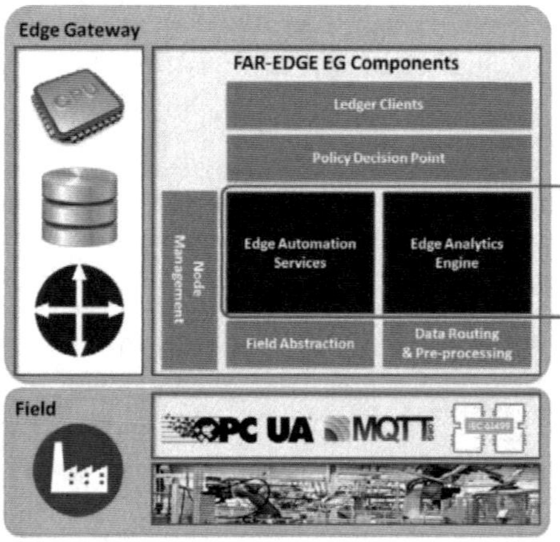

Figure 3. Edge Tier in the FAR-EDGE RA

Deploying computing power and data storage in close proximity to where it is actually used is a standard best practice in the industry. However, this technique basically requires that the scope of individual subsystems is narrow (e.g., a single work station). If instead the critical functionality applies to a wider scenario (e.g., an entire plant or enterprise), it must be either deployed at a higher level (e.g., the Cloud) – thus losing all benefits of proximity – or run as multiple parallel instances, each focused on its own narrow scope. In the latter case, new problems may arise: keeping global variables in-sync across all local instances of a given process, reaching a consensus among local instances on a global truth, collecting aggregated results from independent copies of a data analytics algorithm, etc. The need for peer nodes of a distributed system to mutually exchange information is recognized by the OpenFog RA. The innovative approach in FAR-EDGE is to define a specific system layer – the Ledger Tier – that is responsible for the implementation of such mechanisms and to guarantee an appropriate Quality of Service level.

The Edge Tier is in Plant Scope, located above the Field Tier and below the Cloud Tier. Individual EGs are connected with each other and with the north side of the system, i.e., the globally-scoped digital world in the Cloud Tier – by means of the factory LAN, and to the south side through the shopfloor LAN. From the RAMI 4.0 perspective, the FAR-

EDGE Edge Tier corresponds to the Station and Work Centre levels on the Hierarchy axis (IEC-62264/IEC-61512), while the EGs there contained are positioned across the Asset, Integration and Communication Layers. Edge Processes running on EGs, however, map to the Information and Functional Layers.

The Ledger Tier is a complete abstraction: it does not correspond to any physical deployment environment, and even the entities that it "contains" are abstract. Such entities are Ledger Services, which implement decentralized business logic as smart contracts on top of a distributed ledger. Ledger Services are transaction-oriented: each service call that needs to modify the shared state of a system must be evaluated and approved by Peer Nodes before taking effect. Similarly to "regular" services, Ledger Services are implemented as executable code; however, they are not actually executed on any specific computing node: each service call is executed in parallel by all Peer Nodes that happen to be online at the moment, which then need to reach a consensus on its validity. Most importantly, even the executable code of Ledger Services can be deployed and updated online by means of a distributed ledger transaction.

Ledger Services implement the part of Functional Domains and/or XC Functions that enable the edge computing model, through providing support for their Edge Service counterpart. For example, the Analytics Functional Domain may define a local analytics function (Edge Service) that must be executed in parallel on several EGs, and also a corresponding service call (Ledger Service) that will be invoked from the former each time new or updated local results become available, so that all results can converge into an aggregated data set. In this case, aggregation logic is included in the Ledger Service. Another use case may come from the Automation Functional Domain, demonstrating how the Ledger Tier can also be leveraged from the Field: a smart machine with embedded plug-and-produce functionality can ask permission to join the system by making a service call and then, having received green light, can dynamically deploy its own specific Ledger Service for publishing its state and external high-level commands.

The Ledger Tier lays across the Plant and the Enterprise Ecosystem Scopes, as it can provide support to any Tier. The physical location of Peer Nodes, which implement smart contracts and the distributed ledger, is not defined by the FAR-EDGE RA as it depends on implementation choices.

From the RAMI 4.0 perspective, the FAR-EDGE Ledger Tier corresponds to the Work Centre, Enterprise and Connected World levels on the Hierarchy axis (IEC-62264/IEC-61512), while the Ledger Services are positioned across the Information and Functional Layers.

The Cloud Tier is the top layer of the FAR-EDGE RA, and also the simplest and more "traditional" one. It is populated by Cloud Servers (CS): powerful computing machines, sometimes configured as clusters, which are connected to a fast LAN internally to their hosting data centre, and made accessible from the outside world by means of a corporate LAN or the Internet. On CSs runs that part of the business logic of Functional Domains and XC Functions that benefits from having the widest of scopes over production processes, and can deal with the downside of being physically deployed far away from them. This includes the planning, monitoring and management of entire factories, enterprises and supply chains (e.g., ERP and SCM systems). The Cloud Tier is populated by Cloud Services and Applications. Cloud Services implement specialized functions that are provided as individual API calls to Applications, which instead "package" a wider set of related operations that are relevant to some higher-level goal and often expose an interactive human interface.

The Cloud Tier is in Enterprise Ecosystem scope. The "Cloud" term in this context implies that Cloud Services and Applications are visible from all Tiers, wherever located. It does not imply that CSs should be actually hosted on some commercial cloud. In large enterprises, the Cloud Tier corresponds to one or more corporate data centres (private cloud), ensuring that the entire system is fully under the control of its owner.

In terms of RAMI 4.0, the FAR-EDGE Cloud Tier corresponds to the Work Centre, Enterprise and Connected World levels on the Hierarchy axis (IEC-62264/IEC-61512), while the Cloud Services and Applications are positioned across the Information, Functional and Business Layers.

IV. Reference Use Cases

In following paragraphs we present some indicative use cases that will be supported by FAR-EDGE.

A. *Wheel Alignment Smart Station*

This scenario is centred around the concept of an autonomous cyber-physical system (CPS): a self-contained plant module (workstation) comprising smart machines/tools and locally-scoped monitoring/control logic. Such module operates as a block-box: internally, it implements automated machine/tool configuration and workflows; externally, it integrates with the factory's IT backbone (e.g., MES/ERP) by means of a "public" interface that provides the required functionality while hiding the module's internals.

The concrete use case that the FAR-EDGE project is developing in this scenario targets a wheel alignment workstation for the manufacturing of industrial vehicles. The use case is complex, as it builds on a production process that is currently in place: its full description would go beyond the scope of this paper. To summarise, the added value of introducing the FAR-EDGE platform is this context is twofold. Firstly, it enables smart tools, i.e., an IoT-ready nut driver – to be dynamically deployed on any physical workstation and to be timely reconfigured (torque adjustment) to match fast-changing requirements, as a wide array of truck models is processed along the same production line. Secondly, it allows the entire workstation to be easily relocated to other plants that share the same IT backbone. As a positive side effect, the workstation, being mostly autonomous, is also able to operate with little or no disruption when temporarily disconnected from the network.

According to the FAR-EDGE RA, locally-scoped automation and analytics are Edge Processes belonging to the Edge Tier. From the implementation perspective, Edge

Processes are hosted by an Edge Gateway, which is an integral part of the wheel alignment workstation. In particular, smart tool deployment is in charge of the Edge Automation Services (EAS) component, which communicates with local field devices through the Field Abstraction layer. EAS also interacts with a digital model of the plant in order to retrieve and update information.

B. *Plug-and-Produce Conveyor Belt*

As in the previous example, the foundation of the FAR-EDGE use case is an existing logistic process in a real-world factory. The scenario is that of a large production plant where finished products, stacked on pallets, are moved by a single conveyor belt to a warehouse. Pallets only contain product items of the same type, but each pallet can be different as the conveyor is the outlet of multiple assembly lines working in parallel; the exact product type sequence on the conveyor at any given time is not predictable. When the pallets reach the warehouse, they are dispatched to a number of "exit bays" for immediate shipping, temporary storage or other destinations (e.g., defective products). The dispatching logic should take into account product type on the one hand, bay configuration, capacity and status on the other. In its current implementation, a PLC-based dispatching system does its best to match the input stream (product type ID scanned on pallets) with the output channels (static configuration of exit bays), taking into account the daily production schedule. However, this approach does not allow for any significant schedule change and/or "hot" reconfiguration of the exit bays.

The FAR-EDGE platform is redesigning the above described "primitive" CPS with the introduction of Smart Objects (exit bays with embedded computing power and network connectivity) and of a Ledger Tier (a Distributed Ledger exposing Ledger Services) where *decentralized* configuration and orchestration logic resides. The basic use case is Plug-and-Produce: new bays can be added to the working system, and existing bays can be put offline, at any time: the Ledger Tier is responsible for granting permission and for keeping the digital model of the plant in-sync with the real world. Once online, new bays are immediately able to negotiate with the plant controller their services – e.g., ask for more products of a given type when *actual* processing capacity exceeds the incoming flow. The innovative approach in FAR-EDGE, where blockchain is used to implement Ledger Services, avoids potential single-point-of-failure problems and scalability bottlenecks.

V. CONCLUSIONS

The edge computing paradigm provides many compelling advantages for the implementation of digital automation platforms, including the ability to analyze information close to the field, as well as the ability to flexible (re)configure real-time automation workflows. This is the reason why several edge computing platforms for industrial automation are already under implementation. FAR-EDGE takes these implementations to the next level, through enhancing edge computing implementations with the merits of blockchain technologies, notably in terms of representing and implementing automation and analytics operations as scalable and flexibly configurable smart contracts. Blockchain concepts have already been introduced in the FAR-EDGE RA, which serves as a basis for implementing automation, analytics and digital simulation use cases. In addition to providing open source implementation of FAR-EDGE systems, our project will provide tangible research findings regarding the applicability of blockchain for factory automation.

ACKNOWLEDGMENT

This work has been carried out in the scope of the FAR-EDGE project (H2020-703094). The authors acknowledge help and contributions from all partners of the project.

REFERENCES

[1] P. Leitão, "Agent-based distributed manufacturing control: A state-of-the-art survey", Engineering Applications of Artificial Intelligence, vol. 22, no. 7, pp. 979-991, Oct. 2009.

[2] P. Vrba,., Review of Industrial Applications of Multi-agent Technologies," Service Orientation in Holonic and Multi Agent Manufacturing and Robotics, Studies in Computational Intelligence Vol. 472, Springer, pp 327-338, 2013

[3] F. Jammes and H. Smit, "Service-Oriented Paradigms in Industrial Automation Industrial Informatics," IEEE Transactions on., pp. 62 – 70, vol. 1, issue 1, Feb, 2005.

[4] T. Cucinotta and Coll, "A Real-Time Service-Oriented Architecture for Industrial Automation," Industrial Informatics, IEEE Transactions on, vol. 5, issue 3, pp. 267 – 277, Aug. 2009.

[5] W. Shi, J. Cao, Q. Zhang, Y. Li and L. Xu, "Edge Computing: Vision and Challenges," in IEEE Internet of Things Journal, vol. 3, no. 5, pp. 637-646, Oct. 2016. doi: 10.1109/JIOT.2016.2579198

[6] F. Bonomi, R. Milito, J. Zhu, S. Addepalli, «Fog computing and its role in the internet of things», Proceedings of the first edition of the MCC workshop on Mobile cloud computing, MCC '12, pp 13-16.

[7] Industrial Internet Consortium. 2017. The Industrial Internet of Things Volume G1: Reference Architecture, version 1.8. (2017). [Online], Available from: http://www.iiconsortium.org/IIRA.htm

[8] Industrial Internet Consortium. IIC Edge Intelligence Testbed. 2017. [Online], Available from: http://www.iiconsortium.org/edge-intelligence.htm

[9] EdgeX Foundry Framewok 2017. [Online], Available from: https://www.edgexfoundry.org/

[10] K. Schweichhart. "Reference Architectural Model Industrie 4.0 - An Introduction", April 2016, [Online], Available from: https://ec.europa.eu/futurium/en/system/files/ged/a2-schweichhart-reference_architectural_model_industrie_4.0_rami_4.0.pdf

[11] H2020-703094 FAR-EDGE Project 2017. [Onine], Available from: http://www.far-edge.eu

Implementation of Interactive E-learning System Based on Virtual Reality

SeungJoon Kwon, HyungKeun Jee
Electronics and Telecommunications Research Institute (ETRI)

Daejeon, Republic of Korea
Email: {kwonsj, hkjee}@etri.re.kr

***Abstract*—VR (Virtual Reality)-based e-learning applications have become an important part of the educational program in kindergarten as well as in the National Children's Library (NLCY), in Republic of Korea. As kindergarten pupils and their teachers use the VR-based e-learning system, they can be more visually aware of ongoing course materials and more intuitively aware of getting quick response from event handling on screens. However, the existing VR-based e-learning system consists of complex equipment such as a large screen and beam projector to show the actual scene in 3D, more than two PCs, a forward camera to detect the pupils' movement, and a rear camera to capture the pupils' image. In this paper, we introduce a VR-based interactive e-learning system, which is implemented to enable kindergarten pupils to quickly experience a better sense of reality and immersion in a virtual reality environment without regard to the floor space. Applying technologies such as RTSP (Real Time Streaming Protocol) to the VR-based interactive e-learning system allows users to display the same view on different remote display devices, allowing separate users to share interactive events for collaboration.**

Keywords-e-learning; virtual reality; user interaction.

I. INTRODUCTION

The popularity of VR (Virtual Reality) application systems as e-learning resources has increased significantly. Many e-learning applications have focused on developing online course materials, but VR-based e-learning applications [1][2] mainly have focused on making course materials interactively. VR-based e-learning applications are becoming a key part of the educational program in NLCY (National Library for Children and Young Adults) [3], Republic of Korea. The people who support the library are trying to expand its use of VR-based e-learning system nationwide. In particular, the e-learning system using VR technologies can enhance attention and engagement of kindergarten pupils who have short attention spans [4]. As kindergarten pupils and their teachers use the VR-based e-learning system, they can be more visually aware of ongoing course materials and more intuitively aware of getting quick response from event handling on screens. However, the existing VR-based e-learning system [1][3] consists of complex equipment such as a large screen and beam projector to show the actual scene in 3D, more than two PCs, a forward camera to detect the pupils' movement, and a rear camera to capture the pupils' image. As a result, the process of installing the system becomes complicated, and once the system is installed in a specific place, it becomes impossible to move it to another place. It also requires an isolated and large room to install and operate the system. It is necessary to develop a system to increase the learning efficiency by giving the kindergarten pupils a feeling of immersion in a certain virtual space or situation and providing a vivid virtual experience. Also, it is necessary to develop technologies that enable virtual experiential learning classes held in one kindergarten to be shared with other kindergartens in remote locations in real time, to enable collaborative learning. In terms of the kindergarten administration, the introduction of an interactive virtual experiential learning system, which features a low cost and simple system installation process, is preferable to the existing system.

The rest of this paper is organized as follows. Section II describes the functional components of the proposed system and Section III explains the process of evaluation in terms of the system performance. Finally, in Section IV, we present the conclusions and our future work.

II. SYSTEM DESCRIPTION

The environment of the VR-based e-learning system installed in the NLCY [3] for the purpose of running interactive storytelling programs for kindergarten pupils is shown in Figure 1. This system projects pupils into the background of various fairy tales in VR through large screens and it promotes reading by stimulating the interest in books. The VR-based interactive e-learning system developed in this study is shown in Figure 2.

Figure 1. Interactive storytelling program in NLCY

As an output of the previous project [5], the VR-based e-learning system installed at the NLCY had a very positive effect on kindergarten pupils in that they improved attention, comprehension and retention. By deploying the one-wall full-scale VR-based e-learning system, we can take this to the next level by offering immersive and realistic hands-on virtual learning experiences in which several pupils can participate at the same time.

Figure 2. Proposed VR-based e-learning system: (a) environment, (b) virtual experience to *Santa village* (deployment screen shot)

The disadvantages of the existing system were that the system installation was complicated, a lot of equipment was needed, and space was limited. Also, there was a color image resolution (640x480) issue. In order to overcome these problems, we have developed the VR-based interactive e-learning system that enables kindergarten pupils to experience a better sense of reality and immersiveness in a virtual reality environment, and can be quickly and easily installed by kindergarten teachers or administrators. The system consists of a keyboard, an RGB-D camera (Kinect V2, Full HD), a 64-bit windows desktop PC, and single TV monitor. Through a wireless mobile network, we have expanded to enabling parents or pupils in remote locations to use their mobile screen devices to access the same VR hands-on contents outside of kindergarten. This will enable pupils to conduct virtual learning experience outside of kindergarten before coming to class where teachers can tutor the pupils in VR. The proposed VR-based interactive e-learning system consists of three functional components in terms of design, as shown in Figure 3.

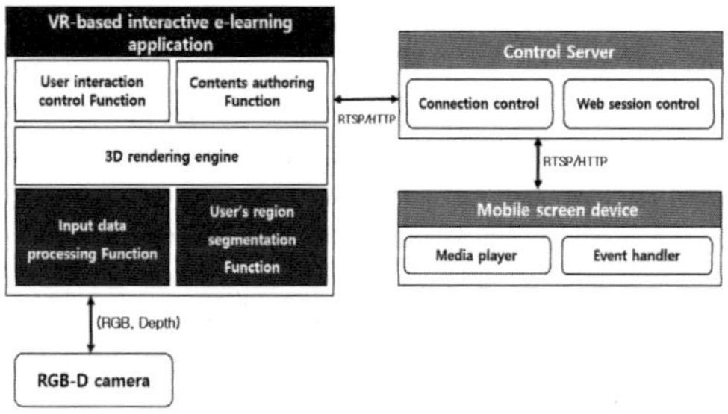

Figure 3. Functional configuration of proposed system

One is a *VR-based interactive e-learning application* including RGB-D camera, another is a *control server*, and the other is a *mobile screen device*. The *control server* processes messages/events such as a session, an access URL, and a contents streaming URL for connection management between the screen device and the e-learning application. The mobile screen device is responsible for functions such as audio/video and user screen transmission of experiential contents, and handles media player and event handler functions for RTSP (Real Time Streaming Protocol)-based content streaming. The *VR-based interactive e-learning application* includes *input data processing function* that receives RGB data and depth data from a RGB-D camera and a *user's region segmentation function* that extracts only a user region through image processing techniques. There is a *user interaction control function* for controlling interaction and event processing between the extracted actual user region data and virtual objects, *and a contents authoring function* for authoring and modifying the experiential contents.

A. *User's region segmentation function*

The *user's region segmentation function* extracts user pixel candidates based on color and depth frame images obtained from the Kinect V2 device. It extracts image objects corresponding to the user's foreground region from the depth frame image, and applies temporal filtering and vectorization processes to minimize outline noise and to correct blinking outline of user's foreground regions. After eliminating the background image objects that are not the user's foreground regions, the resulting images are synthesized into three-dimensional virtual contents. The workflow of the *user's region segmentation function* applied in the proposed system is illustrated in Figure 4.

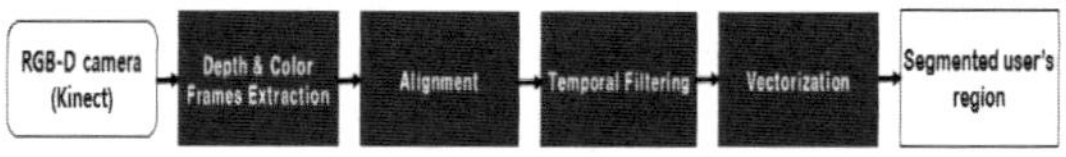

Figure 4. Workflow of user's region segmentation

B. *User interaction control function*

This function consists of two kinds of interaction control processing. One is the interaction control through user speech recognition, and the other is through user gesture recognition. The recognition rate of user speech is different according to the surroundings environment where Kinect is installed and the state of speech signal. In order to process interaction events based on user speech recognition between virtual image objects and real image objects, the Kinect Sensor performs an audio search and locates the sound. After finding the direction of the sound, it recognizes the speech the user has spoken.

According to the recognition result, the interaction event between the user and the virtual object is performed and the result screen is rendered. In general, there are two approaches to user gesture recognition. One is a heuristic approach and the other is a machine learning approach. For this function, we use machine learning based user gesture recognition. The more iterations of the action recording and tagging process for many people, the higher the accuracy of gesture recognition can be. Finally, the gesture recognized and the corresponding event are mapped and the set interaction is performed.

C. *Input data processing function*

The function receives the color image, depth image, audio stream, and skeleton information from the Kinect sensor, and converts it into the required data format. Then, the converted data is input to the user's region segmentation function and user interaction control function.

III. System Performance

In order to build the proposed system, the user's whole body image is extracted in real time and synthesized into three-dimensional virtual contents, and the gesture according to the user's motion and the speech of the user are recognized to process the interaction events between the virtual object and the user. To evaluate the performance of the proposed system, we test the accuracy of *user's region segmentation function* and *user interaction control function* applied inside the system. For the *user's region segmentation function*, we extract the user's body region at 16 FPS (frames per second) in the image frames obtained from Kinect and test the performance of the *user's region segmentation function* as follows. First, we digitize the Full HD color image obtained from Kinect and directly extract the user's whole body region. Through this, a ground truth image (1920x1080 resolution) is prepared, which is divided into a user's body region and a background region, and the accuracy is compared with the result image (1920x1080 resolution) generated by the *user's region segmentation function* of the VR-based interactive e-learning system. In the same dataset range, the ground truth image is paired with the result image of user's region segmentation function. Then, TP (True Positive), TN (True Negative), FP (False Positive), and FN (False Negative) values are calculated for each image frame, and Recall, Precision, and F-measure values are obtained using TP, TN, FP, and FN values. Finally, the *user's region segmentation function* applied to the VR-based interactive e-learning system shows an average of 91.1% F-measure for a total of 20,000 frames of input image. In order to evaluate the performance of the user speech and gesture recognition, we examine the result of recognition event processing by inputting English and Korean data strings. Looking at the front of the Kinect attached to the large screen, a single user shouts tomatoes. The user confirms the virtual tomato object displayed on the screen. The user touches a virtual object (tomato) with one hand, and then performs an action of throwing it in the forward direction, as shown in Figure 5. At this time, when the virtual object is thrown forward, it is judged that speech and gesture recognition is successful. Throughout a total of 50 field tests, the recognition rate of English and Korean data strings for the same object was about 90%. Researchers, not pupils, directly participated in testing the accuracy of the *user's region segmentation function* and *user interaction control function*.

Figure 5. Test for user interaction control (throwing virtual objects) in the proposed system

The proposed system in this study has been developed based on Unity 5.6 64bit. For performance tests, we have used *Nuri curriculum* contents. The *Nuri curriculum* is an educational welfare project targeting the holistic development of children aged 3 to 5 in Republic of Korea. The user interface of the display configuration to experience the content is simple, and the entire system for running the contents can be installed within a few minutes, without the need for large facilities or costly physical equipment. As shown in Figure 6, applying technologies such as RTSP to the VR-based interactive e-learning system allows users to display the same view on different remote display devices, allowing separate users to share interactive events for collaboration.

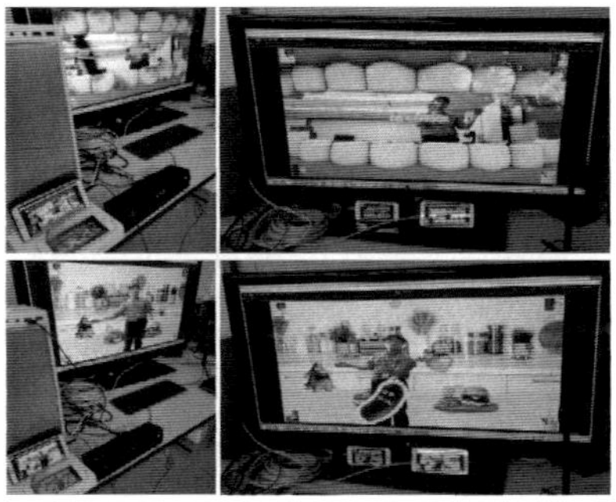

Figure 6. Real-time synchronization of experiencing *Nuri curriculum* content (life safety) across multiple screens

The users can share speech and gesture interaction results for the co-registered virtual objects with other users on a single shared display.

IV. Conclusion and Future Work

In this paper, we propose a VR-based interactive e-learning system, which is implemented to enable kindergarten pupils to quickly experience a better sense of reality and immersion in a virtual reality environment without regard to the floor space. The proposed system is easy to install, easy to use, and easy to configure. A performance evaluation of the proposed system shows that it is effective for speech and gesture interaction to the co-registered virtual objects between users on a single shared display.

In the future, we will install the proposed system in a kindergarten and perform the tests in which the kindergarten pupils participate. Also, we plan to find a method to enhance the high-speed synchronization on display views across multiple smart devices so that virtual learning held in one kindergarten can be shared with other kindergartens in remote locations in real-time.

Acknowledgment

This work was supported by the ICT R&D program of MSIP/IITP [14-811-12-002, Development of personalized and creative learning tutoring system based on participational interactive contents and collaborative learning technology].

REFERENCES

[1] S. Lee, J. Ko, S. Kang, J. Lee, "An immersive e-learning system providing virtual experience". Proc. IEEE International Symposium on Mixed and Augmented Reality (ISMAR 2010), pp.249-250, doi: 10.1109/ISMAR.2010.5643591.

[2] Z. Li, J. Yue, D. Jáuregui, "A New Virtual Reality Environment Used for e-Learning", Proc. IEEE International Symposium on IT in Medicine and Education(ITIME 2009), pp.445-449, doi:10.1109/ITIME.2009.5236382.

[3] S. Kang, Y. Lee, S. Lee, "Kids in Fairytales: Experiential and Interactive Storytelling in Children's Libraries", CHI EA '15 Proceedings of the 33rd Annual ACM Conference Extended Abstracts on Human Factors in Computing Systems, pp.1007-1012, ISBN: 978-1-4503-3146-3, doi:10.1145/2702613.2732826.

[4] J. Yoon, H. Jee, B. Kim, S. Myung, K. Noh, "Trend of u-learning technology", Korean Journal of Information Science, vol.27(7), pp.41-50, July. 2009, ISSN : 1229-6821.

[5] MSIP/KEIT, Project report: Development of learner-participational and interactive 3D Virtual learning contents technology, 2015.

Heads Up Displays (HUD) as a Tool to Contextualize the User in 3D Virtual Worlds

Aliane Loureiro Krassmann, Felipe Becker Nunes, Tito Armando Rossi Filho,
Liane Margarida Rockenbach Tarouco, Magda Bercht
Graduate Program of Informatics in Education
Universidade Federal do Rio Grande do Sul (UFRGS) - Porto Alegre/RS – Brazil
E-mail:{alkrassmann, nunesfb}@gmail.com, rossitito@hotmail.com, liane@penta.ufrgs.br, bercht@inf.ufrgs.br

Abstract—**Virtual Worlds are open 3D environments that can be used to implement virtual laboratories and simulations, improving student interaction. However, it is often seen that their freedom characteristic can cause dispersion for the user, making it difficult to navigate and focus. This paper presents a proposal to reduce the difficulties of this impasse, with a Heads Up Display (HUD) solution that dynamically and constantly senses the locations visited by the avatar, and presents it in the form of a "heat map". An experiment was conducted with 16 individuals that formed the experimental and the control groups (with and without the HUD). The results reveal the usefulness of the HUD, allowing to see that this resource provided a real-time view of the user interaction and places visited, helping him/her navigate the Virtual World.**

Keywords-virtual worlds; heads up display; heat map.

I. INTRODUCTION

Virtual Worlds (VW) are complete 3D environments where virtual laboratories and simulations can be implemented, and users represented by their own avatars can move around, meet and interact with other avatars [1]. According to [2] it opens the possibility for students to perform lab practices at any place, time and at reduced costs and risks of human accidents from eventual problems during experiences. Although the development of these environments is quite a lengthy process, long term benefits of its use may arise, since it can be used several times [3].

VW offers a great level of freedom, as the user not only can chose when to learn, when to enter the environment, but also what to learn and in what order, which is in agreement with active modern pedagogical approaches. Due to the great diversity of didactic materials that can be inserted in this type of environment, such as texts, videos and images, different types of rooms can be created, separated by type of content, so that the user can interact with each topic and their respective educational materials. This opens the possibility for the users to navigate through different locations within the VW.

However, this openness of the environment and freedom received by the users is often seen as a cause of dispersion, leading to several implications, as engagement hindrance or discouragement on the following of their pedagogical trajectory. According to Mayer [4] environments designed to make users discover materials completely on their own are harder to use. Csikszentmihalyi [5] highlights that activities stimulate more flow if they embody certain rules and clearly state what the users should do.

In a complementary way, Sivunen and Nordbäck [6] found that team dispersion could be one of the causes of low social presence among participants. Gütl [7] discovered that if users spend too much time learning to use a complex interface they might leave these environments. In [8], the authors explored how examples of reflective guidance, directive signs, symbols, footprints and notice boards within the environment might be helpful to achieve the learning goals, getting some positive results.

Ubiquitous computing techniques can help overcome these drawbacks. In an educational ubiquitous computing enhanced environment, the fundamental issue is how to provide learners with the right information at the right time in the right way [9]. The so called ubiquitous learning systems aim to provide personalized learning support based on students' preferences, learning status, personal factors as well as the characteristics of the learning contents and learning environments [10].

In this study, we propose the use of ubiquitous computing techniques to provide a context-aware VW, using Heads Up Display (HUD), a device that can be attached to the user's screen for different purposes. Our work dynamically infers user's context, working as a "heat map" that changes the color according to the locations of the 3D environment that the user has visited. It is assumed that this could help with students navigation, decreasing the losing of focus and keeping them aware of the locations they still have to visit. Therefore, the hypothesis of this research is: "using a heat map HUD in 3D VW can facilitate engagement and increase interaction time".

The rest of this paper is organized as follows. Section II presents the related work. Section III explains the research method. Section IV addresses the results analysis and discussion. Section V presents the conclusion.

II. RELATED WORK

Virtual Worlds projected for learning purposes contain a variety of educational resources modelled inside it. In this sense, it is desirable for the user to spend long times navigating it. Users who spend more time in the VW tend to interact more with educational objects [11].

However, one of the most complicated aspects of 3D VW is scaffolding or guidance, since it is very large and flexible [8]. Ubiquitous computing techniques can help overcome this challenge, improving student performance and consequently improving institutional cost effectiveness [12]. One illustrative example of a context-aware 3D VW is an environment for teaching Computer Networks presented by [13], where student's context is used to adapt the materials, tools and information according to their level of expertise.

In consonance with this trend, several researches have benefited from the use of Heads Up Display (HUD) device capabilities to personalize and dynamize VW. Shah, Bell and Sukthankar [14] implemented a recommendation system that suggests places to visit, personalized with the user's destination preferences. To acquire data on users' travel patterns, they developed a custom tracker object using the Linden Scripting Language (LSL), which periodically prompts the user to enter information describing its current location. The tracker object appears as an HUD that can be worn on the right or left of the avatar and monitors the user's current (x, y, z) location.

In the study of [15] participants were each given a HUD that allowed them to indicate up to eight emotional states throughout the presentation (four positive and four negative). The goal of using the device was to identify and analyze which aspects invoked emotional responses and what kinds of information were considered trustworthy or untrustworthy.

One of the promising VW applications that seem to demand such a device is the visit of virtual museums. Sookhanaphibarn and Thawonmas [16] emphasize that personalization can play a key role for increasing the number of return visitors. They have mentioned the idea of using HUD to show personalized recommendations in VW, similarly to what has already been implemented for physical museums, but with the advantages of requesting simple implementation and no additional cost.

Ward and Sonneborn [17] implemented a HUD that provides subtitles of dialogue in many languages, including English, French, German, Spanish, Italian, and Portuguese. Also, the HUD records the avatar's position so users can know where they are in the build and receive audio, pictorial and textual information about what they are seeing on their visit, like a virtual version of the sort of devices used in real life museums.

In the field of displaying locations to situate the user, the Virtual Learning Environment (VLE) MOODLE in more recent versions (2.7 onwards) has a plugin that implements the "heat map" concept to help user navigation, using a color scheme (yellow, orange and red) to represent the "heating". The heat map highlights areas as well as components that highly attracted student's attention by counting the number of mouse clicks [18].

Similarly to the studies presented, in this paper we show the results of the development and application of a context-aware HUD that works as a heat map, "heating" as the locations in the VW are visited more often, allowing the user to be aware of his navigation behavior. The HUD is attached to the user's screen and keeps sensing the places visited, registering into a database and retrieving this information in real time. Our research differs from the ones mentioned because of the heat map characteristic of the HUD, towards investigating an unprecedented hypothesis that this device could help on improving engagement and interaction time. Also, our heat map counts local visitation per user, showing it individually to each one.

III. MATERIALS AND METHOD

This research is an exploratory quasi-experimental study, in which a case study was performed with a convenient sample of university students that had a minimum level of computer skills. To investigate the hypothesis, the sample was separated in two groups: control, who did not use the heat map, just interacted with the VW without this device, and, experimental, who used the VW with the heat map device, and experimental, that used the VW with the heat map device.

A region in a Virtual World from project AVATAR [19] (from the Portuguese of Virtual Learning Environment and Remote Academic Work), on the open source platform Open Simulator was used. Students enrolled in courses at the authors' university and colleagues that work on the project were invited to spontaneously participate in the experiment, which took place on Universidade Federal do Rio Grande do Sul facilities. Singularity [20] and Firestorm [21] viewers were used to enter the VW, because these pieces of software are capable of representing the 3D graphical environment in an appropriate form.

A. *The Virtual World*

Two virtual laboratories were used: Waves and Wireless Networks, which are introduced on [22]. According to the authors, in these virtual labs students from Secondary or Technical education have the opportunity to visualize the practical side of some abstract concepts that are part of their daily life. Figure 1 shows a screenshot of the environment entrance. It can be seen that an instruction manual and a control panel were placed at the beginning of the path, to give the user introductory information about the experiment, for example, on how to move around, use the didactic materials and what is expected in this visitation.

Figure 1 - Waves and Wireless Networks Laboratories entrance.

Due to the comprehensiveness of these two teaching contents it was decided divide them into 12 topics, distributed along 12 specific locations in the two laboratories, which are presented in Table 1.

TABLE I. LOCATIONS AND TOPICS DISTRIBUTION

Location number	Content topic/subject
1	Wave Characteristics
2	AM and FM Radio Waves
3	Wave Phenomena
4	Electromagnetic Spectrum
5	Introduction to Wireless Networks I
6	Introduction to Wireless Networks II
7	Wireless Network Topologies
8	Infrared and Bluetooth
9	Range of Wireless Networks I
10	Range of Wireless Networks II
11	Range of Wireless Networks III
12	Material interference in propagating the wireless network

Didactic materials, such as videos, slides, images, texts, animated digital media, audios, web pages embedded in QR (Quick Response) Code and simulations according to the subjects are available in these locations, each one identified as to their type through luminous plaques.

B. *The heat map HUD*

In the experimental group, a HUD was attached at the top right of the users screen with a numerical map of the environment. The HUD is composed of 12 prims (primitives – 3D object unit) that are linked. Each prim has its own texture that identifies the number and the topic of the location, and its own scripts to change its color, "heating" according to the frequency of access and time elapsed on avatar visitation. To do this, the classification presented in Table 2 was idealized and adopted.

TABLE II. HEATMAP CLASSIFICATION ON HUD

Color	Tag	Frequency	Time elapsed
Yellow	Weak	Second time	2 minutes
Orange	Medium	Third time	3 minutes
Red	Strong	Fourth time	4 minutes

Besides LSL (Linden Scripting Language) programming language, Open Simulator Scripting Language (OSSL) was used to program the HUD. To capture data from each user in real time, sensors programmed with scripts were inserted in each one of the 12 locations of the VW. These sensors collect data and send it through HTTP requests to PHP (Hypertext Preprocessor) files in the server. These PHP files treat the data and insert them in the table created in a MySQL database.

Data stored in the table "Heat map" of the database were as follows: a) user's name; b) name and identifier of the location visited; c) time user remained in that location; d) the current heat map status for the user at that location; e) time records. When visiting a location for the first time, a new complete record is inserted in this table, and only the current heat map status attribute is subsequently updated, according to an incremental analysis of time elapsed.

In this sense, if the user has remained at one of the 12 locations for more than two minutes, it is assumed the user is visiting this location for the second time, so the prim on the HUD that corresponds to this location turns yellow; after three minutes it turns orange and after four minutes it turns red. A sensor checks every five seconds for the presence of an avatar and consults in the database if this specific avatar has already visited the place, registering it after every minute (60 seconds) in an incremental way. The prim also has the ability, by touching it, to tele transport users avatar to each one of the 12 locations.

Figure 2 shows the heat map following the user avatar at different scenarios of the VW. It can be seen, for example, that this user has visited Location 5 very often (red), but Location 3 lacks visiting, as it is still white (top screen). It also shows in the bottom screen that Location 8 is now red, as the user is currently at this location again and probably has spent more 2 minutes observing a simulation (from yellow – 2 minutes; to red – 4 minutes).

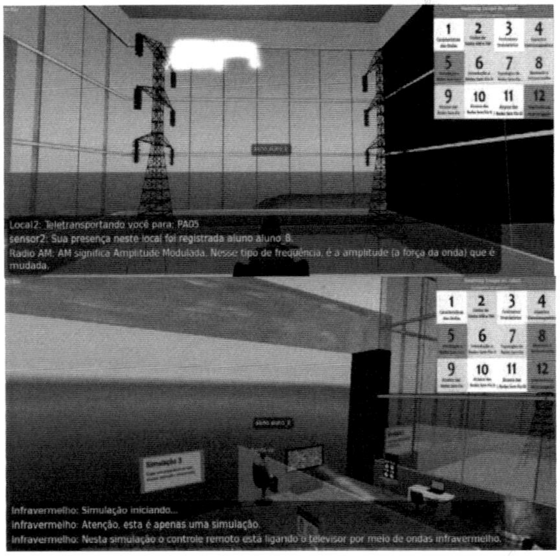

Figure 2 – Heat map HUD under different scenarios.

The locations were signalized with circles on the floor and the sensors are programmed to sense avatars presence in a radius of eight VW meters. Messages are sent to the user about the simulation or educational materials he is currently seeing during this visit.

As mentioned by [21], VWs such as Open Simulator — developed using open-source software — allow developers and teachers to access student logs and retrieve valuable information on learners' in-world behavior and interaction. This possibility, explored in this research, is important not only in terms of assessment: it also facilitates the identification of learner profiles and VW behavior patterns.

C. *The experiment*

Initially, students were informed about the experiment goals, the voluntary aspect of their participation, as well as about the complete confidentiality of any data gathered about them. Each one received an individual login to access the 3D environment. Users were instructed to navigate freely and intuitively in the VW, without any pedagogical path or visitation time previously defined. The purpose of this choice was to provide users with freedom to interact in places they considered appropriate, visiting the desired materials and remaining in a location as long as they were interested.

Immediately after the session, a questionnaire was administered, containing demographic questions about the participants including age, gender, instructional level and VW experience, and items about the navigation in the environment and the impressions regarding the heat map (HUD).

In order to compare the results between control and experimental groups, five questions related to the users impressions concerning the environment characteristics have been evaluated, which can be seen in Table 3.

TABLE III. QUESTIONS RELATED TO THE ENVIRONMENT

Characteristic	Question
Easy and Intuitive Operation	Q1: Was the system operation easy and intuitive?
Easy Navigation	Q2: Were you capable of orienting yourself in the environment?
Provided Information	Q3: Did the system adequately inform you about what was going on?
Provided Instructions	Q4: Did the system clearly indicate what could (or couldn't) be done?
Overall Impression	Q5: Would you like to use virtual labs like these in your area of application?

Additionally to the questions that were administered to both control and experimental groups, a set of questions was answered only by the experimental group, since they were specifically related to the impression about the use of the heat map. These questions can be seen on Table 4.

TABLE IV. QUESTIONS RELATED TO THE HEAT MAP HUD

Characteristic	Question
Localization Support	Q6: Did the heat map help you to orient yourself in the environment?
Information Format	Q7: Did the heat map provide interaction information in an adequate manner?
Timely information	Q8: Did the heat map provide the information in the appropriate time?
Usefulness	Q9: Was the heat map useful?
Design	Q10: Was the heat map design pleasant (colors, format)?
Overall Impression	Q11: Would you prefer to use the environment with or without the heat map?

Except for Question "Q11" that was in multiple choice format, all the others were in the 5-point Likert scale format, with 1 being strongly disagree and 5 strongly agree. The results of the experiment performed are presented as follows.

IV. RESULTS ANALYSIS AND DISCUSSION

A total of 16 individuals participated in this study, as can be seen in Figure 3, which shows the sample's demographic data.

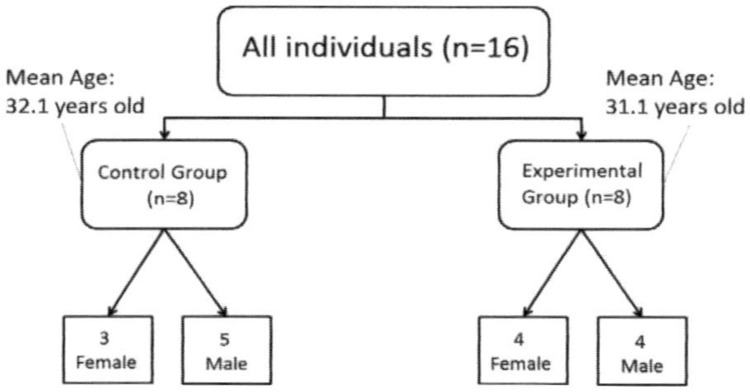

Figure 3 – Sample's demographics.

Regarding the instruction level of the participants, both groups were very similar in this inference: 50% of individuals held Bachelor's or Master's Degree and 50% were Doctoral students. Concerning previous knowledge on VW, individuals of control group had more previous knowledge than the experimental group: while 50% of individuals of control group answered the Likert scale on either levels 4 or 5, only 25% of individuals from the experimental group answered in these levels.

A. *Quantitative Analysis*

The answers related to the evaluation of the experience of exploring the environment (Questions 1 to 5) were positive in general, which can be seen in Figure 4. Out of all responses to the questionnaire, about 78% were positive (levels 4 or 5 of Likert scale), around 13% were neutral (level 3) and only 7.5% were negative (levels 1 or 2). A comparison between control and experimental groups, taking into consideration all responses (Questions 1 to 5), shows a similar result, but there were more responses at level 5 from the experimental group than from the control group (55% versus 40%).

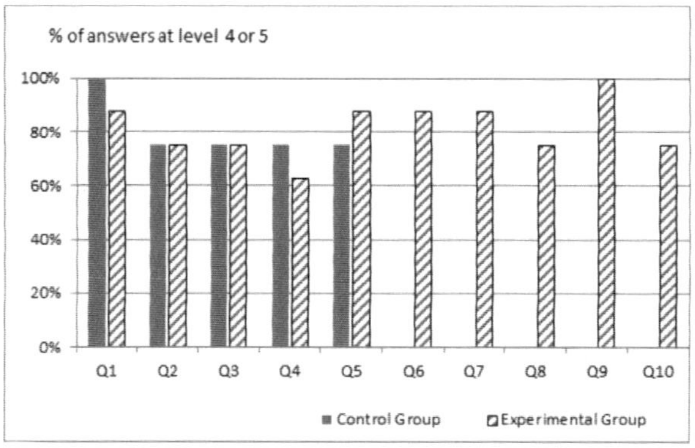

Figure 4 - Summary of questionnaire answers.

In order to test whether the identified differences in responses were statistically significant and therefore could be extrapolated to the population of users, statistical tests have been performed using nonparametric Mann-Whitney test with 95% confidence level. The test checks whether the two groups come from the same population, that is, test whether the two independent groups are homogeneous and have the same distribution [23].

For all questions the null hypothesis (there are no significant differences) tests of the responses medians have not been rejected, since all p-values were above 0.05. However, this must be taken with a proper caution, due to the fact that it was a small sample (only 8 respondents per group).

This result shows that both groups predominantly agreed that: the system operated satisfactorily and its navigation was intuitive (Q1); they were able to locate themselves in the environment autonomously and without major difficulties (Q2); the environment was properly identified, with clear information about the contents and rooms available (Q3); the system has conveniently indicated what should be done and which instructions should be followed (Q4); and finally, users have generally indicated that they would like to use this environment in their domain area (Q5). This reveals an interesting result, showing that both groups well accepted the resources and considered their navigation adequate and that the process of interaction occurred properly.

Concerning the user's impression about the heat map HUD itself, the general responses can also be seen in Figure 4. The experimental group that used the VW with the HUD considered that this device helped them to navigate during their trajectory in the environment (Q6): around 87% of participants gave positive answers (4 or 5 points). The same percentage was obtained for Q7, allowing to infer that experimental group understood that the heat map provided information about their interaction in real time and in an appropriate way. On the other hand, the positivity on answers decrease to 75% on Q8, but reasonably allowing inferring they considered the heat map showed information in an appropriate time. They have unanimously strongly agreed that this device was useful for navigation (Q9). The heat map design characteristic was not so positive according to the answers (Q10). Despite of that, 75% of answers were positive, allowing to conclude that the arrangement of the heat map colors and format was considered adequate. This demonstrates that besides the approval of the environment in both groups, the experimental group indicated a positive tendency regarding the use of heat map HUD, emphasizing that this feature added even more to the quality of interaction in VW.

In addition, all of experimental group participants stated preference on using the Virtual World with the heat map HUD (Q11). The average time spent on visiting the environment was 35 minutes for the experimental group and 32 minutes for the control group.

In this sense, although not statistically proven, some differences between the two groups were identified in the quantitative analysis. There were slightly more positive responses (at levels 4 or 5) from the experimental group than the control group. Considering also that there was a little more time spent in the environment from the experimental group, we can conclude that our hypothesis "using a heat map HUD in 3D VW can facilitate engagement and increase interaction time" is true.

B. *Qualitative Analysis*

The participants from both groups of the study were invited to add comments about their experience at the end of the questionnaire and 75% of them provided inputs to help clarify their ratings and also some suggestions. Among the positive comments from participants of control group they have mentioned the environment is an interesting and productive way of learning, with potential to be a teaching instrument of the highest quality. According to them it is interesting the proposal to visualize some concepts, helping to make it less abstract. One of the participants teaches the same subject of the labs and mentioned he would like to use the environment in his class.

Among the negative comments in control group, they have mentioned there is some information overload, with many warnings and messages overlapping, disrupting the interaction. Some revealed that although intuitive enough, at times they did not know where to go or what to do, highlighting the need for more tips or indications. In this context, a user feedback is transcribed below:

"There are arrows on the floor that indicate the direction, but after each 'section' ends, there is no indication of where we should go (I believe it to be intentional, giving the student freedom), but it could be suggested to the student."

Among the positive comments from participants of experimental group, some of them mentioned the heat map helped them navigate, being very useful. As mentioned by most of them, the environment is of easy interaction and location, well intuitive, with beautiful and nice design. They revealed that they had a great user experience, finding the labs and the simulations very interesting. One participant has mentioned he wanted to participate in the test of the next version of the VW. A clipping of a participant comments is presented below.

"It was very interesting for a first experience, a very interactive way to learn. I had some difficulty locating myself in a few moments but the heat map helped me."

Among the negative comments, participants from the experimental group mentioned that sometimes the heat map in a specific position covered important parts of the screen, reducing the visibility. In this sense, they have suggested the heat map could be hidden in those cases. Some participants revealed the system does not clearly state what should be done, because the chat box where the instructions and explanations are sent is in a barely visible place in the left corner. On the other hand, it was also mentioned by other users that there is information overload when the dialog (information) appears on the whole screen, even if it is transparent. One of the suggestions was to dedicate half of the screen for the chat box.

In this qualitative analysis, the usefulness of the heat map can be seen. While the control group highlighted the need for more indications or suggestions about where to go in the environment, the experimental group pointed out the device helped them navigate, and no comment of this kind (loss of direction) was received from them.

IV. Conclusion And Future Work

The use of context information from user interaction in VW can be useful in different application scenarios, one of them being educational. The access of students' logs facilitates assessment and the identification of learner profiles and patterns [24]. The collecting of information from users behavior in the environment can allow the accomplishment of different types of actions to assist the students during their interaction.

In this way, the study presented in this paper focused on the use of context information of users to present a real-time heat map, in HUD format, of their activities in the environment. The objective was to help user navigation in the environment, highlighting the places visited and how often, working as a tool to contextualize the user in 3D Virtual Worlds.

The results from the experiment demonstrated the acceptance of the hypothesis that using the heat map HUD in 3D VW can facilitate engagement and increase interaction time, as we have collected important indications about the implications of using this device, in which the users emphasized the usefulness of knowing their on navigation pattern to aid in their interaction. On the other hand, the users who did not have the HUD device coupled to their screen complained about loss of directions and the need for more guidance.

The HUD showed to be flexible, as it can be attached to particular users and it functions individually. Flexible guidance (guided and unguided navigation) can also be provided to meet the needs of different students' learning styles and levels of knowledge [8]. The device can be used in other Virtual Worlds, by importing the HUD 3D object. This type of application can benefit especially new users, helping on guidance in this new environment.

As a limitation of this research, it can be mentioned the sample size relatively small, consisting of sixteen respondents, which limits the degree of external validity and generalizability of the results. This study could be reelaborated in the future to include a greater number of participants to increase validity. Also, data could be captured in other VW, from other areas, to compare the results among different environments. As a future research we intend to analyze the records from the database and establish an automatic way to give feedback to students and to allow teachers to see reports of users behavior, as well as compare the registers with pre and post tests of knowledge, to see if certain navigation patterns could be connected to good learning performances.

References

[1] D. J. H. Burden, "Deploying embodied AI into virtual worlds", Knowledge-Based Systems vol. 22, no. 7, pp. 540-544, 2009.

[2] F. B. Nunes, M. C. Zunguze, F. Herpich, F. F. Antunes, A. G. Nichele, L. M. R. Tarouco, and J. V. De Lima, "Perceptions of pre-service teachers about a Science Lab developed in OpenSim", International Journal for Innovation Education and Research, vol. 5, no. 5, pp. 71-94, 2017.

[3] A. Mastrokoukou and E. Fokides, "Development and Evaluation of a 3D Virtual Environment for Teaching Solar System's Concepts", Procedings from the 3rd International Symposium on New Issues on Teacher Education, vol. 2, 2015.

[4] R. E. Mayer, "Multimedia learning", Psychology of learning and motivation, vol. 41, pp. 85-139, 2002.

[5] M. Csikszentmihalyi, "Finding flow", 1997. http://wiki.idux.com/uploads/Main/FindingFlow.pdf

[6] A. Sivunen and E. Nordbäck, "Social Presence as a Multi - Dimensional Group Construct in 3D Virtual Environments," Journal of Computer - Mediated Communication, vol. 20, no. 1, pp. 19-36, 2015.

[7] C. Gütl, "The support of virtual 3D worlds for enhancing collaboration in learning settings", Techniques for fostering collaboration in online learning communities: Theoretical and practical perspectives, pp. 278-299, 2010.

[8] O. Baydas, T. Karakus, F. B. Topu, R. Yilmaz, M. E. Ozturk, and Y. Goktas, "Retention and flow under guided and unguided learning experience in 3D virtual worlds", Computers in Human Behavior, vol. 44, pp. 96-102, 2015.

[9] H. Ogata, and Y. Yano, "Context-aware support for computer-supported ubiquitous learning", the 2nd IEEE International Workshop in Wireless and Mobile Technologies in Education, pp. 27-34, 2004.

[10] J. G. Hwang, "Definition, framework and research issues of smart learning environments-a context-aware ubiquitous learning perspective", Smart Learning Environments, vol. 1, no. 1, pp. 4, 2014.

[11] J. Cruz-Benito, R Therón, F. J. García-Peñalvo, and E. P. Lucas, "Discovering usage behaviors and engagement in an Educational Virtual World", Computers in Human Behavior, vol. 47, pp. 18-25, 2015.

[12] V. Kellen, A. Recktenwald, and C. Bumgardner, "P–An Open Source Personalization Platform for Higher Education", University of Kentucky, Lexington-USA, https://pdfs.semanticscholar.org/1e5b/8023cbfa9d281a2ce4ed71577d2eadc0b4ce.pdf , 2010.

[13] F. Herpich, G. B. Voss, F. B. Nunes, R. R. Jardim, and R. D. Medina, "Immersive virtual environment and artificial intelligence: A proposal of context aware virtual environment", In The Eighth International Conference on Mobile Ubiquitous Computing, Systems, Services and Technologies (UBICOMM), 2014.

[14] F. Shah, P. Bell, and G. Sukthankar, "A Destination Recommendation System for Virtual Worlds", in FLAIRS (Florida Artificial Intelligence Research Society) Conference, pp. 475-476, 2010.

[15] J. Keelan, L. B. Ashley, L. B., Morra, D., Busch, V., Atkinson, K., and Wilson, K. "Using virtual worlds to conduct health-related research: Lessons from two pilot studies in Second Life. Health Policy and Technology", vol. 4, no. 3, pp. 232-240, 2015.

[16] K. Sookhanaphibarn, R. Thawonmas, "Digital Museums in

3D Virtual Environment, Handbook of Research on Methods and Techniques for Studying Virtual Communities: Paradigms and Phenomena", Information Science Reference, vol. 1, 2010.

[17] T. B. Ward, and M. S. Sonneborn, "Creative expression in virtual worlds: Imitation, imagination, and individualized collaboration", Psychology of Popular Media Culture, vol. 1, pp. 32-47, 2011.

[18] Rakoczi, G., "Cast your eyes on moodle: An eye tracking study investigating learning with Moodle", In Proceedings of the 4th International Conference Moodle. Si, 2010.

[19] AVATAR Project. Universidade Federal do Rio Grande do Sul. http://www.ufrgs.br/avatar/.

[20] Singularity Viewer Official website. http://www.singularityviewer.org/.

[21] Firestorm Viewer Official website. http://www.firestormviewer.org/.

[22] A. L. Krassmann, T. A. Rossi Filho, L. M. R. Tarouco, and M. Bercht, "Initial Perception of Virtual World Users: A Study about Impacts of Learning Styles and Digital Experience", International Journal for Innovation Education and Research, vol. 5, no. 5, pp. 95-112, 2017.

[23] N. Nachar, "The Mann-Whitney U: A Test for Assessing Whether Two Independent Samples Come from the Same Distribution", Tutorials in Quantitative Methods for Psychology, vol. 4, no. 1, pp. 13-20, 2008.

[24] A. Balderas, A.Berns, A., Palomo-Duarte, M., Dodero, J. M., and Ruiz-Rube, I., "Retrieving Objective Indicators from Student Logs in Virtual Worlds", Journal of Information Technology Research (JITR), vol. 10 no. 3, pp. 69-83, 2017.